Karl Barth's Emergency Homiletic, 1932-1933

Karl Barth's Emergency Homiletic, 1932-1933

*A Summons to Prophetic Witness
at the Dawn of the Third Reich*

Angela Dienhart Hancock

WILLIAM B. EERDMANS PUBLISHING COMPANY
GRAND RAPIDS, MICHIGAN / CAMBRIDGE, U.K.

© 2013 Angela Dienhart Hancock
All rights reserved

Published 2013 by
Wm. B. Eerdmans Publishing Co.
2140 Oak Industrial Drive N.E., Grand Rapids, Michigan 49505 /
P.O. Box 163, Cambridge CB3 9PU U.K.

Library of Congress Cataloging-in-Publication Data

Hancock, Angela Dienhart, 1965-
Karl Barth's emergency homiletic, 1932-1933: a summons to prophetic witness
at the dawn of the third Reich / Angela Dienhart Hancock.
pages   cm
Includes bibliographical references and index.
ISBN 978-0-8028-6734-6 (pbk.)
1. Preaching. 2. Barth, Karl, 1886-1968. Homiletik.   I. Title.

BV4211.3.H365   2013
251 — dc23
2013013485

www.eerdmans.com

Contents

Preface	viii
Acknowledgments	xi
Introduction	xiii

1. **Karl Barth's Theological Existence**	1
Liberalism to *Romans*	3
Revelation in Motion: *Romans* to *Church Dogmatics*	8
Theological Existence and the Singular Science of Theology	18
Two Signature Leitmotifs	26
Word for World	30
Conclusion	37
2. **Theological Existence in the Weimar Years: Three Lenses**	38
The Political and Social Dynamics of the Weimar Experiment	39
The Politics of Karl Barth	52
The Ecclesiastical Lens	62
The Academic Lens	76
Conclusion	90
3. **Theological Existence and the Rhetoric of Weimar**	92
The Rhetoric of Politics in Weimar	93

CONTENTS

    Political Propaganda and the Protestant Church in Weimar   112

    Karl Barth and the Rhetoric of Political Reaction and Revolution   119

    Conclusion   134

4. **Theological Existence and Protestant Proclamation in Weimar**   137

    The German Homiletical Inheritance   139

    If God Be for Us, Who Can Be Against Us?   157

    The Modern "Theme" Sermon and the End of Weimar   163

    Karl Barth and the Modern Sermon   176

    The *Sermon Exercises* as Emergency Principle and Material Homiletic   189

    Conclusion   191

5. **Karl Barth's *Predigtvorbereitung* in Context: Winter Semester 1932-1933**   193

    May to November 8, 1932   194

    November 8 to 29, 1932   200

    November 29, 1932, to January 24, 1933   207

    January 24 to February 21, 1933   219

    February 21 to 28, 1933   229

    Conclusion   234

6. **Karl Barth's *Predigtvorbereitung* in Context: Summer Semester 1933**   237

    February 28 to May 9, 1933   238

    May 9 to 16, 1933   260

    May 16 to 23, 1933   267

    May 23 to 30, 1933   275

    May 30 to June 13, 1933   284

    June 13 to 20, 1933   288

    June 20 to 27, 1933   296

Contents

June 27 to July 11, 1933   304
July 11 to 18, 1933   313
July 18 to 25, 1933   316
Conclusion   321

Postscript: Rereading Karl Barth's "Homiletics"   324
Appendix   329
Glossary of Selected German Terms   334
Bibliography   338
Index   349

Preface

Nico Smith, the late South African Afrikaner minister and professor of theology at Stellenbosch University, frequently told the story of his "conversion" with regard to the issue of apartheid. The decisive factor in his change of heart, Smith said, was a conversation he had with Karl Barth in the early 1960s. Smith was a staunch supporter of apartheid at the time.

He describes the key moment of the exchange as follows:

> Barth then looked at me and said: "May I ask you a personal question before you leave? Are you free to preach the gospel in South Africa?"
>
> "Of course," I said. "I'm completely free as we have freedom of religion in our country."
>
> Barth immediately responded by saying that that was not the type of freedom he had in mind. He wanted to know whether I, if I came across things in the Bible that were not in accordance with what my friends and family believed, would be free to preach about such things?
>
> I was once again embarrassed and said I really did not know as I had never yet had such an experience.
>
> Barth then leant a little forward in his chair, and said, "But you know, it may become even more difficult. You may discover things in the Bible that are contrary to what your government is doing. Will you be free to preach about such issues?"
>
> Once again I had to say I really did not know.
>
> Barth then just said: "It's OK. You may go."
>
> In the tram back to the city center, I thought about Barth's question: "Are you free?" I said to myself, "I'm sure Barth thinks we in

South Africa are Nazis and he wanted to warn me against apartheid." In some way I felt like Peter whom Jesus asked three times, "Do you love me?" But since that day, the question of whether I was free kept returning to my mind and I could not get rid of it.[1]

Barth's question to Smith near the end of his own life demonstrates his continued understanding that Christian preaching finds its proper prophetic voice only as it listens well to the way of witness of the biblical text, only as it does its work in reference to the Godness of God. It is precisely in this "captivity" that Christian preachers find true freedom in relation to every hegemonic impulse, especially their own.

This book is written in the conviction that the implications of Karl Barth's work for the task of proclamation, particularly its prophetic character, have barely been explored.

During my time as a pastor, I found Barth's theology a tremendous resource in my preaching and teaching. Not because — preserve us! — I was quoting copiously from the *Church Dogmatics* in my sermons, but because Barth's rigorous and imaginative engagement with Scripture and situation prompted me to do the same in my own work.

But when I entered a doctoral program in practical theology, I was surprised to find that Barth's theology was often identified as something responsible practical theologians must overcome if they want to engage real people and real issues. I did not recognize the "neo-orthodox" Barth I was introduced to in homiletical textbooks and practical theological treatises, a Barth so intent upon the Bible that he has no interest in the world around him. Where did this "Barth" come from and why was he so ubiquitous in academic practical theological texts, particularly those focused on the task of preaching?

Such questions eventually led me to Barth's *Übungen in der Predigtvorbereitung* (Exercises in Sermon Preparation) of 1932-33. The disserta-

---

1. Nico Smith, "Experiences of a Dissenter," in *Maintaining Apartheid or Promoting Change? The Role of the Dutch Reformed Church in a Phase of Increasing Conflict in South Africa*, ed. Wolfram Weisse and C. A. Anthonissen (New York: Waxmann, 2004), pp. 103-4. Smith became a passionate opponent of apartheid, for some years living among the impoverished and segregated blacks of Mamelodi. After the fall of apartheid, he helped to build a multiracial congregation in Pretoria. When Smith died in 2010, the African National Congress praised him as "a gallant fighter" for his efforts to end apartheid. See "ANC Pays Tribute to Nico Smith," *Mail & Guardian*, June 21, 2010; http://www.mg.co.za/article/2010-06-21-anc-pays-tribute-to-nico-smith.

tion that emerged included significant research on the reception of Karl Barth's theology in North America, particularly in the field of homiletics, and concluded with a response to the dominant reading of Barth based on a thoroughly contextual interpretation of the *Predigtvorbereitung* artifacts. Readers who wish to explore that argument in detail are directed there. This book sets aside that more "local" argument in order to let the story of what happened in Barth's preaching classroom in the turmoil of Germany in the early 1930s take center stage.

It is my hope that this study is the first of many that will offer a close reading of Barth's writings, his sermons, and especially the artifacts of his teaching in the 1920s and early 1930s embedded in a "thick description" of his context. Only then will become clear all the ways in which his saying is also a doing.

ANGELA DIENHART HANCOCK
Pittsburgh, Pennsylvania
August 2012

Acknowledgments

I am grateful to the members of my dissertation committee at Princeton Theological Seminary where this study was born: James F. Kay, Bruce L. McCormack, and Sally A. Brown. James F. Kay was a true *Doktorvater* who shaped my thinking in countless ways, and is the kind of disciplined scholar I hope to become. Bruce McCormack first introduced me to the music of Barth's theology and demonstrated that reading Barth genetically and contextually could change everything. Sally A. Brown read my manuscripts with a practical theologian's eye and helped me keep those "on the ground" questions in view in the midst of so many competing threads.

My work has also been enriched by conversation with other members of the Princeton Theological Seminary faculty, student body, and staff over the years; in particular I mention Daniel Migliore, Charles Bartow, Carol Belles, Michael Brothers, Elsie McKee, Mark Lewis Taylor, Nancy Lammers Gross, Kate Skrebutenas, Rick Osmer, and Clifford Anderson, though there are many others.

Thanks are also due to those who were of invaluable assistance to me while conducting research in Germany and Switzerland. Many thanks to the director of the Karl Barth-Archiv, Dr. Hans-Anton Drewes, who provided wise counsel and a warm welcome during my time in Basel, and to Dr. Bernhard Christ and his family, who graciously invited me into their home. Dr. Eberhard Busch and Dr. Gerhard Sauter were fascinating guides to Göttingen and Bonn respectively, and my work benefited greatly from their insights.

I am also very grateful to Dieter Zellweger of the *Nachlaß Kommision* of the Karl Barth-Archiv for permission to use the manuscripts and letters so crucial to this study.

This book would not have been possible without the support of my husband, Trent, who spent countless hours editing the various versions of the manuscript, endured my endless lectures on theology, rhetoric, and politics in the Weimar Republic, and, along with our children Alexander and Tess, cheerfully attended German classes just to keep me company.

Finally, I am forever indebted to Dr. Seth Berk, the nursing staff of Virtua Medical Center in Mount Holly, New Jersey, and the hundreds of individuals who donated the blood and platelets that sustained me during my battle with leukemia.

This book is dedicated to them.

Introduction

It touches me personally to speak about his work, because Karl Barth made preaching courageous and joyful when we were his students — I know that I can say this for many. The sermon exercises which he gave thirty years ago in Bonn, together with the sermons which we heard from him there in the Schloßkirche, sustained us as preachers and helped us to stand our ground in the confusion which we saw closing in on us with the entrance to the Predigerseminar and the pastorate.

Walther Fürst, student at the University of Bonn, 1932-33[1]

In the fall of 1932, Karl Barth began holding "Exercises in Sermon Preparation" *(Übungen in der Predigtvorbereitung)* at the University of Bonn. No one asked him to do so; in fact, someone else was responsible for teaching the official homiletics course at the university. The 110-plus young people who showed up for those emergency sessions were children when the Great War devastated Europe and teenagers during the upheavals of the Weimar Republic. Most of them did not question the nationalistic piety they inherited from their parents, pastors, and teachers, and they largely shared the political fears and longings of their elders. At least some of the

---

1. Walther Fürst and Klaus-Peter Jörns, *Predigt und Gebet: Theologische Beiträge* (Göttingen: Vandenhoeck & Ruprecht, 1986), p. 28.

students in that Bonn classroom thought they had found an answer to Germany's troubles in the National Socialist Party and the commanding presence of its Führer. Barth — a foreigner, an outspoken critic of nationalism, and a member of the despised Social Democratic Party — was an unlikely candidate to change these particular hearts and minds.

What does a theologian say to young preachers at the dawn of the Third Reich? What Barth did say and how he said it and why he said it at that time and place is the subject of this study. It is the story of how a preaching classroom became a place of resistance in Germany in the firestorm of 1932-33, a story that has not been told in its fullness. This book, then, is above all a work of recovery, the excavation of something lost to the theological imagination, brought back out into the light.

But how can one say that Barth's *Predigtvorbereitung* lectures have been lost in the English-speaking world when some of the artifacts of it are so readily available, published in English as *The Preaching of the Gospel* (1961) or more recently in the little purple paperback entitled *Homiletics* (1991)?[2]

For the practical theologians — homiletical theorists in particular — who are quite naturally interested in what Barth has to say while trespassing on their territory, the true nature of the *Predigtvorbereitung* lectures is obscured not only by the fact that they are usually read acontextually as "Karl Barth's (universal) homiletic," but also because they are interpreted in light of the tenacious "neo-orthodox" caricature of Barth as someone who was so taken with God that he had no room for human beings and their little concerns, be they rhetorical, practical, or political. The slim purple volume is proof-texted with zeal to establish that Barth, for all his genius, is ultimately an unhelpful conversation partner for contemporary constructive homiletical theorizing.[3] Barth's "universal" homiletic, thus divorced from its context and containing its share of provocative statements, functions as a sort of cautionary tale — what happens when dogmatic theologians overextend themselves.

For the theologian or Barth scholar, the *Predigtvorbereitung* exercises

---

2. Karl Barth, *The Preaching of the Gospel* (Philadelphia: Westminster Press, 1963); and Karl Barth, *Homiletics,* trans. G. W. Bromiley and D. E. Daniels, foreword by David G. Buttrick (Louisville: Westminster John Knox, 1991).

3. For a detailed account of the reception of Karl Barth in North American homiletics, see Angela Dienhart Hancock, "Preaching 'As If Nothing Had Happened': Karl Barth's Emergency Homiletic, 1932-1933" (Ph.D. dissertation, Princeton Theological Seminary, 2011), pp. 6-63.

Introduction

are lost in a different way: they are simply overlooked. If one wants to understand Barth's doctrine of revelation, for example, one looks to the first two part-volumes of the *Church Dogmatics* or perhaps the Göttingen dogmatic cycle or maybe one of Barth's early addresses on the subject. Few theologians imagine that Barth's venture into the messy details of how to preach in 1932-33 might illuminate or even extend what he says in his systematic writings. In this way, too, the unique perspective of Barth's emergency homiletic is lost from view.

Finally, for the pastor or seminary student or curious layperson who sets out to read some Karl Barth and seizes upon *Homiletics*, drawn to its virtues of brevity and wit, the true nature of the *Predigtvorbereitung* is also obscured. Not because such readers initially come to the text armed with objections to its content or because they devalue its practical concerns, but rather because of the foreword penned by David Buttrick, which not only tells the reader very little about the story behind Barth's efforts nor the students in front of him, but also concludes with the damning assertion that if Karl Barth had been in South Africa and not Prussia, he would have told a figure like Desmond Tutu to keep quiet about apartheid.[4] Thus stripped of its context and charged with abetting crimes against humanity, Barth's *Predigtvorbereitung* is obscured, muffled at the outset, drained of its power.

The present work aims to change that.

This study is structured as follows:

Chapters One through Four are designed to prepare the reader for the contextual interpretation of the *Predigtvorbereitung* artifacts themselves, presented in Chapters Five and Six. An initial orientation to the theological, political, ecclesiastical, academic, rhetorical, and homiletical dimensions of Barth's context is critical if one is to understand the dynamics in each domain as they overlap, change, and intensify during the course of the sermon exercises in the years 1932-33.

Chapter One offers the reader an orientation to Barth's theological existence, how he came to affirm what he did about the Godness of God and particularly the relationship between that affirmation and the intellectual and theological climate of the Weimar years.

Chapter Two provides an overview of German political, ecclesiastical, and academic developments in the years leading up to the sermon exercises and Barth's participation in and reaction to key events in each domain.

4. David Buttrick, foreword to Barth, *Homiletics*, p. 9.

Chapter Three explores the rhetorical dimensions of Barth's political context and traces the dynamics of his response to the propaganda of Weimar in the overlapping spheres of German society and church.

Chapter Four situates the *Predigtvorbereitung* within the broad sweep of the German homiletical tradition and the inherited practices of preaching that shaped sermons in the Weimar period, describing Barth's reception of this tradition both as a dogmatic theologian and as a practicing preacher.

With these contextual complexities in view, Chapters Five and Six present the story of Karl Barth's *Übungen in der Predigtvorbeitung*, based on the extant artifacts of the event.[5] To facilitate this contextual reading, these chapters move chronologically through the sermon exercises week by week. The accounts of the material covered in a given week are interspersed with sections that describe the changing context, both in terms of the broad dynamics of the German situation and with regard to Barth's own struggles and concerns.

Finally, the book concludes with a call for a reconsideration of Barth's sermon exercises in North America and beyond.

All translations of German texts are mine, unless otherwise indicated.

---

5. For a description of these source documents and the history of their redaction and publication, see the Appendix.

CHAPTER ONE

Karl Barth's Theological Existence

For Karl Barth, theology was not just a vocation or an intellectual activity but an *existence*, that is to say, it involved every aspect of life in its conversation and concern. To think and live *von Gott aus* entails the acknowledgment that nothing exists in isolation from what the God who is God has done, is doing, and will do. Therefore, to understand why Barth embarked on an emergency excursion into homiletics in 1932, it is appropriate to begin with the theological center of Barth's life and thought — but it cannot stop there. While this chapter consists of an exposition of Barth's theological existence in the years leading up to the *Predigtvorbereitung* lectures in relation to the intellectual and theological climate of the time, it is only a beginning. The themes explored here are by no means exhaustive; rather, the chapter provides the basic background and theological orientation needed to prepare the reader for the contextual interpretation that is to come. The fullness of what Barth was doing theologically in 1932-33 will only become visible in relation to the broader dynamics of the overlapping political, ecclesiastical, academic, rhetorical, and homiletical contexts in which Barth self-consciously did his work.

This chapter is structured as follows:

First, a brief account of Barth's pilgrimage from theological liberalism to a theology of revelation and the nature of his rediscovery of the Godness of God; second, a discussion of the development of Barth's concept of revelation from the *Romans* period to the first volume of the *Church Dogmatics*, with attention to the threefold form of the Word; third, an exposition of Barth's emerging understanding of the nature of the discipline of theology in the 1920s and 1930s; fourth, the introduction of two motifs which are indispensable for interpreters of Barth's theology and may be discerned in nearly every session of the sermon exercises: the *Realdialektik* and the *analogia fidei;* fifth, a consideration of the implications of Barth's affirmation of the Godness of God for his thinking about human life and action, particularly in relation to questions of culture and ethics. Finally, the chapter concludes with a few comments regarding the designation of Barth's theology as a theology of "crisis."

The basic contours of Barth's theological development from the conversion evidenced by the two Romans commentaries to the publication of the first part-volume of the *Church Dogmatics* are now well-established in the literature. The long-dominant paradigm most famously championed by Hans Urs von Balthasar, which posited a second "break" in Barth's thinking in 1930 with his work on Anselm, has been successfully dismantled.[1] The new interpreters stress the continuity of Barth's theological thinking, viewing the developments of the 1920s and 1930s as the outworking, extending, testing and deepening of the insights first expressed in the Romans commentaries, rather than evidence of a some sort of second "revolution."

Perhaps even more significant for the task of this study is the fact that these newer interpretations stress to varying degrees that what *did* change dramatically in the 1920s and early 1930s was the *context* in which Barth did his theological work and to which he self-consciously responded in theological terms. This recognition is shared by another, sometimes overlapping group of contemporary scholars who have taken up the task of reading Barth with careful attention to various aspects of his context.[2]

But before we turn in detail to that multifaceted context and Barth's equally complex response, we begin with a brief recounting of the nature

---

1. The key text is Bruce McCormack, *Karl Barth's Critically Realistic Dialectical Theology: Its Genesis and Development, 1909-1936* (Oxford: Clarendon Press, 1997). See also Ingrid Spieckermann, *Gotteserkenntnis: Ein Beitrag zur Grundfrage der neuen Theologie Karl Barths* (Munich: Chr. Kaiser Verlag, 1985); and Michael Beintker, *Die Dialektik in der "dialektischen Theologie" Karl Barths: Studien zur Entwicklung der barthschen Theologie und zur Vorgeschichte der "Kirchlichen Dogmatik"* (Munich: Chr. Kaiser Verlag, 1987).

2. Examples include George Hunsinger, *Karl Barth and Radical Politics* (Philadelphia: Westminster, 1976); Timothy Gorringe, *Karl Barth: Against Hegemony* (Oxford: Oxford University Press, 1999); Gary J. Dorrien, *The Barthian Revolt in Modern Theology: Theology without Weapons* (Louisville: Westminster John Knox, 2000); Frank Jehle, *Ever against the Stream: The Politics of Karl Barth, 1906-1968* (Grand Rapids: Eerdmans, 2002); and, most controversially, Friedrich-Wilhelm Marquardt, *Theologie und Sozialismus: Das Beispiel Karl Barths*, 3rd ed. (Munich: Kaiser, 1985).

and trajectory of the dialectical theology that originated with Barth's encounter with Paul's letter to the Romans from the *Pfarrerhaus* in Safenwil.

Liberalism to *Romans*

As a theology student, Barth gently defied the wishes of his pietist preacher father by tempering the theological conservatism he encountered in Bern and Tübingen with a sojourn in the ferment of Berlin. His appetite for modern theology thus whetted, the young Barth eventually made his way to Marburg in 1908, where theological liberalism was in full flower. Over the course of his theological education Barth became a thoroughgoing "modernist" and ultimately a devoted disciple of Wilhelm Herrmann, whose influence on Barth would never completely disappear.[3]

Marburg

Theology at Marburg, as elsewhere in Germany, had long been preoccupied with the theological implications of the scientific, naturalist, and materialist perspectives that so dominated the broader intellectual landscape in Germany. Occasional idealists argued against the poverty of what was, in their view, reductive thinking, but it was an uphill battle. Rüdiger Safranski describes the pragmatic zeal of the reigning zeitgeist:

> The victorious advance of materialism was not halted by clever objections more especially because it had a metaphysical admixture: belief in progress. If we analyze objects and life down to their most elementary components, then — this belief in progress claims — we shall discover nature's secret of operation. Once we discover how everything is done, we shall be able to copy it.[4]

Intellectuals, including liberal theologians, largely embraced the promise of scientific ways of knowing and shared in the widespread confi-

---

3. For a nuanced discussion of Herrmann's thought and its influence on Barth, see McCormack, *Critically Realistic Dialectical Theology,* pp. 49-68.

4. Rüdiger Safranski, *Martin Heidegger: Between Good and Evil* (Cambridge: Harvard University Press, 1998), p. 30.

dence in human potential. But the triumph of the scientific method raised certain thorny epistemological questions, especially for disciplines traditionally engaged with the "meta"-physical realm, such as religion, ethics, aesthetics, theology, and philosophy.

On what grounds might a human subject claim to have true knowledge of God, of self, of history, of ethical norms, of the material world? Were there limits to the scientific way of knowing, and was it meaningful to speak of "knowledge" with regard to objects to which science had no direct access? Is everything that is "known" reducible to the contents of one's own mind or experience (idealism), or is there a material world that exists outside human conceptions of it (realism)? If such a world exists, can humans ever know it "as it is" in itself, on its own terms, or is "knowledge" limited to the knowledge of the contents and categories generated by the human psyche?

These were, of course, questions inherited from Kant, and they were intensified at Marburg due to the presence of the neo-Kantian philosophers Hermann Cohen and Paul Natorp, who along with the other neo-Kantians struggled to assert the continuing necessity of the discipline of philosophy as the methodological and ethical conscience of science.[5]

Most of Barth's teachers at Marburg accepted the basic philosophical framework inherited from Kant, stood firmly in the theological tradition of Schleiermacher, and were disciples of Albrecht Ritschl. They considered religious experience the unifying ground of the individual self, understood religion to be the foundation for human moral and cultural achievement, and imagined a fruitful symbiosis between church and state. They largely understood "revelation" as a reference to the historical man Jesus of Nazareth, who could be detected behind and among the Gospel texts, especially in his exemplary moral and spiritual vitality. Further, the Marburgers identified Christianity as the religion most able to function as a catalyst for human flourishing. This commitment to the superiority of the Christian faith necessitated constant attention to the questions raised by nineteenth-century historicism.

Historicists affirmed (to varying degrees) that all knowledge is historically conditioned, and therefore subject to change. Events and beliefs

---

5. For Barth's reception of Marburg neo-Kantianism in relation to *Romans* and beyond, see Johann Friedrich Lohmann, *Karl Barth und der Neukantianismus: Die Rezeption des Neukantianismus im "Römerbrief" und ihre Bedeutung für die weitere Ausarbeitung der Theologie Karl Barths,* Theologische Bibliothek Töpelmann (Berlin: W. de Gruyter, 1995).

can and must be explained in terms of their direct material causes, and history must be approached "objectively" and "scientifically" without judgment or speculation, proceeding from the evidence alone.[6] But for all this stress on objectivity in historicist thought, there is often the assumption of some kind of underlying continuity of experience or "nature" among human beings, regardless of when or where they lived. If an event is attributed to a cause with which the contemporary historian has no experience, e.g., witchcraft, then the historian must look for an alternative explanation. It is not difficult to discern that this overlapping set of convictions posed no small threat to the intellectual guardians of a religion whose founder rose from the dead.[7]

Though "objectivity" was certainly valued by historicists as a corrective to the romantic hagiographic historiographies of former generations, there was also a recognition that history, as an examination of the human world, required interpretation. Part of the historian's task, as understood by seminal thinkers like Ranke and Dilthey, was not just to accurately depict "what really happened" but *why* it happened. Historians were to discern the *meaning* of history. But by the early twentieth century, a new skepticism began to fester within the household of historicism. The idea that history *had* meaning — that history told a coherent story — was itself called into question.

In Barth's student days, the theological discussion at Marburg largely centered on the relationship between the claims of faith and the various claims of the historicist perspective outlined above. Could the dogmatic beliefs of the Christian church regarding Jesus Christ be justified in historical, "scientific" terms? Could the Bible's depiction of the historical person Jesus of Nazareth or of a God who is somehow involved miraculously or "naturally" in human history be rationally defended?

Ernst Troeltsch, erstwhile student of Ritschl, said a persuasive "no" to all these questions by the end of the nineteenth century, thereby founding a thriving school of his own, which set out in the name of historicism and

---

6. This scientific objectivity was a goal of most forms of nineteenth-century historicism, but not surprisingly its practitioners pursued this goal largely within the confines of their own ideological commitments. In the case of the "founder" of objective historiography, Leopold von Ranke (1795-1886), as with many of his "school," these commitments included liberalism, nationalism, and anti-Catholicism.

7. "Historicism," in *Dictionary of the History of Ideas Online* (New York: Charles Scribner's Sons, 1974); and "Historicism," in *Routledge Encyclopedia of Philosophy Online* (London: Routledge, 1998-2011).

objectivity to eradicate all vestiges of dogmatism from Christian theology and to understand Christianity first and foremost in its relationship to other religious traditions. If Christianity was indeed the highest form of religion, it would have to be shown as such in broad, "objective" terms, not internal dogmatic ones. Even then, the possibility that a better religion might come along someday could not be ruled out.[8]

Troeltsch's willingness to throw so much overboard scandalized the older, ecclesiastically-oriented Ritschlian liberals and left a generation of young liberals like Barth searching for a way to undermine the epistemological assumptions of "historicism" itself, without leaving intellectual rigor behind. In Wilhelm Herrmann some of them found a way to do so. Herrmann offered a spiritually vital alternative to the seeming dead end of Troeltschian skepticism and relativism.

Herrmann

Like all of Barth's liberal teachers, Herrmann accepted that neither the Bible nor basic Christian tenets can be established as sources of knowledge in strictly scientific terms. In fact, Herrmann was not interested in establishing a rationally respectable place for Christian convictions at all. Herrmann wanted nothing to do with what he considered an essentially apologetic enterprise. According to Herrmann, Christianity is a matter of "faith," and faith is a unique kind of knowledge because it has a unique object. Faith is not established by scientific evidence and it doesn't need to be. Faith happens to a person, and by its nature it is an experience that cannot be denied or explained. Faith is "self-authenticating." It is historical both because it happens to people in history, and because it is somehow connected to the "historical" life of Jesus of Nazareth — not to his "outer" life which is subject to the criteria employed by historians, but to his "inner" life, which remains beyond the limits of their expertise. In the experience of faith, mediated by the pictures of Jesus' inner life preserved and com-

---

8. As far as Troeltsch was concerned, "to wish to possess the absolute in an absolute way at a particular point in history is a delusion." Ernst Troeltsch, *The Absoluteness of Christianity and the History of Religions* (Richmond: John Knox, 1971), p. 122. Quoted in Mark Chapman, *Ernst Troeltsch and Liberal Theology: Religion and Cultural Synthesis in Wilhelmine Germany* (Oxford: Oxford University Press, 2001), p. 52. On Troeltsch's understanding of the task of *Glaubenslehre*, see Chapman, *Troeltsch and Liberal Theology,* pp. 69-73.

municated by other Christians, individuals encounter the *personality* of Jesus, and thus are changed.

Herrmann sought to sidestep the critiques leveled by historicism with this categorical shift from "knowledge" to "faith" while still grounding Christian belief in something he could describe as "historical." While Herrmann's explanation did not satisfy critics like Troeltsch, it satisfied his student Barth, at least for a while.

Safenwil

Barth left Marburg with the awareness that a "modern" theological perspective like the one he adopted from Herrmann would not import well into parish life, given the much more conventional beliefs of the average village congregation. Nonetheless, the young theological graduate was confident that it was the only possible responsible answer for him.

But once Barth ventured out from the academic world (after serving a year as an editorial assistant for the liberal flagship journal *Die Christliche Welt*) and into the challenges of the pastorate — first as assistant in Geneva, then as pastor in Safenwil — new concerns begin to take center stage.

First, there was Barth's introduction to the burgeoning Religious Socialist Movement in Switzerland, an encounter that was all the more significant given his ongoing practical efforts on behalf of struggling workers in his local community. Second, there was the challenge that the practices of preaching and teaching in the local church posed to Barth's theological commitments, especially with regard to his inherited stance vis-à-vis the Bible.

Both the longing for a more just society and the precarious experience of preaching week by week ate away at Barth's confidence in his theological assumptions. The bourgeois political conservatism of his liberal teachers was hardly compelling in the midst of the working-class squalor that Barth encountered in Safenwil. He found that the clinical approach to the Bible he learned from scholars like Harnack was a feeble resource when he taught confirmation or stepped into the pulpit.

But Barth's disillusionment became irreversible with the outbreak of the Great War in 1914, more specifically, with the discovery that his revered teachers, Herrmann included, had signed a manifesto endorsing the Kaiser's war aims. Barth was horrified that they would conflate God's will with

Germany's aggression or at least, in the case of Martin Rade, with Germany's "spirit of unity" in the face of their enemies. Though he would not articulate an alternative publicly for some time, the wheels of revolution were set in motion.

In the midst of his theological identity crisis, Barth embarked on, of all things, a Bible study. For months and ultimately years, Barth wrestled feverishly with the book of Romans (with side trips to Kierkegaard, Doestoevsky, Overbeck, Kant, and Plato), producing two passionate commentaries that commanded the attention of church and academy and resulted in his appointment as Honorary Professor of Reformed Theology in Göttingen in 1921. Barth left Safenwil with compassion for the plight of the working poor, appreciation for the impossible situation of the preacher, considerable anxiety about donning an academic robe, and a new way of thinking, interpreting, and existing theologically.

Revelation in Motion: *Romans* to *Church Dogmatics*

Barth's initial discovery (or recovery) was the recognition of the reality, subjectivity, and freedom of God — the *Godness* of the living God, in contrast to an un-god who could be constituted by human thought or undialectically read off the face of human history or inferred from the depths of "inner" experience.[9] Barth's discovery asserted the unthinkable for the liberal constructive spirit: an unbridgeable chasm between God's self-constituting, holy, and wholly mysterious eternal being and finite, created, and distorted human being. This "infinite qualitative distinction" between God and humanity confounded every effort to manufacture a bridge across this universe from the human side — including the efforts Barth called "religion."

Yet for all this early emphasis on negation, distance, and transcendence, Barth simultaneously insisted that God *can* be truly known by hu-

---

9. Herrmann, too, spoke of the wholly otherness of God and affirmed revelation as an event of grace and the only source of knowledge of God. But for Herrmann, individuals somehow, miraculously, have a direct experience of Jesus' personality. This experience, which includes awareness of sin and subsequent regeneration, makes a permanent impression on their spirit. For Barth, God remains hidden even in revelation, and revelation is actualistic, i.e., it does not become something inscribed on the human spirit or consciousness, but must occur again and again by God's gracious act if it is to occur at all. See Dorrien, *Barthian Revolt*, p. 23.

man beings in God's gracious act of revelation. The genuine *Gottserkenntnis* that is revelation never becomes a "thing" that human beings possess and control, but is always a miraculous event that breaks into human consciousness by God's power and at God's pleasure. Even as it is disclosed, it remains hidden, veiled, mysterious, impossible, and free. Revelation is something that human beings have no inherent capacity to access or intuit or hold on to — it is not a grasping but a being grasped.

What exactly *is* the revelation Barth has in mind? What exactly is revealed?

It is not surprising that Barth is careful (nearly 500 pages' worth of carefulness in the first volume of the *Church Dogmatics*!) about naming the *content* of revelation, for to name it generally or abstractly or undialectically would be to deny its very nature as an event that never becomes a human possession.[10]

Barth circles around the *Sache* of revelation repeatedly in his cycles of dogmatics, delineating some of the edges, thinking after its implications, gesturing toward its center but always insisting "revelation" cannot ultimately be extracted from God's decision to communicate to particular people at particular times. He writes,

> what God says to us specifically remains His secret which will be disclosed in the event of His actual speaking.... We can only cling to the fact — but we must cling to it — that when He spoke it was, and when He will speak it will be, the Word of the Lord, the Word of our Creator, our Reconciler, our Redeemer.[11]

But because it is *this* God who speaks, what Barth *can* affirm about the "what" of revelation is this: because this God is God, and only God is capable of knowing Godself, revelation can only be understood as an event in which human beings are (temporarily, impossibly) enabled to participate in the Self-knowing, Self-communicating, Self-interpreting activity of the Triune God.[12] Indeed, the very affirmation that God reveals God's own Self assumes God's dynamic Tri-unity.

Therefore, even in his first cycle of dogmatics lectures at Göttingen

---

10. This is among the reasons why "proof-texting" from Barth's writings to demonstrate his definition of a term as central to his thought as "revelation" is fraught with peril.

11. Karl Barth, *Church Dogmatics*, ed. Geoffrey W. Bromiley and T. F. Torrance (Edinburgh: T&T Clark, 1956-75) (hereafter cited as CD), I/1, p. 143.

12. "Revelation is the self-interpretation of God." CD I/1, p. 311.

in 1925, Barth recognized that one could not talk about revelation without considering the doctrine of the Trinity. God is Revealer, Revelation, and Revealedness: "*God* reveals Himself. He reveals Himself *through Himself*. He reveals *Himself*."[13] God the Father speaks, and what God speaks *is* Jesus Christ the Son, and the Holy Spirit *from inside us* speaks our "yes" to the spoken Son of the speaking God.[14]

Revelation means the Word of God spoken, constituted, and heard by God in such a way that a human being is taken up in the conversation, is addressed personally and, by the power of the Spirit, responds. The facticity of this event *is* God's decision toward us, the enemies of God.[15] The Word of God is at once promise, judgment, reconciliation, claim, blessing, grace. It tells us something we could not tell ourselves. "In it, it is decided who we are."[16] Though it is a personal encounter it cannot be reduced to a mystical pre- or post-cognitive silence — revelation has a *content*, something is communicated, something is said.[17] It is rational even as it remains inconceivable.

Does Barth mean that revelation cannot be described as something like an experience, a feeling, or a vision? On the contrary, Barth recognizes it could and does include such categories, but he insists that participation in revelation is not just a "something more" than those categories but a "something *infinitely* more." Barth certainly recognized that the "eventing" of revelation will affect the human psyche and change the course of a person's life and therefore history at large — these effects are important *signs* that mark a site of revelation and point to the Revealer. But Barth stresses that revelation is not to be confused with the signs that accompany it.[18]

---

13. CD I/1, p. 296.

14. "God's revelation is Jesus Christ Himself." CD I/1, p. 452. "The Spirit guarantees man what he cannot guarantee himself, his personal participation in revelation. The act of the Holy Ghost in revelation is the Yes to God's Word which is spoken by God Himself for us, yet not just to us, but also in us." CD I/1, p. 137.

15. The "work of the Son or Word is the presence and declaration of God which . . . we can only describe as revelation. The term reconciliation is another word for the same thing. . . . [T]o the extent that God in the fact of His revelation treats His enemies as His friends, to the extent that in the fact of revelation God's enemies already are actually His friends, revelation is itself reconciliation." CD I/1, p. 409.

16. CD I/1, p. 161.

17. "The personalizing of the concept of the Word of God, which we cannot avoid when we remember that Jesus Christ is the Word of God, does not mean its deverbalising." CD I/1, p. 138.

18. The effects of revelation in terms of human psychology or biography are a human

The Threefold Form of the Word

What, then, *is* the content of this communication to the degree it can be identified at all? Most simply: God is with us. "Revelation means the incarnation of the Word of God," Barth writes.[19] The identification of revelation and incarnation proscribes any disembodied abstract speculative path to "knowing" God, or better, any path at all. God comes to us and meets us in Jesus Christ, and promises to come again in the witnesses, ancient and contemporary, who are enabled moment by moment to point to him.

Revelation is a *spiritual* event, but it happens only in conjunction with specific *physical* events: the preaching of a sermon, the testimony of the prophets and apostles, and most importantly in the actuality of the baby in the manger in Bethlehem.[20] As such, God is veiled in flesh in this threefold form, in human nature, in human writing, in human speaking, even when God unveils Godself. Barth understands this decision too as an act of grace, for humans cannot see God face to face and live.[21]

This threefold Word is the regular way God promises to speak. Barth's understanding of the nature of this one Word begins and ends with Jesus Christ, in his particular history from his primal begetting to his life, death, and resurrection, his ongoing eventful presence in the Spirit, and his promised future which is sure but not yet visible. All three forms of the Word are grounded in this first form: the objective history of Jesus Christ, and thus Jesus Christ *as his history* functions as the criterion with which the other two forms are tested and confirmed. It pleased God to give the church a witness to Jesus Christ, a witness that, as a concrete piece of literature, is able itself to function as a norm for the church's preaching, albeit in a relative way. Preachers are not the prophets and apostles, Barth argued, and the witness of the latter-day preacher is bound to theirs, even as

---

sign "not to be treated lightly." But the sign remains a sign "which may fade again and disappear. But the Holy Spirit remains the Holy Spirit." See CD I/1, p. 465.

19. CD I/1, p. 168.

20. The Word of God is spiritual, distinct from natural events. But "there is no Word of God without a physical event. The fact that preaching and sacrament belong to it is also a reminder of this. So, too, is the letter of Holy Scripture. So finally and supremely is the corporeality of the man Jesus Christ." CD I/1, p. 133.

21. "It is good for us that God acts as He does and it could only be fatal for us if He did not, if He were manifest to us in the way we think right, directly and without veil. . . . It would not be love and mercy but the end of us and all things if the Word were spoken to us thus. . . . In its very secularity it is thus in every respect a Word of grace." CD I/1, p. 169.

they wrestle with their words in relation to the Word, Jesus Christ, himself. Francis Watson summarizes Barth's view:

> The Word of God that is uttered at the center must pass through the inner circle in its outward movement into the world; that is, it must be mediated by the Word of its first addressees. Because the content of the Word of God is the particular divine action constituted by the history of Jesus, in fulfillment of the prior history of the covenant with Israel, some people find themselves in more immediate proximity to the divine communicative action than others. Like Jesus himself, these people are Jews, Jesus' contemporaries and predecessors. Their hearing of the divine word entails a commission not only to hear but also to speak: to their own contemporaries, but also, through the medium of writing, to unborn generations and to the end of the earth.[22]

Unlike Jesus Christ — fully human *and* fully divine — Scripture and preaching are fully divine only by God's commandeering of them, moment by moment. But Barth was clear that they are fully human all the time — this is why he doesn't speak of the divine/human nature of Scripture and preaching in Chalcedonian terms, but rather in terms of their *function*. Like John the Baptist, the second and third forms of the Word always point away from themselves to Christ. For Barth, the Bible is not the Word of God any more than preaching is *in and of itself*. It is by God's grace alone that Scripture and proclamation are made faithful witnesses.

Of course, Barth argues repeatedly that we cannot claim that God can *only* speak in these three forms. Barth affirms that God can speak anywhere through anything — God is *God* — but this extraordinary speaking that Barth calls "parables" or "signs" would only be recognizable as occasions of revelation by the continuity of their witness with the way of God with us in Jesus Christ as attested in Scripture and confessed in the church's proclamation — the places where God has spoken in the past and promises to speak again. It must be stressed again that this by no means suggests a naïve confidence in the faithfulness of the church's speech about God, for example, or even the words of Scripture in and of themselves. All human words remain inadequate, broken and feeble in relation to the Word of God Jesus Christ, even when and if God chooses them as wit-

---

22. Francis Watson, "The Bible," in *The Cambridge Companion to Karl Barth*, ed. J. B. Webster (New York: Cambridge University Press, 2000), p. 60.

nesses. As we shall see, these qualifications would take on increasing importance as the situation in Germany deteriorated in the early 1930s.

Word in the Second Case: Scripture

The fact that Barth claimed he came to his theological conclusions from his study of the Bible, not just initially in his Romans commentaries but consistently from then on, was mystifying, in itself, to many of his contemporaries. The charge of "biblicism" emerged early and resurfaced regularly.[23] By "biblicism" Barth's German critics meant a slavish attention to the words of the biblical text and a corresponding neglect of the wisdom provided elsewhere by historicism or experience or some other discipline like philosophy.[24]

But it wasn't just Barth's attentiveness to the text of the Bible in all its ungainliness but also his assumption that it had something to say here and now, something that went beyond what biblical scholars were willing to say themselves, that drew fire.[25] From his first Romans commentary onward, Barth repeatedly colored outside the lines drawn in the name of "objectivity" and "science" when he read the Bible, not accidentally, but ardently.

23. In addition to "biblicism," Barth was variously charged with gnosticism, Alexandrianism, Marcionism, dogmatism, impressionism, enthusiastic revivalism, hostility to biblical criticism, pride, presumption, and arrogance by members of the theological establishment in their reviews of *Romans I*. See Richard E. Burnett, *Karl Barth's Theological Exegesis: The Hermeneutical Principles of the Römerbrief Period* (Grand Rapids: Eerdmans, 2004), pp. 15-19. Some of the reviews of *Romans II* express similar sentiments. Jülischer went so far as to call Barth's preface to *Romans II* "evidence of a disturbed disposition." For a summary of these reviews, see Burnett, *Barth's Theological Exegesis*, pp. 20-22. For the two versions of the commentaries on Romans, see *Der Römerbrief (Erste Fassung) 1919*, ed Hermann Schmidt (Zürich: Theologischer Verlag Zürich, 1985), and *Der Römerbrief, 1922* (Zürich: Theologischer Verlag Zürich, 1940). For the English translation of *Romans II*, see Karl Barth, *The Epistle to the Romans*, 6th ed., trans. Edwyn Clement Hoskyns (London: Oxford University Press, 1968).

24. Barth was willing to accept the charge of "biblicist," but only as he defined it: "Taken precisely, all the 'biblicism' which I can be shown to have consists in my having the prejudice that the Bible is a good book, and that it is worthwhile to take its thoughts at least as seriously as one takes one's own." Karl Barth, "Preface to the Second Edition," in *The Epistle to the Romans*.

25. The eminent professor of New Testament and church history at Basel, Paul Wernle, was surprised that Barth did not "distinguish and choose" only what was "eternal" in Paul's message but took seriously "the most modest remnant." See Burnett, *Barth's Theological Exegesis*, pp. 16-17.

All of this entailed something of a revolution in biblical exegesis and hermeneutics. In a theological environment where the historical-critical method exerted a nearly unchallenged authority over what the Bible could and could not say, Barth demoted historical-critical research from a final word to a helpful and necessary tool, a first step toward engaging the Bible, a first step on the way to listening for the Word to which the Bible points.[26] Barth offered a corrective to the tendency to reduce the text to a source of information about something in the past and a challenge to the assumption that the best exegesis is done by disinterested and clinical observers. At a time when biblical scholars were trained to scrutinize biblical texts from a safe distance with their own version of what is now known as a hermeneutic of suspicion, Barth rehabilitated a hermeneutic of trust.[27] "There is a river in the Bible," Barth said in a lecture in 1916, "that carries us away — once we have entrusted ourselves to it — away from ourselves to the sea."[28]

In his study of Barth's hermeneutical approach in the *Römerbrief* period, Richard Burnett conclusively demonstrates that Barth articulated a strategy of interpretation from the time of his first Romans commentary, though he was slow to make it public.[29] With Schleiermacher (and the

---

26. Barth was not, as he stated and demonstrated repeatedly, an enemy of historical criticism, or any other kind of critical tool in relation to the Bible. It was a question of expanding the range of critical inquiry to include the "meta" questions of meaning, rather than contracting it. This is why descriptors like "pre-critical" or even "post-critical" in reference to Barth's exegetical approach are misleading. Eberhard Jüngel's term, "meta-critical," is a more accurate characterization. See Eberhard Jüngel, *Barth-Studien* (Zürich: Benziger; Gütersloh: Mohn, 1982), pp. 83-97.

27. To be sure, the "hermeneutic of suspicion" Barth encountered in the biblical scholars of his day was not exactly that of the group Paul Ricoeur called "the masters" of the hermeneutics of suspicion: Karl Marx, Friedrich Nietzsche, and Sigmund Freud — a method of interpretation which assumes that the surface-level meaning of a text conceals the hidden interests, particularly the political interests, of its creators. The purpose of interpretation is thus to unmask or demystify those interests. See Paul Ricoeur, *Freud and Philosophy: An Essay on Interpretation* (New Haven: Yale University Press, 1970), pp. 32-35. Nonetheless, there is some overlap: many German biblical scholars questioned the reliability of the "surface" of the biblical text, and believed that the biblical authors and redactors produced the texts they did for particular reasons.

28. Karl Barth, "Die neue Welt in der Bibel," printed as "The Strange New World within the Bible," in Karl Barth, *The Word of God and the Word of Man*, trans. Douglas Horton (Boston: Pilgrim Press, 1928), p. 34.

29. Burnett argues that Barth's reluctance to publish explanations of his exegetical and hermeneutical approach along with his Romans commentaries contributed to the mis-

Marburg neo-Kantians), Barth recognized that there can be no presuppositionless exegesis. What one considers the whole Bible to be about, what one understands its subject matter *(Sache)* to be, will profoundly affect the way one interprets any of its parts. If the Bible is a source of information about human piety or history or religious experience, as most of Barth's teachers at least implicitly assumed, information about human piety or history or religious experience is what will be discerned.

But why would one assume the Bible is primarily about some aspect of human being? Even if that aspect is the human personality of Jesus?

Barth returned again and again to the question of the whole, the *Sache*, in the midst of his wrestling match with the epistle to the Romans:

> What is there within the Bible? What is the significance of the remarkable line from Abraham to Christ? What of the chorus of prophets and apostles? And what is the burden of their song? What is the one truth that these voices evidently all desire to announce, each in its own tone, each in its own way? . . . What is there behind all this that labors for expression? It is a dangerous question. We might do better not to come too near this burning bush.[30]

Barth's study of Romans led him to the realization that what consumed Paul and every other prophet and apostle in the Bible was a desire to point to something — not religious experience or history or morality or their own pious personality — but to God. The interpreter stands with the author, with the witness, looking where they are looking, rather than standing over against them, parsing their psyche or mythology instead of taking their words seriously.[31]

Barth recognizes, of course, that every biblical witness, whether

---

taken perception that his way of reading was arbitrary. See Burnett, *Barth's Theological Exegesis*, pp. 14-15.

30. Barth, "Strange New World," pp. 31-32.

31. This must be seen in relationship to the hermeneutical tradition that began with Herder and flowered in Schleiermacher, namely, that the empathy required for good interpretation must be based on a universal, intuitable human nature, which one can access by looking inside oneself. Barth did not set out with the goal of "understanding the author better than he understood himself" but to understand the subject matter that concerned the author. Rather than assuming the sameness of human being that undergirded both romantic and historicist ways of reading, Barth adopted an exegetical method that affirmed the otherness of others. For a nuanced discussion of Barth's hermeneutic in relation to the broader tradition of philosophical hermeneutics, see Burnett, *Barth's Theological Exegesis*, especially pp. 184-220.

prophet, apostle, editor, or redactor, writes within and to a particular context. Indeed, Barth argues, this is precisely how revelation happens, one concrete event at a time.[32]

Yet the witness to a given event of revelation is not something that historical criticism can unearth or reconstruct somehow in the shadows behind the text. This witness is inextricably bound to the very words and sentences of the text itself. What is in the text matters. Again, it is not that the words of the Bible *are* revelation. Barth, in fact, thought the doctrine of verbal inspiration was "deplorable" in that "it does not just put scripture in the pope's place but makes it a pope, a paper pope, from which we are to get oracles as we get shoes from a shoemaker."[33] The Bible can *become* the Word of God to us, but even when it does, like all events of revelation it remains mysterious, indirect, veiled. Its holiness remains incognito in its secularity:

> When God speaks to man, this event never demarcates itself from other events in such a way that it might not be interpreted at once as part of these other events. . . . The Bible is also in fact the historical record of a Near Eastern tribal religion and its Hellenistic offshoot. Jesus Christ is also in fact the Rabbi of Nazareth who is hard to know historically and whose work, when he is known, might seem to be a little commonplace compared to more than one of the other founders of religions and even compared to some of the later representatives of His own religion. . . . Even the biblical miracles do not break through this wall of secularity. From the moment they took place they were interpreted otherwise than as proofs of God's Word, and obviously they can always be interpreted in a very different way. The veil is thick. We do not have the Word of God otherwise than in the mystery of its secularity.[34]

---

32. "[T]hat Cyrenius the governor of Syria cannot be left out of the Christmas story and Pontius Pilate has an authentic place in the Creed — all this signifies that when the Bible gives an account of revelation it means to narrate history, i.e., not to tell of a relation between God and man that exists generally in every time and place and that is always in process, but to tell of an event that takes place there and only there." CD I/1, p. 326.

33. Karl Barth, *The Göttingen Dogmatics: Instruction in the Christian Religion*, vol. 1, ed. Hannelotte Reiffen, trans. Geoffrey W. Bromiley, 1st English ed. (Grand Rapids: Eerdmans, 1991), p. 217. There is nothing remotely accommodating for some form of literalism or "inerrancy" here, as Barth's most conservative critics have long recognized.

34. CD I/1, p. 165.

Not surprisingly, then, Barth's hermeneutic does not come with any guarantees. All human interpretation is and always will be provisional, for biblical scholar, theologian, and preacher alike.

Word in the Third Case: Proclamation

Barth's attention to the question of revelation not only included but often commenced with a dramatic emphasis on the activity of preaching, its (im)possibility and character. Barth explored the plight of the preacher specifically in early lectures such as "The Need and Promise of Christian Preaching" (1922) and "The Word of God and the Task of the Ministry" (1922), and he returned to it again and again in each cycle of dogmatics in the 1920s and early 1930s as he worked out the implications of a theology of the Godness of God. We will explore Barth's relationship to the praxis of preaching — his own preaching, his reactions to the preaching of others, and his approach to questions of method in practical theology — over the course of this study. But here we must briefly consider the material reasons for Barth's relentless attention to the activity of proclamation.[35]

Why does the situation of the preacher have such *theological* significance for Barth? Several factors are worth noting:

First, and most obviously, Barth's attention to preaching is due to his affirmation of the Reformed belief that the preaching of the Word of God is the Word of God.[36] As such, it looms large in a theology rooted in the conviction that God has spoken, does speak, and promises to speak to human beings.

Second, in his quest to begin with particularity and not generality, with concreteness and not abstraction, Barth finds in the activity of preaching a compelling immediacy:

> The Spirit makes revelation as present and close to us as history does holy scripture, not, of course, without holy scripture, but in and by it, and yet in it and by it it is the Spirit making revelation itself present and close. . . . Here we need say only that God's Word today as a com-

---

35. By which he meant not only preaching but also the administration of the sacraments.
36. Echoing the Second Helvetic Confession, 5.004.

mon work of scripture and Spirit is not something abstract but something concrete — the preaching of the Christian church.[37]

Barth repeatedly balances his interest in the "there and then" of past revelation with the insistence that God speaks here and now, breaking into time from eternity. Proclamation is the "eschatological miracle."

Third, the juxtaposition of the conviction that preaching is (actualistically) the Word of God and the prosaic reality of human preachers functioned as a vivid demonstration of the "fearful situation" that faced *anyone* who dared to speak of God, theologians included.

Fourth, Barth understood proclamation as the one thing of all possible things that was uniquely the church's commission. He recognized the very great temptation that faced the church to devote itself to anything, everything, but this one thing.

Finally, Barth's attention to preaching stems from his understanding of the nature of theological inquiry. Dogmatics serves preaching and has no function without it. Because Barth was a dogmatic theologian, by his own definition his task was to support and critique the church's speech about God, especially its proclamation.

Theological Existence and the Singular Science of Theology

Barth's rediscovery of the Godness of God had a profound effect on the way he understood the task of theology. With the "war theology" of his liberal teachers fresh in his mind, Barth turned from a theology that sought to preserve, legitimate, and strengthen the values of nation and culture, and began to imagine a theology free enough to call into question every ideology, every hegemony, and every claim to ultimacy that arose from the human sphere, even if it arose from the sphere of the church.

Barth was helped along the path to a liberated theology by his attention to an odd triumvirate of prophets as he made his way through his commentaries on Romans: the pietist Johann Blumhardt, Blumhardt's charismatic socialist son Christoph, and the skeptical church historian Franz Overbeck.[38]

---

37. Barth, *Göttingen Dogmatics*, vol. 1, p. 37.
38. For a detailed study of the influence of Blumhardt and Overbeck on Barth's early theology as well as the development of his thought regarding theology as "science," see Clif-

Voices in the Wilderness

Barth first encountered Christoph Blumhardt as a theology student during his brief sojourn at Tübingen in 1907, but it was not until he was rethinking everything in Safenwil that the message of the Blumhardts began to take hold. Both father and son shared a conviction that God was present and powerful, and that the coming kingdom of God would mean the transformation of the world. There were reports of exorcisms and healings by the elder Blumhardt in the nineteenth century, while the younger was known for his passionate preaching and decidedly non-ideological socialist activism in the twentieth.

What attracted Barth to the Blumhardts? It was both the fact that they always began their reflections with the reality of God, without apology or qualification, and the hopeful, expectant, and prayerful rhythm of their lives. As Eberhard Busch writes, describing the influence of Christoph Blumhardt on Barth after their meeting in 1915:

> The way in which Blumhardt combined an active and eager search for signs and "breakthroughs" of the kingdom of God with a tranquil, patient "waiting" on God, and the decisive action which he alone could perform, was evidently important for Barth. Even more important was the fundamental connection in Blumhardt's thought between knowledge of God and the Christian hope for the future; through this he learnt to understand God afresh as the radical renewer of the world who is at the same time himself completely and utterly new. For Barth this could be — and had to be — the starting point for further developments.[39]

It would not be until about 1920 that Barth would discover a strangely complementary counterpoint to the Blumhardts in the writings of Franz Overbeck.[40] The fact that Overbeck was a good friend of Nietzsche perhaps makes the historian's anti-theological stance less of a surprise. According to Overbeck, the religion that sprang into existence with Jesus *(Urchristentum)* could not develop or "make progress." Like death,

---

ford Blake Anderson, "The Crisis of Theological Science: A Contextual Study of the Development of Karl Barth's Concept of Theology as Science from 1901-1923" (Ph.D. dissertation, Princeton Theological Seminary, 2005).

39. Eberhard Busch, *Karl Barth: His Life from Letters and Autobiographical Texts* (Philadelphia: Fortress, 1976), p. 85.

40. Franz Overbeck (1837-1905), professor of church history, University of Basel.

Urchristentum was a boundary that marked the limit of human knowledge and history. It perpetually announced the end of the world and demanded immediate and dramatic decision — now.

Thus Overbeck argued that it was impossible to reconcile this eschatological faith with secular science. Attempts to do so were disastrous not only for faith but also for the discipline of science. When "science" gets a hold of raw, vibrant religious experience, it ruins it by explaining it away and reducing it to something generic or propositional. The spell is broken.

Likewise, when theology tries to use "science" to bolster its own claims, it only manages to corrupt it with its hidden and not-so-hidden metaphysical assumptions, not to mention its general ineptitude.

With regard to this latter sin, Overbeck took aim at liberal Protestantism on the one hand and so-called "positive" theology on the other. Overbeck loathed the desperate attempts of neo-Protestants to make faith palatable to the scientific community and baptize the culture — "to decorate the world with the predicates of Christianity," he scoffed.[41] Equally worthy of scorn in Overbeck's view were the "positive" apologists with their amateur efforts to *prove* Christianity by taking up historical-critical and other scientific tools.

Needless to say, Overbeck was a disturbing figure to the theological establishment, but as Barth made his way through Romans a second time, he was drawn to the radical nature of Overbeck's critique. Barth, like Overbeck, was dissatisfied with the academic tendency to domesticate revelation. If there was to be such a thing as theological "science," then it would have to be motivated by something other than the desire for respectability in the intellectual world. It would have to have room for the kind of radical eschatological expectancy he found in the Blumhardts. It would have to be a "science" that allowed for the miracle of revelation, and it would, therefore, have to be a *singular* science, unlike any other, because its object was completely dependent on the grace of its Subject. Although Barth argued that theology had a proper place on the edges of the university — as a sign of the limits of all human knowing — it was a science bound to the Church and its work of proclamation.[42] As Clifford Anderson summarizes, "Barth certainly did not want to foster the possibility of

---

41. Franz Overbeck, *Kirchenlexikon*, quoted in Anderson, "Crisis of Theological Science," p. 398.

42. "But materially I have tried to show that from the very outset dogmatics is not a free science. It is bound to the sphere of the Church, where alone it is possible and meaningful." CD I/1, p. xiii.

an extra-ecclesial theological science, but used Overbeck (and Blumhardt) to shift the locus of theological science from historical theology to practical theology."[43]

Bound to the Church

For Barth, theology is only necessary because the church is commanded to proclaim the Word of God. Because preaching is done by human beings who are indubitably *simil justus et peccator*, their speaking about God requires both appreciation and testing. It requires criticism. Theology is the name for the science that devotes itself to asking about the faithfulness and fittingness of the church's speaking about God in relation to the Word of God, Jesus Christ, and the witness of the Old and New Testaments.[44]

This conception of theology does not seem very grand compared to, say, the late medieval designation of theology as the "queen of the sciences," yet for Barth it is this event — the homely, fleshy miracle of God's word on human lips — that theology is charged to strengthen, purify, and support by its dogmatic and critical activity.[45] Theology does not exist to satisfy intellectual curiosity or help Christianity appear credible to modern skeptics or to luxuriate in religious contemplation:

> No, the fact is that what is under debate in dogmatics is the Church's fundamental relation of obedience to its Lord in respect of its proclamation. It is not a matter of offering a little truth to those who feel especially uneasy on this score while in all else they are as satisfied as all the rest. It is a matter of the will of God whose acknowledgment or nonacknowledgment in the Church's proclamation is something that should truly unsettle the whole Church, the Church as such and in all its members. The Church stands or falls with the object of dogmatic enquiry. Hence it has to undertake this enquiry. It cannot pursue dogmatics or not pursue it. A dogmatics which it might not pursue, in whose enquiry it did not wholly participate as in the enquiry about its

---

43. Anderson, "Crisis of Theological Science," p. 409.

44. "Scientific dogmatics — and now we come to the decisive point — enquires into the agreement of Church proclamation with the revelation which is attested in Holy Scripture." CD I/1, p. 283.

45. "But the normal and central factum on which dogmatics focuses will always be quite simply the Church's Sunday sermon of yesterday and tomorrow." CD I/1, p. 81.

whole existence, a dogmatics which might let itself be crowded into the corner of religious intellectuals or the intellectually religious, could only be a poor, useless and tedious dogmatics which it would be better not to pursue at all. We pursue dogmatics because, constrained by the fact of the Bible, we cannot shake off the question of the obedience of Church proclamation.[46]

As those charged to test the church's past and present words in relation to the Word, theologians will often find themselves taking on the role of disturber of the peace.[47] But lest one think that Barth finds some sort of secure vantage point in theology's critical vocation, he is quick to acknowledge the permanent bankruptcy of theology alongside every other human endeavor. A theology by grace alone can only be a *disturbed* disturber of the peace.

Barth's conviction that the knowledge of God is always indirect and eventful rather than direct and permanent results in the radical relativization of all human endeavors — political, religious, ideological, ethical, cultural but also, certainly, theological. Theology must begin its work again and again from the beginning, never secure in its own conclusions, humble, self-critical, and dependent on the grace of God. It does not attempt to justify itself. Theology is without weapons, as Herrmann also affirmed (though on different grounds), even when it shakes the foundations.[48] It comes to its work again and again with empty hands, beginning again from the beginning:

> Thus the real results of dogmatics, even though they have the form of the most positive statements, can themselves only be new questions, questions to and fro between what the Church seems to proclaim and

---

46. CD I/1, p. 274.

47. "But dogmatics cannot be only exposition. Its scientific character consists in unsettling rather than confirming Church proclamation as it meets it in its previous concretions and especially in its present-day concretion." CD I/1, p. 281.

48. "I repeat a quotation: 'Knowledge of God is the expression of individual experience and is without weapons.' 'Without weapons' is excellent! But 'expression of individual experience' is certainly not good. For before the Divine on which Herrmann obviously means here to make a claim, neither 'individual experience' nor its 'expression' is entitled to anything at all. Herrmann's 'weaponlessness' is not the weaponlessness of the *divine*." Karl Barth, "The Principles of Dogmatics According to Wilhelm Herrmann," in *Theology and Church: Shorter Writings, 1920-1928* (New York: Harper & Row, 1962), p. 259.

the Bible seems to want proclaimed, questions which can be put only with the greatest modesty and a sense of supreme vulnerability if they are perhaps serious and significant questions.[49]

A Scholastic Turn?

Barth read, absorbed, and wrestled with the writings of an astonishing number of thinkers in the 1920s, each of whom merits consideration beyond the scope of this study. We might mention in passing Feuerbach, Luther, Hegel, Dostoevsky, Kant, Plato, Aquinas, Calvin, Anselm, D. F. Strauss, and, always, Schleiermacher. Barth's appointment as Professor of Reformed Theology in 1921 also led to his first methodical exploration of the writings of older Reformed theologians, and he also delved into the works of orthodox Lutheran, medieval, and patristic theologians.

In Göttingen in 1924 Barth delivered his first cycle of lectures on dogmatics. He tried again in Münster in 1926, and he started over from the beginning again when he got to Bonn in 1931.[50]

Barth's new attention to historical and doctrinal theology came as something of a shock not only to his critics in the theological world, but also (especially!) to many of his allies. As Barth's cycles of dogmatics appeared one after another in the 1920s the lament rang out from some quarters that the once enthralling prophet of *Romans* had become another stodgy "scholastic" in the end. An occasional reference to Luther was one thing, but Aquinas? As Barth observed in 1932, "It would seem that Church history no longer begins for me in 1517. I can quote Anselm and Thomas with no sign of horror."[51] The same could not be said for many of Barth's critics.

Some of the resistance to Barth's dogmatic project from otherwise receptive neo-Protestants can perhaps be traced to the legacy of Herrmann. Herrmann was rabidly anti-traditionalist, meaning he was not just indifferent to, but opposed to, dogmatic theological work. For Herrmann, the point is that religious awakening happens in us, now. As Barth wrote of Herrmann and doctrine in 1927:

---

49. CD I/1, pp. 268-69.
50. This third cycle he would not complete, though some thirty years and 10,000 pages were devoted to the task.
51. CD I/1, p. xiii.

If he scented this enemy (and he was always on the watch for him), then he had no hesitations. . . . It can be taken for granted that wherever Herrmann was speaking of the problem of revelation, he would stress the negative limitation: revelation is not doctrine. This was more important than all else.[52]

But among Barth's "dialectical" colleagues — Brunner, Bultmann, Gogarten, and we might include (with some qualification) Tillich — some of the disappointment over Barth's "scholastic" turn was fueled by the role that existentialist philosophy played in their respective theologies. The similarity to Herrmann's position with respect to the matter is unmistakable. Existentialists also placed the decision of the individual vis-à-vis Jesus Christ here and now at the center of their concern. How could those distant fathers and long-ago disputes be much help in understanding the unique anxieties of the modern self?[53]

It was, then, a major departure for Barth to listen with critical appreciation to the ancient and modern stewards of doctrine and to engage them as contemporaries. He was well aware that in taking the broader Christian tradition and its *loci* seriously he was swimming against the stream, but he did not back down, even finding a way to affirm the leprous

---

52. Barth, "Principles of Dogmatics," p. 248.

53. We have not said much thus far about the other young theologians who joined Barth in his revolt against the liberal consensus, and we cannot say much here. In brief, Barth's *Romans* commentaries brought together a group that included Eduard Thurneysen, Georg Merz, and Friedrich Gogarten. The journal *Zwischen den Zeiten*, founded in 1923, served as the mouthpiece for the movement. Emil Brunner and Rudolf Bultmann were also associated with "dialectical theology" and contributed to the journal on occasion. Two of the impulses that brought and kept the group together (for a while) were their dissatisfaction with the theology of their teachers and their interest in theological themes that had their roots in Kierkegaard — the "infinite qualitative distinction" between God and humanity being the most obvious of these. These shared elements had a tendency to obscure the differences between them, even to them, for some time. But from Barth's vantage point in the late 1920s, all of his erstwhile theological companions (with the exception of Thurneysen) were increasingly advocating positions with which he did not agree and which he eventually thought (at least indirectly) could be used to justify the kind of theology practiced and preached by the nascent "German Christian" movement. At least some of the reasons for the ultimate incompatibility of the group as a whole have to do with their varying opinions regarding the place of philosophy in theological work, and most particularly in the vast differences in their respective appropriation of the thought of Kierkegaard in particular and existentialism in general. Brunner, Bultmann, and Gogarten had existentialist sympathies of one sort or another that Barth and Thurneysen did not share.

label "scholasticism."[54] He acknowledges the perceived liabilities of the enterprise at the beginning of his lectures on dogmatics in Göttingen:

> Is not the word "dogmatics" an ominous one, a bogey that causes the children of light [cf. Luke 16:8] as well as the children of the world to shudder? Not arbitrarily might we not think of the dark and musty wigs of the 17th century on the one hand and head-shaking natural scientists on the other? Dogmatics and the youth movement — an unheard-of and insulting combination, is it not? . . . As regards all this, I can only note first that the task of dogmatics, whether put early or late, has always placed students in an anxious, precarious, and as already stated, dangerous situation, and it will always do so.[55]

In other quarters, it was not only the fact that Barth turned to the tradition that generated controversy — it was how he did so. One aspect of Barth's 1923 debate with church historian Adolf von Harnack illustrates the point.[56] In his penultimate salvo of the exchange Harnack complains that Barth treats Luther (and Paul) as subjects in their own right, not objects to be analyzed "scientifically."[57] Hermeneutics is once again at issue.

For Barth, the decision to read *with* rather than *over against* the prophets and apostles extends also to the approach to the writings of subsequent witnesses to revelation down through the centuries. This hermeneutic is grounded in the conviction that Christ is contemporaneous both with us and with them. This communion of the saints teaches us "to see and understand the man of the past, be he Jeremiah or Jesus or Paul, or Luther, as a fellow-man, to criticize him as such, but also to respect and love him, in short, to treat him as companion of one and the same time."[58]

---

54. From CD I/1, p. 279: "Nothing that can claim to be truly of the Church need shrink from the sober light of 'scholasticism.' No matter how free and individual it may be in its first expression, if it seeks universal acceptance, it will be under constraint to set up a school and therefore to become the teaching of a school. Fear of scholasticism is the mark of a false prophet. The true prophet will be ready to submit his message to this test too."

55. Barth, *Göttingen Dogmatics*, vol. 1, pp. 4-5.

56. Adolf von Harnack (1851-1930), professor of church history, Berlin.

57. See Adolf Harnack, "Nachwort zu meinen Offene Brief an Herrn Professor Karl Barth," in Karl Barth, *Gesamtausgabe*, ed. Hinrich Stoevesandt and Hans Anton Drewes (Zürich: Theologischer Verlag, 1971), V.35, p. 87. ET: "Postscript to My Open Letter to Professor Karl Barth," in *The Beginnings of Dialectic Theology*, ed. James McConkey Robinson (Richmond: John Knox Press, 1968), pp. 186-87.

58. CD 1/1, p. 146.

Barth is clear that this interpretive approach did not preclude criticism. He had no intention of repristinizing the Christian tradition or any members of it.[59] As we would expect, Barth reads the tradition sympathetically but critically: testing it, questioning it, and often transforming its claims in surprising ways. In all of Barth's dogmatic ventures in the 1920s and 1930s, there is evidence of what Daniel Migliore calls Barth's "open, experimental spirit."[60]

The results of Barth's attention to the breadth and depth of the Christian tradition and its concerns would prove to be a rich resource for resistance as a new kind of nationalist ideology took root in the German university, giving rise to an increasingly parochial and *völkisch* scholarship, even among theologians. Barth certainly affirmed that dogmatic theologians, like preachers, must have a word to say to their present context; they must not "think and speak timelessly as though they were people of the fourth or sixteenth century," they must "sympathetically bear the burdens" of those around them right now.[61]

But at a time when the *Augenblick* — the present moment of decision, the urgency of the here and now — loomed larger by the day, Barth insisted on the need for German theology to widen its horizon to include the world beyond its temporal and national borders. We might even say, by way of anticipation, that Barth called them to look "beyond the hill" of what looked like "relevance."[62]

Two Signature Leitmotifs

Barth wrote a massive continent of material, which is imposing enough for any would-be interpreter. But equally challenging is Barth's *way* of think-

---

59. "I must now say what I do not mean by confessionalism. I do not mean a repristination of the older Christian or Reformed dogmatics. . . . Confessionalism denotes a rule of thought, not its content. . . . As regards content, it is a free and not a captive science." Barth, *Göttingen Dogmatics*, vol. 1, p. 294.

60. Daniel Migliore, "Karl Barth's First Lectures in Dogmatics: Instruction in the Christian Religion," in Barth, *Göttingen Dogmatics*, vol. 1, p. lxii.

61. Barth, *Göttingen Dogmatics*, vol. 1, p. 295.

62. One of the most controversial passages in Barth's *Homiletics* (1991) reads: "All honor to relevance, but pastors should be good marksmen who aim their guns beyond the hill of relevance." Karl Barth, *Homiletics*, trans. G. W. Bromiley and D. E. Daniels, foreword by David G. Buttrick (Louisville: Westminster John Knox, 1991), pp. 118-19.

ing — it is thinking that allows for tension without the need for synthesis or reduction or finality. It is a way of thinking that is always on the move, circling back around through the same ideas and concerns again and again from different starting places — constantly beginning again at the beginning with God's concrete deciding to be with and for humanity in Jesus Christ. It is a constant movement of listening, arguing, looking back, leaning forward, imagining. This means determining Barth's "position" with regard to any particular issue involves an awareness of the dynamics of Barth's broader argument, not just the parsing of any one text in isolation.

Barth's particular way with words presents an interpretative challenge, not only because there are so *many* words, but because amid all their complexity it is easy to overlook the recurring patterns of thought (*Denkformen*) that constitute what we might think of as the deeper music which underlies Barth's words. Failure to recognize the presence and broader implications of these patterns can sometimes lead an interpreter astray. Given the scope of this study, we can only take a brief look at the two most significant leitmotifs, both of which make regular appearances in the artifacts of the *Predigtvorbereitung* lectures: dialectic and the analogy of faith.[63]

Dialectic

Barth uses several forms of dialectic in his early writings, but we will concern ourselves here with two of them in particular, both of which endure in Barth's thinking into the 1930s and beyond: dialectical method and *Realdialektik*.

In his 1922 lecture "The Word of God and the Task of the Ministry," Barth offers a rare account of his thinking with regard to method in theology. He affirms (with the qualifications we might expect) (1) a dogmatic approach that upholds positive descriptions of God, (2) a self-critical approach — which Barth equates with a mysticism that can only be silent regarding God — and finally, (3) his preferred (though not exclusive) method, that of "dialectic." A dialectical method takes up the tasks of the other two types — making positive statements about God but then imme-

---

63. For an examination of these and other *Denkformen* in Barth's work, see George Hunsinger, *How to Read Karl Barth: The Shape of His Theology* (New York: Oxford University Press, 1991).

diately insisting on the inadequacy of this human (and any human) activity. There is no attempt to synthesize these two movements into something stable and static and controlled. The theologian must not set up camp but keep on moving forward, affirming and negating, on this "narrow ridge of rock."[64] It is easy to see why Barth would be attracted to such an approach given his theological commitments and his recognition of the failures of theologies right and left that all too readily detect God's will in current events or current passions. As Daniel Migliore observes:

> [Barth's] dialectical approach arose in response to the ethical crisis of the time. It was a means of resistance to the easy identification of God with popular movements and dominant ideologies in contemporary culture. Dialectic is the attempt to respect God's freedom, mystery, and hiddenness in all of God's relations with the world. To speak of an action of God without acknowledging its worldly incognito would mean that God had ceased to be God.[65]

But although Barth did consider "dialectic" a superior way in 1922 — in that it acknowledged the *Realdialektik* (see below) of God's concealment even and precisely in God's self-revealing — he did not of course think that any method, dialectical or otherwise, guaranteed knowledge of God. It was a human attempt to "think after" an event of revelation, nothing more.

In contrast, the second form we will consider is neither a method nor most accurately a pattern but itself a witness to the Wholly Otherness of God in relation to humanity in the event of revelation. As such it is a "real" dialectic, grounded in God's activity of Self-revealing against the backdrop of the ontological difference between God and human beings. As Bruce McCormack has demonstrated, it is a dominant theme in *Romans II* but it persists directly or indirectly in all of Barth's writings from then on. The *Realdialektik* is the very dynamic we discussed above in our consideration of revelation; namely, that God remains veiled in human words, human actions, and the human Jesus of Nazareth *even and precisely as* God gives Godself to be known. *Realdialektik* means that knowledge of the living

---

64. Karl Barth, "The Word of God and the Task of the Ministry," in *The Word of God and the Word of Man* (Boston: Pilgrim Press, 1928), p. 207.

65. Migliore, "Karl Barth's First Lectures in Dogmatics," in Barth, *Göttingen Dogmatics*, vol. 1, p. xxxi.

God never becomes a human possession, tool, or weapon. The steady drumbeat of this *Realdialektik* — the veiled-ness of unveiled-ness — has practical consequences for the Christian preacher, a fact that will become apparent as this study unfolds.

The Analogia Fidei

The motif known as the analogy of faith, characteristic of Barth's mature theology, has been discerned *in nuce* as early as *Romans II* and is also in evidence in Barth's first dogmatics lectures in Göttingen.[66]

What is the *analogy fidei?*

McCormack defines it as a relation of correspondence between "the act of divine Self-revelation and the human act of faith in which that revelation is acknowledged. More specifically, the analogy between God's knowledge of Himself and human knowledge of Him in and through human concepts and words."[67]

It is crucial to grasp that this likeness of action *(analogia fidei)* is *not* grounded ontologically — God and human beings do not share in a third thing called "being" that "naturally" enables humans to recognize and respond to the revelation of God *(analogia entis)*. Rather, the *analogia fidei* is a recognition of the *miracle* that by the grace of God a human subject can in fact really participate in the event of revelation. Barth is clear that the faith and the power to do so are a gift — revelation is *God's* possibility through and through. Yet the human being who acknowledges God in faith is "not at all a block or stone," Barth insists, but a "self-determining" person.[68]

What must be noted here, as McCormack points out, is that the *analogia fidei* could not possibly supplant the *Realdialektik* as Barth's thought developed — as has been argued by many in the past — because the *Realdialektik* of God's veiling in unveiling is its presupposition.[69] *Realdialektik* is the basso continuo — the indispensable underlying chord structure — *analogia fidei* the melody.

66. On the *Urgestalt* of the *analogia fidei* in *Romans II* see McCormack, *Critically Realistic Dialectical Theology*, p. 261. On analogy in the *Göttingen Dogmatics* see Migliore, "Karl Barth's First Lectures in Dogmatics," pp. xxxii-xxxiii.
67. McCormack, *Critically Realistic Dialectical Theology*, pp. 16-17.
68. CD I/1, pp. 244-45.
69. See McCormack, *Critically Realistic Dialectical Theology*, pp. 16-18.

It is only against the background of the *Realdialektik* of hiddenness in revealedness that the affirmation of human correspondence expressed by the *analogia fidei* shows up as a *miracle*:

> Christ does not remain outside. And it is true enough that man must open the door (Rev. 3:20). But the fact that this takes place is *quoad actum* and *quoad potentiam* the work of the Christ who stands outside. Hence it is also unconditionally true that the risen Christ passes through closed doors (Jn. 20:19f.).[70]

Any time Barth is describing the relationship between divine and human action, readers should expect to find the motifs of the *Realdialektik* and the *analogia fidei* somewhere in the vicinity, whether they are named as such or not. Many a flatfooted reading of Barth has isolated some of Barth's words regarding something like God's transcendence, but missed the "Nevertheless!" of this deeper music. It is critical to recognize Barth's overarching intention to sound both of these notes at this juncture in this study, because there will be times that circumstances will compel Barth to "one-sidedly" ring out one of these bells more vigorously than the other, especially in the early 1930s.

Word for World

One of the most persistent criticisms leveled against Barth is the charge that his theology is an abstract, otherworldly affair that results in the negation of human culture and action. In some quarters, he has been described not only as one who has little use for culture but is positively anti-culture, contemptuous of the human world.[71]

In other quarters, it is the projected consequences of Barth's emphasis on the Godness of God in the realm of ethics that are lamented. One contemporary critic voices the latter longstanding complaint nicely: "Barth's separation of the human and divine realms led to passivity, to acquiescence, and ultimately to acceptance of the status quo because it re-

---

70. CD I/1, p. 247.

71. Gabriel Vahanian, "Karl Barth as Theologian of Culture," *Union Seminary Quarterly Review* 28, no. 1 (1972): 37. Vahanian includes Schubert Ogden and Reinhold Niebuhr in this category.

fused to sanction any action in the social world as unquestionably that of the Gospel."[72]

Because these critiques have shaped the reception of Barth in many contexts, it is necessary before we continue to consider the place of culture and ethics in Barth's thought from the time of his break with establishment theology to his emergency decision to add practical theology to his teaching responsibilities in 1932.

Of course, we can only offer a rough sketch of Barth's thinking with regard to questions of culture and ethics leading up to the time of the *Predigtvorbereitung* lectures here. Nonetheless, this sketch will serve as an introduction of themes which we will return to in subsequent discussions of Barth's reaction to the dissolution of Weimar and the threat of National Socialism.

Culture

Romans I and *II* constituted a thorough rejection of the church's idolatry of culture, typified in the liberal German theologians who publicly declared their support for the Great War. Notice that it was primarily a critique of the *idolatry* of culture by the Christian church, not an attack on culture itself. By "culture" Germans understood everything worthy that is wrought by human beings — science, aesthetics, ethics, education, government. Barth could certainly speak a critical word regarding those spheres as well, but it was the religious *legitimation* of the values and practices of the nation, among other things, that drove his early jeremiad against "religion."

From the point of view of the representatives of so-called "culture Protestantism," Barth sounded like he was indeed unconcerned for the welfare of the culture they worked so tirelessly to preserve from a descent into atheism, materialism, and various sorts of degradation. Adolf von Harnack said as much in 1923 in one of his "Fifteen Questions to the Despisers of Scientific Theology":

> If God is simply unlike anything said about him on the basis of the development of culture, on the basis of the knowledge gathered by cul-

---

72. Douglas J. Cremer, "Protestant Theology in Early Weimar Germany: Barth, Tillich, and Bultmann," *Journal of the History of Ideas* 56 (1995): 296. Like most who level this charge, Cremer offers no evidence, empirical or otherwise, to support his claim.

ture, and on the basis of ethics, how can this culture and in the long run one's own existence be protected against atheism?[73]

Barth replied to Harnack with thinly veiled sarcasm:

> Statements about God derived from "the development of culture, from the knowledge gathered by culture and from ethics" may as expression of special "experiences of God" (e.g. the experiences of the War) have their significance and value in comparison with the experiences of primitive people who do not yet know such great treasures. (Consider, for example, the significance and value of the statements of the War-theologians of all countries.) *These* statements can definitely not be considered as the "preaching of the gospel." Whether they *protect* culture and the individual "against atheism" or whether they *sow* atheism ... would remain an open question in each individual case.[74]

Barth not only restates his opposition to the idea that knowledge of God can be derived from culture, but suggests that attempting to do so is actually detrimental to it. To collapse revelation undialectically into some aspect of culture is to, in some sense, abandon culture.

Throughout the 1920s and right up to his 1931 dogmatics lectures in Bonn and beyond, Barth remains adamantly opposed to any sort of theology that deifies culture, and yet he was certainly not anti-culture or indifferent to the so-called "problem of culture" which was a frequent topic of theological discussion in Weimar. Barth wrote in 1931: "The problem of culture is the problem of being human, which undoubtedly exists for the theologian too, since theology is a specific activity of humanity."[75] As we have observed, he is also open to the possibility, grounded in the freedom of God, that "parables of the kingdom" can occur in the cultural sphere:

> There can be no thought of a general sanctifying of cultural achievement ... but there is even less place for a basic blindness that culture may be revelatory, that it can be filled with the promise. The Church

---

73. Adolf von Harnack, "Fifteen Questions to the Despisers of Scientific Theology," reprinted in Martin Rumscheidt, *Revelation and Theology: An Analysis of the Barth-Harnack Correspondence of 1923* (Cambridge: Cambridge University Press, 1972), p. 30.

74. Karl Barth, "Fifteen Answers," reprinted in Rumscheidt, *Revelation and Theology*, p. 33.

75. CD I/1, p. 284.

will need to consider carefully whether it knows what it is doing when in a concrete case it affirms the presence of the promise.... The Church will not see the coming of the kingdom of God in any human cultural achievement, but it will be alert for the signs which, perhaps in many cultural achievements, announce that the kingdom approaches.[76]

Barth does not, like Harnack and his peers, lament the secularity of culture but instead urges it to be *more* secular, in that it does not claim to represent "eternal" values or take itself with ultimate seriousness.

In Barth's view, both church and culture are comprised of sinners; both church and culture are sustained by God's reconciling grace. God is *for* them, church *and* world. "It is not at all true," Barth writes, "that the Church is outside with God and the world is inside without God."[77] Therefore, while the church is commissioned to be a witness to God's promise to the culture which surrounds it, it does not do so across some great divide but from within the culture itself, and on the basis of God's promise to make all things new:

> With this eschatological anticipation, the Church confronts society. Not with an undervaluation of cultural achievement, but with the highest possible evaluation of the goal for which it sees all cultural activity striving. Not in pessimism, but in boundless hope. Not as a spoilsport, but in the knowledge that art and science, business and politics, techniques and education are really a game — a serious game, but a game, and *game* means an imitative and ultimately ineffective activity — the significance of which lies not in its attainable goals but in what it signifies. And the game might actually be played better and more successfully, the more it was recognized as a game. Our earnestness could not be impaired by making clear to ourselves that the game can never be ultimately serious, and never is; that the right and possibility of being wholly in earnest is God's alone.[78]

Barth's strong "no" to any form of deification of the culture frees it from "tower of Babel" aspirations, creating a genuine and properly secular

---

76. Karl Barth, "Church and Culture (1926)," in Karl Barth, *Theology and Church: Shorter Writings, 1920-1928* (New York: Harper & Row, 1962), p. 344.
77. CD 1/1, pp. 154-55.
78. Barth, "Church and Culture (1926)," p. 349.

space for the play of human creativity and ingenuity. The stark contrast between this vision and that of the *Reich* soon to come will become blindingly apparent as we proceed.

Ethics

Barth formally addressed the question of ethics several times after *Romans I*, beginning with the Tambach lecture in 1919, and he spent two semesters lecturing on ethics, first at Münster in 1928-29 and then again in Bonn from 1930-31. Our exposition here must be limited to a few characteristics of Barth's thought on ethics in the late 1920s and early 1930s that are particularly relevant for understanding his theological and practical reaction to the events surrounding the *Machtergreifung* of 1933.

It does not need to be said that Barth interpreted his teachers' endorsement of war in 1914 as an ethical as well as a theological disaster. It was all the more ironic given that morality — based particularly on Jesus' teaching on the "brotherhood of man" — was high on their list of concerns.

What are the characteristics that distinguish Barth's ethical approach from that of the German Protestant theological establishment?

First, it must not be forgotten that Barth worked and taught in a predominately Lutheran environment while in Germany, especially during his sojourn as the vastly outnumbered Professor of Reformed Theology in Göttingen. As Barth became acquainted with the Reformed tradition he increasingly began to claim the distinctive features of that tradition as his own. Though he remained attentive to and appreciative of Luther's thought throughout his life, certain aspects of Lutheranism began to trouble him.[79]

One of these aspects is the traditional Lutheran understanding of the relationship between law and gospel, a theme we will revisit throughout the course of this study.[80] Put rather crudely: the primary function

---

79. On the influence of Luther in Barth's theology, see George Hunsinger, "What Barth Learned from Martin Luther," in *Disruptive Grace: Studies in the Theology of Karl Barth* (Grand Rapids: Eerdmans, 2000), pp. 279-304.

80. The matter is complicated further by the addition of Luther's understanding of the world as comprised of "two kingdoms": the secular and the spiritual. According to Luther, the law has the positive function of preserving order in the secular kingdom, but in the spiritual kingdom it is only understood as a threatening demand which drives the sinner to repentance. The so-called "third use of the Law," which would grant the Law a positive use in

of the law in orthodox Lutheran theology is to bring sinners to despair over their inability to keep God's commands, and thus drive them to accept the gospel of grace, being justified through faith. As so conceived, the ordering "law/gospel" is irreversible — law precedes gospel — thereby preparing the sinner for grace. For the believer, law has been superseded by grace through faith, and the justified sinner is freed from the demands of the law.

But Barth, taking up and magnifying a theme of Calvin, argues that the proper response to the grace of God is not only faith, but also obedience. God does not only justify sinners — God sanctifies them as well:

> Alongside the gospel, without in the least suspending its character as gospel, there stands with equal dignity the law, alongside the proclamation of grace the demand for repentance, in this order and not the reverse as in Lutheranism. . . . We cannot accept God's answer without placing ourselves under the question that is put to us. We cannot recognize God without accepting his authority. We cannot have knowledge in relation to God without action.[81]

With that Barth turns the Lutheran formula on its head: gospel precedes law. Thus for Barth, the question of ethics is always an intrinsic part of dogmatic reflection.

In addition to this Lutheran law/gospel backdrop, Barth's ethics must also be considered in relation to the neo-Kantian theological approach of his teachers. In brief, thinkers like Ritschl and Harnack presumed in the teaching of Jesus a universal moral code which could be extracted from its context and applied by autonomous human subjects.

In contrast, Barth relocates ethics from the realm of timeless principles and the rational consciousness of self-determining agents to the particular relationship God constitutes between God and human beings in the event of revelation, understood within the overarching activities of the Triune God in creation, reconciliation, and redemption. The command of God, then, always comes as something concrete, a Word addressed to an individual in a particular time and place. As John Webster points out, this

---

the "spiritual kingdom" as a guide to the life of faith (which some claim can also be found among Luther's writings and others trace to Melanchthon), has long been and remains a disputed issue in the Lutheran tradition.

81. Barth, *Göttingen Dogmatics*, vol. 1, p. 172.

does not mean that Barth is "an occasionalist with a merely punctilliar understanding of what it means to be a moral agent. It is more that Barth is drawing back from any idea of God's command as a general truth, an empty form to which we give content."[82]

Does Barth give an answer to the question "What do we do?" in his early ethical reflections? Just as Barth is careful with regard to naming the specific content of revelation too glibly, so too he is careful with this question. But there are two observations that will help clarify Barth's position.

First, as we saw in his thinking about the content of revelation, Barth draws our attention to who God is *for us*. God our Creator, our Reconciler, our Redeemer — this God calls into being — in the event of revelation — a person who is right then a reconciled creature, heir to the eschatological promise. As such, Barth seeks to "think after" this event to consider the kinds of attitudes and actions that might correspond to each of these relations. What does it look like to live in relation to our Creator, our Reconciler, our Redeemer, here and now?

Second, none of Barth's work on ethics should be separated from what has already been said about the nature of revelation as the Word of God in its threefold form. Every event of revelation with its grace and promise includes God's judgment and command, and this judgment and command is not empty any more than revelation itself is empty.[83] It is not empty, but personal, contextual, and concrete.

---

82. J. B. Webster, *Barth's Moral Theology: Human Action in Barth's Thought* (Edinburgh: T&T Clark, 1998), p. 51.

83. "How necessary it is to be clear about this twofold movement of the Word of God and the faith that follows it may be seen finally from the fact that one has only to extend the lines a little on both sides to move from the concepts of veiling and unveiling, or form and content, to other opposing concepts, namely, Law and Gospel, demand and promise, or in another direction letter and spirit, or in yet another God's wrath and judgment and God's grace. The Word of God in its veiling, its form, is the claiming of man by God. The Word of God in its unveiling, its content, is God's turning to man. The Word of God is one. In the claim there takes place the turning, and the turning does not take place without the claim. When man is truly and seriously put under the Law he comes to the Gospel, and when he comes to the Gospel by revelation and faith, he is truly and seriously put under the Law. God's wrath and judgment is only the hard shell, the *opus alienum* of divine grace, but the man who knows grace, the *opus Dei proprium*, he and he alone knows what is God's wrath and judgment. The letter of proclamation and the Bible is the bearer of the Spirit, but it is the Spirit that constantly brings us back to the letter." CD I/1, p. 179.

Conclusion

There is no doubt that Germany was in a time of crisis from the beginning of the Great War to the death throes of Weimar and beyond. To Barth's theological contemporaries, the sense of crisis extended from the political and economic upheaval to their fears regarding the decay of German cultural and moral values, the rising tide of atheism and materialism, the steady decline of church attendance, the precarious position of theology in the university, and the existential anxiety of the modern person. To these theologians, these overlapping crises of nation, culture, faith, church, theology, and individual could be solved, one way or another, by Christianity, if only the right path could be found.

For Barth, the "crisis" of the theology he first scribbled out in Safenwil and thought through in the following decades was not of this sort. Revelation, Barth thought, brought its own crisis, and properly so. The fact that we are not in charge of God, we do not "have" God's revelation as a tool or a weapon or a persuasive piece of propaganda means a certain perpetual insecurity, an eschatological unrest, an escapable self-questioning. This is not a crisis to be fixed or transcended, but one to be embraced.

Barth was well aware that Germany was in a time of crisis when he volunteered to hold sermon exercises in 1932. He was intimately involved in the swirl of discussion, debate, and struggle of those days in many different contexts. But as the next chapter will demonstrate, Barth's response to the multifaceted German crisis had its ground and hope in the *real* crisis, the *Realdialektik*, wrought by the undomesticated and undomesticatable Word.

CHAPTER TWO

Theological Existence in the Weimar Years: Three Lenses

It was early spring at the University of Bonn, and the summer semester was already under way. Professors were planning which courses would be offered the following term, and one professor in particular decided to add a new responsibility to his already full schedule. Not only was the subject of this course not in the professor's own field; it was a course that had been in the past, and would be in the upcoming year, taught by someone else — a faculty member who had been teaching at the university for a very long time.

The someone in question was the longtime professor of practical theology and apologetics at the university, one Emil Pfennigsdorf, and the newcomer who aimed to trespass on Pfennigsdorf's territory was, of course, Karl Barth.

It is a matter of some delicacy, one professor informing another of such a plan. In this case it was done by letter, written on May 7, 1932.

The letter reads as follows:

> Highly esteemed colleague!
>
> Before the schedule with the announcements of our faculty for the next winter semester is published, I want you to know that I intend to hold "Exercises in Sermon Preparation." I ask you sincerely to receive this in a friendly way.
>
> The students have been asking for such exercises for several semesters. And it is understandable to me that some among the advanced students, who have attended my systematics lectures and exercises with interest, wish to hear from me what I think precisely at the

point which I have always stressed as the bottom line, namely, the sermon, the intersection of [theology and] church praxis.

On the other hand I repeatedly hear the lament about the supposedly practical inadequacy of my particular students, so also for that reason I need to take part in practical instruction — within certain bounds.

In outstanding regard
Your very loyal[1]
[Karl Barth]

Why did Barth initiate this breach of academic protocol in the spring of 1932?

The purpose of this chapter is twofold: to shed light on the reasons behind Barth's unprecedented decision to add practical theology to his teaching load in 1932, and to prepare us to interpret the artifacts of Barth's venture with a clear grasp of the contexts that influenced his approach to the task.

With these goals in mind, this chapter will examine the relationship between Barth's theology and its context from three vantage points, each chosen for their particular relevance for the interpretation of the *Predigtvorbereitung* lecture notes: the political, the ecclesiastical, and the academic.

This structural arrangement is necessary for clarity of presentation, given the complexity of each of these situations, but it must be said that there was of course constant overlap and interaction between these various domains. Barth himself was aware that the boundaries between them were blurred and, in the most fundamental sense, nonexistent. The initial orientation provided here is necessary in order to understand the dynamics in each domain as they change and intensify during the course of the sermon exercises in the years 1932-33.

In the conclusion to the chapter, we return to the question of the motives that led Barth to volunteer to teach preaching in 1932.

The Political and Social Dynamics of the Weimar Experiment

The broad outlines of Weimar's disintegration and the eventual triumph of National Socialism are now well-established. There is, however, a lesser

---

1. Karl Barth to Emil Pfennigsdorf, May 7, 1932, original in Karl Barth-Archiv, Basel, Switzerland. Used with permission.

degree of consensus in the scholarly community when it comes to the question of the reasons for these developments, though there is more agreement than in decades past. The hegemony of the *Sonderweg* theories so plentiful in twentieth-century German historiography have largely given way to accounts that attempt to balance analysis of the broad political and social factors with close research into the daily lives of "regular" people *(Alltagsgeschichte)*.[2] The present study, with its focus on Barth in his context, is to some degree of this latter sort.[3]

The task of this section is to orient the reader to the changing political and social landscape of the period more generally and then to examine Karl Barth's political thought and action both as an expression of his theological existence and in relationship to these often tumultuous developments.

The Romance of the Iron Chancellor

Like all countries, Germany had its share of legendary figures that remained on the national stage — symbols not only of what had been but also what could be. We might include Charlemagne, Frederick the Great, and Martin Luther in this category, but historians have long observed that the heroic figure that may offer the most insight into the ideals of many Germans in the early twentieth century is the nineteenth-century states-

---

2. *Sonderweg* interpretations of German history stress the uniqueness of German culture, character, geography, etc., arguing that the feature in question set Germany on the "path" that led to fascism. In its late-twentieth-century form, *Sonderweg* historians used the tools of political, social, and/or economic theory to analyze the differences between the Weimar experiment in liberal democracy and other, "regular," Western liberal democracies, perhaps most influentially by Hans-Ulrich Wehler. Because they focused on sweeping patterns and massive structures over long periods of time, *Sonderweg* histories had difficulty accounting for the many exceptions to their rules that emerged as scholars began to examine complex, "thick" local histories. See Jürgen Kocka, "Asymmetrical Historical Comparison: The Case of the German *Sonderweg*," *History & Theory* 38, no. 1 (1999): 40-50.

3. The current exemplar of this balancing act between broad dynamics and local histories is historian Richard Evans, particularly in his masterful and critically acclaimed three-volume narrative history of Weimar and the Third Reich. The historical account offered above relies heavily on his analysis, particularly that of his first volume. See Richard J. Evans, *The Coming of the Third Reich*, 1st American ed. (New York: Penguin Press, 2004); Richard J. Evans, *The Third Reich in Power, 1933-1939* (New York: Penguin Press, 2005); and Richard J. Evans, *The Third Reich at War, 1939-1945* (New York: Allen Lane, 2008).

man, aristocrat, and imperialist Otto von Bismarck. Bismarck, the "Iron Chancellor," was credited with uniting the loose confederation of Germanic states into one nation, a "Second Reich" to be compared with the splendor of the Roman Empire, and doing so with a pragmatic blend of diplomacy and military force.[4] Though Bismarck was recognized as a master of Realpolitik, he did not hesitate to act, sometimes brutally, upon his strong ideological biases against socialism, egalitarianism, parlimentarianism, and Catholicism — all things Bismarck considered a threat to the state as he envisioned it.[5] In the midst of the upheaval, pluralism, and fragmentation that came with the early decades of the twentieth century, many Germans longed for a leader like Bismarck: an aggressive defender of a united, glorious, thoroughly *German* empire.

The long-term political consequences of the persecution Bismarck initiated in the nineteenth century against German socialists and Catholics in particular were devastating. Because the liberals supported Bismarck in these repressions (in the name of national security), neither the Catholics nor the socialists would trust them again. The Catholic "Centre Party" would vote against liberals and with nationalists to prove their patriotism and avoid future persecution. The socialists, reforming as the Social Democratic Party in 1890, would refuse to cooperate with the liberal middle-class parties even when there were clear benefits to doing so. Thus by 1914 there were six major political parties in Germany: the Social Democrats, two liberal parties (the National Liberals and the Progressives), two conservative parties (the Conservative and Free Conservative), and the Centre Party.[6] With so many parties competing for every vote in *Reichstag* elections, campaigning was fierce and voter participation extremely high.[7]

But for all the issues that divided them, what most of these parties had in common was an unquestioning and unquestioned nationalism.

---

4. From the time of unification until 1918, executive power in Germany was held by the emperor *(Kaiser)* and his advisor, the chancellor. A two-tiered parliament consisting of the *Bundesrat* (representatives appointed by the state government) and the *Reichstag* (democratically elected representatives, though only males over 25 could vote) had the power to veto, though not initiate, legislation. The chancellor was appointed by the Kaiser, not elected.

5. Evans, *Coming of the Third Reich*, p. 2.

6. Evans, *Coming of the Third Reich*, p. 16.

7. Evans cites a rate of 85 percent of eligible voters in 1912. Evans, *Coming of the Third Reich*, p. 16.

The Great War and Its Aftermath

In the years leading up to the war, Germany was the most powerful economy in Europe, a leader in technology, agriculture, and industry, and a place full of artistic, academic, scientific, and literary creativity. But for all the benefits that came with innovation and growth, there was also fear of what these changes would mean. Amid this ferment and uncertainty, an unimaginable series of events rapidly unfolded.

In the summer of 1914, Germany found itself at war. Due to a complex web of alliances, most of Europe was suddenly mobilizing for battle on an unprecedented scale, and other continents would sooner or later join it. On the one side the Central Powers: the German Empire, the Austro-Hungarian Empire, the Ottoman Empire, and the Kingdom of Bulgaria; and on the other the Allied Powers, which included the Russian Empire, the United Kingdom, France, Canada, Australia, Italy, the Empire of Japan, and the United States.

Given Germany's military and economic strength, most Germans expected to win the war, and some early dramatic victories only increased their confidence. There was speculation, some of it from the government itself, about the particular territories Germany should annex when they had triumphed. The great wave of patriotism and unity that swept through Germany (the "Spirit of 1914") included the veneration of military figures, the most beloved of whom was the ex-retired general, later field marshal, Paul von Hindenburg, lauded for his many successes on the Eastern Front. Hindenburg would be named Chief of Staff in 1916, and along with his deputy, General Erich Ludendorff, would exercise increasing authority over not only the war but also domestic policy. In the name of winning the war, it was the two generals who would place restrictions on civil liberties, restructure the Germany economy in support of the war effort, and begin aggressive incursions into neighboring countries, who would not forget these humiliations when the war was over.

Red Tide Rising

While Germany continued to do well on the Eastern Front, this onslaught facilitated the collapse of the Russian imperial monarchy in 1917. This provided the opportunity for which the Bolsheviks had waited. Lenin and his comrades surged to power in 1917, violently and rapidly dismantling the old Russia and imposing the new communist one. The Bolsheviks also formed an organization to facilitate communist movements in other parts of the world. The reaction of upper and middle-class Germans to the bloodbath of the Russian revolution was sheer terror, and their panic would eventually result in a willingness to do whatever was necessary to stop such a thing from ever happening in Germany. The formation of the German Communist Party in 1918 and the scattered revolutionary uprisings from the left which occurred in Germany in 1918-19 only increased the anxiety level. Even the Social Democrats, who largely supported moderate reform rather than revolution, would be regarded with suspicion by right-wing Germans from then on.[8]

Meanwhile, it had become clear on the field of battle that Germany could not prevail as American reinforcements kept coming and war-weary soldiers began to surrender. The German press, as instructed, did not tell the public the truth about Germany's situation, nor did the Kaiser in his official statements. When the inevitability of defeat was finally acknowledged, people were stunned and horrified, and when the punitive terms of the Treaty of Versailles were negotiated and presented in 1919, they were outraged. General Ludendorff and other government officials had hoped their public support for the democratization of the German system of government (once they realized the war was lost) would result in a kinder, gentler treaty with the Allies. But this was far from the case.

The "Stab in the Back" Mythology

The Treaty of Versailles called for Germany to accept full responsibility for the war, dismantle most of its military, give up a substantial amount of territory, offer up some of its citizens (including the Kaiser) to trial for war crimes, and pay a massive sum in reparations to several other countries. Far from functioning as a peace treaty, to many Germans Versailles was simply "prolonging the war by economic means."[9] Not only did Germans find Allied demands excessive and unfair, some did not even accept that the Allies had actually won the war. In fact, a persistent and powerful rumor began to circulate in the days immediately after the armistice, an al-

---

8. Evans, *Coming of the Third Reich*, p. 57.
9. Michael Burleigh, *The Third Reich: A New History* (Basingstoke: Macmillan, 2000), p. 48.

ternative account of why Germans now suffered the humiliation of defeat. They had *not* been overcome by their opponents on the battlefield, but betrayed from within — stabbed in the back by those within Germany who wanted the state to collapse. This legend of sabotage was circulated among army officers and popularized by statements made by Hindenburg and Ludendorff themselves.

What kind of citizens would commit such treason? Citizens deemed to have international ties — communists, socialists, Catholics, Jews. The liberal politicians who benefited politically from the end of the monarchy and the establishment of Weimar were also included in this group of what became known as the "November criminals." Though the political coalition that founded Weimar had nothing to do with the Versailles negotiation, they were nonetheless tainted by association right from the start. A number of Germans found the "stab in the back" version of events more palatable than the alternative, particularly among those who themselves fought in the Great War.

Naturally, many soldiers had difficulty transitioning back to peacetime under the circumstances, and militarism — a positive view of the use of force and the celebration of "soldierly" virtues — was widespread throughout Germany during the Weimar years.[10] Although the Treaty of Versailles reduced Germany's massive military to a remnant of 100,000 soldiers, German society had no shortage of men in uniform, many of them armed. There were countless militias, paramilitary organizations, and veterans' groups like the *Stahlhelmer* (Steel Helmets) who participated in regular marches and rallies. Political parties formed their own armed squads who served as bouncers for political meetings, paraded through towns and cities in demonstration of their prowess, and frequently engaged the representatives of other parties in bloody street brawls.[11] Unable to attack Germany's external enemies, these peacetime soldiers focused their energies on what they considered her internal ones.

In the years immediately following the war, those who subscribed to the "stab in the back" myth were outnumbered by the majority of Germans who, although they also felt the terms of Versailles were unfair, wanted to forge a democratic Germany with a social conscience and cultural freedom. But the "stab in the back" interpretation of the end of the

---

10. Militärgeschichtliches Forschungsamt, ed., *Germany and the Second World War* (Oxford: Oxford University Press, 1990), p. 15.

11. Evans, *Coming of the Third Reich*, p. 73.

war simmered beneath the surface of Germany's fledgling democracy, and it would gain broader political traction as the 1920s drew to a close.

The Structure of Weimar

Even before the Kaiser abdicated the throne at the end of the war, the news of defeat bred chaos and violence in the streets all over Germany. In the tumultuous period after the Kaiser's departure, the Social Democrats rallied behind Reichstag delegate and pragmatist Friedrich Ebert, forged alliances with the left-liberal Democrats and the Centre Party, and with them gained a majority in the 1919 nationwide election to name delegates to the assembly in Weimar that was charged to draft a new constitution after the war.

Why did the coalition led by the Social Democrats prevail in the elections? Even voters who disagreed with them politically believed that the compromise represented by parliamentary democracy would provide the best protection against a Russian-style communist revolution in Germany.[12] Fear of Bolshevism would prove an enduring feature of postwar political reasoning, and when the threat of revolution seemed to diminish in the mid-1920s, the willingness of some voters to stand behind the Republic diminished accordingly. The next time fear of Bolshevism gripped the nation many Germans would seek a different kind of solution.

The Weimar Constitution replaced the Kaiser with a democratically elected president, while the office of chancellor remained, appointed by and responsible to the president alone.[13] Reichstag members were now elected by men *and* women over age 20 and seats were distributed in proportion to the votes each party received. Article 48 of the new Constitution, which allowed the president to bypass the legislature and rule by decree in the event of an "emergency," would prove to be its most unfortunate feature. Ebert's presidency was relatively short-lived (he died in 1925),

---

12. Evans, *Coming of the Third Reich*, p. 79.
13. While the chancellor was appointed by the president, the decision was not without political constraints. The choice of chancellor needed to reflect the majority party or majority alliance within the Reichstag itself. Hence, as the balance of power in the Reichstag changed with nearly every election cycle, chancellors and their governments rarely remained in office for very long during the Weimar years. Although there were only two presidents during the period 1919-1933 (Ebert and Hindenburg), there were no less than fourteen chancellors, the longest remaining in office only two years, and even more cabinet upheavals.

but some of his decisions placed Weimar democracy in a precarious position right from the beginning. His copious use of Article 48 set an ominous precedent. His decision to keep imperialist judges and civil servants of all kinds in their posts for the sake of an orderly transition and his appeasement of the powerful officer corps with their monarchist ideals weakened Weimar in the long run.

In the early 1920s ordinary Germans were filled with anger over the extent of reparations, ruined by the devastating hyperinflation, and furious when French troops set up camp in the Ruhr valley. By the mid-1920s, however, the situation had improved. The economy recovered, France withdrew, and Germany joined the League of Nations. Some were taken with the creativity and novelty of the emerging Weimar cultural scene. But the suffering of the early 1920s was indelibly associated with the Republic, and not everyone was pleased by innovations like jazz, cabaret, and street theatre.

Ebert's duly elected successor, the former Field Marshal Paul von Hindenburg, was himself a monarchist, and his military credentials and conservative imperialism fostered cooperation between the otherwise fragmented right-wing parties. Hindenburg operated within the bounds of the Weimar Constitution, but it became increasingly clear that he did so halfheartedly. His skepticism was shared not only by key constituents like the army and the civil service but also by large numbers of ordinary Germans who suffered through the tremendous economic upheavals of the early 1920s. Weimar democracy had failed them in those years of hyperinflation and starvation as it had failed them in its capitulation to the demands of Versailles in the first place. Many believed the Republic's commitment to tolerance and pluralism led to what they considered the decadence of Weimar popular culture. And as another economic disaster made landfall in Germany at the close of the 1920s, one particular alternative to the perceived weaknesses of the Social Democrats and their Republic looked increasingly promising to many.

National Socialism and Its Sympathizers

The National Socialist German Worker Party (NSDAP or "Nazi" Party) was barely visible on the political radar for much of the 1920s. It achieved some notoriety as a result of its failed attempt to overthrow the German government in 1923 and the subsequent trial and imprisonment of its leader, the intense former army corporal turned political activist Adolf Hitler. From his prison cell Hitler wrote his manifesto, *Mein Kampf*, which introduced his fiercely anti-communist, anti-Semitic, nationalistic, and anti-intellectual ideas to a wider audience. Nonetheless, the Nazi Party was officially banned in Germany until February of 1925, and even when it reemerged and restructured itself in 1927-28, its electoral prowess was hardly impressive.

In 1928, the NSDAP garnered a meager 2 percent of the vote in the Reichstag elections. Yet only four years later, they managed to achieve a stunning 37 percent of the vote. How did a fringe movement like the Nazi Party move so quickly from the sidelines to a position of political dominance?

Multiple factors contributed to their sudden rise to power.

First, National Socialist ideology tapped into deep currents that existed in Germany long before anyone had heard the name Adolf Hitler. The longing for a decisive leader like Bismarck, the hope for a restored and expanded German Reich, the anger over the humiliation and injustice of Versailles, the fear of a communist revolution, the identification and demonization of "enemies" within Germany itself (Marxists, communists, exploitative capitalists, and Jews),[14] the interpretation of history as a struggle between races, the glorification of all things military, disdain for the "materialism" of the West versus the "spirituality" of the German character, the celebration of an idealized traditional German peasant life, dismay over the immorality of modern culture, nostalgia for the euphoric "Spirit of 1914" that united all Germans in a common and noble purpose, contempt for the endless compromise and ineffectuality of democracy in general and Weimar democracy in particular — all of these were notes the Nazis struck loudly and repeatedly. Opposition to the dreaded "Young Plan" in 1929 resulted in a new collaboration between the Nazis and the conservative nationalist political parties, a state of affairs that proved advantageous for the National Socialists.[15]

Second, the Nazis wedded these inherited themes with the authoritative language of science, adopting biological and evolutionary metaphors to describe the life of the nation. This gave what might have been seen as a

---

14. Sometimes these labels were conflated; thus terms like "Jewish Bolsheviks" and "Jewish capitalists" were commonplace in the rhetoric of the right. That it was illogical for one group to be both Marxist revolutionaries and capitalist oppressors apparently made no difference to those who employed them.

15. The Young Plan was an American proposal to reduce Germany's reparation debts. The right opposed it because they were opposed to the idea of reparations, period.

purely reactionary conservative movement a progressive, forward-looking veneer. The brand of racial Darwinism the Nazis advocated included the belief that the state had a responsibility to insure the survival and productivity of the German people both by safeguarding its racial purity and minimizing elements that might weaken the gene pool. There was a clinical and secular quality to this that, as Richard Evans observes, would never appeal to traditional conservatives or members of established religions.[16] Yet the idea of racial or social "hygiene" was increasingly a subject of discussion in the Weimar years, especially among scientists, physicians, social workers, and criminologists, and the Nazis joined in this cutting-edge debate.

Third, by co-opting some of the rhetoric of the left, the Nazi Party used the economic crisis of the late 1920s and early 1930s to their advantage. Ever since Germany's rapid industrialization in the nineteenth century, organized labor had been a major force in German politics. The Social Democrats were the primary party of labor, while the young Communist Party attracted much of the remainder. But with the onset of the depression in 1929 and massive unemployment that followed, the "party of labor" appeared unable to address the crisis effectively. While the Communist Party greeted the ensuing chaos as a hopeful sign that revolution was near, most Germans, even liberals, simply wanted jobs, bread, and order. The Nazis took up the label "socialist" for themselves (though they simultaneously condemned socialists, Marxists, and communists) and constantly celebrated the virtues of the ordinary worker in their propaganda, claiming they alone could rescue the unemployed and underemployed from the economic disaster Weimar had brought upon them. Yet the "socialism" espoused by the Nazis was markedly different from that of the left. Instead of pitting the classes against one another, Hitler promised the end of class warfare altogether. He offered relief from economic hardship yet shrewdly avoided all talk of the redistribution of wealth, thus placating an otherwise wary middle class.[17] This was a "socialism" the landed right could embrace. Many voters responded to Hitler's vision of a Germany unified in a common purpose, where every part of the national, racial "body" had dignity and value in contributing to the greater good of the German *Volk*.

Fourth, the Nazis terrorized their political enemies, intimidated would-be critics, and gained adherents enamored with "action" by their

---

16. Evans, *Coming of the Third Reich*, p. 38.
17. Burleigh, *Third Reich*, p. 135.

merciless but strategic use of violence. Following Hitler's failed putsch in 1923, he publicly resolved to achieve his political goals by legal means, rather than by force of arms. But this calculated restraint was only part of the story. From the beginning, Nazi militias and gangs (like the bands of thugs from other right-wing groups) were involved in street fights, political assassinations, and general mayhem in many parts of Germany.[18] But crucially, the Nazi squads did *not* attack representatives of the state as the Communist terrorists regularly did. Instead, the Nazis focused their attacks on political enemies: mostly Social Democrat and Communist politicians and supporters. The Nazis were skillful at either blaming the Communists for Nazi atrocities or portraying their actions as justifiable retaliation for Communist action against them. Because so many people were terrified of a Communist revolution, especially as the street violence escalated in the early 1930s, the violence that was attributed to the Nazi gangs was considered by many to be a helpful defense against the red menace.[19] In this way, Hitler was seen as a leader who had the will and means to bring law and order to Germany's streets, in spite of the ironic fact that the Nazis themselves systematically contributed to the continued disorder and lawlessness.[20]

Finally, the Nazis were unparalleled campaigners, an issue we will explore more fully in the next chapter. What is important to note here is that Hitler was careful to keep his vision of the Third Reich vague enough to allow for multiple interpretations depending on the demographic in question. Nazis carefully tailored their message, telling each group of voters exactly what they wanted to hear. They didn't succeed in wooing a majority of the electorate, but given Weimar's system of distribution, that was not necessary. The Nazis managed to make major inroads with the civil service, small businessmen, women, the young, the old, and, crucially, middle- and upper-class conservatives and rural voters.

---

18. There were three hundred and fifty political assassinations by right-wing groups during the Weimar years. Burleigh, *Third Reich*, p. 53.

19. Evans, *Coming of the Third Reich*, p. 265.

20. Hitler and other Nazi leaders were also very careful never to give their subordinates direct orders to commit violent acts. Their rhetoric was certainly incendiary, but deliberately vague. This led some middle-class Germans to disassociate Hitler and his immediate associates from the atrocities committed by overzealous lower level Nazi gangs. See Evans, *Coming of the Third Reich*, p. 230.

To the Brink of Revolution (1929–May 1932)

On October 24, 1929, the American stock market crashed, and in short order took the German economy down with it. What was already a difficult situation in Germany became exponentially worse. The National Socialists seized the moment and campaigned as never before. This frenzy of activity paid off in a way few anticipated. The Nazi Party earned 107 seats in the Reichstag in the 1930 elections, up from a mere 12 in 1928, and it did so by garnering votes from a broad spectrum of (primarily Protestant) social groups, becoming the "catch-all party of social protest" against Weimar, its culture, and its policies.[21]

The Nazi breakthrough not only resulted in a further escalation of their violence on the streets; it brought the already combative atmosphere of the Reichstag to a new level of incivility and finally outright anarchy.[22] It convened less and less frequently and by 1931 no longer functioned as a legislative body. Policy decisions were made by President Hindenburg and his advisors and put into effect by the power of Article 48.

But the ancient Hindenburg was near the end of his term as president, and because the Nazis refused to support a constitutional revision to extend his term, he was forced, at age 84, to put himself before the voters in a general election early in 1932. Among his rivals for the office of President was the gifted and popular Communist Party nominee Ernst Thälmann and, standing up for the National Socialists, none other than Hitler himself. The campaigning was feverish and the desperation palpable on all sides.

By February 1932, 33 percent of the German workforce was unemployed, and many others suffered severe cuts in pay and hours.[23] The unemployed roamed the streets, their haggard presence a constant reminder to many of the failure of the Weimar "system." Michael Burleigh's description of the situation is worth quoting at length:

> By 1932, the German suicide rate stood at 260 per million (as against 85 in Britain and 133 in the United States). Since women were paid less than men, they found it easier to get jobs and worked while their husbands and sons brooded at home, an inversion of the gender roles nor-

---

21. Evans, *Coming of the Third Reich*, p. 264.
22. Evans, *Coming of the Third Reich*, p. 275.
23. Burleigh, *Third Reich*, p. 122.

mal at the time that made for domestic fractiousness. Hopelessness spread to children, who absorbed their parents' despair. . . . In big cities, some teenagers went around in anti-social packs. . . . There was a rise in juvenile crime, prostitution, vagrancy and vandalism, and also in the population in remand homes and the juvenile wings of prisons. . . . [S]ome four hundred thousand people took to the roads in search of work, which stimulated further anxieties about tramps and vagrants. Those dependent on meager local benefits lived on bread and potatoes or whatever they could beg or steal, with heating fuel scratched off the slagheaps. . . . There was a shocking increase in cases of impetigo, rickets, and pulmonary illnesses. As the proportion of income spent on housing rose from 10 to 50 percent, the number of evictions mounted, and many unemployed workers moved to squatter settlements in the suburbs. Former industrial workers went back to being subsistence gatherers and farmers, stealing or scratching food from allotments. An enterprising few tried to make a go of it by selling beer, fruit, or razor blades on street corners. This vicious circle of self-help by the unemployed undercut small businesses, already suffering from a drop in demand. And the poverty of urban workers affected the countryside.[24]

Both the Nazi and Communist Parties benefited politically as things deteriorated. Such massive problems required dramatic and visionary solutions. Communist activists evangelized among the frustrated and bitter unemployed, often with success. "Red" gangs were a visible, threatening presence in the slums of German cities. While in retrospect their fears were unfounded, many middle-class Germans saw Communist agitators proselytizing and were once again convinced that a Bolshevik revolution was about to overwhelm the nation.[25] As in the past, this fear of the left led some voters to abandon their own political party for one that promised to keep the revolution at bay.

While Hitler did not win the presidency in the general election of 1932, he held his own even against a military icon like Hindenburg. The Nazi Party as a whole had done even better, achieving their highest percentage of votes ever in the Reichstag elections. As the spring of 1932 unfolded, political tensions were high, the Republic was in disarray, and the

24. Burleigh, *Third Reich,* p. 126.
25. Evans, *Coming of the Third Reich,* pp. 242-43.

Nazis were poised to take the stage. They would not have to wait long, though no one knew that at the time. This was the broader political situation in May of 1932, when Barth decided it was imperative that he add practical theology to his teaching responsibilities.

The Politics of Karl Barth

Any investigation of Barth's political commentary in the Weimar period must begin by acknowledging at least three dynamics: the socialist ethos Barth brought with him from Switzerland; the close relationship between his theological discoveries and his reaction to political developments in Germany; and the strategy of indirect critique he employed at the end of the 1920s and early 1930s. The third we will explore in detail when we discuss Barth and rhetoric in Chapter Four; the first two will occupy us here.

The Socialist Trajectory

Barth's political awakening began with his discovery of Swiss religious socialism during his time as pastor in Safenwil. Barth had already become acquainted with poverty firsthand while he was an assistant pastor in Geneva, and he had been involved in various kinds of relief work during that period. He was certainly aware of what was known as "the social question" even before that, as evidenced by his essay in a student newspaper while still at university, but he did not appear to have examined the issue of systemic economic injustice deeply, hardly surprising given the individualism and political conservatism of the Marburg school.[26] That would all change when Barth got to Safenwil.

Safenwil had become an industrial village and many in Barth's congregation worked in its textile mills and factories. Times were hard when Barth arrived, and they became worse after 1914 when the war began to have an impact. Food rationing, mandatory service, and tax increases all took their toll on the working-class population.

The Religious Socialist Movement in Switzerland was sparked by

---

26. In 1906 Barth wrote "Zofingia and the Social Question," in which he argued that the membership fees for Zofingia (a student organization) effectively shut out the poorer students and issued a call for reform and greater diversity in the union membership.

Herrmann Kutter's 1903 book *Sie Müssen*, which argued that the socialist movement, in spite of its atheism, embodied the gospel. Kutter urged a complacent, bourgeois Swiss Church to join the Marxists in their struggle for a just society. Leadership of the movement was shared by pastor Leonard Ragaz, and together they founded a journal *(Neue Weg)* to disseminate their views. There was a tremendous response from the Swiss church, particularly among young pastors. Barth was no exception.

In his Safenwil years Barth pored over key socialist and economic texts, became an expert in factory conditions and safety laws, and devoured trade union newspapers. He was shaken by the depths of human sinfulness he encountered and deeply troubled by the exploitation of the poor that went well beyond individual actions to the structures of society. He had not learned much about this at Marburg. He got involved in disputes in the town, negotiating with factory owners on behalf of workers. He held evening classes for working women and men on issues related to the labor movement and social democratic strategy and hosted a book group on "Socialism and the Social Movement" in the manse.[27] During those years he was instrumental in the formation of three new labor unions. All in all, Barth gave forty-three addresses related to socialism during his time in Safenwil, and the subject regularly came up in his preaching.[28] His "red" activities were not welcomed by everyone.[29]

Barth remained committed to the goals of socialism all his life.[30] But his initial commitment to religious socialism was challenged by the outbreak of the war. Not only did his theological heroes sign their names to the war manifesto, but the Socialist International was also caught up in war madness, in spite of their promises to work for peace.[31] Barth was an-

---

27. Frank Jehle, *Ever against the Stream: The Politics of Karl Barth, 1906-1968* (Grand Rapids: Eerdmans, 2002), p. 30.

28. Timothy Gorringe, *Karl Barth: Against Hegemony* (Oxford: Oxford University Press, 1999), p. 31.

29. In 1913, five out of the six members of the *Kirchenpflege* resigned in protest over his sermons and socialist activism. See Mark R. Lindsay, *Covenanted Solidarity: The Theological Basis of Karl Barth's Opposition to Nazi Antisemitism and the Holocaust*, Issues in Systematic Theology (New York: Peter Lang, 2001), p. 92. At one point there were calls for his resignation.

30. Gollwitzer argues that, from Safenwil on, Barth identified God's kingdom with "true socialism." What he came to reject was the identification of the socialism human beings create with the kingdom of God, though he affirmed the potential correspondence of human efforts toward the just society envisioned by socialism. George Hunsinger, *Karl Barth and Radical Politics* (Philadelphia: Westminster Press, 1976), pp. 79-80.

31. The Socialist International was a large organization of socialist and labor parties,

gry that the German Social Democratic Party succumbed to nationalism as well. By 1915, though he remained committed to work for a just society and insisted on solidarity with the poor, Barth was clearly uneasy with any undialectical conflation of socialism and the kingdom of God.

But in spite of Barth's disappointment with the socialist movement, he did not think it was possible to remain neutral and uninvolved. He joined the Swiss Social Democratic Party in 1915 and was involved locally and regionally in various ways until he immigrated to Germany, arguing against the influence of militarism, nationalism, and Bolshevism in the party.

Barth continued to follow the developments within the Religious Socialist Movement as well as the secular one. He noted differences in the way Kutter and Ragaz reacted to the war, and weighed the merits of each approach.

Kutter saw the gospel as a critique of all ideologies, and urged people to wait and pray for wisdom amid political turmoil. Rather than trying to "Christianize" the Social Democratic Party, he thought pastors could best prepare people for a new kind of society through faithful proclamation.[32] Kutter had a strong appreciation for what he considered the "spiritual" nature of German culture, and he supported the German war effort.

Ragaz, on the other hand, stressed immediate and courageous political activism and considered Kutter's approach quietistic. Ragaz reacted to the war with increasing condemnation, taking a pacifist stand. He ultimately sided with the Allied powers.

Barth was torn between them in many ways during the early months of the war as he tried to make sense of events. While Barth did not agree with Kutter's position vis-à-vis the German war effort, he eventually recognized that Kutter's exhortation to wait on a Word from God in a time of crisis *could* be a more radical position than Ragaz's call to action. Barth agreed that it might be harder to listen well, might be harder to discern what is right, in an emergency situation.[33]

But Barth was also drawn to Ragaz's emphasis on praxis. The hearing of the Word could not be separated from obedient, grateful action. But what kind of action? Should the church lose itself in socialist activism or

---

with participants from a number of countries. They had issued a "declaration of war on war" in 1912. Bruce McCormack, *Karl Barth's Critically Realistic Dialectical Theology: Its Genesis and Development, 1909-1936* (Oxford: Clarendon Press, 1997), p. 103.

32. McCormack, *Critically Realistic Dialectical Theology*, p. 118.
33. Lindsay, *Covenanted Solidarity*, p. 96.

Theological Existence in the Weimar Years

was the witness of socialism a summons to the church to get on with its own unique task?³⁴

When Barth wrote *Romans I*, widespread revolution looked possible in Europe, and indeed was already under way in Russia.³⁵ Socialists everywhere were excited that the long awaited change had finally come. But Barth was cautious, even ambivalent, about revolutionary action in the first edition of *Romans*. Readers are exhorted to participate in political life, but not with ultimate seriousness. Even the best political judgment is flawed and frail — to be politically active is to sin boldly, Barth argues. One must participate, but under no circumstances is a political ideology to be pronounced divine.

As the dust of revolution settled and the war neared its end, Barth's cautiousness was vindicated. The results of the Bolshevik revolution were now becoming clear. What had been accomplished? One dictatorship was replaced by another. An evil may have been overcome, but only by another evil. A police state was not the answer.

Tambach, 1919

With the end of the war, Switzerland experienced its own upheaval and confusion. The General Strike was under way. Barth was busy lobbying the Swiss Social Democrats, urging them not to join the Third International under the circumstances. Then, in September of 1919, Barth received a last-minute invitation to speak at Tambach, a conference devoted to fanning the relatively feeble flames of religious socialism in Germany.³⁶ It was a strange place for Barth to argue *against* religious socialism, but that is exactly what he did.³⁷

---

34. Despite Barth's disagreements with each, both Kutter (Neumünster) and Ragaz (Zürich) wanted Barth to succeed them at their respective universities when they retired.

35. McCormack argues that the identification of sin as the desire for autonomy and self-realization in *Romans I* was a critique (though not a rejection) of political liberalism and decidedly anti-bourgeois in tone. McCormack, *Critically Realistic Dialectical Theology*, p. 167.

36. Barth was called in after both Ragaz and Kutter turned down the invitation.

37. Barth knew it would be hard for him to gain a hearing at Tambach given the "mood of religious and social enthusiasm, in which the cry 'God for Kaiser and Fatherland' still echoed." Barth to Thurneysen, July 8, 1919, in Karl Barth, *Gesamtausgabe*, ed. Hinrich Stoevesandt and Hans Anton Drewes (Zürich: Theologischer Verlag, 1971), V.3, pp. 336-37.

Barth gave the pastors, students, and laypeople gathered there dialectical and nuanced marching orders. Political action, protest, and even participation in revolution are vital for Christians, he told them. But not for a moment can the church claim that what it does is somehow the equivalent of *God's* action, protest, and revolution. The resurrection demonstrates what is truly radical. Neither the establishment nor the revolution can lay claim to our worship. Barth argued against a "two kingdom" theology where the state is autonomous and the church sticks to its own internal affairs. God cannot be corralled in some "religious" pasture, he said. The whole of society, humanity, and world belongs to Christ, is *in* Christ. Christians are not only free but called to the trenches of politics, to move forward making relative judgments, taking risks for the sake of others, but do all this without idolizing a cause or divinizing an agenda. Barth urges them to act on a God-given restlessness. Join in alongside other democratic socialists, Barth tells the Germans gathered there, and work to support the fledgling German Republic with no illusions of grandeur.

> Have we actually *heard* the call that has come to us? Have we *comprehended* that which we have understood — that the challenge of our day is not to stand in opposition to life or its details but to orient nothing less than our *entire* lives toward God? Have we comprehended that this orientation must be guarded and proved in its entirety by our frank criticism of the particulars, by making courageous resolutions and taking steps, by taking on ruthless challengers, by patiently doing the work of reform, which in our day in particular requires that we take an open-hearted, broad-minded and honest attitude toward *social democracy*, precisely not as disengaged onlookers or critics *of* it but as hope-sharing and guilt-bearing players and comrades *within it*?[38]

The only basis for action now is the recognition of God's eschatological power, Barth argues:

> We put our energy toward both daily and banal business and tasks, but also toward a new Switzerland and a new Germany *precisely because* we are waiting for the new Jerusalem to come down from God out of the heavens [Rev. 21:2].[39]

---

38. Karl Barth, "The Christian in Society," in *The Word of God and Theology* (London: T&T Clark International, 2011), p. 64.

39. Barth, "The Christian in Society," p. 67.

By the time Barth was writing *Romans II*, revolution had failed in Germany and evidence of the brutality of the Russian situation continued to mount. In the second edition of *Romans* neither the status quo nor Bolshevism is legitimated — in fact, Barth argues that the Russian revolution is the more dangerous of the two because its goals are closer to the truth.

> Far more than the conservative, the revolutionary is overcome of evil, because with his 'no' he stands so strangely near to God. That is the tragedy of revolution.[40]

So what should one do when faced with revolutionaries who threaten to fight evil with evil? Barth articulates a strategy of nonviolent protest: Deprive revolution of its pathos.[41] Supplement this deprivation by acts of love, "undertaken as the protest against the course of this world."[42] Politics is only possible as game, Barth writes, the very metaphor he will use to discuss participation in culture more generally later on.[43]

In Safenwil Barth had been consumed with practical political activism, made a serious study of socialism and related issues, and paid close attention to events on the world stage — a "Red Pastor" as he was known in the Safenwil community. But what would happen when Barth was transplanted not only to the completely different environment of academia but to a new position vis-à-vis his context? How would Barth's political praxis change once he was viewed as an outsider by those around him?

Barth and Politics in Weimar

The nature of Barth's political involvement did indeed change after he arrived in Germany. There are several reasons for this. First, as he began his work in Göttingen, Barth's panic over his unpreparedness took its toll. Much of his time was devoted to catching up to the academic mandarins all around him and preparing his lectures. Second, all the positive and negative attention generated by his *Romans* commentaries also brought with it

---

40. Karl Barth, *The Epistle to the Romans*, 6th ed., trans. Edwyn Clement Hoskyns (London: Oxford University Press, 1968), p. 480.
41. Barth, *Romans*, p. 483.
42. Barth, *Romans*, p. 492.
43. Barth, *Romans*, p. 489.

the recognition that he had more substantive work to do. The seeds planted in *Romans* would need roots and leaves and branches. He, as the representative of what was now known as dialectical theology, would need to explain himself more fully. Barth was invited to share his theological discoveries in a staggering number of lectures and addresses in Germany and beyond. As a result, by the end of the 1920s Barth was an international figure in the theological world. Third, there is the fact that Barth's appointment to Göttingen came with conditions, one of which was that Barth had to agree that, as a professor in Germany, he would not "agitate" for his political perspective.[44] Finally, as a Swiss citizen, Barth was conscious of his status as an outsider vis-à-vis his host country. Martin Rade warned Barth to stay out of German politics for this very reason.[45]

It is not surprising, then, that Barth did not engage in the sort of political activism that characterized his life in Safenwil. But his interest in current events and efforts to address political questions continued, albeit in a more reserved form.[46]

Barth often found the political views of his theological faculty colleagues jarring. In general, he avoided open conflict on such matters during his early years in academia. When he did enter the fray he was often (as Rade had expected) berated and dismissed for his lack of German-ness.[47]

But while it was clear he would not make much headway in direct debate with his German nationalist colleagues, Barth did not abandon efforts to contribute to the future of Weimar democracy. He turned his attention to what he hoped was the more receptive ground of the students themselves, hosting open evenings at his home which were often devoted to the

---

44. McCormack, *Critically Realistic Dialectical Theology*, p. 242.

45. McCormack, *Critically Realistic Dialectical Theology*, p. 301.

46. Later Barth would attribute his relative political reserve in much of the Weimar years both to the intensity of his theological work and to his Swiss identity. See his letter of July 8, 1945 ("To the German Theologians Held Prisoner of War") in Karl Barth and Ernst Wolf, *Karl Barth zum Kirchenkampf: Beteiligung, Mahnung, Zuspruch*, Theologische Existenz Heute (New Series) (Munich: Kaiser, 1956), p. 92. Quoted in Gorringe, *Karl Barth*, p. 84.

47. Barth observed to Thurneysen in January 1923: "The German professors are really true masters at finding ingenious Christian and moral grounds for brutalities. . . . Also Hirsch was bad, speaking of the *una sancta* (the German *Volkes*). . . . I had a frightful scene with him after that, in which 'Swiss! Foreigner! Agitator! Disturber of the peace!' flew around my head." Barth, *Gesamtausgabe* V.4, p. 131. In a letter to *Die Christliche Welt* in 1927, Otto Ritschl went so far as to dismiss *all* of Barth's theology as an expression of his Swiss "neutrality" and "pessimism." Otto Ritschl, "Vierundzwanzigsten Brief," *Die Christliche Welt* 41 (1927): 844. See also McCormack, *Critically Realistic Dialectical Theology*, p. 376, note 3.

discussion of politics and cultural events.[48] He would continue this practice in the mid-1920s when he went to Münster. There Barth led the students through a series of biographies and autobiographies of many contemporary political figures (including the Kaiser!). And in the following semester they turned to the question of the motives and connections that underlay the various political positions. Through the course of such meetings, Barth modeled both a theologically grounded critique of politics and the civil discourse so vital to democracy.[49]

In addition to these relatively circumscribed efforts, Barth would also take up themes with political implications in many lectures and writings over the course of these years, sometimes explicitly. In a speech at a conference in Wales in 1925 (and delivered shortly thereafter in Germany), for example, Barth explained why a new universal Reformed creed was unlikely:

> A church which today desired to confess its faith must have the courage to express the insight currently won from Scripture on the problems of life which today beset its members. It cannot wait until its statement comes thirty years too late, like the Social Manifesto of the Bielefeld Church Assembly. It must act while the problem is still 'hot', while the Church can speak its word upon it where the word of the Church belongs, at the outset of the problem. The Church must have the courage to speak today (I mention only one specific problem) upon the fascist, racialist nationalism which since the war is appearing in similar forms in all countries. Does the Church say yes or no to this nationalism? Does the Church, deliberately and in principle, say Yes to war, or has it, in spite of all practical considerations, a final, principled No to set on the lampstand? A No which is unqualified and fully audible, not a pacifist's No, but a specifically Christian No against the war?

---

48. Marcus Barth reports that Barth "observed with horror a strong rightist movement" during the time he taught in Germany, not only among his colleagues, but also among the students. Marcus Barth, "Current Discussions on the Political Character of Barth's Theology," in *Footnotes to a Theology: The Karl Barth Colloquium of 1972*, ed. Martin Rumscheidt (Waterloo: Corporation for the Publication of Academic Studies in Religion in Canada, 1974), p. 78.

49. Barth describes his open evenings in May of 1924 in a letter to Thurneysen, noting that they had read the political autobiographies of Alfred von Tirpitz and Karl Liebknecht, and would continue with Georg Michaelis, the Kaiser, Philipp Scheidemann, the Crown Prince, Erich Ludendorff, Theobald von Bethmann-Hollweg, and Matthias Erzberger. Barth explained that he encouraged the students to question the motives behind the actions of the various politicians and to explore their political relationship to one another. Barth, *Gesamtausgabe* V.4, p. 252.

Does the Church intend to affirm and establish by a creed in all lands the unambiguously militaristic position which it took in 1914?[50]

Barth could not vote in German elections while he was at Göttingen, but with a regular appointment to Münster he was granted dual citizenship, which included voting rights.[51] Barth reports to Thurneysen that he voted for the Social Democrats in the spring of 1928.[52] As it turned out, the elections of May 1928 had gone fairly well for the Social Democratic Party. For all its problems it looked like the Republic could survive. Barth seemed to think so. This hope would live on for a while.

In his ethics lectures of 1928-29, Barth again supported neither reactionary nor revolutionary political action, but instead spoke warmly of democracy. In the lectures Barth supported women's right to vote, rejected imperialism and argued against any sort of state suppression on the grounds of race or class. As Frank Jehle observes, these were not typical positions in Germany or even in the wider European context.[53] Barth would repeat these arguments in his ethics lectures once he got to Bonn in 1930-31, when the political situation had intensified.

By the end of the 1920s Barth was aware of the increasingly visible right-wing revolutionaries in Germany, including the Nazis, but he, like so many others, could not imagine that they would prevail. He remembered later,

> I was thoroughly wrong at that time in not perceiving danger in National Socialism, which had already begun its ascent. From the very beginning its ideas and methods and its leading figures all seemed to me to be quite absurd. I thought that the German people were simply too sensible to fall prey to that possibility.[54]

50. Barth, "The Desirability and Possibility of a Universal Reformed Creed," in *Theology and Church: Shorter Writings, 1920-1928* (New York: Harper & Row, 1962), p. 133.
51. McCormack, *Critically Realistic Dialectical Theology*, p. 302.
52. See Barth, *Gesamtausgabe* V.4, p. 607.
53. Jehle, *Ever against the Stream*, p. 4. In Lutheran circles the "two kingdom" theology led some prominent figures to argue against not only revolutionary movements but democracy itself, favoring instead the authoritarianism of monarchy. In the 1920s, Paul Althaus called democracy "a disaster" and the monarchy an "ethical necessity." See Jehle, *Ever against the Stream*, p. 39. According to the "two kingdom" model, the church must submit to the demands of the state. But in a democracy, who is one "submitting" to? Not the *state* but the *majority*. This was a troubling thought to Lutherans at the time.
54. Karl Barth, "Zwischenzeit," *Kirchenblatt für die reformierte Schweiz* 118 (1962): 38.

McCormack argues that Barth probably recognized that the Republic was in real danger in the aftermath of the September 1930 elections, when the National Socialists made their dramatic gains.[55] While Barth's differences with his dialectical comrades had been simmering for years, from this point on he began to take steps to distance himself from them.[56]

Once again Barth directed his political efforts toward his students. The open evenings at his home in Bonn in the winter of 1930-31 were all about politics, and large crowds of students would gather for discussion of the platforms and ideologies of the Weimar parties.[57] In May 1931, he joined the Social Democratic Party in a show of solidarity. He explained to a friend in 1932:

> . . . early last year, in view of the fact that right-wing terror was gaining the upper hand, I thought it right to make it clear with whom I would like to be imprisoned and hanged.[58]

Barth was aware that things were spinning out of control.[59]

From the final months of 1931 on, Barth entered the public debate. He advanced his argument in the course of various church controversies and in a highly visible academic dispute ("the Dehn case"), each of which were simultaneously political struggles. We will explore these situations in more detail below.

What is important to note here is that when Barth wrote to Pfennigsdorf in May of 1932, Barth took the fascist threat seriously. He was engaged in active resistance, even defiance, on multiple fronts. Encroaching on Pfennigsdorf's territory by teaching preaching himself was certainly one of them.

At the heart of Barth's theological and political critique of National

---

55. McCormack, *Critically Realistic Dialectical Theology*, p. 414.

56. McCormack argues that Barth promoted the idea of a "break" between *Die christliche Dogmatik* and the first part-volume of the *Church Dogmatics* in 1933 as a means to declare his unequivocal independence from his erstwhile friends and any theology that might lend credence to the view that God's revelation could be found in *Volk, Vaterland*, or *Führer*. McCormack, *Critically Realistic Dialectical Theology*, pp. 446-47.

57. Eberhard Busch, *Karl Barth: His Life from Letters and Autobiographical Texts* (Philadelphia: Fortress, 1976), p. 203. Barth, *Gesamtausgabe* V.34, pp. 47-48.

58. Karl Barth to Hans Asmussen, January 14, 1932, quoted in McCormack, *Critically Realistic Dialectical Theology*, p. 414.

59. Barth told Thurneysen in November 1931 that the German political situation was like "sitting in a car which is driven by a man who is either incompetent or drunk." Quoted in Busch, *Karl Barth*, p. 217.

Socialism and its Christian sympathizers were the very factors that disillusioned him with liberal theology and ideological socialism in the first place. Idolatrous nationalism and its corresponding inhumanity, the legitimation of violence, confidence in the human ability to discern God or destiny in historical events or natural "orders" — these dynamics could only lead to political and every other kind of disaster. The only way to counter National Socialism, Barth thought, was to challenge these underlying dynamics, especially as they took root and spread in the church and the academy.

The Ecclesiastical Lens

Mapping the Landscape

In 1910, there were approximately 40 million Protestants, 24 million Catholics, 600,000 Jews, and a smattering of adherents to other Christian denominations in Germany.[60] The Protestant *Land* (regional) churches were either Lutheran, Reformed, or Union (an alliance of the two), but the vast majority were Lutheran.

In the decades leading up to the Great War, most German Protestant church leaders accepted the basic premises of liberal theology to a large degree, and like many of the liberal theologians that dominated the academic sphere, they were also politically conservative and extremely patriotic. The majority were monarchists, and remained so even when the monarchy was no more. The "two kingdoms" theology bequeathed by Lutheranism encouraged them to submit to the authority of the state and stay out of matters which did not directly concern them.[61] Though church leaders were certainly aware of the challenges posed by industrialization and the growing labor movement, they struggled to find resources within their theological understanding to do much beyond seconding the minor reforms attempted by the state.[62]

---

60. Ernst Christian Helmreich, *The German Churches under Hitler: Background, Struggle, and Epilogue* (Detroit: Wayne State University Press, 1979), p. 36.

61. Franz Feige advances the theory that it was the fact that the Reformation in Germany took place with the support and protection of the territorial princes that contributes to the idea in Lutheranism that rebellion against authority is a sinful act. Calvinism grew up in a more hostile environment; hence, resistance to authority is more comprehensible as an act of faith for the Reformed. Franz G. M. Feige, *The Varieties of Protestantism in Nazi Germany: Five Theopolitical Positions*, Toronto Studies in Theology (Lewiston: E. Mellen Press, 1990), p. 9.

62. Helmreich, *German Churches*, p. 41.

Theological Existence in the Weimar Years

German children were enrolled in the church automatically at birth, so the membership rolls of the *Landeskirchen* were enormous. Church attendance was another matter. Indeed, it was commonplace for clergy to complain about poor church attendance in the decades leading up to the First World War. Individuals had the right to withdraw formally from the church, thus exempting them from paying the church tax. Until 1906, additions exceeded withdrawals most of the time. But from 1906 onward (with the exception of the war period 1915-17) the withdrawal numbers began to climb, eventually exceeding the additions.[63] Sometimes Socialists actually launched public relations campaigns urging people to withdraw, much to the chagrin of church leaders.[64]

With the war came a revival of sorts as the Spirit of 1914 swept the churches. Ministers preached of the war as God's will and extolled the superior nature of the German *Geist* vis-à-vis the West.[65] The eventual defeat of Germany was incomprehensible given these assumptions. The end of the war precipitated a spiritual crisis, and subsequent events only confirmed the gravity of the situation.

The revolution of 1918 and the subsequent establishment of Weimar were widely perceived as a threat to the existence of the church. There were persistent demands from Social Democrats for a greater separation of church and state, demands which, in the minds of those in the church, jeopardized longstanding practices: government subsidies for the churches, the church's right to tax its members, religious instruction in the schools, funding for theological faculties, and government sponsored chaplaincies, among other things. But the Social Democrats were well aware that they did not have a majority without the support of their coalition partners, and they also discerned that public opinion strongly favored continuity on the church/state question. Even Germans who were not particularly religious and did not participate in the organized church themselves did not support abolishing the tradition of state-sponsored religion.[66] As it turned out, the

---

63. Helmreich, *German Churches*, p. 37.
64. Helmreich, *German Churches*, p. 41.
65. Klaus Scholder quotes from Ernst von Dryander's sermon on Romans 8:31 ("If God be for us, who can stand against us"), which opened the Reichstag on August 4, 1914: "we know that we are going into battle for the roots of our strength, we know that we are going into battle for our culture against the uncultured, for German civilization against barbarism, for the free German personality bound to God against the instincts of the undisciplined masses." Klaus Scholder, *The Churches and the Third Reich*, vol. 1 (Philadelphia: Fortress, 1988), p. 6.
66. Helmreich, *German Churches*, pp. 41-42.

Weimar Constitution did not do any of the things the church leaders had feared. Continuity carried the day.[67]

But the new situation did bring changes of a different sort to the structure of the *Landeskirchen*. Because there was a reduction in the number of states after the war, so too there was also a decrease in the number of *Landeskirchen*.[68] Now that the princes were no more, the remaining twenty-eight found themselves with a new and unanticipated autonomy. They were self-governing in ways they had not been before. As long as the state continued its financial support, this independence was welcomed.[69] Most *Landeskirchen* began the work of drafting new constitutions in response to the changed situation, which resulted in a variety of localized governing models and terminology.[70] Most of the *Landeskirchen* tried to produce a constitution that would facilitate the involvement of the laity in the decision making.[71] What they did not attempt to do was to separate themselves from the state and its financial support.

Most Protestants understood it to be the duty of the state to support religion in the same way it would support any means of cultural enrichment. While there was, and had long been, a desire for a single unified *Reichskirche* in some quarters, this was not a majority view. Nevertheless, there was strong consensus that there should be *some* sort of connectional relationship between the *Landeskirchen* which would present a united Prot-

---

67. In spite of this, fears remained that the provisions of the Weimar constitution ("the constitution without God") would eventually erode state support of the church. Scholder, *Churches and the Third Reich*, vol. 1, p. 20.

68. The *Landeskirche* of the Old Prussian Union dwarfed the others, with close to nineteen million members. The church of Saxony, the second largest, had only four and a half million. Scholder, *Churches and the Third Reich*, vol. 1, p. 32.

69. Owing to their status as public corporations, while the Weimar *Landeskirchen* were self-governing, they did so under the supervision of the state. Helmreich, *German Churches*, p. 121.

70. Seven of the *Landeskirchen*, for example, established the office of bishop, others called for a general superintendent, still others for a *Land* president. Helmreich, *German Churches*, p. 68.

71. Helmreich, *German Churches*, p. 68. The call for a more "democratic" church with full participation of the laity *(Volkskirche)* and a unified *Reichskirche* was sounded most clearly in the early days of Weimar by liberals such as Martin Rade. See Scholder, *Churches and the Third Reich*, vol. 1, p. 9. While this *Volkskirche* movement did not result in a radical restructuring of *Landeskirchen* governments nor a *Reichskirche* in the early 1920s, it did contribute to a grassroots revival of sorts with themes of *Volk* and unity that would be vigorously taken up by the German Christian movement later in the decade. Scholder, *Churches and the Third Reich*, vol. 1, pp. 28-29.

estant front in the pluralistic Republic. This resulted in the formation of the German Evangelical Church Confederation *(Deutscher Evangelischer Kirchenbund)*, which thus functioned as the public voice of German Protestantism. We cannot go into detail regarding the bureaucratic intricacies of the *Kirchenbund's* three governing bodies, but it is important to note that the most powerful of these bodies was the thirty-six-member *Kirchenausschuss*, led by the president of the largest of the *Landeskirchen*, that of Prussia. The *Kirchenausschuss* was one of the key forums where the church-political drama of 1932-33 would play out.

Meanwhile the individual confessions (Lutheran, Reformed, and United) continued to maintain their own organizations in addition to participating in the Confederation.

In the years immediately after the war the church had plenty of reasons to be unhappy: the economic chaos had a dire impact on church finances, the strong church attendance of the war years had faded away, there was a slight decline in marriage and communion figures, and the church withdrawals had increased.[72] The Marxists in particular were blamed for the exodus from the church, with at least some justification.

In spite of these declines, or maybe because of them, there was a proliferation of periodicals directed to Protestants during the Weimar years, along with a number of new or newly strengthened church societies, clubs, and organizations.[73]

The Politics of the Protestant Church in Early Weimar

While there were certainly a variety of theopolitical positions among clergy in the Weimar years, we can generalize about the dominance of two traits: conservatism and nationalism.[74] Their conservatism was slightly

---

72. Helmreich, *German Churches*, p. 81. The exception to this trend was the increase in theology students during the Weimar years, from 2,089 men in 1926 to 6,791 in 1931, an oddity that provoked concern over where to put them all once they graduated. The numbers of women studying theology also increased dramatically. Helmreich, *German Churches*, p. 82.

73. The importance of the church-related newspapers and magazines should not be underestimated. As Helmreich observes, they could function as a "strong and significant agency of instruction and propaganda." Helmreich, *German Churches*, p. 86.

74. Helmreich quotes a popular saying from the 1920s: "The church is politically neutral, but it votes German National." Helmreich, *German Churches*, p. 77. It is estimated that

tempered by the recognition that the church was losing the working class to the Communists and Socialists in the 1920s, so there were some efforts to address the "social question." Religious socialism garnered modest interest in some quarters. However, any desire to reach out to the working classes was undermined by the complete antipathy that the majority of *Landeskirchen* and their leaders had toward anything that resembled Marxism, socialism, or communism, all of which they equated with atheism.[75] The Weimar government itself was never embraced by the vast majority of Protestants; at best it was only grudgingly accepted. A few prominent liberals, notably Martin Rade and Otto Baumgarten, urged the church to make the best of the new situation and see the bright side of the new Republic.[76] But few Protestant leaders were persuaded. Unlike the Catholic Church with the Centre Party, the Protestants could claim no one political party as *the* Protestant party. Their allegiance tended to be split between the parties of the right, who offered the necessary combination of nationalism and anti-Marxism.

Triumphalism

By the mid-1920s, as the economy stabilized and it became clear that the Protestant church could hold its own even under a "godless" constitution and without the protection of princes, a new confidence emerged. The atheists had not succeeded in marginalizing the church in German society. With skillful church leadership German Protestantism had prevailed, some proclaimed. In fact, with the erosion of morality everywhere in evidence the importance of the church had never been more clear: they were

---

the percentage of conservative national clergy in Weimar held steady at between 70 and 80 percent. Feige, *Varieties of Protestantism*, p. 59.

75. Helmreich, *German Churches*, p. 78.

76. This attitude of resignation to Weimar was known as *"Vernunftrepublikanismus"* and is evident in this quote from Otto Baumgarten in 1918: "I admit that until the war I belonged to the enemies of democratization and politicization of the people and still doubt if the gain which they yield in activity and feeling of responsibility will compensate for the enormous damage to tranquility and warmth and solidity of social life, but . . . I do not feel justified in defiantly renouncing cooperation in the new era. Let us make the best out of the unavoidable!" Otto Baumgarten in *Evangelische Freiheit: Monatschrift für die Kirchliche Praxis in der gegenwartigen Kultur* 18 (October 1918): 314, 318. Quoted in Frank J. Gordon, "Liberal German Churchmen and the First World War," *German Studies Review* 41, no. 1 (1981): 60.

to use their new-found freedom and boldness to guard the ethical soul of the nation.[77]

This view of the matter was shaped and stoked by a popular book on church life, *Das Jahrhundert der Kirche*, written by the youthful and energetic superintendent of the Prussian church, Otto Dibelius, in 1926. It was this self-satisfaction regarding the church's "success" and the nature of its task that would put Dibelius and those who shared his perspective on a collision course with Barth.

Barth's 1930 article "Quousque Tandem?" was a direct critique of the reigning Protestant nationalist ecclesiology, which congratulated itself that it had triumphed over the atheists with its dexterous leadership, delighted in the natural appetite for religion "in the soul of the German people," and read God's vindication of the German Protestant Church in this turn of events.[78] Barth attacked the complacency, arrogance, and self-centeredness of such a perspective, as if the church's institutional power and prosperity was the point and God's will could be so easily discerned in history. How could the church be so focused on its own flag-waving, "as if there were no housing shortage and no unemployment in Germany"?[79]

The article was published in *Zwischen den Zeiten* early in 1930, before the Nazi electoral breakthrough. Barth concluded the essay with the plea that the German church retrace its steps and return to costly, humble preaching of the gospel, rather than making "all the exhortation, comfort, and teaching of the Bible and the Reformers water for her own little mills."[80]

Needless to say, the critique was not well received by the Protestant establishment, and the public debate about the nature and mission of the church that began as a result of Barth's essay would take on new significance as the political situation became increasingly polarized in the

---

77. Klaus Scholder explains that this belief — that the role of religion is to defend and preserve the moral character of the nation — was one conviction that both conservative, nationalist, and liberal German Protestants shared, in spite of differences in the specific content of the "morality" in question. Scholder, *Churches and the Third Reich*, vol. 1, p. 40.

78. The Latin phrase means "how long?" and most famously appears in a speech by Cicero against the corrupt politician Catiline. The entire sentence from the speech reads in English: "How long, Catiline, will you abuse our patience?" Karl Barth, *"Der Götze wackelt": Zeitkritische Aufsätze, Reden und Briefe von 1930 bis 1960*, ed. Karl Kupisch (Berlin: Käthe Vogt, 1961), p. 211.

79. An excerpt of "Quousque Tandem?" in English is printed in Peter Matheson, *The Third Reich and the Christian Churches* (Edinburgh: T&T Clark, 1981), pp. 2-4. For the complete German text see Barth, "Quousque Tandem?" in *"Der Götze wackelt,"* pp. 27-32.

80. Barth, "Quousque Tandem?" p. 31.

months and years that followed.[81] Indeed, with the results of the September 1930 elections, the debate about the church was simultaneously and inextricably also one about politics.

But to understand the dramatic transformation of the Protestant church in the early 1930s, we must back up and consider three of the factors that made the church vulnerable to the baptized version of National Socialism: the "German Christians."

The Völkisch Movement

The *völkisch* ideology that animated many by the early 1930s in Germany had its roots in a number of sources in the nineteenth century. For our purposes a rough sketch of the outlines of the *völkisch Weltanschauung* as it took shape on the fringes of the Protestant church in the 1920s will suffice: a dualistic view of ethics, a celebration of the "German spirit" and its destiny, an ontological understanding of race which had as its focus the "struggle" between Germans (Aryans) and Jews, the belief that Jesus was himself Aryan, and the conviction that Christianity must be rescued from the superstitions of the Old Testament and the distortions of the Jewish Paul.[82] For the *völkisch* ideologues, so-called "Positive" Christianity meant this "purified" Christianity.

While the passionate nationalism, calls for law and order, anti-Marxism, heroic piety, and general moral outrage of *völkisch* prophets did

---

81. Dibelius responded promptly to "Quousque Tandem?" in a report to the Prussian General Synod, arguing that Barth's critical stance toward the church could be sustained only in the context of "a Christian state" but not in a time when the state was "religionless," i.e., in the context of a government like Weimar. Only the church and its moral witness could keep the entire national community from sliding into atheism. Scholder, *Churches and the Third Reich*, vol. 1, p. 123. Barth wrote many years later of the church's "unmistakable bias towards the black-white-red reactionaries" in those days; he added that because of the restructuring that came with Weimar "for the first time [the church] had found its own feet in independence from the state" and "developed a remarkably pompous self-importance which did not seem to be matched by the content and profundity of its preaching. Here and there could already be found 'bishops' of the kind who loved being bishops . . . and some of them, pooh-poohing the malice of the time and the storm-clouds in the heavens, saw the star of a whole 'century of the church' rising on the horizon. I could not see either of these tendencies as being of any use to the cause of the church, and opposed them as well as I could." Quoted in Busch, *Karl Barth*, pp. 190-91.

82. Scholder, *Churches and the Third Reich*, vol. 1, pp. 74-84.

have broad appeal among many postwar Protestants, it is critical to note that the fixation on race in particular was not a dominant characteristic of the Protestant church in the 1920s. This is not to say that there was not a subtle (or not so subtle) anti-Semitic prejudice in place, but that regardless of this there was discomfort with and most often outright rejection of the *völkisch* version of Christianity with its Aryan Jesus and truncated Bible.

Instead, the primary targets of church leaders in the 1920s were Bolshevism, secularism, and immorality, though the *völkisch* disciples increasingly succeeded in placing something identified as "the Jewish problem" even on the ecclesiastical agenda.[83] When anti-Semitism was later openly embraced within the mainstream of the Protestant church (as in the broader society), it was most often conflated with one or more of the perceived threats to the German *Volk* — Bolshevism, secularism, materialism, internationalism, pacifism — in other words, it was in the name of some version of nationalism. This nationalism is the underlying dynamic Barth relentlessly challenges.

"Political Theology"

The vision of the *völkisch* movement converged with that of some influential younger Lutheran theologians, most significantly Paul Althaus and Emanuel Hirsch, on the romantic concept of *Volk*.[84] One is born into a particular people with a particular destiny, these scholars argued, and that corporate racial identity is a gift from God, an "order of creation" to be celebrated and protected. Theologians must serve the *Volk* by pointing out the spiritual and political mission that is their destiny. The church, too, has the well-being of the national community *(Volksgemeinschaft)* as its focus.[85]

This view of the matter is somewhat confusingly referred to as "Political Theology" because it was preoccupied with obedience to God in "political" (meaning German-national) terms, and identified revelation with particular historical-political events. Though preoccupied with the rights and

---

83. Helmreich, *German Churches*, p. 125.

84. The concept of *"Volk"* has a lengthy pedigree in German thought. It was first given its metaphysical connotation (as a "national soul" evident in all peoples) by Johann Gottfried Herder (1744-1803). Johann Fichte (1762-1814) and Ernst Moritz Arndt (1769-1860) would associate the term particularly with the German people and their destiny. Feige, *Varieties of Protestantism*, pp. 21-22.

85. Scholder, *Churches and the Third Reich*, vol. 1, p. 103.

value of the German *Volk,* Political Theology was a resounding rejection of democracy. True leaders were divinely appointed, not elected.[86] Individuals were absorbed into a corporate "will," that of the *Volk,* and were summoned to heroic, selfless devotion to the Fatherland. The survival of the German *Volk* was a matter of obedience to the God who brought it into being for a special, holy reason.

Unlike the *völkisch* movement with its unpalatable eccentricities, Political Theology emerged in the heart of Protestantism and legitimized many *völkisch* ideas with its relatively moderate tone. As Klaus Scholder observes:

> One cannot understand how Christians were ready to accept the flood of hate and vulgarity which *völkisch* antisemitism spewed forth without realizing that the beginnings of political theology had made the right of the *Volk* the embodiment of the divine will in creation.[87]

In 1927 Althaus summarized the agenda for the church as "serving the *Volk* as *Volk*" in a speech before the Königsburg *Kirchentag,* and argued that this entailed two tasks: "a truly German proclamation of the gospel, and the entering of the church into the organic forms of life and living customs of *Volkstum.*"[88] The time had come to "sanctify" *völkisch* ideas for the sake of the Kingdom of God, and the church must now "have an eye and a word for the Jewish threat to our *Volkstum.*"[89] It would be a few more years before Althaus' claims would be echoed in large portions of the Protestant church, but the baptism of *völkisch* racism by Political Theology marked an important turning point in the 1920s.

There were certainly those who argued against Political Theology and the claims of the *völkisch* movement during the mid-to-late 1920s, Karl Barth among them.[90] Dialectical theology was itself a subject of debate in

---

86. Scholder, *Churches and the Third Reich,* vol. 1, p. 105.
87. Scholder, *Churches and the Third Reich,* vol. 1, p. 107.
88. Quoted in Scholder, *Churches and the Third Reich,* vol. 1, p. 112.
89. Scholder, *Churches and the Third Reich,* vol. 1, p. 113.
90. Two notable contributions in this regard: Otto Baumgarten's pamphlet "Cross and Swastika" (1926), which was distributed to every Protestant pastor in Germany, and Eduard Lamparter's series of articles in 1927-28 entitled "Evangelical Church and Judaism" (later published in book form). Both texts were clear and theologically grounded rejections of *völkisch* anti-Semitism in German church and society. The latter book by Lamparter included a foreword in which twelve prominent theologians and church leaders commended the work, notably Martin Rade, Paul Tillich, and Karl Barth. Scholder, *Churches and the Third Reich,* vol. 1, pp. 115-17.

ecclesiastical circles during the same period, but it did not claim many adherents among the longstanding leaders of the Protestant church. It was largely rejected by the liberal establishment, the Religious Socialists, and the conservative Lutheran nationalists.[91]

But if dialectical theology did not claim a majority in the Protestant church as the 1920s unfolded, neither did Political Theology. The evidence suggests that the majority of Protestant *Land* churches remained largely unmoved by the *völkisch* appeals of the Lutheran Political Theologians even in the late 1920s.[92]

But the problem, Scholder argues, was this: when the climate shifted in the early 1930s, Political Theology was seen as a sensible middle ground between those who condemned racism and nationalism (the Religious Socialists, dialectical theologians, and liberals) on the one hand and the extremist fringe (represented by a small group of rabidly *völkisch* "German Church" pastors) on the other.[93]

By the early 1930s, as it became clear that *völkisch* ideology was gaining currency in German society more broadly, church leaders posed the question of the relationship between "Germanhood" and Christianity with increasing urgency. With National Socialist fervor marching visibly through the streets, the old anxieties that marked the beginning of Weimar returned. Would the church be left behind in the new revolution?

Bystanders to the Revival

The September 1930 election made it clear to Protestant leaders that they would need to take National Socialism with its nominally Roman Catholic *Führer* seriously if they did not want to be relegated to the sidelines of the *Volk* revival now under way.[94] As Klaus Scholder observes, the Nazi Party

---

91. Scholder, *Churches and the Third Reich*, vol. 1, p. 49.

92. In a 1928 survey, only the *Landeskirche* of Berlin considered the *völkisch* movement to be significant for the church. On the other hand, there was widespread concern about the "atheism" of Social Democracy. Scholder, *Churches and the Third Reich*, vol. 1, p. 120.

93. Scholder, *Churches and the Third Reich*, vol. 1, p. 117.

94. Scholder quotes a pastor from Berlin who expresses a concern with regard to Catholicism and the National Socialist Movement that was common at the time: "The Evangelical Church has to be careful to secure for itself the same towering influence in the movement as have the Catholic members." Scholder, *Churches and the Third Reich*, vol. 1, p. 131.

was the youth party, full of energy and promise.[95] The image of young Germans rising up and committing themselves wholeheartedly to Hitler's vision was a powerful incentive for the church to remain open to the possibility that the Nazis could be the answer to Germany's woes. No church likes its young to abandon it. Lutheran church leaders believed that they could have a positive influence on the Nazis, shaping their raw enthusiasm and passion in a Christian direction.[96] From 1930 onward National Socialism and aspects of its ideology dominated discussion in the German Protestant church and its publications.[97]

In the 1931 meeting of the *Kirchenbundesrat*, an entire day was devoted to the discussion of the "German Church." How should they handle the most radical pastors who preached the *völkisch* gospel from Protestant pulpits?

While a resolution was proposed that would forbid pastors from speaking or acting "in contradiction to the confession of faith and the ordinances of the church," it failed miserably.[98] Why?

Even though there was still discomfort with those who wanted a "purified" Christianity and the recognition (as evidenced by the resolution itself) that *völkisch* thought did indeed constitute heresy at least on some points, there was a deeper dynamic at work: "fear that the public might suspect that 'the church rejected the German idea, indeed fought against it.'"[99] The church did not want to be left behind. It needed to be "relevant" in the way that National Socialism was clearly relevant to many people. Moreover, the leading Political Theologians began to speak of National So-

---

95. Scholder, *Churches and the Third Reich*, vol. 1, p. 130.

96. Scholder, *Churches and the Third Reich*, vol. 1, p. 137. The idea that one could accept aspects of National Socialism, such as its *völkisch* philosophy, while rejecting what were seen as its cruder elements, or praising Hitler while rejecting the violence of some of his henchmen, was common among Protestant leaders and political theologians. Again, it reinforced the impression that their "yes and no" to the Nazis represented a sensible middle ground. The thought that the church might have an indispensable part to play as the conscience or spiritual corrective for the obviously God-sent movement was difficult to resist.

97. This openness on the part of the Protestant Church to consider National Socialism must be contrasted with the position of the Catholic Church in Germany, which unambiguously condemned Nazi ideology in the early 1930s and forbade Catholics from joining the NSDAP. This would be the case until the agreement between the Holy See and Hitler, the *Reichskonkordat* of July 1933.

98. Scholder, *Churches and the Third Reich*, vol. 1, p. 118.

99. Scholder, *Churches and the Third Reich*, vol. 1, p. 118. Scholder quotes the archived transcript of the assembly.

cialism in a new way in the wake of its triumph at the polls. It had proven itself to be *more* than a political movement. How could it be doubted that *God himself* was speaking in the courage of the brown battalions, the earnestness of the enraptured youth, and the spellbinding presence of its Leader? Hirsch and Althaus began to back away from notions of a universal Christian fellowship, rejecting international ecumenical relationships as a betrayal of the German *Volk*.[100] If the church was not careful, they warned, it would increase the degree of alienation from the Protestant church that was already evident "among nationally-minded, morally earnest people."[101]

Thus the terms of the debate were set. Barth himself returned to the question of ecclesiology with a lecture that he delivered in Berlin, then Bremen, and finally Hamburg in January of 1931 on "The Need of the Evangelical Church." There was new urgency regarding the question of the church's identity and purpose in the wake of the Nazi electoral surprise — an urgency demonstrated by the 1400 people who showed up to hear Barth in Berlin, crowding in for two hours to hear the speech.

Barth argued against the assimilation of the message of the gospel to categories like fate, authority, order, and "the hyphen linking Christianity and *Volkstum*, Protestant and German."[102] The need was for a truly *protestant* church *in* Germany, Barth argued, not for a *German* protestant church.[103]

Otto Dibelius gave his own lecture in Berlin in the same venue only days later for the purpose of answering Barth. He argued that Barth was just a theorist and did not understand the practical demands of the hour. What use was theology at such a time as this? "We are forced into a battle more serious than any conducted since the cross of Christ was first carried upon German soil. In this battle, no one sends notes of excuse based on theological scruples."[104] What was the battle of which Dibelius spoke?

The battle was for the moral soul of the German nation, a *Seele* which the Communists, Marxists, and Social Democrats threatened to destroy. The *Swiss* Barth could not possibly understand the needs of the *German* spirit, Dibelius reasoned.

For Barth of course, the idea that the church was called to or capable

---

100. Scholder, *Churches and the Third Reich*, vol. 1, p. 169.
101. Quoted in Scholder, *Churches and the Third Reich*, vol. 1, p. 169.
102. Karl Barth, "Die Not der evangelischen Kirche," in *"Der Götze wackelt,"* p. 56.
103. Barth, "Die Not der evangelischen Kirche," p. 57.
104. Quoted in Scholder, *Churches and the Third Reich*, vol. 1, p. 125.

of saving society from unbelief and serving as its moral compass was a dangerous one. Barth's response to Dibelius returned to the theme he would sound again and again in his interactions with church leaders who were sure they already knew and already did the will of God: humility, repentance, and utter dependence on the free Word of God.

National Socialism, the "German Christians," and the Protestant Church

The National Socialist platform in the 1920s affirmed the freedom of the church in Germany with two important caveats: the various confessions were free to practice their faith so long as that practice did not threaten the existence of the state or conflict with the "manners and moral sentiments of the Germanic race."[105]

From this early date the Nazis co-opted the term "Positive Christianity" to describe the version that met with their approval — namely a "Christianity" that was anti-Marxist and anti-Jewish. But their primary concern in the late twenties and early thirties was on getting votes from as many people as possible. To that end they stayed out of church affairs and took a neutral position with regard to the various confessions until the early 1930s in Prussia, when they began a more aggressive campaign for Protestant votes. Nazi leaders instructed the brownshirts to attend church en masse in uniform and meddle in church elections. Some weddings and funerals became opportunities for political demonstrations, with banners flying and slogans in the air.[106] Protestant church administrators were not comfortable with this turn of events, but had little authority to intervene decisively. The "worship guidelines" issued in some quarters and statements proclaiming that the church was "above parties" did little to defuse the highly charged situation.[107]

For some time before this there had been efforts by pastors in a number of *Landeskirchen* to form National Socialist church parties to gain seats in church elections and influence local policy. They were, not surprisingly, most successful in areas where Religious Socialists were concentrated.[108]

---

105. Wolfgang Treue, Deutsche Parteiprogramme 1861-1954, p. 146, quoted in Helmreich, *German Churches*, p. 123.
106. Scholder, *Churches and the Third Reich*, vol. 1, p. 144.
107. Scholder, *Churches and the Third Reich*, vol. 1, p. 145.
108. Scholder, *Churches and the Third Reich*, vol. 1, p. 196.

While there would continue to be other *völkisch* and pro-Nazi groups in the German Evangelical church, it was the Prussian church elections in the fall of 1932 that launched the group that would become known as the "German Christians."[109] With the support of Nazi chief Gregor Strasser, the German Christians campaigned furiously for pro-Nazi church candidates in the massive *Landeskirche* of Prussia. As the leader of the group, Wilhelm Kube, wrote in an article of January 1932: "National Socialists! Do not let the doors of your church be slammed in your faces! . . . Take your church and fill it with the living Christian spirit of the awakened German nation!"[110] Using a structure similar to that of the broader National Socialist organization, the German Christians had spread to *Land* churches throughout the Reich by early June 1932.[111]

The German Christians publicly announced their "guidelines" for the party and its candidates in the spring of 1932. The guidelines included a number of *völkisch* themes: rejecting parlimentarianism in the church, describing "race, *Volk*, and nation" as "orders of existence," calling for one unified *Reichskirche*, praising "Positive" Christianity, the "spirit of Luther," and "heroic piety," identifying Jews as "a grave danger" to the nation, and condemning Marxism, internationalism, and pacifism.[112] A memorandum accompanying the guidelines instructed party members that "discussions on 'dogmatic questions' were to be avoided at all costs."[113]

By the time Barth wrote to Pfennigsdorf in the spring of 1932, the battle lines within the church vis-à-vis National Socialism were clearly visible. On the pro-Nazi side there were the older Nationalist Protestants, those influenced by the younger Lutheran Political Theologians, and the *völkisch* fringe groups, including the German Christians themselves. Groups that resisted the Nazi ideology in the church included some left-wing liberals like Martin Rade, who found Hitler's doctrines morally incompatible with Christianity; the Religious Socialists, who argued against the Nazis on political and ideological grounds; and Karl Barth, most of his dialectical colleagues, and his students. Klaus Scholder argues that of these

---

109. This was not the only *völkisch* group that called itself "German Christians" at the time, but it became the most famous.

110. Wilhelm Kube, quoted in Scholder, *Churches and the Third Reich*, vol. 1, p. 203.

111. Helmreich, *German Churches*, p. 127.

112. "The Guiding Principles of the Faith Movement of the German Christians" can be found in Arthur C. Cochrane, *The Church's Confession under Hitler* (Philadelphia: Westminster, 1962), pp. 222-23.

113. Quoted in Scholder, *Churches and the Third Reich*, vol. 1, p. 208.

resistors, it was only Barth and theologians who shared his perspective that were able to persuade significant numbers of the undecided at this juncture, precisely because of their attention to the underlying theological issues.[114] Simply countering one ideology with another (especially one as threatening to most Protestants as Marxism) was ineffective. A deeper basis for resistance was needed in the context of a politicized church. Though Scholder may underestimate Barth's support of Weimar democracy, he summarizes the strength of Barth's position well:

> No more radical critique of ideology has been developed in the twentieth century than that made by dialectical theology. . . . This criticism clearly and impressively persisted through all the transformations of Barthian theology. For the Weimar period, this criticism was ambivalent, at least in its political effects. It hit the attempts to establish and to preserve the Republic on the basis of feelings of Christian responsibility just as hard as the designs of the opponents. . . . But this was the price to be paid for the presence in the field at the decisive moment of a theology which could establish theologically, and therefore in a way that the entire church could understand, why Christian theology could not now ally itself with National Socialism and why, therefore, the German Evangelical Church did not have to attach itself to the brown battalions.[115]

The Academic Lens

The typical German university in the early 1930s was less like an ivory tower and more like a tinderbox. The reasons for this have to do with the attitude of the professoriate on the one hand and the activism of the student body on the other.

Germany's world-renowned universities had long been a source of pride for the nation, and one would expect that academic freedom would have been a cherished value among faculty members.[116] But the ethos

---

114. Scholder, *Churches and the Third Reich*, vol. 1, p. 143.
115. Scholder, *Churches and the Third Reich*, vol. 1, p. 51.
116. The principle of academic freedom — that one should be free to follow truth wherever it leads without interference from the state — was central to the German scholarly tradition and a founding principle of the University of Berlin in the nineteenth century. Alice Gallin, *Midwives to Nazism: University Professors in Weimar Germany, 1925-1933* (Macon: Mercer University Press, 1986), p. 67.

shared by the vast majority of university professors across all disciplines in the Weimar years led them to embrace something else altogether. Once again the dominant characteristic in evidence is nationalism, a commitment traceable through generations of German academics, and a tendency only strengthened by the advent of the war and the humiliation of Versailles. Perhaps the extent of their chauvinism and resulting intolerance is not so surprising when one considers that most full professors had been appointed when imperial Germany was in full flower. The world they had known and loved had evaporated.

But another dynamic was also at work. With the triumph of the scientific method came increasing specialization in academic disciplines and an identity crisis of sorts as academics tried to demonstrate that their analytical and compartmentalized work was still related to the "whole person," that it could contribute to a *Weltanschauung* that would provide meaning in an industrialized society, and that it was relevant to the concerns of modern people.[117] They still wanted to be engaged in *Bildung* — the formation of the cultivated, cultured person — even as *Wissenschaft* had splintered them. As a group they seized upon opportunities to strengthen and unify the enfeebled German soul and to demonstrate their indispensability in preserving the *Volk*. They resisted the democracy which reduced the German people to squabbling factions.[118] For most German academics, seconding the nationalist passion evident in the wider German society came naturally: faculty members issued collective statements in support of Germany's war efforts, as we have seen; many spoke publicly against the Peace Settlement in 1919; many penned scathing condemnations of the French occupation of 1923; and a smaller group of professors began writing about the "threat" posed by the (supposedly) increasing numbers of Jewish professors and Jewish students in the Weimar years.[119] Like their counterparts in many other professions, German academics made no secret of the fact that they longed for the return of the monarchy, despised Marxism in all its forms, and considered democracy with its majority (read: mob) rule a threat to German culture, morality, and spirit.[120]

117. With unity, wholeness, and synthesis of meaning held in high esteem, few scholars were interested in taking risks to preserve and defend things like academic freedom, freedom of speech, or pluralism. Gallin, *Midwives*, p. 59.

118. For a discussion of these developments, see Gallin, *Midwives*, pp. 53-60.

119. Evans, *Coming of the Third Reich*, p. 132.

120. Academics often spoke of democracy in general and Weimar in particular as promoting the "unGerman" values they associated with the French Revolution, such as freedom

Given this perspective, it is not surprising that only a small number of left-leaning and/or pro-democratic professors were appointed during the course of the Weimar Republic.[121]

Naturally there was little motivation among such faculties to make the kind of philosophical, pedagogical, and curricular changes that would be necessary to equip the rising generation with the skills to contribute to a healthy constitutional democracy.[122] At best the professors were *Vernunftrepublikaneren*, grudgingly going along with the inevitable.[123] While they (like many other groups in Germany) described themselves as above politics *("unpolitisch")*, this self-understanding only betrays the depth of their nationalist, monarchist, and anti-democratic assumptions. Their strategy was largely to bide their time — they would not throw themselves into the political fray of Weimar, but keep the German spirit and culture alive through their academic work until a government worthy of the *Volk* arose

---

and equality, both of which they thought would lead to cultural relativism. Gallin, *Midwives*, p. 17. Barth himself recalled that, in the 1920s, "I found that with very few exceptions, the professors whom I came to know socially, in common rooms, sessions of the Senate and elsewhere, had what I can only describe as an attitude of sabotage towards the poor Weimar Republic. They did not even give it a fair chance. . . . They poured scorn on the notion that the year 1919 might have been a liberation for Germany." Busch, *Karl Barth*, p. 189.

121. The full professors *(Ordentlicher Professoren)* of a given faculty constituted the senate. This elite group nominated individuals for professorships, submitting three names for each post with the final selection made by the regional Ministry of Culture and Education. Even in the unlikely event that the Ministry officials in a particular *Land* were inclined to select a candidate with democratic or socialist leanings, few such candidates were presented to them by the faculty. A Ministry could challenge the slate of candidates, but of course then they would be accused of "politics." Gallin, *Midwives*, p. 46.

122. Historian Alice Gallin interviewed architect and former Nazi Minister of Armaments and War Production Albert Speer regarding his time as an instructor at the Technical University of Berlin when he was a young man. When asked why he became a Nazi at the time, Speer faulted the German educational system of the period, arguing that "he had not received the tools he needed to argue with the very talented and articulate National Socialist students" he was instructing. "He and other young people were very depressed by the political weakness and economic inadequacy of the Weimar government, and without really studying the writings and platform of the Nazis, he responded to the enthusiasm he witnessed among them." Gallin, *Midwives*, p. 3. Gallin's excellent study investigates the way in which most university professors passively or actively contributed to an intellectual climate easily exploited by the National Socialists.

123. The exceptions to this rule included the few socialists, political liberals, and Social Democrats already entrenched at a university or too well-respected in a particular discipline for a Minister of Culture to ignore. Many of these would be among the first to go once Hitler seized control.

once again.[124] Though emphatically maintaining that they remained "above parties," they did not hide their views from their students.

But if German academics as a whole did little to nothing to support Weimar democracy, a significant number of university students took matters even further. Resistance was not enough. It was time for revolution.

Why were many students so hostile to the Republic?

The students entering universities in the 1920s and 1930s were shaped by the ethos and values of the *Wandervogel* movement which began at the turn of the century — an idealistic, romantic pietism that turned from the spirit-numbing ugliness of modern industrial society to the divine beauty of the natural world. This movement, and the broader youth movement spawned by it, was comprised of a number of clubs and societies that gathered for activities like poetry recitations, long hikes, and patriotic sing-alongs around the campfire (often in uniform). It claimed large numbers of participants even before the Great War, but naturally the youth groups were readymade for the "Spirit of 1914" and continued to enjoy a robust following during the course of the Weimar Republic. Most groups were, as a rule, "hostile to the Republic and its politicians, nationalist in outlook, and militaristic in character and aspirations."[125] They idealized the soldiers who had fought in the Great War, were steeped in the "stab-in-the-back" mythology, and shared in the indignation over Versailles and the French occupation of the Ruhr. The participants were also mostly male, Protestant, and middle-class — the very demographic most likely to attend Germany's elite institutions of higher learning.

Once these young men arrived at the universities, they joined any number of student clubs and organizations, many of which were also conservative, monarchist, and nationalist — and passionately so. In 1919, in hopes of diluting the influence of the most extreme of these groups, the Republic made participation in newly founded, democratically-structured General Student Unions mandatory for all students. Regardless of the intentions, it was not long before the leadership of these Unions was also

---

124. Gallin, *Midwives*, p. 16. It should also be noted that the organizational structure of the university was itself hardly democratic. While the full professors (about a quarter of the instructional staff in some large universities) enjoyed security and power, the younger teachers — the *Ausserordentlicher, Nichtordentlicher* (assistant and associate professors) and *Dozenten* (unsalaried lecturers) — had a precarious existence financially and otherwise, competing for the patronage of the established professors in hope of future advancement. It was not a situation that encouraged open communication or institutional change.

125. Evans, *Coming of the Third Reich*, p. 130.

dominated by right-wing students, soon on a par with the tenor of the older dueling clubs and fraternities.[126] Unfortunately, the faculty played no role in overseeing these campus groups, though the fraternities often remained in contact with the *alte Herren* (alumni members), relationships which were "one of the channels through which the nationalistic and anti-Semitic sentiments of one generation were handed on to another."[127]

With the end of the war came a dramatic increase in the number of university students, which waned slightly in the mid-1920s during the brief period of economic stability, only to burgeon again once the economy took a nosedive at the end of the decade.[128] Unfortunately, the universities themselves were not able to keep up with the runaway enrollment. In some schools, standing-room-only lecture halls and overrun libraries were the order of the day. While they were required to take all qualified students, the universities were given no additional funding to accommodate them.[129] By the early 1930s, perhaps this overcrowding contributed to the feeling that everything was coming apart at the seams and Weimar and its failed policies were somehow to blame.

As we have seen, most professors sympathized with the nationalistic perspective of the students and some fanned the flames. By the mid-1920s, faculty members who challenged the university zeitgeist were often subject to persecution — not usually by their fellow faculty members (though they often did little to defend their embattled colleagues) — but by the students themselves. Professors who expressed openness to ideas like socialism, pacifism, or anything else deemed unGerman were subject to protests, jeering, demonstrations, slander, and threats from right-wing student organizations. Such events were already occurring well before the official Nazi student group became a significant presence at most univer-

---

126. Evans, *Coming of the Third Reich*, p. 132.
127. Gallin, *Midwives*, p. 51.
128. In 1914, the university enrollment in Germany was 61,000, after the war (in spite of casualties and territories lost) the enrollment was 72,000, and by 1931 the enrollment was 95,780. The increase is owing partly to the Weimar government's efforts to make higher education accessible to students from a wider range of backgrounds and, some argued, partly because the massive unemployment rates brought some young people to the university who would otherwise have joined the workforce immediately. Gallin, *Midwives*, pp. 48-49.
129. Like professors, students moved freely between universities and often attended classes at several during the course of their studies. This mobility made it difficult for schools to anticipate problems stemming from overcrowding. It also meant that in many cases student loyalties were less tied to a particular university than to the system-wide student organizations to which they belonged. Gallin, *Midwives*, p. 50.

sities.¹³⁰ If nationalist students did not join the Nazi Party in the early 1930s, they were certainly well-disposed toward it, and the party made inroads with the professors as well.¹³¹

The theological faculties were by no means immune to the tenor of the times. In December 1930, Martin Rade reported with dismay that in the North German universities "about 90 percent of the Protestant theologians appear at lectures with the National Socialist party badge."¹³²

The theological faculty which made the greatest contribution to the rise of National Socialism was undoubtedly that of Erlangen, where during the war Professor Karl Holl had promoted a vigorous recovery of a neo-conservative, politically-relevant Luther. Holl's most brilliant student was Emanuel Hirsch, who became the primary representative of the "Luther Renaissance" from his lectern at Göttingen University, and with the like-minded Paul Althaus fueled the National Socialist revolution in the academy as well as the church with their Political Theology.¹³³ Althaus joined the Erlangen faculty in 1925.

Both Althaus and Hirsch were increasingly popular, drawing students to their respective institutions and openly railing against their liberal and dialectical rivals. But maddeningly, there was one theologian who managed to draw large numbers of students in spite of the fact that he swam against the nationalist tide drowning many a university. For that we must head west to one of the few universities where at least some faculty and students would not go down without a fight: Bonn.

The University of Bonn

Barth began teaching at Bonn in March of 1930. By this time he was internationally known, and students thronged to the theological faculty to

---

130. By the winter semester of 1929-30, Nazi students already constituted an absolute majority at both Erlangen and Greifswald. Scholder, *Churches and the Third Reich*, vol. 1, p. 128.

131. Of the established parties, the Nazis were by far the youngest, with an average age of twenty-five to twenty-six in the years between 1930 and 1933. Less than 8 percent of Social Democrats were under twenty-five in 1930. Scholder, *Churches and the Third Reich*, vol. 1, p. 131.

132. Martin Rade, *Christliche Welt* 44, no. 23 (December 1930), quoted in Scholder, *Churches and the Third Reich*, vol. 1, p. 131.

133. Feige, *Varieties of Protestantism*, p. 64.

study under him. Barth's arrival marked, in Eberhard Busch's words, "the dawn of an unforgettable heyday for the Protestant theological faculty" in Bonn.[134]

It would be short-lived.

The majority of Barth's students in Bonn were German Protestant men, but growing numbers of women, foreign students, and Roman Catholics were also among the crowds.[135] The number of theological students actually doubled following his arrival (from 170 to 340), with about 400 in attendance by 1933.[136] His main lectures were held in the second-largest lecture hall at Bonn (capacity 322), and the room was often overflowing. He had to limit the number of students in his seminars, and did so according to performance on a pre-course exam. The "open evenings" he held in his home were packed, and he added discussion groups *(Sozietät)* to accommodate the throngs of students.[137]

We might assume that the vast majority of these students were disciples of Barth, strongly in agreement with his theological position. But the evidence suggests that the situation was more complex. Some of them were zealous or not-so-zealous "Barthians" — a group Barth sometimes poked fun at — but others were there to compare Barth's teaching to that of their mentors at other schools.[138] We know still others were strongly nationalist in outlook — there are reports of *Stahlhelmer* (Steel Helmets) and Nazis attending Barth's lectures in Bonn in uniform.[139] Most likely many of Barth's German Protestant students came to Bonn with the nationalist views so characteristic of their peers elsewhere.

Barth knew how precarious professor-student relations could be during those years. Nowhere was this better illustrated for him than in the famous (or infamous) "case of Günther Dehn," which erupted at the end of 1930.

---

134. Busch, *Karl Barth*, p. 199.
135. Busch, *Karl Barth*, pp. 202-3.
136. McCormack, *Critically Realistic Dialectical Theology*, p. 415.
137. Busch, *Karl Barth*, p. 202.
138. Some of them were there fresh from hearing Bultmann or Gogarten, hoping to hear Barth's side of the ongoing debates between the scholars. Busch, *Karl Barth*, p. 203.
139. Barth told Hirsch and Dörries in 1932 that he had "many" National Socialist and like-minded students in attendance at his lectures and seminars in Bonn. Barth, *Gesamtausgabe* V.35, pp. 175-76. See also Charlotte von Kirschbaum to Eduard Thurneysen, June 2, 1933. Barth, *Gesamtausgabe* V.34, p. 420.

The Dehn Affair

Günther Dehn was a former Religious Socialist, an early adherent to dialectical theology, and a friend to Barth. To understand how Dehn ended up in big trouble in the early 1930s, we have to back up to an event in November of 1928, when Dehn was a pastor in Berlin.

In a lecture in Magdeburg, Pastor Dehn condemned militarism and the glorification of war, urged the church to work for reconciliation between nations, and finally, crucially, Dehn wondered aloud whether it was appropriate that war memorials were displayed in churches. Soldiers who perished in battle died with the intent to kill others, Dehn argued. Death for the Fatherland could not be compared (as it often was in those days) with Christian martyrdom.[140]

Word of Dehn's remarks spread. There were complaints to Dehn's superiors. *Völkisch* organizations protested publicly that Dehn was denigrating Germany's fallen heroes. After Dehn was duly scolded by the Consistory, it seemed the matter was over.

But in December 1930, Dehn was called to the Chair of Practical Theology at the University of Heidelberg. Before he arrived to take up his post, the editor of the *Eiserne Blätter* saw fit to write an editorial detailing Dehn's controversial comments from two years earlier.[141] The Heidelberg faculty, afraid their students would riot as they had already done against a Jewish professor, refused to grant him a "declaration of confidence." Only one lone professor (New Testament professor Martin Dibelius) stood up for him.[142]

Dehn turned the Heidelberg job down only to receive another offer from the University of Halle, courtesy of Prussian *Kultusminister* (and Religious Socialist sympathizer) Adolf Grimme. Though the faculty found Dehn's scholarly contributions unimpressive, they grudgingly agreed.[143]

But Dehn's woes were only just beginning.

By February 1931 the National Socialist student union was distributing pamphlets at Halle, claiming that Dehn "wants to educate German children in the crassest and most cowardly pacifism. Are we supposed to look on as such a person receives a chair at our university?"[144]

---

140. Scholder, *Churches and the Third Reich*, vol. 1, p. 172.
141. Scholder, *Churches and the Third Reich*, vol. 1, p. 173.
142. Scholder, *Churches and the Third Reich*, vol. 1, p. 174.
143. Jack Forstman, *Christian Faith in Dark Times: Theological Conflicts in the Shadow of Hitler* (Louisville: Westminster/John Knox, 1992), p. 181.
144. Scholder, *Churches and the Third Reich*, vol. 1, p. 174.

Dehn's first lecture was interrupted by rioting both inside and outside the hall. Students chanted, "Germany awake, Judah perish, Dehn perish!," fireworks were thrown, and the doors of the lecture hall were broken by the raucous crowd.[145] Threats of disciplinary action by the president of the University and the police had only limited effect.[146] Dehn's few lectures at Halle were filled with disruptions, insults, and threats. Klaus Scholder explains: "This was the distinctive form of anonymous, political mass terrorism against individuals which developed at the German universities in this period."[147] The debacle was all over the press.

By mid-November, the younger instructors at Halle (*Assistenten* and *Dozenten*) went public with their support — not of Dehn, but of the rioting students. Right-wing students from Halle as well as other nearby universities "poured into Jena and held a mass demonstration against Dehn and the Minister of Culture."[148]

At that point, Karl Barth felt it was time to do something publicly to support the young professor. He circulated a petition indicating "personal and material solidarity" with Dehn among his colleagues, to be published in the *Theologische Blätter*. Barth could get only four others to sign the document — Karl Ludwig Schmidt, Martin Dibelius, Otto Piper, and Georg Wünsch — and Wünsch qualified his support "on theological grounds," saying he could only support Dehn "personally," not "materially."[149]

---

145. Friedemann Stengel, "Wer Vertrieb Günther Dehn (1882-1970) aus Halle?" *Zeitschrift für Kirchengeschichte* 114, no. 3 (2003): 391.

146. Forstman, *Christian Faith*, p. 182.

147. Scholder, *Churches and the Third Reich*, vol. 1, p. 174.

148. Forstman, *Christian Faith*, p. 182. Dehn also wrote these prescient words in his postscript: "Perhaps what happened in Heidelberg and Halle is only a prelude to coming events, where a state, purely orientated on power politics, which knows nothing of its responsibility towards God, will either demand complete obedience from the church or will declare it to be a danger to the state. It is possible that the church of the present stands on the threshold of the most difficult struggles with modern nationalism, in which case its very existence will be challenged. . . . Here resistance must be offered." Quoted in Scholder, *Churches and the Third Reich*, vol. 1, pp. 174-75.

149. Forstman, *Christian Faith*, p. 182. The full text of the brief declaration can be found in Barth, *Gesamtausgabe* V.35, p. 161. Bultmann and Gogarten both declined to add their names to the *Theologische Blätter* statement. Bultmann wrote to Barth that he could not endorse Dehn's theological position and was not sure he should be appointed at Halle. He expressed a willingness to sign the declaration if Barth would rewrite it to reflect either simple (not material) solidarity with Dehn or just condemn the student rioters. Barth did not modify the statement. Instead, Bultmann was among the more than thirty professors of theology who signed a subsequent declaration that condemned "the attempt of student cir-

Theological Existence in the Weimar Years

Meanwhile, the Halle faculty managed to calm things down on campus. They ostensibly stood behind Dehn yet quietly appointed another professor of practical theology to teach alongside him, thus providing an alternative for students dead-set against the embattled new professor. By December this stony cease-fire continued in Halle, but just before Christmas Dehn published some documents related to the controversy. In the postscript he repeated his warnings about the dangers of "fanatical love of the Fatherland, tinged with pseudoreligious coloring," and the truce was over, both on the campus and in the press.[150]

On January 27, 1932, two big guns joined the fray in support of the student protesters. Professors Emanuel Hirsch and Hermann Dörries, both of Göttingen, published their own manifesto on the Dehn controversy in a right-wing newspaper, the *Deutsche Allgemeine Zeitung*. In it they argued that the Dehn affair had nothing to do with academic freedom, but was a question of what qualified one to teach theology or even to offer an opinion on a matter such as the Halle controversy. The qualifications, Hirsch and Dörries explained, were these:

> First, a recognition that the nation and its freedom, for all the questionableness of creaturely life, are also regarded by the Christian as being sanctified by God and demanding total surrender of heart and life; and, following on this recognition, acknowledgment of the passionate will for freedom in our *Volk*, enslaved and violated by power-hungry and avaricious enemies.[151]

In other words, the only people qualified to teach or speak on public issues were those who shared the nationalist *völkisch* perspective of the Political Theologians.

Though Barth was initially reluctant to reenter the public debate, he heeded the call from Martin Rade and others to challenge Hirsch and Dörries directly.[152] Barth's article of February 15 urged the two Göttingen

---

cles to debar Dr. Günther Dehn from academic teaching." It was sent to the Rector of Halle University a few days later. Karl Barth et al., *Karl Barth–Rudolf Bultmann Letters, 1922-1966* (Grand Rapids: Eerdmans, 1981), p. 67.

150. Forstman, *Christian Faith*, p. 182.

151. Quoted in Scholder, *Churches and the Third Reich*, vol. 1, p. 175.

152. The complete German text of Barth's article in response to Hirsch and Dörries may be found in Barth, *Gesamtausgabe* V.35, pp. 174-83.

masters to come clean and admit that the debate behind the debate over Halle had to do with two competing theological claims: their German nationalist views versus the dialectical perspective that fueled Dehn's critique of runaway nationalism. Why pick on poor Dehn and not the theology that prompted his convictions?

Barth pleaded with the professors to join him in having a substantive debate about the church and the gospel and Holy Scripture rather than the political sloganeering and the "rime of barbarism" that had characterized the conflict to date. Could not the Halle students and their academic defenders "act in a scholarly way, even if with passion"?[153]

Barth observed in his article that he himself had made claims similar to Dehn's about issues of war and peace in his ethics lectures at Münster and at Bonn, and there had been no uproar, even though there were many Nazi and nationalist students in the audience. Things did not need to be this way.[154] Barth also noted that the Halle students had praised a statement by Adolf Hitler in their university newspaper in relation to the Dehn appointment. Hitler's statement read:

> if the theoretician says the NSDAP is a superficial party, then I can only answer him: you are only a theoretician: *Right now is a time for battle and not for the study of the science of war.* We have no time at this point to train highly educated intellectual people.... *Now our concern must be that no one takes power but us. Therefore we have no time for theoretical problems.* That was the nineteenth century. This century must surrender everything for success.[155]

Barth could not believe that scholars like Hirsch and Dörries could agree with such sentiments.

Hirsch responded to Barth in short order in the pages of the nationalist *Deutsches Volkstum*. Among other things Hirsch argued at length that Barth, as a Swiss citizen, could really have nothing to say about the German situation, politically or theologically or in any way. And the idea that it would be possible for Hirsch to have a theological discussion that would somehow transcend his national identity was not only ridiculous but offensive to him:

---

153. Scholder, *Churches and the Third Reich*, vol. 1, p. 176.
154. Forstman, *Christian Faith*, p. 187.
155. Barth, *Gesamtausgabe* V.35, p. 180.

Do you wish to deny that integration into *Volk* and state and into the historical hour and historical task of *Volk* and state is so interwoven with my existence as a human being that I could deny it only by being disobedient to the one who has placed me in it, and could fail to make it the fundamental point of that understanding of *Volk*, state and war which is my task as a theologian only by lapsing into non-existential, i.e. theologically insignificant, chatter?[156]

To speak of God or church or Scripture and not his Germanness would be positively sinful, Hirsch complained.

As for the Hitler quote that the Halle students embraced, it *would* be problematic if a *theologian* had written the statement, Hirsch agreed. But if you consider the larger situation, he continued, Hitler was right that "intellectuals who are alienated from the *Volk*" have nothing to offer. It is the young with their passion for *Volk* and freedom who have something to teach *us*, Hirsch concluded.[157]

Though Barth wrote a response to this letter and Hirsch answered with a concluding letter of his own, nothing new was added to the substance of the debate. Barth pleaded again that they have a discussion concerning the theological assumptions that grounded their respective views, while Hirsch (in a letter to the editor of the *Deutsches Volkstum*, not to Barth) reiterated his argument that Barth could not possibly understand what it meant to be a Christian in Germany and clearly he did not want to understand.[158]

As for Dehn himself, he resigned from Halle in the fall of 1932, though mercifully he was granted a one-year sabbatical.[159]

The Dehn affair was only one of several "cases" where students launched campaigns against what they considered objectionable professors in the years leading up to the National Socialist revolution.[160]

---

156. Scholder, *Churches and the Third Reich*, vol. 1, p. 177.

157. Barth, *Gesamtausgabe* V.35, p. 196.

158. Hirsch's letter to the editor may be found in Barth, *Gesamtausgabe* V.35, pp. 203-7.

159. Scholder, *Churches and the Third Reich*, vol. 1, p. 177. Later Dehn would take up a teaching position in the Confessing Church.

160. Other examples of professors subject to student protest for their "unGermanness" in the Weimar years include Heidelberg mathematics professor Emil Gumbel, Munich law professor Hans Nawiasky, Breslau law professor Ernst Cohn, and Leipzig economist Gerhard Kessler. We might also mention Kiel theologian Otto Baumgarten in this category, though he was already retired when National Socialist students began their campaign against

When one considers that broader landscape, Bonn University as a whole stands out as something of an anomaly among the universities of the time, its students remarkably reasonable when compared to the hoodlums and hecklers of Halle. The Nazi student organization so successful elsewhere struggled to get off the ground in Bonn.[161] The Nazis would eventually gain traction with the students in the months ahead, but Bonn would always lag behind their runaway successes elsewhere. If there was any place where Barth might be able to persuade young people to resist the wave of nationalism, it was there. What pedagogical strategies did Barth bring to the task? What sort of teacher was he?

Karl Barth, Teacher

Alexander J. McKelway, a former student of Barth, identified two characteristics of his pedagogical approach in his seminars and discussion groups. First, he noted how Barth constantly posed questions to his students and regularly appointed students to read material and pose questions themselves for the class to consider. This practice of questioning was a way to challenge assumptions, to dispossess the knower, and to cultivate receptivity, reconsideration, and deep listening. As McKelway explains, "It was not right answers, but right questions that interested Barth."[162] This questioning was for Barth not an intellectual exercise but a serious investment on the part of the questioner — one must "risk the exposure of true conviction" that allows for self-questioning.[163]

Second, McKelway describes Barth's reaction to the aggressive partisan debates that sometimes erupted in the classroom. Barth was of course

---

him, following a sermon he delivered in 1930. For more on Baumgarten, see Scholder, *Churches and the Third Reich*, vol. 1, p. 173.

161. This may be owing in part to the strong Catholic student groups on campus and the influence of a popular rector (and Centre Party politician), Heinrich Konen. Catholics as a rule had a more positive assessment of Weimar democracy. Hans-Paul Höpfner, *Die Universität Bonn im Dritten Reich: Akademische Biographien unter Nationalsozialistischer Herrschaft*, Academica Bonnensia (Bonn: Bouvier, 1999), pp. 111-12. Regardless of the reasons, of all universities in Germany, the Nazi *Studentbund* had its poorest showing in the student society elections of February 1930 in Bonn, getting only 8.2 percent of the vote compared to 50 percent in some other institutions. Höpfner, *Universität Bonn*, pp. 111-12.

162. Alexander Jeffrey McKelway, "Magister Dialecticae Optimarium Partium: Recollections of Karl Barth as Teacher," *Union Seminary Quarterly Review* 28, no. 1 (1972): 94.

163. McKelway, "Magister Dialecticae Optimarium Partium," p. 96.

more than willing to express criticism of other theological positions, yet he was unhappy when students were unwilling to listen earnestly and well to the positions of others before venturing a response. He was constantly asking them to consider what might be worthwhile among the grand sweep of the theological tradition right down to their contemporaries, to be open to what they might learn, even from unlikely sources. And Barth modeled this attitude of expectation himself, something Dietrich Bonhoeffer observed after participating in Barth's Schleiermacher seminar in Bonn: "He has an openness, a readiness to listen to any pertinent criticism, and at the same time an intense concentration on the subject, whether a suggestion is made proudly or modestly, dogmatically or quite tentatively."[164]

Both these emphases — on good questions and deep listening — point to Barth's broader strategy as a teacher. Rather than simply transmitting information about the tradition or his own doctrinal views, Barth was intent on giving students the skills they needed to think for themselves, to get to the heart of the matter, to identify what was at stake there at the twilight of Weimar.[165] From the open evenings where Barth facilitated discussion on the fundamental differences between Weimar's political parties, to the way he encouraged students to make their own charts depicting cultural and political events in relation to various theologians in his lectures on nineteenth-century theology, to the many informal discussions on controversial matters he had with students while at Bonn, Barth sought to cultivate a thoughtful, critical, and self-critical habit of mind among them.[166]

The evidence suggests that Barth may not have been the only one with these kinds of pedagogical goals on the theological faculty at Bonn.[167] We do know Barth enjoyed good working relationships with his colleagues there and found many kindred spirits among them.

There were two exceptions to this happy rule: the systematic theologian Johann Wilhelm Schmidt-Japing and the professor of practical theol-

---

164. Bonhoeffer quoted in Busch, *Karl Barth*, p. 215.

165. Barth's pedagogical goal can be discerned in §7 of the *Church Dogmatics* when he writes that instruction is to be "guidance to independent dogmatic work, and not just the imparting of the specific results of the work of a specific teacher." CD I/1, p. 276.

166. There is certainly dialectical tension in Barth's educational goal. Students (and theologians) should think for themselves, but always be ready to let themselves be called into question. It is intellectual courage coupled with intellectual humility. For one of many examples of Barth's warnings to his Bonn students about the perils of overconfidence, see CD I/1, pp. 162-63.

167. Höpfner, *Universität Bonn*, p. 148.

ogy and apologetics, Emil Pfennigsdorf. Both would become German Christians in due course, but it is Pfennigsdorf in particular who merits a few final comments here.

Emil Pfennigsdorf joined the Bonn faculty in 1913, after many years in the pastorate. He was a "throne and altar" monarchist who wrote critically of Weimar and called for a new *Volkstaat* and *Führer*.[168] He shared the Political Theologians' convictions regarding the "orders of creation" and the revelatory nature of historical events. He joined the first pro-Nazi group to appear in Bonn in 1929. The *Kampfbund für deutsche Kultur* was not itself National Socialist, but with its radical nationalism and *völkisch* anti-Semitism it was certainly sympathetic to its agenda.[169] It was Pfennigsdorf — the embodiment of so much that troubled Barth in those days — who was responsible for teaching Bonn's young theological students how to preach. By the spring of 1932, Barth felt the time for intervention had come.

Conclusion

As we have seen, Barth's venture into practical theology occurred in the midst of political instability, economic hardship, and violence. In both church and academy the nationalism, fear, and intolerance so easily exploited by the National Socialists was everywhere apparent. Barth, with his socialist background, his Swiss citizenship, his Social Democratic voting record, and his radical theology of the free and Wholly Other God, was an unlikely candidate to win a hearing under the circumstances. And yet, even as rioting erupted in lecture halls in other parts of Germany, Barth had been able to keep substantive conversation alive in Bonn, pushing his students of all persuasions to dig down deep into the heart of things, to measure the ever-present claims regarding nation, race, *Volk,* and church by the one Word that calls them all into question.

Is it surprising that Barth would want to extend that effort to include the practical matter of what these young people would say in the name of God in the not so distant future when they stood in pulpits all over Ger-

---

168. Höpfner, *Universität Bonn,* p. 48.

169. The *Kampfbund* was founded by Alfred Rosenberg in 1928 with the purpose of rallying intellectuals to the cause of protecting German culture from everything deemed "unGerman." It soon spread to many parts of the country and persisted until 1937, when it was assimilated into a Nazi organization.

many and addressed the church? Barth's emergency homiletic was born of the conviction that *how* these novice preachers went about their task as Weimar crumbled *mattered*. Any responsible interpretation of the artifacts of the "sermon exercises" of 1932-33 must begin with the recognition of all that was at stake, for Barth and for his students.

But before we turn to the artifacts themselves, there is one further set of interpretative lenses we cannot ignore. The conflict that festered and then exploded in Germany society, church, and academy cannot be understood by looking only at political events or election statistics. This conflict was enjoined in language itself. We cannot hope to interpret Barth's choices in the *Predigtvorbereitung* lectures rightly without considering how words functioned in Weimar and facilitated its demise, and how the church's speech about God, in particular its preaching, was infiltrated by the propaganda pressing in on all sides. How did Barth respond to this linguistic fascism in his own use of language? How did his theology of proclamation function in relation to the nationalist homiletic often second-nature to many a post-war German pastor?

Chapters Three and Four will explore precisely these issues.

CHAPTER THREE

Theological Existence and the Rhetoric of Weimar

"Words can be like tiny doses of arsenic," German Victor Klemperer wrote in the 1930s. "They are swallowed unnoticed, appear to have no effect, and then after a little time the toxic reaction sets in after all."[1]

Klemperer was uniquely qualified to make observations about the rhetoric of German political and social life under the influence of the extreme right. A Jewish Protestant professor of literature and former soldier with conservative nationalist political leanings, Klemperer was also trained as a philologist. In addition to the copious diaries he kept throughout the period, he also began to catalogue the language of the Third Reich, keeping track of the way particular words and constellations of words functioned to reinforce the *Weltanschauung* of National Socialism. He called his lexicon *Lingua Tertii Imperii*, the Latin title itself a parody of Nazi grandiosity. For Klemperer, language could commandeer human emotions, it could "write and think" for its users and dictate belief to the less vigilant.[2]

---

1. Victor Klemperer, *The Language of the Third Reich: LTI, Lingua Tertii Imperii; A Philologist's Notebook*, trans. Martin Brady (London: Athlone Press, 2000), pp. 15-16.

2. Klemperer traces his view of language to Schiller. While Klemperer's claims regarding the power of language remain controversial, the value and poignancy of his eyewitness testimony is undisputed. On Klemperer's linguistic philosophy, see John Wesley Young, "From LTI to LQI: Victor Klemperer on Totalitarian Language," *German Studies Review* 28, no. 1 (2005): 45-64; Heinz L. Kretzenbacher, "Language Reveals All," *Monthly Review: An Independent Socialist Magazine* 55, no. 7 (2003): 47-51; and Roderick H. Watt, "Landsersprache, Heeressprache, Nazisprache? Victor Klemperer and Werner Krauss on the Linguistic Legacy of the Third Reich," *Modern Language Review* 95, no. 2 (2000): 424-37.

Theological Existence and the Rhetoric of Weimar

One need not subscribe to Klemperer's philosophy of linguistic determinism — indeed, such a view will be explicitly rejected in what follows — to acknowledge the role of political rhetoric in shaping public perceptions. By the end of the Weimar years, the vocabulary of public discourse in Germany was dominated by the categories, complaints, and catchwords of the nationalist right and the far left, drowning out the center. Some of the words, symbols, and tropes that prevailed on the streets found their way into Protestant pulpits, where inherited homiletical practices proved all too hospitable to theologically-legitimated reactionary visions and chauvinistic fears.

Because Barth conducted his "sermon exercises" in this time of feverish campaigning and unrelenting propaganda, this chapter serves to orient the reader to the rhetorical dimensions of Barth's political context and to trace the dynamics of his response in the overlapping domains of German society and church. Consideration of the rhetoric of Weimar in relation to the homiletical traditions and practices of the German Protestant church, Barth's homiletical orientation, and his response to the preaching of his day will be taken up in the chapter to come.

The tasks of this chapter unfold as follows: first, an exposition of the nature, development, and content of propaganda and political rhetoric in the time of Weimar, with particular attention to the role of the German press and the rise of National Socialism; second, an account of the reception of the rhetoric of Weimar politics in the Protestant church and the church's own venture into the propaganda wars; and finally, a description of the strategy Barth articulated with regard to the challenge of political propaganda in church and academy, looking back to *Romans II* and forward to the *Theologische Existenz heute!* of 1933.

The Rhetoric of Politics in Weimar

In the years following the Second World War, the news of the extent and nature of the atrocities committed by the Germans horrified the international community. Even as the rubble was being cleared and Allied "denazification" procedures were under way, Germans began offering their first interpretations of why Hitler happened. In these early efforts at what came to be known as *Vergangenheitsbewältigung* (overcoming, or coming to terms with, the past), Germans largely avoided any acknowledgment of guilt or complicity in the course of events and emphasized instead that the German

Volk had also been victims of the National Socialist regime. The argument that most Germans should be viewed as victims of Hitler and his henchmen, or at least no worse than the people of any other nation whose leaders ordered violent acts, persisted for decades, especially in West Germany, though student rebellion in the late 1960s prompted renewed discussion of the matter of German guilt.[3] Even well-respected German historians such as Friedrich Meinecke and Gerhard Ritter offered explanations that largely left the role of the German population out of the equation.[4]

In more recent years there is evidence that the question of responsibility for National Socialism in general and the Holocaust in particular remains a live issue for Germans, not only in light of the *Historikerstreit* of the late 1980s but also in the more recent debates over the "Denkmal für die ermordeten Juden Europas" (Memorial to the Murdered Jews of Europe) which finally opened in Berlin in 2005.[5]

Germans were not the only ones to exaggerate the irresistible nature of National Socialist tactics. The argument that National Socialism was "totalitarian," and thus to be equated with Communism served American Cold War political interests, and was taken up with considerable enthusiasm by some politicians and historians.

These interpretations did not remain unchallenged. The counter-arguments to the idea that National Socialism was an aberration that victimized a passive German populace initially arose in the form of various *Sonderweg* theses that attributed the roots of National Socialism to aspects of the German "character" or to longstanding historical, cultural, and intellectual factors. While popular accounts such as William Shirer's wildly inaccurate *The Rise and Fall of the Third Reich* only confused matters, subsequent scholarly studies of the rise of National Socialism have been able to demonstrate that historical, cultural, and intellectual currents, while significant, were only pieces of a larger context — a larger context that in-

---

3. For an orientation to the *Vergangenheitsbewältigung* controversy in the 1960s, see Konrad H. Jarausch, "Critical Memory and Civil Society: The Impact of the 1960s on German Debates about the Past," in *Coping with the Nazi Past: West German Debates on Nazism and Generational Conflict, 1955-1975*, ed. Philipp Gassert and Alan E. Steinweis (New York: Berghahn Books, 2006), pp. 11-30.

4. Peter D. Stachura, ed., *The Nazi Machtergreifung* (London: Allen & Unwin, 1983), p. 2.

5. For a detailed analysis of the issues at stake in the *Historikerstreit*, see Richard J. Evans, *In Hitler's Shadow: West German Historians and the Attempt to Escape from the Nazi Past* (London: I. B. Tauris, 1989).

cluded the agency and role of the German public.[6] But this recognition reflects a degree of perspective that was simply incomprehensible to most Germans in the late 1940s.

The German people were, in fact, suffering at the end of the war and had difficulty seeing beyond their own grief and hardship. But the question of complicity could not be avoided forever. It arose with increasing intensity as images from the concentration camps were circulated. Why did so many of them vote for Hitler in the first place?[7] Sometimes it was claimed that Germans were simply unprepared to deal with the political situation in the last years of Weimar, that as a *Volk* they were largely *unpolitisch*, and that they were manipulated by the silver-tongued demagogue, his theatrical vision, his satanic powers, and his magical words. The nobility, morality, and rationality of the German *Volk* had been violated, interrupted, and possessed by a cunning alien force.[8] This rhetoric of de-

---

6. In recent years the claim of Daniel Goldhagen — that ordinary Germans not only knew about but were complicit in the murder of the Jews — while largely discredited by historians in its particulars, raised the issue of everyday complicity anew and reignited the discussion of "guilt," particularly in the German context. See Daniel Jonah Goldhagen, *Hitler's Willing Executioners: Ordinary Germans and the Holocaust* (New York: Knopf, 1996). For an overview of the problems with Goldhagen's thesis and its reception in Germany, see Ian Kershaw, *The Nazi Dictatorship: Problems and Perspectives of Interpretation*, 4th ed. (London: Arnold, 2000), pp. 251-62.

7. For the purposes of the present study, we must distinguish between the rhetorical situation *prior* to the Nazi *Machtergreifung* in January of 1933 and the very different environment that resulted from the systematic and centralized efforts to control public discourse that took place afterward. National Socialist propaganda functioned differently once those publicly offering alternative views were progressively eliminated, marginalized, or intimidated. Yet another dynamic comes into play once the economy recovered in 1936 and Hitler could claim that he had delivered on his promise of work and bread. Our focus in this chapter is political and theological discourse in the last years of Weimar. The changes in the rhetorical situation that accompanied the transition to fascism will be addressed in Chapter Six, as they occurred in relation to the ongoing *Predigtvorbereitung* class meetings.

8. This type of explanation was common inside the Protestant church, even among the minority who came to oppose the National Socialist regime. Walter Künneth, a member of the Confessing Church, explained in 1947: "All good powers of the German people were being constrained by this propaganda apparatus and misused in an unsurpassable way. . . . Only under the sign of a religious demonic possession is the 'true diabolical refinement' comprehensible. . . . This propaganda reached its goal, namely the *Gleichschaltung* of the soul of the German *Volk*. As a substitute for the lost Christian nourishment a new 'faith' arose, the 'faith in the word of the *Führer*,' in the message of propaganda. Through this method of radical dishonesty it succeeded in executing a godless spell on the soul of the German people. The demonization took place in great style through a psychological defor-

monic infiltration still arises in some quarters, no matter how many scholarly studies appear that challenge its satisfying simplicity and outrage.[9]

But even if we remove such exalted metaphysical claims from the equation, the questions remain: Were Germans really naively *"unpolitisch"* in the Weimar years? Was the general population or, for that matter, the educated elite easy prey for a skilled Nazi propaganda machine?[10] How significant was the hyperbolic style of public discourse in Weimar in paving the way to the Third Reich? As we might expect, the situation is considerably more complicated than theories of linguistic determinism will allow.

Long before Victor Klemperer began compiling his lexicon in earnest, politics had been part of the fabric of German *Alltag*. In the years leading up to the Great War, Germany was humming with vigorous political debate, fed by a multiplicity of partisan daily newspapers and populist orators.[11] Election turnout was extremely high — from 84 percent in 1907

---

mation of the people, so that a will-less mass became an organized *Volk.*" Walter Künneth, *Der grosse Abfall, eine geschichtstheologische Untersuchung der Begegnung zwischen Nationalsozialismus und Christentum* (Hamburg: F. Wittig, 1947), pp. 99-100. For a discussion of the use of "demon" metaphors with regard to National Socialism by German intellectuals in the 1960s, see Joachim Scholtyseck, "Conservative Intellectuals and the Debate over National Socialism and the Holocaust in the 1960s," in Gassert and Steinweis, eds., *Coping with the Nazi Past,* pp. 244-45.

9. Cf. Wolfgang Mieder's more recent claim: "There can and must be no doubt that the devilish and propagandistic misuse and perversion of the German language played a significant role in changing Germany from a democratic and decent nation to one of terror, persecution, and death." Wolfgang Mieder, foreword to Robert Michael and Karin Doerr, *Nazi-Deutsch/Nazi-German: An English Lexicon of the Language of the Third Reich* (London: Greenwood Press, 2002), p. xv.

10. The idea that it was not just the average German but the intellectual who was ill-equipped to contest populist agitation or demagoguery because of a "timidity" in public speaking has been championed by those advocating the reintroduction of some version of classical rhetorical instruction in German education. Hans Bestian articulated the argument in the early 1950s, when theories of German victimization abounded, and it has been reiterated by subsequent campaigns for rhetorical education. That there is little empirical evidence that Germans suffered from a lack of confidence or weak persuasive skills does not seem to give the rhetoricians pause. See Hans Bestian, "Redeübungen im Deutschunterricht," *Wirkendes Wort* 1, no. 3 (1950): 166.

11. Politicians and intellectuals in Imperial Germany had long been concerned about left-wing demagogues stirring up the masses, as evidenced by the censorship laws of 1836 (the *Demagogenverfolgung*). Liberals also expressed concern about the way right-wing agitators appealed to the baser instincts of the crowd. The charge of "demagoguery" was frequently leveled by liberals against conservatives in the decades immediately preceding the Great War, most famously and prolifically by Max Weber. David Blackbourn, *Populists and*

Theological Existence and the Rhetoric of Weimar

and 1912 to as much as 94 percent at state and local levels — and crowds actually haggled for black market tickets to the Reichstag gallery to watch the partisan fireworks.[12] This political fervor was by no means limited to formal campaigns or election seasons — the social lives of many citizens also revolved around their particular party affiliation. Choirs, sports clubs, libraries, youth groups, women's organizations, dramatic societies — even pubs — identified themselves in political terms: as Social Democrat, nationalist, Centre, and so forth.[13] The characterization of Germans as *"unpolitisch,"* an idea sometimes promoted by Germans themselves, cannot be sustained.[14] If anything, they were hyper-political, and while partisan bickering was temporarily stilled by the unifying "Spirit of 1914," political engagement remained high in the years after the war.[15]

The politicization of social existence continued during the Weimar Republic for many members of the older generation, but the young, interrupted by the war and lured by the proliferation of new leisure activities, were markedly less invested in the particular political parties they inherited from their parents.[16] They were weighing their options. Some reveled in the new freedoms and experimental tone ushered in with the Republic.

But the ironic spirit which characterized the cutting edge of Weimar cultural life did not resonate with the majority. As we have seen, the young people reared with the romantic sensibilities of the *Wandervogel* tribes dreamed of heroic sacrifice and patriotic glory, and their elders on the political right were far from immune to such visions. The outrage over the

---

Patricians: Essays in Modern German History (London: Allen & Unwin, 1987), p. 220. For their part the conservative elites, while repulsed by the "beer-bench" politics and "demagogic chauvinism" of populist rabble-rousers, realized it would be foolish not to harness such energy for their own ends. Blackbourn, *Populists and Patricians*, pp. 230-31. Whatever else we might say about their readiness to meet the challenges of democracy, Germans were by no means naïve or uninformed when it came to the danger of rhetorical manipulation in the political sphere in the decades before the Great War.

12. Blackbourn, *Populists and Patricians*, p. 222.

13. Richard J. Evans, *The Coming of the Third Reich*, 1st American ed. (New York: Penguin Press, 2004), p. 84.

14. For a discussion of the meaning of "unpolitical" among German professors, see Alice Gallin, *Midwives to Nazism: University Professors in Weimar Germany, 1925-1933* (Macon: Mercer University Press, 1986), pp. 16-18. "Unpolitical" usually meant anti-Republican.

15. "Whatever Germany suffered from in the 1920s, it was not a lack of political commitment and belief, rather, if anything, the opposite." Evans, *Coming of the Third Reich*, p. xxvi.

16. Evans, *Coming of the Third Reich*, p. 85.

outcome of the war, the trauma of hyperinflation, rapid cultural change, fear of a Russian-style revolution, brutally high unemployment rates, and the advent of democracy itself intensified the language of political debate as the 1920s unfolded. Military metaphors, hyperbole, slogans, insults, dire predictions, and threats were everywhere, mixed with sweeping utopian promises and punctuated by the politically-motivated violence that broke out in the back alleys and beer halls of Germany's cities.

But though there were all kinds of factors that contributed to the extreme style of political discourse in Weimar's final years, this rhetorical and sometimes physical mayhem was encouraged and fueled by the deployment of a relatively new weapon in the battle for political power: the "science" of propaganda.

The New Science of Propaganda

The term "propaganda" can be traced to a seventeenth-century Catholic committee of cardinals charged by Pope Gregory XV with "propagating" or "disseminating" the Christian faith.[17] But this fairly neutral sense of the word has long since given way to a more sinister one in common usage. Propaganda often is used as shorthand for things like manipulation, brainwashing, distortion, and, more recently, "spin." Scholars in the relevant fields continue to argue over what exactly propaganda is, and whether or not the concept always merits the suspicion it arouses.[18] Some definitions emphasize that propaganda is deliberate and systematic, others that it is persuasion directed toward a mass audience, still others that it is designed to change public perception in ways that benefit the propagandist (and not necessarily the public).[19]

---

17. T. F. Hoad, ed., *The Concise Oxford Dictionary of English Etymology* (Oxford: Oxford University Press, 1996).

18. In some ways, the contemporary debates about the ethical status of "propaganda" parallel the millennia-long arguments over "rhetoric," and indeed, there is considerable overlap between these two conceptions of the art of persuasion. Plato's objections to sophistic rhetoric — that it appealed to emotion over reason and was indifferent to the question of truth — are also regularly invoked with regard to propaganda. Christoph Classen wryly observes that "propaganda" is simply the word used to describe "whatever one's opponent is up to." Christoph Classen, "Thoughts on the Significance of Mass-Media Communications in the Third Reich and the GDR," *Totalitarian Movements & Political Religions* 8, no. 3/4 (2007): 552.

19. Garth Jowett and Victoria O'Donnell, *Propaganda and Persuasion*, 3rd ed. (Thousand Oaks: Sage Publications, 1999), p. 3.

Others are more concerned with describing the defining features of propaganda, arguing that it appeals to emotions and prejudice rather than reason, for example, or highlight its use of simple, memorable slogans and images. No doubt the meaning of the term itself will continue to be contested. Rather than attempt a comprehensive general definition from the overlapping suggestions noted above, our purpose here is perhaps better served by considering what Germans understood by "propaganda" in the years after the Great War, and how they interpreted their experiences of it in the context of Weimar political life.

Prior to the war, Germans were familiar with the term "propaganda," but it was simply used as a synonym for "advertising" *(Reklame)*, and not necessarily associated with politics.[20]

What prompted its redefinition?

As we have seen, many Germans refused to believe that the war had been lost in the trenches of the Western Front, preferring the idea that Germany had been defeated by enemies from within. But the "stab in the back" was not the only influential alternative explanation for Germany's defeat. Alongside and often along with the theory of internal traitors there was a recognition that public opinion, both foreign and domestic, had contributed to the outcome of the war. Some Germans complained that the German government had only managed haphazard attempts at taking charge of the situation via mass communication, but the British had excelled at public relations, both at home and abroad.[21] Not only were the British able to cast themselves in the role of the unjustly persecuted and portray the Germans as marauding Huns to the world, they were also able to sow seeds of doubt in the German soldiers themselves. Germans felt their government's efforts at public persuasion were feeble compared to the British blitz — the government had only succeeded in keeping the civilian population in the dark as victory slipped away day by day.

Once the war was over, Germans marveled at the power of propaganda. The idea that public relations techniques could so mislead the masses was stunning and terrifying. The widespread consensus among Germans — that Germany had failed in the battle to win hearts and minds and

---

20. Corey Ross, "Mass Politics and the Techniques of Leadership: The Promise and Perils of Propaganda in Weimar Germany," *German History* 24, no. 2 (2006): 186.

21. Though tenaciously held, the postwar belief in the vast superiority of British propaganda techniques and the relative incompetence of the Germans is not supported by the evidence. David Welch, *The Third Reich: Politics and Propaganda* (London: Routledge, 1993), p. 11.

that it needed to do better — is evidenced by the large numbers of books, articles, and other writings which appeared on the subject of propaganda in the years after the war, not only in German academic contexts, but also in the popular press. As historian Corey Ross explains, this belief in the power of propaganda often brought with it a correspondingly condescending view of the German public as passive and easily seduced, especially now that women had joined the electorate.[22] If a stable and unified democratic state was to be established under such conditions, some would-be propagandists reasoned, then the educated elite would need to intervene to protect the German masses from manipulation, counteract the fracturous tendencies of parliamentary democracy, and defuse the threat of revolution. In this way, propaganda, even if it used "tendentious or misleading rhetoric," could serve the greater cause of democracy.[23] Given the complexities of modern industrial society, mass politics, and new media, the science of propaganda was seen as an essential tool, and institutes and think tanks were founded to facilitate research in the field. But not everyone was interested in the science of propaganda as a means to strengthen democracy.

Adolf Hitler was among the many who were convinced that Allied propaganda had made the difference in the outcome of the war, and he was determined to use this weapon himself. Two chapters of his manifesto *Mein Kampf* are dedicated to the subject. Hitler's theoretical statements on propaganda and mass psychology appear to originate from the then-popular French social psychologist Gustave Le Bon, though this cannot be directly established.[24] Hitler himself credits his appreciation for the "art" of propaganda not only to his observation of British wartime tactics but also, grudgingly, to the *Zauberkraft* ("magic") exhibited by Marxist propagandists.

What persuasive strategy does Hitler articulate in *Mein Kampf*?

Propaganda, he explains, should be directed toward the masses, not the elite. It should be simple and vivid, with lots of repetition, appealing to strong emotions like love and hate. And it should be relentless.[25] Once Hitler was released from prison and the bans on National Socialist campaigning were lifted, Hitler set about putting his theories into practice. He began by taking up a tool that was a part of daily life for citizens of Weimar: the press.

22. Ross, "Mass Politics," pp. 188-90.
23. Ross, "Mass Politics," p. 188.
24. Gerhard Paul, *Aufstand der Bilder: Die NS-Propaganda vor 1933* (Bonn: J. H. W. Dietz, 1990), p. 30.
25. See Adolf Hitler, *Mein Kampf*, 13th ed., trans. James Murphy (London: Hurst & Blackett, 1942), pp. 318-26.

The Press and German Politics

Propaganda took many forms in the last years of the Weimar Republic. Though there has understandably been great scholarly interest in the emerging media of late Weimar (radio, film), in the dramatic spectacles of mass politics (staged rallies, military parades), and in the visual media that greeted citizens at every turn (campaign posters, party fliers, pamphlets), it was, in fact, newspapers that remained the dominant form of mass communication throughout the 1920s and early 1930s. For most people, newspapers were their primary source of information about political issues, even if they only encountered the press indirectly.[26] The massive proliferation of newspapers began in the final decades of the nineteenth century, and the number of newspaper titles in Germany had increased from about 2,400 in 1881 to over 4,700 in 1932.[27] The reasons for the sheer number of newspaper titles in Weimar Germany were threefold.

First, newspapers had become reliant on advertising income from local businesses, so the German press was highly regionalized. No town was too small for its own paper, and the larger the community the more newspapers it produced.[28] Second, the postwar introduction of *Boulevardzeitung* — daily tabloids that were primarily sold on the street rather than by subscription — added another layer to an already crowded market for printed news.[29] Third, like much else in Weimar society, the press was thoroughly politicized, decentralized, and fragmented. Not only did every political party have its own newspaper, but every newspaper had its own politics.

In his comprehensive study of the press and German politics in Berlin during the Weimar Republic, Bernhard Fulda explains that in the Weimar press the news "was reported highly selectively; stories were given

---

26. As we have seen, the social lives of many Germans were entwined with their political identity. Even if a particular individual did not read the newspaper regularly, its content would surely be reported around the table at the pub, at a church event, or on the walk home from choir practice.

27. Bernhard Fulda, *Press and Politics in the Weimar Republic* (Oxford: Oxford University Press, 2009), p. 13.

28. Berlin had the largest number of daily newspapers, with thirty different citywide papers and another thirty to forty serving particular local districts. Fulda, *Press and Politics*, p. 17.

29. To lure impulse buyers, the tabloids relied on over-the-top novelty and sensation, eventually forcing their more traditional competitors to adopt their aggressive, eye-catching style. Fulda, *Press and Politics*, p. 34.

a strong slant and edited with the papers' different political outlooks."[30] This subjectivity was not an unreflective bias, but was actively embraced by the publications themselves as a journalistic goal.[31] This *Weltanschauungs-journalism* was not a new phenomenon but a longstanding tradition in the German press, and it had only intensified in the context of the Great War. In those heady times, journalists saw themselves as participants in the national "struggle" for victory and had little interest in reporting "what really happened." The advent of postwar democracy had a splintering effect on the press, who continued to embrace their role as advocates, but now as advocates for partisan, rather than national, political goals.[32] Journalists, editors, and publishers saw themselves as *educators*, not mere informers, and no commitment to "objectivity" hindered the political crusades that marched across the pages of their publications.[33] They were convinced that their influence could make all the difference, and in this belief they were not alone.

Laments or celebrations of "the power of the press" were frequently heard in Weimar well beyond journalistic circles, and, as with the convictions regarding "propaganda" more generally, this observation included a view of the "public" as a helpless subject at the mercy of an all-powerful press. "Greater than the influence of priests and scholars is the influence of journalists," intoned a popular book of the period.[34] Although this belief

---

30. Fulda, *Press and Politics*, p. 18.

31. Fulda, *Press and Politics*, p. 18. The fact that the German press made little effort at "objectivity" must certainly be taken into account when interpreting Barth's oft-cited comment to the effect that preachers should prepare "with the Bible in one hand and the newspaper in the other." For Barth was very aware of the power of the press. In a *Time Magazine* interview in 1963, Barth explicitly drew attention to this dynamic as he remembered the 1920s. The journalist from *Time* wrote of the interview: "Barth recalls that 40 years ago he advised young theologians to 'take your Bible and take your newspaper, and read both. But interpret newspapers from your Bible.' Newspapers, he says, are so important that 'I always pray for the sick, the poor, journalists, authorities of the state and the church — in that order. Journalists form public opinion. They hold terribly important positions.'" "Theologians: Barth in Retirement," *Time*, May 31, 1963.

32. Every paper had recognizable political loyalties, and the newspaper directories compiled for distribution among potential advertisers listed the political perspective of each paper, as reported by the publisher. Most were critical of Weimar democracy. Fulda, *Press and Politics*, p. 19.

33. About half of the employment contracts of German newspaper editors in 1927, for example, included the requirement that the editor express only the political perspective of the publication in his or her work. Fulda, *Press and Politics*, p. 42.

34. Joseph Eberle, *Grossmacht Presse, Enthüllungen für Zeitungsgläubige: Forderungen*

about the susceptibility of the masses to the influence of the press was largely unquestioned, studies have shown that individual Germans thought themselves immune or resistant to its power, even as they assumed the weakness of their neighbors.[35] This belief in the power of the press in shaping *public* opinion coupled with the assertion of *personal* immunity to its charms is a critical factor in the surprising way the press *did* in fact shape political behavior in Weimar.

Regardless of public perception at the time, the evidence suggests the correlation between a specific editorial endorsement of a political candidate by a newspaper and the voting behavior of its readers was relatively weak. Though readers were often loyal consumers of particular papers, they did not necessarily follow the paper's recommendations at election time, at least in markets where alternative news sources were readily available.[36] This is not to say that the press did not have an impact on voter behavior. It certainly did. But its influence was most powerful when it was indirect. This indirect influence took at least three forms.

First, the Weimar press was extremely influential when it came to the behavior of politicians, who, in the absence of any opinion polling, regularly read the newspapers as if their lives depended on it. Politicians shared the public's view of the power of the press and often (mistakenly) assumed that the average citizen read as widely and obsessively as they did themselves. This being the case, they reacted aggressively to the increasingly sensationalized and scandal-heavy coverage of the Weimar papers, particularly when that coverage showed them in a negative light.[37] Politicians would respond to muckraking headlines with hyperbolic language of their own, which then became news itself.[38] The politicians from the parties associated with Weimar received the brunt of the onslaught, but they were not the only ones. The degree of panic among politicians regarding the effects of journalistic attacks is evident in the frequent attempts by politicians to create legislation that would effectively limit the freedom of the press. By the early 1930s, temporary bans of particular newspapers by emergency decree were commonplace.[39] The vicious tone of these relent-

---

für Männer, 3rd ed. (Vienna: Verlagsanstalt Herold, 1920), p. 19. Quoted in Fulda, *Press and Politics*, p. 9.

35. Fulda, *Press and Politics*, p. 9.
36. Fulda, *Press and Politics*, p. 12.
37. Fulda, *Press and Politics*, p. 205.
38. Fulda, *Press and Politics*, p. 104.
39. Fulda, *Press and Politics*, pp. 219-21.

less public attacks and counterattacks contributed to the wider breakdown of reasoned public discourse in Weimar. The newspapers spoke a hostile language of slogans, insults, stereotypes, and labels, legitimating its use elsewhere.

Second, while the press did not directly control what readers did in the voting booth via their endorsements, it did control and frame the political agenda.[40] The amount of coverage given to a political issue or figure in the press indicated what was important, and, of course, the way a particular figure or event was portrayed could not help but affect a reader's opinion of the matter.[41]

Finally, the press was instrumental in promoting the idea that Germany was in crisis, on the verge of civil war, on the brink of disaster, and that Weimar democracy was an abject failure. The impotence, corruption, and stupidity of the Republic and its traitorous politicians was a constant theme in the right-wing press. The newspapers played on public fears, encouraged outrage, and exerted pressure on their readers to do something — or else.

Of course, none of this would have had much effect if things had not in fact been very difficult for the average German, especially when the global financial crisis decimated an already precarious economy. There was plenty to be unhappy about. But most unsettling to middle-class voters were the reports of violence on the streets, or rather, what they were told that violence meant. With the Bolshevik revolution still haunting the bourgeois imagination, even a minor street fight could look an awful lot like the beginning of the end. The newspapers were happy to stoke these alarmist fires — not only did it sell papers, but many editors believed they were offering a public service in sounding the alarm.[42]

So despite the fact that acts of political violence were committed by members of several parties, not least by the National Socialists, it was Communist violence that received unrelenting attention in many publications. It was front-page news that served to confirm the widespread opinion that between the radical right and the radical left, it was the radical left

---

40. Fulda, *Press and Politics*, p. 73.

41. The extensive and often sympathetic coverage of Hitler's trial in the mid-1920s in the right-wing press not only put him on the map with conservative nationalists; it also influenced Hitler's view of himself as someone destined to be more than a cheerleader for his party. He saw that he *was* the *Führer* — the press told him so. Fulda, *Press and Politics*, p. 74.

42. Though many believed that a Communist revolution or civil war was at hand in the final years of Weimar, neither was a likely event.

that posed the greater threat.[43] The primary beneficiary of this impression was the National Socialist movement.

The Press, Propaganda, and the National Socialist Revolution

Hitler understood that in order to succeed at the polls, he needed to utilize every available means to reach the voters directly. To coordinate the party's campaign strategy, Hitler appointed Joseph Goebbels head of party propaganda in November 1928, in recognition of his significant success as *Gauleiter* of Berlin. With their limited financial resources, it was not easy in the beginning to implement Goebbels's vision. But as the party membership increased, so did the money. Under Goebbels's oversight, the Nazis continued to stage demonstrations, organize parades, and plaster up posters, and they began an innovative direct mail and pamphlet distribution campaign which tailored their message to particular types of voters, usually distinguishing them by occupation.[44]

From their observation of Marxist agitation, both Hitler and Goebbels were convinced of the power of the spoken word, which could overcome "the resistance of the emotions" in a way that a printed text could not.[45] This being the case, the Nazis were constantly hosting tightly controlled and well-publicized political meetings and rallies in towns and cities all over Germany, each one with a featured Nazi speaker.[46] Alongside this public face of National Socialist propaganda, there was a more discreet "private" campaign that included frequent street brawls, destroying the campaign materials of other parties, and regularly disrupting the political meetings of their opponents.[47]

---

43. Fulda, *Press and Politics*, pp. 213-14.

44. The exception to this was the relatively late NSDAP appeal to women, who were lumped together as a gender, not differentiated by profession. For a description of Nazi propaganda directed to women in the 1932 campaigns, see Julia Sneeringer, *Winning Women's Votes: Propaganda and Politics in Weimar Germany* (Chapel Hill: University of North Carolina Press, 2002), pp. 242-43.

45. Paul, *Aufstand der Bilder*, p. 42.

46. The National Socialists developed training programs for their speakers, as did several other parties, including the SPD. Thomas Childers, "The Social Language of Politics in Germany: The Sociology of Political Discourse in the Weimar Republic," *American Historical Review* 95, no. 2 (1990): 338.

47. As time went by, some of the behind-the-scenes guerilla tactics of the NSDAP actually became a celebrated part of their public image, and they often received accolades

Hitler and Goebbels also knew they could not afford to neglect the press. The NSDAP had its own party newspapers, of course, but these partisan publications never had much success in reaching beyond the circles of the already-converted.[48] But in the end this lackluster performance did not matter, because by 1930 the Nazis had muscled their way onto the front pages of nearly every major newspaper, and they were there to stay. How had they managed to steal the limelight?

Changes in press coverage can be detected in the months leading up to the 1930 elections. The depictions of violence, especially Communist violence, were more plentiful, as were references to the supposed threat of civil war. At the same time, the National Socialists enjoyed increased and largely positive coverage, which came in one of two forms. First, the NSDAP was often portrayed as *the* anti-Communist party, courageously defending Germany with their bare hands on the street when necessary.[49] Second, their well-attended mass rallies also attracted the attention of the press, in particular the incredible 7,000 events the Nazis staged in October of 1929.[50]

In the days leading up to the 1930 election the Nazis worked to get every possible vote, even making what turned out to be a futile attempt to woo working-class voters. But it was middle-class nationalist voters that were "ideologically available" for mobilization, and all the right-wing parties were courting them.[51] Thematically there was little difference between these competing conservative factions. They all denounced Weimar, Marxism, the "November criminals," internationalism, and materialism; sported a *völkisch* anti-Semitic underbelly; and extolled the virtues of a re-

---

when they "defended themselves" from Communist aggressors on the streets. In 1930, the Nazis managed to get the antiwar film *Im Westen nichts Neues* banned all over Germany by rioting at every showing. Some in the nationalist press hailed them as heroes. Welch, *The Third Reich*, p. 13.

48. The Nazi Party's own national paper, the *Völkischer Beobacheter,* relaunched in 1925. Goebbels founded the weekly newspaper *Der Angriff* in 1926 while he was *Gauleiter* of Berlin, which would become a daily paper in late 1930. By the September 1930 elections, the Nazis had six daily newspapers in various parts of the country, with *VB* distributed in both Munich and Berlin. Welch, *The Third Reich*, p. 13.

49. Fulda, *Press and Politics*, p. 144.

50. The dramatic increase in attendance at the rallies, and hence the heightened interest on the part of the press, stems from Hitler's decision to join the other nationalist parties in opposing the Young Plan. Fulda, *Press and Politics*, p. 146.

51. Ian Kershaw, "Ideology, Propaganda, and the Rise of the Nazi Party," in Stachura, ed., *Nazi Machtergreifung*, p. 165.

stored, economically stable, and unified *Volksgemeinschaft* in their respective propaganda efforts. But the Nazis distinguished themselves from their competitors in several ways, not least by their emphasis on Hitler himself, framing him as a symbol, not just a person. Hitler was not a politician like the despised squabblers in the *Reichstag*, but a *Führer* who transcended political parties.[52] He was building a movement that was greater than politics. It was an unstoppable force that would sweep away the broken "system" of Weimar with its failed economic policies, immoral culture, and endless bickering. He would usher in the new Reich. The Nazis took the basic platform of the right, personified it in a dynamic central figure, and presented it with a degree of aggression that dwarfed the other conservative parties. The brownshirts seemed to be everywhere.[53] With their military bearing, confrontational stance, and youthful demographic, they succeeded with those already leaning to the right in creating an image of vigor, power, and life, while the other right-wing parties appeared weak by comparison.[54] And that made all the difference. For the question on many a mind as the chaotic 1930 election drew near was this: Who would be strong enough to restore order to Germany's streets?

Once the votes were counted, it was clear that the NSDAP was a force

---

52. In presenting himself as the "Leader," Hitler consciously connected himself to Bismarck. The Second Reich was not founded by a democratic majority, the Nazis argued, but by a strong, ruthless leader like Bismarck. It would take another like him to usher in the Third. Richard Evan Frankel, *Bismarck's Shadow: The Cult of Leadership and the Transformation of the German Right, 1898-1945* (Oxford: Berg, 2005), p. 157. Bismarck was greatly admired by the right for his "struggle against everything unGerman," and a Bismarck cult of sorts thrived during the Weimar years. By the mid-1920s there was a noticeable increase in the size and frequency of Bismarck celebrations. Frankel, *Bismarck's Shadow*, p. 142.

53. In this regard, the Nazis benefited from right-wing nationalist and *Deutschnationale Volkspartei* leader Alfred Hugenberg's acquisition of the largest German film company, *Ufa*, in 1927. From then on the National Socialists were regularly featured in the newsreels that accompanied feature films in a vast network of *Ufa* cinemas. Welch, *The Third Reich*, p. 13.

54. The National Socialists used the language of *Kampf* with its social Darwinistic and racial connotations to highlight their gladiatorial disposition. The term figures prominently in Houston Stewart Chamberlain's influential book *The Foundations of the Nineteenth Century*, which envisioned idealistic Germans and materialistic Jews locked in an eternal power struggle, with the fate of humanity hanging in the balance. Evans, *Coming of the Third Reich*, pp. 33-34. For the Nazis, politics, society, life itself was struggle — a battle that required strength in body and will. *Kampf*, then, was code for spiritual and physical violence. It indicated that the National Socialists would do whatever was necessary to preserve the *Volk* from what they considered its internal and external threats. Kershaw, "Ideology," pp. 165-66.

to be reckoned with. Their electoral gains brought increased financial resources as private industry donations began to flow. The press was paying attention. But now that attention was not so positive. Naturally all the leftist and left-leaning papers were highly critical of the newly ascendant Nazis, but now so were the publications representing the traditional right-wing parties, who saw their own electoral chances slipping away. From 1931 to the end of the Republic, as the depression deepened and the violence escalated, politicians, the press, and the public engaged in an all-out war of words.[55] Public spaces were plastered and replastered with campaign posters, party "gangs" looked for trouble in the alleyways, uniformed party militias marched through the streets as if to war, and the papers screamed partisan accusations. Nearly every public venue was a breeding ground for agitation, demonstration, or proselytizing. Even in most of the universities, as we have seen, it was often impossible to express support for things like democracy or pacifism without enduring heckling, rioting, and libelous attacks.

After the 1930 elections, the political operatives of all parties knew that the Nazis were the ones to beat. For this reason, much of the political rhetoric of the time consisted of borrowings from, or reactions to, the tropes the Nazis had themselves co-opted and popularized. Perhaps first among these was the constellation of meanings surrounding the German word *"Volk." Volk* could mean simply "people" in a generic sense and it sometimes did, but in the political context of Weimar it was more commonly a specific reference to the *German* people, a people constituted as a *Volk* not on the basis of geographical proximity, citizenship, or constitutional loyalty, but by shared blood, history, culture, "spirit," and language. The term *"Volk"* was attached to a host of other terms in order to specify their Germanness. Hence *Volkstum* (German folklore, identity), *Volksgeist* (the German way of thinking/feeling), *Volksseele* (the soul of the German people), and so forth. The oft-evoked ideal of the *Volksgemeinschaft* posited a mystical bond between members of this national German-Aryan community. It was this bond that could overcome the divisions wrought

---

55. Fulda, *Press and Politics*, p. 169. The political environment was so volatile that President Hindenburg tried to defuse the situation by ordering a political cease-fire for Christmas 1931. Hindenburg's "Schutz des inneren Friedens" forbade all public political gatherings, posters, flyers, and pamphlets from December 10, 1931, to January 3, 1932. Barth refers to the cease-fire in his Christmas meditation published in a Munich newspaper in 1931. See Karl Barth, *Gesamtausgabe*, ed. Hinrich Stoevesandt and Hans Anton Drewes (Zürich: Theologischer Verlag, 1971), V.I.8, p. 632. See also Paul, *Aufstand der Bilder*, p. 95.

by partisan politics and class warfare, and restore Germany to its rightful place as the leader of nations.⁵⁶ The members of this idealized *Volksgemeinschaft* put the common good before individual, party, or class interests, in contrast to the selfishness of Western and Marxist "materialists."⁵⁷ The euphoria of the first days of the Great War had been a foretaste of what Germany would be like if it could transcend the divisions wrought by democracy.⁵⁸

Corresponding to the positive vision of the *Volksgemeinschaft* was the incessant denunciation in right-wing and right-leaning propaganda of those considered *Volkfremd* (alien to the German *Volk*, unGerman) and/or *Volkverräter* (traitor to the German *Volk*). As we have seen, groups who were thought to have international ties or a "materialist spirit" were portrayed as a threat to the survival of the *Volk*. Nationalist propaganda attacked Communists, Marxists, and Social Democrats as well as other "unGerman elements" such as capitalist "moneybags," the "November criminals" who supposedly capitulated to the Allies, and Jews, who were sometimes linked to any or all of the above.⁵⁹ The flaws of the Weimar "system" itself increasingly became the focus of election campaigns, and its Social Democrat politicians were lambasted as corrupt and immoral "*Bonzen*" (fat cats), incapable of running the country or preventing a Bolshevik-style bloodbath.⁶⁰

Meanwhile, Communist propaganda also aimed its guns at the "system," the Social Democrats tried to frighten voters into standing by the Republic by emphasizing the violent nature of both the Nazis and the Communists, and the Catholic Centre Party joined the conservative nationalist parties in including regular appeals to religious voters, particularly women.⁶¹

---

56. Peter Fritzsche, *Rehearsals for Fascism: Populism and Political Mobilization in Weimar Germany* (New York: Oxford University Press, 1990), p. 212.

57. Michael and Doerr, *Nazi-Deutsch/Nazi-German*, p. 423.

58. The Nazis in particular called for a sleeping national-community to wake up and take back their *Heimat*, and Hitler's mass rallies were intended to give participants a "*Volksgemeinschaft* experience" that would bind them to the NSDAP in a way no rational argument could. Paul, *Aufstand der Bilder*, p. 42.

59. Barth was called "unGerman" in the aftermath of his manifesto "Quousque Tandem?" Karl Wilhelm Dahm, *Pfarrer und Politik: Soziale Position und politische Mentalität des deutschen evangelischen Pfarrerstandes zwischen 1918 und 1933*, Dortmunder Schriften zur Sozialforschung (Cologne: Westdeutscher Verlag, 1965), p. 194.

60. Paul, *Aufstand der Bilder*, p. 11.

61. The SPD also had a positive side to their propaganda: the promise of a peaceful

Given the dire economic times, all of the parties also included promises of *"Arbeit und Brot"* (work and bread) in their appeals.[62] Attention to the plight of the worker had of course long been a feature of the propaganda of the Marxist parties, but by the early 1930s the Nazis had taken it up as well. The National Socialist leaders considered the working class "biologically sound, honest dupes of Marxist 'false consciousness,'" and thus they began imitating the left-wing practice of featuring a giant "worker" on their campaign posters.[63] As a result, the images emblazoned on the campaign posters of the different parties in the final years of the Republic were remarkable similar: a giant naked man (the German worker) stepping on a squabbling mob. The "mob" in question usually represented Weimar democracy, which the "worker" (representing either the proletariat or the *Volksgemeinschaft*) would crush beneath his noble feet. If the poster was designed by the SPD, of course, the squabbling mob would instead be composed of rabid Nazis and rampaging Communists.

In the midst of this propaganda blitz, the National Socialists looked like the party with momentum, and indeed, for a while, they had it. The July 1932 election was the high point for the National Socialists, who lured large numbers of voters away from the other nationalist conservative parties. But the Social Democrat (SPD), Communist (KPD), and Centre parties had also intensified their own propaganda efforts, and their voters remained immune to Nazi appeals.

It was true that the National Socialists had made dramatic electoral gains, and it seemed that their propaganda efforts had not been in vain. But it is important to note that already by November 1932, just as the *Predigtvorbereitung* exercises commenced, support for the NSDAP had begun to erode. By the time Hitler was appointed chancellor in January 1933, Ian Kershaw observes, it was "a time of propaganda failure, not success."[64] Richard Bessel argues that, on the basis of mounting historical evidence, historians must retire the tropes of an irrational population duped by Nazi

---

socialist *Volksgemeinschaft*. Nonetheless, the party tended to minimize the significance of religion and culture in its vision of the national community. Sneeringer, *Winning Women's Votes*, pp. 202-5.

62. Paul, *Aufstand der Bilder*, p. 247.

63. Michael Burleigh, *The Third Reich: A New History* (Basingstoke: Macmillan, 2000), pp. 121-22.

64. Kershaw, "Ideology," p. 178. As Kershaw argues, many studies that focus on the propaganda itself simply presume its effectiveness and neglect the more difficult question of how these efforts were in fact received. See Kershaw, "Ideology," p. 163.

Theological Existence and the Rhetoric of Weimar

sleight of hand in favor of the thesis that people supported the Nazis because under the particular circumstances of the early 1930s, they came to the (rational) conclusion that the NSDAP was most likely to protect their interests.[65]

This shift to the acknowledgement of a "rational" voter does not necessitate the claim that propaganda had little effect, nor does it fund a vision of German voters in general and Nazi voters in particular as dispassionate citizens thoughtfully weighing the political options and carefully parsing the ideological grammar that confronted them. On the contrary, there is no doubt that Germans were under great stress at the time, that emotions ran high, and that the raging propaganda wars often drowned out nuanced political debate. Campaign rhetoric, pageantry, and revival-meeting fervor certainly played a role, especially among the core fanatics and the young.[66]

But, broadly speaking, National Socialist propaganda did not function as some sort of irresistible force. Voters made a choice in 1932, and they had their reasons.

For the activist base of the party, *völkisch* anti-Semitism was a central motivation. But anti-Semitism was not the basis of the broader appeal of the party; in fact, it was conspicuously absent from much of their propaganda in the early 1930s. The Nazis used it only where it "worked" — among their activist base and in the relatively limited areas of the country with strong anti-Semitic traditions. On the other hand, Hitler's rabid anti-Semitism was no secret. No one who cast a vote for Hitler could claim ignorance of it.[67]

Most of those who opted for the NSDAP at the height of its popularity in 1932 already had conservative nationalist fears, grievances, and longings. With regard to those matters no convincing was required. Instead, they cast their lot with the Nazis because they were persuaded that among

---

65. Bessel notes that Nazi voters did not respond to National Socialist propaganda in the years before 1930, and their support for the party was already in decline by late 1932. Of course, one might point out in response to Bessel that many voters made the judgments they did largely based on the information they gleaned directly or indirectly from propaganda! Nonetheless, Bessel succeeds in shifting the focus from awe at a Nazi propaganda machine back to the voters themselves and their reasons for deciding for the NSDAP. See Richard Bessel, "The Rise of the NSDAP and the Myth of Nazi Propaganda," *Wiener Library Bulletin* 33, no. 51 (1980): 20-29.

66. Kershaw, "Ideology," p. 176.

67. Kershaw, "Ideology," pp. 167-68.

the choices at the time the NSDAP was "the most powerful adversary of Marxism and the most radical and forthright exponent of the belief in national and social renewal (the 'national community' idea, which was itself of course in essence outrightly anti-Marxist)."[68] In other words, Nazi aggression could get the job done.[69]

Hitler's electoral success in the early 1930s, then, cannot be attributed to mass psychosis, irresistible propaganda, or a passive, naïve, or apolitical population.[70] If anything, it was the wider rhetorical climate itself — born of suspicion, desperation, fear, prejudice, and partisanship, and haunted by the specter of actual or threatened physical violence — that made rational debate about political choices so difficult at the time.[71]

We might think that a different kind of discourse would prevail in the German Protestant Church. How would the church react to the escalating propaganda wars swirling around it? Perhaps in Protestant circles, "above parties," a thoughtful testing of the political spirits would be the rule.

Political Propaganda and the Protestant Church in Weimar

Prior to the advent of Weimar, the German Protestant church had little reason to think of itself as a political agent. Certainly it lamented unwelcome developments in the wider society such as encroaching secularization, the erosion of moral values, and the anticlericalism of "godless" socialists. But in spite of these and other worries, the church enjoyed the protection, financial support, and approbation of the Wilhelmine state, and hence did not perceive a need to utilize political means to achieve its desired ends. With the Weimar revolution, all that would change. The

---

68. Kershaw, "Ideology," p. 168.

69. For the definitive study of why people voted for Hitler see Thomas Childers, *The Nazi Voter: The Social Foundations of Fascism in Germany, 1919-1933* (Chapel Hill: University of North Carolina Press, 1983).

70. Less than half the electorate had ever, or would ever, cast a vote for Hitler in a free election, but ultimately that did not matter. When Hitler launched his next propaganda campaign in March 1933, he made sure he had the stage all to himself.

71. As Julia Sneeringer argues, Weimar political campaigns were "oriented around sweeping ideological pronouncements rather than concrete proposals.... Because Germans voted for party lists rather than individual candidates, they were further removed from their representatives, making voting increasingly an expression of protest.... In short, Weimar politics was combative and theatrical; the successive jolts of inflation, a harsh stabilization, and the depression made it combustible." Sneeringer, *Winning Women's Votes*, pp. 6-7.

"Christian" monarchy was replaced with a "religionless" constitution, and the *Volkskirche*'s existence as a *Volkskirche* was suddenly called into question.[72] All the rights, privileges, and benefits it held dear were now at risk in the democratic free-for-all. As Wesley Smith explains, after 1918 the German Protestant church "had to compete with other worldviews, without the sanction of the state, to shape the moral life of society."[73] Surely they should do something about this.

But direct political activism was an uncomfortable prospect for many. The church had long proclaimed its separation from what it considered the questionable world of politics. But under the changed circumstances, some argued, a quietist position would only strengthen the new godless state and play into the hands of the socialists, who wanted to confine religion to the "private" sphere anyway.[74] No, the church needed to stand up for itself and its claims by whatever means necessary. What it should *not* do, Protestant leaders thought, was engage in what it considered partisan politics. It should be "above parties."

But, as we have seen, "above parties" was anything but a statement of neutrality in relation to the political situation of the day. What church leaders meant by "above parties" was in one sense a statement of their intent to be a sort of "state within a state," the "one structure that remained true to Germany's historic traditions" in contrast to the selfish partisanship encouraged by the Republic.[75] The desire to "remain true to Germany's historic traditions" placed it firmly in the camp of the conservative nationalist right.[76]

---

72. In its most basic sense, the designation *"Volkskirche"* indicates comprehensive membership, i.e., one belongs to the church because one has been born into the *Volk*. See Daniel R. Borg, *The Old Prussian Church and the Weimar Republic: A Study in Political Adjustment, 1917-1927* (Hanover: University Press of New England, 1984), p. 2. This meant, of course, that a church tax was levied on all German citizens unless they formally withdrew from the church. The broader concept of *"Volkskirche"* included the longstanding idea that the Protestant church played an indispensable role in German society — as steward and custodian of public morality and culture.

73. B. Wesley Warren Smith, "Pastoral Care to the Soul of the Nation: Ludwig Ihmels and Germany's Domestic Crises, 1902-1933" (Ph.D. dissertation, Princeton Theological Seminary, 1998), p. 142.

74. Borg, *Old Prussian Church*, p. 28.

75. John S. Conway, "National Socialism and Christian Churches," in Stachura, ed., *Nazi Machtergreifung*, p. 128.

76. "Above parties" in a broad sense, then, is code for "anti-democracy." In a democracy, interest groups ("parties") vie for power and influence, but the church claimed to stand

Thus the Protestant church — still "above parties" — began to mobilize to protect its interests. As the largest nongovernmental institution in Germany, there is no doubt that the church was a powerful political force in Weimar. And it did not enter the public arena in the early years of Weimar without some prior experience: during the Great War the church mounted a systematic campaign to strengthen the will to victory among the *Volk*.[77] With their access to the vast networks of the *Landeskirchen* church leaders could reach large numbers of people, and a multiplicity of church-related newspapers, newsletters, pamphlets, and other publications were already in place. In Germany's countless small towns, pastors were among the elite "opinion leaders" who had great political influence in their local communities, and pulpit pronouncements in support of the war effort were commonplace, as we shall see.[78]

The national and local Protestant political campaigns of the 1920s were devoted to opposing school reform and the disestablishment of the church on the one hand and promoting Sunday "blue laws" and various kinds of morality legislation on the other.[79] Early in the Weimar years, church organizations began sending questionnaires to the various political parties, asking pointedly about their respective positions on issues relating to church and state with the "promise or threat" that the church press would publish the results.[80] Protestants founded or supported organiza-

---

"above" such a system, preserving the spirit of the monarchy until it could be restored. In terms of Weimar's political options, the parties of the left were out of the question for most Protestants — the majority associated socialism with atheism and immorality — and the Centre party was of course for Catholics. Practically, then, "above parties" meant a reluctance to identify the Protestant church with one *specific* right-wing party, but its location on the political spectrum was clear. In fact, at the end of the war, many pastors, church newspapers, and church districts went so far as openly to endorse the right-wing Fatherland party, simultaneously arguing that "allegiance to the Fatherland could scarcely be construed as partisan." Borg, *Old Prussian Church*, p. 42.

77. Borg, *Old Prussian Church*, p. 37.
78. Fulda, *Press and Politics*, p. 210.
79. To these ends, the German *Volkskirche* Federation *(Volkskirchenbund)* was formed in 1919. Borg, *Old Prussian Church*, p. 72. Chairman Arthur Titius summarized the mission of the *Bund*: "In politics today one has respect only for the masses.... For a number of years the federation will have the task of revealing the existing forces [of Protestants] and allowing them to be politically effective." Quoted in Borg, *Old Prussian Church*, p. 73. They were later joined in these efforts by the work of the Church Federation *(Kirchenbund)* of the *Landeskirchen* (constituted in 1922), which also lobbied with regard to issues important to the church. Borg, *Old Prussian Church*, p. 77.
80. Borg, *Old Prussian Church*, p. 83.

tions devoted to swaying public opinion in the church's favor. There were petition drives, campaigns for particular candidates (though not "parties"), get-out-the-vote efforts, special "pre-voting" worship services, and pro-church propaganda campaigns, disseminated through an ever-expanding number of church-related publications.

The political struggle over confessional education and the church/state relationship would continue for years. But by the mid-1920s it was clear that the church had managed to garner widespread public support for much of its primary agenda. Some form of Christian instruction would remain in the schools and the *Landeskirchen* would keep their funding. Church leaders were not convinced the battle was really over, and they still found much to lament as they catalogued the doleful effects of democracy on the German *Geist*. They read the "boulevard" press. They insisted that the moral leadership of the Protestant church was needed now more than ever. Nonetheless, they could claim a measure of victory against what many considered to be the systematic attempt of the left to marginalize the church.[81] Their foray into the world of political activism had made a concrete difference. From then on the discussion of political questions, domestic and foreign, held a prominent position in most church-related periodicals and had become the highlight even of church gatherings.[82]

With the shifts in electoral fortune, the furor over the "Young Plan," and the collapse of the economy, what had already been vigorous political engagement by the Protestant church in the 1920s would only intensify in the volatile climate of the early 1930s. Not only was this true for the church vis-à-vis the political world beyond its walls but also with regard to the church's internal dynamics. National Socialism became a frequent topic of debate among Protestants after the Nazis' 1930 electoral gains, and many

---

81. It is precisely this mixture of triumphalism and call to continued self-promotion that is typified in Otto Dibelius's two-volume *Das Jahrhundert der Kirche*. Barth critiques the first volume in his "Quousque Tandem?"

82. "At church meetings religious questions are attended to respectfully and often with interest and understanding. The spirits come alive at once, though, when the political area is touched. Suddenly everybody has his own opinion; everybody feels personally involved; heckling occurs. Political enthusiasm dominates everything." Dibelius, *Nachspiel*, quoted in Franz G. M. Feige, *The Varieties of Protestantism in Nazi Germany: Five Theopolitical Positions*, Toronto Studies in Theology (Lewiston: E. Mellen Press, 1990), p. 101. On the political activism of pastors at the end of Weimar, see Kurt Nowak, *Evangelische Kirche und Weimarer Republik: Zum politischen Weg des deutschen Protestantismus zwischen 1918 und 1932* (Göttingen: Vandenhoeck & Ruprecht, 1981), pp. 210-15.

were torn between appreciation for much of the Nazi platform and discomfort with their coarse rhetoric and aggressive style of campaigning.

But it proved difficult to denounce the National Socialists on tactical grounds when some of the most respected theologians in the country were prone to inflammatory rhetoric themselves. As John Conway observes, the influential Political Theologians "deplored the revolutionary excesses of the extremists, but seemed unaware how much their virulent incitements to hatred and denunciations of their opponents debased the level of theological argument."[83] Nationalist Protestants argued among themselves over the best right-wing party to lead Germany beyond Weimar while dissenting voices from the minority left-wing of the church, whether Religious Socialist, left-liberal, or dialectical were met with increasing hostility. Part of the reason for this polarization had to do with the fact that the National Socialists began systematic efforts to influence and infiltrate some of the church elections beginning in 1931, with notable success in some cases.[84]

To understand the state of political and theological discourse in the church at the time Barth convenes his sermon exercises, three dynamics merit further comment here. First, in the early years of Weimar, many of the *Landeskirchen* had enacted regulations to govern the political activity of their pastors. This was the formal expression of the "above party" ethos. The guidelines from the Synod of Old Prussia are representative of others. In Old Prussia, pastors could, of course, express their political views as private citizens — indeed, they were virtually required to do so as clergy when an issue relating to the church was at stake — but the rules forbade clergy from campaigning *as clergy* for a particular party, especially when they did so in the context of their duties, for example, in a sermon.[85] In the deteriorating situation of the early 1930s, then, regional church leaders had the

---

83. Conway, "National Socialism," p. 140.

84. The NSDAP began interfering in the Bonn *Kirchenwahlen* in 1932, recruiting German Christian candidates to run for office (most of whom had not been active in the church until then) and vigorously promoting their candidacy. Notably, these earliest efforts were largely unsuccessful in Bonn, with German Christians winning only a small number of seats. Pastors and lay presbyters alike denounced the "politicization" of the church elections by the agitation of the NSDAP, at least in 1932. Annette Hinz-Wessels, *Die evangelische Kirchengemeinde Bonn in der Zeit des Nationalsozialismus (1933-1945)* (Cologne: Rheinland-Verlag, 1996), p. 466.

85. Shelley Baranowski, *The Sanctity of Rural Life: Nobility, Protestantism, and Nazism in Weimar Prussia* (New York: Oxford University Press, 1995), p. 173. For a discussion of the practical problems that came with church oversight of the political activities of clergy see Borg, *Old Prussian Church*, pp. 272-76 and 284-90.

Theological Existence and the Rhetoric of Weimar

difficult task of enforcing the "above party" policy at the local level, as increasing numbers of complaints were lodged against crusading right-wing preachers, "red" agitators, and/or politicized worship services. The practice of "telling" on activist pastors became another form of partisan warfare within the church. Not surprisingly, the evidence suggests that the consistories did try to enforce the regulations, but when the accused was a conservative nationalist, they did so with reluctance and considerable sympathy.[86] After all, they did not want to appear anti-nationalist at a time when a nationalist revival was under way.

This concern for appearances is related to the second dynamic that compromised the church's ability to talk thoughtfully about politics, namely, that by the last years of Weimar, church leaders were very anxious about their public image.[87] They wanted the Republic to collapse, but they certainly didn't want a Communist revolution. When they looked to their obvious political home, the right, the Nazis were the ones who looked unstoppable. That being the case, as was argued in Chapter Two of this study, many in the hierarchy believed they must demonstrate the church's value to the coming regime. If they were to survive and thrive, they needed to be "relevant" in the Reich to come. Even among those who in other circumstances might be persuaded to reconsider, the desire to emphasize the church's anti-Communist, pro-*Vaterland* credentials at what seemed like a perilous moment was a formidable barrier to genuine dialogue between the dominant right wing of the church and the Religious Socialist, left-liberal, or dialectical minority. If church leaders were not adamant about their nationalism, would they lose the younger generation, as they lost the workers in the past?[88] For the sake of the *Volk*, they needed to ensure that the historic relationship between Christianity and nationalism remained intact. How else could the church fulfill its vocation as moral leader of the culture?

Finally, discourse in the church deteriorated by the end of Weimar because there was little common ground on which the right and left wings

---

86. For examples of this bias in the context of specific cases in the Old Prussian Church, see Baranowski, *Sanctity of Rural Life*, pp. 173-75.

87. For an account of the varied and often conflicted ways this anxiety came to expression among leaders of the *Landeskirchen* and their changing views of the NSDAP, see Jonathan Richard Cassé Wright, *"Above Parties": The Political Attitudes of the German Protestant Church Leadership, 1918-1933*, Oxford Historical Monographs (New York: Oxford University Press, 1974), pp. 74-98.

88. Borg, *Old Prussian Church*, p. 177.

of Protestantism could test the political spirits together. They could no longer articulate a shared Christian identity that transcended political commitments. Indeed, for the many Protestant leaders influenced by the Political Theologians, the difference between theological speech and political speech had largely disappeared. Consciously and unconsciously, the church's language about God and itself had been infiltrated by the dominant political rhetoric of the day. Even the more moderate among the right-wing churchmen used the words of the radical right without specifying their intended or qualified meaning.[89] The language of *Volk* and *Kampf* permeated everything. With the National Socialists, many Protestants longed for rebirth, renewal, revival, *Volksgemeinschaft*, leadership, and unity. And along with those shared longings, references to the shared "unGerman" enemies of the *Volk* were usually not far behind.[90] The doctrine of the orders of creation gave the dominant faction in German Protestantism a theological reason to sanctify the nationalism it felt so deeply, to take up the political rhetoric of the right, and to demonize any who questioned its claims. Natural theology — their God-given Germanness — became the basis of theopolitical solidarity in the church at the end of Weimar, and as such, there was little room for discussion with dissenters. Leaders of many of the *Landeskirchen* watched as the political pathos that dominated the rest of the society became a feature of church life as well, but they could do little to stop it.[91]

---

89. Alice Gallin argues that university professors were also imprecise in their use of the language of the right, thus legitimating the National Socialist enthusiasm among their students. Gallin, *Midwives to Nazism*, p. 31.

90. Nowak, *Evangelische Kirche*, p. 298.

91. The degree to which communication in the church had deteriorated is evidenced by the fact that many of the *Landeskirchen* leaders issued statements about partisan rhetoric in the context of the church in the early 1930s. Among the most dramatic is the following plea issued from the pulpit by Landesbishop D. Bernewitz at the *Volkstrauertage* of 1932: "In great sorrow concerning the conscience and the future of our *Volk* I appeal to everybody, on the commemoration day for our brothers and sons who fell for the freedom of Germany in the world war, I appeal to the fellow believers and fellow *Volk* in self-examination to stop the dishonorable speech, hate, and murder. How can one party believe that in order to damage others, they attack their defenseless members? Thus they only make it so much more acrimonious, and one hate breeds others. How can a newspaper believe that they serve the truth, if they write lies which gloss over the crime or make the innocent guilty? . . . In times of decision everyone is permitted to argue for what seems to him to be the best for *Volk* and *Vaterland*, but in honest *Kampf* with the means of integrity and truth, not with the poisonous weapons of the vulgar and with deceitfully drawn daggers. You should not become an evil character! You should not bear false witness! You should not kill! — Whoever sows to

This volatile power struggle was the rhetorical situation in German society, academy, and church when Barth decided to intervene directly in the education of a new generation of preachers. Given his theological existence, his Swiss background, and his well-known political sympathies, what strategies did he employ to gain a hearing in a climate where so much of the discourse inside and outside the church had become polarized, politicized, and paralyzed?

Karl Barth and the Rhetoric of Political Reaction and Revolution

In John McDowell's review essay on Timothy Gorringe's *Karl Barth: Against Hegemony*, he notes that Gorringe sees precisely in Barth's "silence" regarding political events in the early 1930s a calculated response to those events. But McDowell complains in an aside that Gorringe "does not ask with any conviction why Barth follows such a style."[92] That is the question to be answered in what follows.

It is true that Barth did not set out to generate a theory of communication, a rhetorical strategy, or a pedagogical method in response to the propaganda wars of the early 1930s. Given the rapidly changing situation, improvisation was often necessary. But that does not mean he was not intentional about his words, his style, and his tone in those years. Barth understood that language mattered, and he paid close attention to the words of others as well as his own.[93] The worse things got, the more alert he be-

---

the wind will reap the whirlwind. I appeal to our honor, for the sake of our conscience, for the sake of our *Volk*, for the sake of God, that we lead honestly and gallantly in the *Kampf* for a better future of our afflicted *Volk*, that we still again would be what we were in the best times of our history: a united *Volk* of brothers." Hermann Sasse, *Kirchliche Zeitlage* (Gutersloh: C. Bertelsmann, 1932), p. 164. The alert reader will note that the rhetoric of the nationalist right is present, even here in Bernewitz's call to civility. For other statements of concern regarding political discourse in the early 1930s issued by leaders of other Landeskirchen, see Sasse, *Kirchliche Zeitlage*, pp. 126-68.

92. John McDowell, "Timothy Gorringe's Contextualised Barth: An Article-Review," *Evangelical Quarterly* 74, no. 4 (2002): 340.

93. Barth later observed of this period: "I followed the efforts of the few thoughtful people, the small groups of men of good will who took the 'Weimar Republic' and its constitution seriously and wanted to build up German social democracy. . . . I also saw and heard the so-called 'German nationals' of the time — in my memory the most undesirable of God's creatures whom I have ever met. They had learnt nothing and forgotten nothing, and torpedoed absolutely every attempt to achieve the best that was possible on that basis. With

came. And given his theological existence, this is hardly surprising. Indeed, we should not forget that the problem of communication, specifically communication about God, had consumed Barth since his Safenwil days.

While Barth did not attempt to offer a comprehensive statement regarding his rhetorical strategy at the end of Weimar, it is possible to trace certain features of his approach that come to expression in his writings of the period. What follows is a brief survey and analysis of some key themes that provide insight into Barth's theologically grounded approach to the problem of communication in revolutionary times, particularly in those that turned out to be the last years of Weimar. Not only will they prepare us to understand the way Barth communicated with his politically diverse *Predigtvorbereitung* students, but they will also illuminate how he encouraged and prepared *his students* to communicate as they took up their places as leaders in the partisan environment of the Protestant church at the end of the republic.

"Deprive Them of Their Pathos"

To understand Barth's response to the propaganda of revolution, right and left, that dominated the discourse of late Weimar, it is instructive to look back to an earlier instance when Barth wrote about the question of the church's relationship to the rhetoric of ideology and revolution — in the second edition of his *Romans* commentary. At the time Barth was writing the second edition of the commentary, in 1921, the German church's endorsement of the war, the grim aftermath of the Bolshevik revolution, and the potential for similar bloody revolutions elsewhere weighed heavily on his mind. These concerns are evident in Barth's exegesis of Romans 12–13, where both the relationship of church and state and the question of the ethics of revolution come to the fore. Most illuminating for our purposes here is Barth's advice to would-be revolutionaries, that is, Christians who are (rightly) dissatisfied with the existing order of the state. Because Barth's reading of Paul leaves no room for either reactionary conservatism or left-wing revolution (although he affirms that the "red" revolutionary is

---

their inflammatory speeches they probably made the greatest contribution towards filling to the uttermost a cup of wrath which was then poured out on the German nation over the next two decades." Eberhard Busch, *Karl Barth: His Life from Letters and Autobiographical Texts* (Philadelphia: Fortress, 1976), p. 189.

more dangerous because "nearer to the truth"), he concentrates on the proper form that the Christian's resistance to absolute claims on the part of the state (or any other human institution, including the church as an institution itself!) should take.[94]

> It is evident that there can be no more devastating undermining of the existing order than the recognition of it which is here recommended, a recognition rid of all illusion and devoid of all the joy of triumph. State, Church, Society, Positive Right, Family, Organized Research, and so forth live off of the credulity of those who have been nurtured upon vigorous sermons-delivered-on-the-field-of-battle and other suchlike solemn humbug. Deprive them of their PATHOS, and they will be starved out; but stir up revolution against them, and their PATHOS is provided with fresh fodder.[95]

What Barth means by "pathos" is clear from his earlier exegesis of the seventh chapter of Romans. In his exposition of Romans 7:5 for example — "For when we were in the flesh, the sinful passions, which were through the law, wrought in our members — to bring forth fruit unto death." — Barth uses the word "pathos" in describing human "passions" whether erotic, political, ethical, or aesthetic, but most particularly, religious.[96] It is religion which is the "crowning of all other passions [*pathos*] with the passion [*pathos*] of eternity, the endowment of what is finite with infinity, the most exalted consecration of the passion [*pathos*] of men, and their most secure establishment."[97]

Barth later argues that religion has been invoked ("triumphantly") in connection with science, art, ethics, socialism, the State, the youth movement, and race, "as though we had not had abundant experience of the

---

94. Karl Barth, *The Epistle to the Romans*, 6th ed., trans. Edwyn Clement Hoskyns (London: Oxford University Press, 1968), p. 478.

95. Barth, *Romans*, p. 483. Barth's interpretation challenges the ultimacy of every state, including that of Weimar. That Barth was *not* thinking of the Republic but of Imperial Germany in this text is clear from the reference to the battlefield sermons, but it is certainly true that the Weimar state would not be exempt from Barth's critique. No state is to be identified with the Kingdom of God. Nonetheless, in contrast to the religious pretensions of the Second Reich, it seems likely that the Weimar constitution's matter-of-fact secularity met with Barth's approval.

96. Barth, *Romans*, p. 235.

97. Barth, *Romans*, p. 236.

waste land of 'Religion and . . .'"⁹⁸ It is difficult not to think ahead to the situation at the end of the Republic as Barth continues:

> Is it possible to justify these strange prophets [*Führers*], when we see hosts of men and women flocking to enlist willingly under their banners, eager to lay hold of religion, in order that their complacent capacities may be sanctioned, developed, and consecrated; when we behold them zealous to add to their passions [*pathos*] one further emotion, the emotion [*pathos*] of eternity . . . ?⁹⁹

People who seek to improve the world, Barth explains, will

> do their best to prevent the intrusion of religion into that world. They will lift up their voices to warn those careless ones, who, for aesthetic or historical or political or romantic reasons, dig through the dam and open up a channel through which the flood of religion may burst into the cottages and palaces of men.¹⁰⁰

To deprive the state of its pathos, then, means to keep eternity out of it. Deny its ultimacy. Starve it ideologically. It is a strategy of nonviolent resistance that meets the pathos of conservatism with what Barth calls the "Great Positive Possibility" — love of the other — and not with the pathos of revolution, which returns evil for evil and incites ideological warfare.¹⁰¹

Here, as in his later lectures on ethics at Münster and Bonn, political activity, while important and necessary, does not have *eternal* significance and should not be baptized as such. It is a *game* that is played in full and vigilant awareness of its relativity:

> Calm reflection has thus been substituted for the convulsions of revolution — calm, because final assertions and final complaints have been ruled out, because a prudent reckoning with reality has outrun the insolence of warfare between good and evil, and because an honest humanitarianism and a clear knowledge of the world recognize that the strange chess-board upon which men dare to experiment with men

98. Barth, *Romans*, p. 267.
99. Barth, *Romans*, p. 267.
100. Barth, *Romans*, p. 267.
101. This love of the other "ought to be undertaken as the protest against the course of this world, and it ought to continue without interruption." Barth, *Romans*, p. 492.

and against them in State and Church and in Society cannot be the scene of the conflict between the Kingdom of God and Anti-Christ. A political career, for example, becomes possible only when it is seen to be essentially a game; that is to say, when we are unable to speak of absolute political right, when the note of "absoluteness" has vanished from both thesis and antithesis, and when room has perhaps been made for that relative moderateness or for that relative radicalism in which human possibilities have been renounced.[102]

But it is not only the state that is to be denied religiously funded *pathos*. *Romans II* also argues that any would-be revolutionaries should also be deprived of the holy legitimation they need to "storm the heavens."[103] Any political ideology that claims divine sanction is denied it.

In his 2007 essay on Barth and the Nazi revolution, Arne Rasmusson is quite right in his claim that "deprive them of their pathos" is a useful lens for interpreting Barth's reaction to the National Socialists themselves once they are in power.[104] But it is also helpful in understanding Barth's perspective in relation to the situation in the Protestant church at the end of Weimar, namely, in relation to the nationalist right on the one hand and the Religious Socialists on the other. In either case, "pathos," i.e., granting an ideology absolute significance, has resulted in an escalating exchange of theopolitical propaganda. Because their respective political views are held with deadly "eternal" seriousness, neither critical distance nor reasoned dialogue about politics is possible. To deprive these partisans of their pathos would be to oppose them on a wholly other ground, not, say, on the soil of baptized Social Democratic principles.[105]

When it comes to purely political questions, then, pathos in substance or in style would not be a faithful witness to the Godness of God for

---

102. Barth, *Romans*, p. 489.

103. Barth, *Romans*, p. 485. Barth makes a similar argument with regard to any number of movements and causes that take themselves with ultimate seriousness: "Deprive a Total Abstainer, a really religious Socialist, a Churchman, or a Pacifist, of the PATHOS of moral indignation, and you have broken his backbone." Barth, *Romans*, p. 509.

104. Arne Rasmusson, "'Deprive Them of Their Pathos': Karl Barth and the Nazi Revolution Revisited," *Modern Theology* 23, no. 3 (2007): 369-91.

105. "Of course, there is within the Church an Evangelical theology which is to be affirmed and a heretical non-theology which is to be resolutely denied. But I rejoice that *in concreto* I neither know nor have to know who stands where, so I can serve a cause and not a party, not working either for or against persons." Preface to CD I/1, p. xv.

Barth. But this does not mean that Barth thinks that nothing should be communicated with ultimate seriousness or passion. For Barth, proper pathos is reserved for the question of the theological reality underneath, behind, and beyond any particular political position. And it will be a pathos expressed in and through thoughtful, rigorous, scholarly work. As Barth exhorted a student group in 1926: "Do not let us think poorly of thought; do not let us share in the anti-intellectualism of these days! We cannot act without thinking! The great demand that the mercy of God imposes on us is primarily the demand of right thought, of a knowledge out of which then the right action must come!"[106]

Barth's intention is to change the conversation from the pathos of politics to the pathos proper to the way of witness to Jesus Christ. This is plainly seen, for example, in the course of his *Auseinandersetzung* with Emanuel Hirsch over the Dehn case.[107] In that exchange, Barth pleads for two things in the context of the partisan mudslinging that prevailed among the students (and faculty!) in Halle: on the one hand the relocation of "passion" from politics to theology and on the other hand a more thoughtful, scholarly, "scientific" debate over the theological basis of the political positions under dispute. If we were to identify two dominant features of Barth's approach in the early 1930s, it would be this tenacious pursuit of the theological heartbeat tacit in every political claim and the simultaneous desire to engage in substantive, rational, critical, and self-critical discussion regarding the relationship of that theological claim to the gospel.[108]

It is not surprising, then, that Barth's most passionate rhetoric and most intense writing in the early 1930s is reserved for debates concerning the theological claims used to justify political ideology, especially (in that context) those on the right. What are the doctrines that fund, facilitate, or foster nationalist politics and everything that comes along with them? The orders of creation. The "point of contact." Natural theology.

---

106. Karl Barth, *Vom christlichen Leben*, in Barth, *Gesamtausgabe* I.31, p. 468.

107. For a complete discussion of the Dehn case, see Chapter Two.

108. Barth has a "word of caution" (which he also directs to himself) regarding the folly of "confidence" in theology. He observes that the theological conversation of the early 1930s was all too "positive," meaning too "sprightly," too "sure of its object." It is the *style* that is problematic — a "certain assurance of voice, speech and attitude" indicating that a theologian is not genuinely open to debate, self-criticism, reconsideration. "To what extent is our theological dialogue no real discourse?" he wonders, "*C'est le ton qui fait la musique.*" [It's the tone that makes the music.] CD I/1, pp. 162-63. This call for theological humility would be issued again when Barth turned his attention to the young preachers of 1932-33.

Theological Existence and the Rhetoric of Weimar

For this reason Barth relentlessly and deeply challenges their validity again and again — we might even say (looking over the course of the 1930s) most completely in a 1,400-page treatment of the doctrine of the Word of God. For the sake of gaining a hearing in a politicized church, Barth the Social Democrat (mostly!) restrains himself from joining the partisan free-for-all with regard to political issues, channeling his energies to fight the theological battle at the root of the political one.[109]

Saying the Same Thing Differently

Commentators have long noted the contrast between the rhetoric of Barth's *Romans* commentaries and that of the successive dogmatic cycles that issued forth from Göttingen, Münster, and Bonn. Indeed, the charge of "scholasticism" leveled by many of Barth's contemporaries in the 1920s encompassed both his burgeoning interest in the broader theological tradition *and* the predominance of a new, more measured tone in his published writing. Some contemporary interpreters have argued that this change is perhaps best understood in the context of the transition between the broad artistic and literary movement in Weimar Germany known as Expressionism, with its efforts to shatter surface appearances to expose a hidden reality, to the *Neue Sachlichkeit* — the sober, even cynical, realism — that followed it.[110] There are surely general similarities between Barth's hyperbolic style in *Romans II* and the literature dubbed "expressionistic," but in the end this does not tell us nearly as much about why he wrote the

---

109. In this he was not always successful. He had strong feelings regarding the political situation (as his contemporaries were well aware) and sometimes these slipped out. In a 1928 lecture on the concept of the church to a group of pastors, for example, Barth made a polemical remark about the Bismarck cult and "unleashed a small storm of indignation, as though here I had attacked the holy of holies ('These are your gods, O Israel!')." See Busch, *Karl Barth*, pp. 179-80. When Barth did offer a direct critique of fascism in the Weimar years, he usually included a critique of other ideologies as well, making it clear that he was not speaking as a Social Democrat, but as a theologian. See, for example, Barth's December 1931 article in *Zofinger Zentralblatt* (which was reprinted in a German publication in 1932). Barth was highly critical of fascism with its "Race, *Volk*, Nation!", but also of Communism and "Americanism." See Karl Barth, "Fragen an das 'Christentum,'" in Karl Barth, *Theologische Fragen und Antworten* (Zollikon: Evangelischer Verlag, 1957), pp. 93-99.

110. The most systematic effort to make this case with regard to *Romans II* is Stephen H. Webb, *Re-Figuring Theology: The Rhetoric of Karl Barth* (Albany: State University of New York Press, 1991).

way he did as does an examination of the immediate context of war and the aftermath of war, the dramatic literary company he was keeping at the time, and the exuberant urgency of one who has just happened upon a buried treasure.[111]

Still less does the movement toward a "New Objectivity" among some Weimar artists and writers help us in understanding Barth's (public) rhetorical choices in the deteriorating situation in society, church, and academy in the 1920s and early 1930s.[112]

For that, we do best to begin with the clues from Barth himself. Initially there is of course Barth's recognition that once he had entered the academic world, he must begin the hard work of thinking through the Godness of God, explaining and testing the insights he discovered in Safenwil, considering them again in the wider context of the Christian tradition, and constantly poring over the Scriptures. The question of what this thinking-through should *sound* like in his context was not unknown to him.[113]

And in addition to all of the above dynamics, Barth had also been

---

111. We might include Overbeck, Blumhardt, Kierkegaard, and, above all, the great "expressionist" himself, the apostle Paul.

112. This change in style evident in much of Barth's formal theological writing of the early 1930s must be distinguished from the continued drama, irony, and wit of his private and occasional writing and speaking. When Barth turned his attention to the question of the theological heart of the matter (the Godness of God [grace!] and thus the relativity of all human "ologies"), his approach was increasingly precise, direct, "scientific" (in the German sense of that word), and comprehensive. It was there — in a methodical thinking-after the reality of God's revelation in Jesus Christ as witnessed in the Scriptures — that he hoped to establish a common basis for ongoing theological discussion in church and academy. It is not surprising, then, that in the context of his theological writings he resisted comments that might be seen as a mere reflection of, say, his own partisan political views. When he did speak forcefully against fascism in the early 1930s, the critique usually included the immediate concession that all "isms," even the ones Barth found most compelling, are deprived of their pathos as well. In the context of the fears, resentments, and longings at the end of Weimar and in the early stages of the revolution that followed, the basis of a call to the Protestant church to resist the claims of National Socialism must be broader, deeper, and harder to ignore than the (then) highly suspect views of a Swiss citizen and a member of the SPD.

113. In 1922, for example, as Barth worked on a lecture on ethics, he wrote to his friend Georg Merz of his struggle to determine not only *what* he wanted to say but *how* he wanted to say it: "not academically-theologically (to the devil with that way of doing it!), not pious-biblicist and not in the hysterical postwar *(hysterisch-nachkriegzeitlich)* period style but also not down from the damned Hellenistic heights, as both my brothers like to do." Karl Barth to Georg Merz, September 14, 1922, in Barth, *Gesamtausgabe* V.4, p. 97, quoted in Timothy Gorringe, *Karl Barth: Against Hegemony* (Oxford: Oxford University Press, 1999), p. 89.

paying attention to the changing situation in German society, academy, and church, and listening carefully to his readers. As early as the preface to the second edition of *Romans* we find Barth referring frequently to the various sorts of feedback he received with regard to his first effort; he even cited these responses as one of the reasons why he needed to write the commentary again: "I am bound to say that the more favorable reviews have been most valuable in compelling me to criticize myself. Their praise has caused me such dismay that I have had sometimes to express the matter otherwise, sometimes even to adopt an entirely different position."[114] This pattern — revision in response to a misreading or misunderstanding — would occur again and again over the course of the period.

The most significant instance of this type of revision for our purposes is Barth's decision in the spring of 1930 to abandon the plan to continue the dogmatic cycle he began in Münster *(Christliche Dogmatik)* and offer instead a revised and expanded form of the doctrine of the Word of God under the auspices of a *Kirchliche* dogmatics.[115] As he explains in the preface to CD I/1 (written in August 1932), he wanted to say what he had said at Münster, but he could say it only "in a very different way."[116] Why does Barth think this change in the "how" is required of him?

With regard to the dramatic *expansion* of his Münster effort, Barth explains that this was essential in order to "make more extensive soundings and lay broader foundations." He is concerned that readers, especially those who would not have easy access to cited sources, can "hear the voices which were in my own ears as I prepared" above all with regard to the biblical text, "the basic text upon which all the rest and everything of our own can only wait and comment."[117] But as for the need to *revise* the earlier text, it is again the comments of critics (and fans!) of the Münster volume, particularly in their relation to the changed political and church-political situation, that are foremost in Barth's mind. More specifically, in this "second draft" Barth explains that he has "excluded . . . anything that might appear to find for theology a foundation, support, or justification in philosophical

---

114. Barth, *Romans*, p. 4.

115. For a full discussion of Barth's reasons for the revision of the Münster cycle in relation to the book on Anselm (with special attention to the complex question of Barth's later interpretation of the revision as a "retraction"), see Bruce McCormack, *Karl Barth's Critically Realistic Dialectical Theology: Its Genesis and Development, 1909-1936* (Oxford: Clarendon Press, 1997), pp. 434-48.

116. Preface to CD I/1, p. xi.

117. Preface to CD I/1, p. xii.

existentialism."[118] Did he think he *had* grounded theology in philosophical existentialism in the previous volume? No. But some of his readers (very publicly) claimed that he had. And in light of the particular situation of the early 1930s, Barth simply had to make it clear that Protestant theology could never claim a "foundation, support, or justification" in a given, natural "order," not even if that order was rooted in the gripping rhetoric of existentialism. Why? To deprive the Political Theologians of their pathos.[119]

Barth had, indeed, used existentialist language in the Münster text in discussing the situation of the hearer in the event of preaching — a topic we will consider more fully in the chapter that follows. But Barth was at great pains to stress that this use of certain existential words, concepts, and images was not intended as a philosophical foundation for the doctrine of the Word of God.[120] Nonetheless, Barth's readers had shown him that his linguistic borrowing had (in this case) been a mistake, and he excised the unhelpful sections. He could say what he wanted to say — indeed, at that point he *needed* to say what he wanted to say — without them.[121]

Barth's efforts to purge his own writing of any "eggshells" that might be used to justify an ideological position extended even to particular words. By the early 1930s he had backed away from the language of the "orders of creation," for example, and even expressed concern about the word "Christian" itself.[122] The change in the title of his dogmatics from the "Christian"

118. Preface to CD I/1, p. xiii.

119. The existentialist emphasis on subjective human experience and (sometimes) decisionism made some adherents vulnerable to the pathos of the fascist movement, as the case of Martin Heidegger amply demonstrates. (Heidegger very publicly joined the NSDAP on May 1, 1933). At best, existentialist philosophy offered little ground for resistance. On what basis could an existentialist question the authentic testimony of those who had discovered "deep religious significance in the intoxication of Nordic blood and their political Führer"? Preface to CD I/1, p. xiv.

120. CD I/1, p. 126.

121. On the one hand, Barth argues that philosophical categories come and go and theologians inevitably make use of them. Because of this, one should not simply dismiss theologians of earlier periods solely on the grounds that their philosophical language appears outdated. Instead, it is better to ask what they were "really trying to say in the vocabulary of their philosophy." CD I/1, p. 378. On the other hand, as far as Barth is concerned, a theology that bases its *material* decisions on *philosophical* grounds has ceased to be theology.

122. "Supposing we decide . . . to proceed with caution when we use the adjective 'Christian,' and to use the word in a way quite other than is the vogue in our victorious modern Christendom. What, then, is meant by such phrases as 'Christian' view of the universe, 'Christian' morality, 'Christian' art? What are 'Christian' personalities, 'Christian' families, 'Christian' groups, 'Christian' newspapers, 'Christian' societies, endeavors, and institutions? Who gives us

dogmatics of Münster to the "Church" dogmatics in Bonn is a reflection of those reservations: "In substituting the word Church for Christian in the title, I have tried to set a good example of restraint in the lighthearted use of the great word 'Christian,' against which I have protested."[123]

In other words, Barth was challenging the rhetorical sanctification of human activities (even theology!) with the attachment of the word "Christian," depriving them of their pathos.[124]

With the title change, Barth had not only abandoned the word "Christian." He also made it clear to whom he was speaking when he turned his attention once again to the doctrine of the Word of God.

Karl Barth and Church Propaganda

By the end of the 1920s, Barth was increasingly troubled by what he heard from church leaders, what he heard from Protestant pulpits, and what he read in church papers. The language, the pathos, the self-promotion sounded all too familiar. He recognized the rhetoric of Weimar politics taking hold in the church's life.[125] In a number of addresses and writings

---

permission to use this adjective so profusely? Especially when we must know that to confer this adjective, in its peculiarly serious import, is withdrawn altogether from any authority we have? This, if you like, unimportant misuse of language: does it not become evil to anyone who reflects at all? . . . Ought not a serious consideration of the office of the Holy Spirit to the pardoned sinner to have this small result, at least, namely: to make it more difficult in the future for such an adjective as this to drip from our lips and our pen? And could not this tiny check draw after itself sundry different and very real insights and thus be a hopeful sign that in the churches of Luther and Calvin men should begin to understand once more what the word 'Christian' means?" Karl Barth, *The Holy Spirit and the Christian Life: The Theological Basis of Ethics*, trans. R. Birch Hoyle, with a foreword by Robin W. Lovin (Louisville: Westminster/John Knox, 1993), pp. 37-38.

123. Preface to CD I/1, p. xiii.

124. For similar reasons, Barth also had begun to distance himself publicly from his former dialectical colleagues. In his view, Brunner and Gogarten, each in his own way, were producing theological work that was vulnerable to exploitation by the Political Theologians or the German Christians.

125. In the fall of 1929, not long before Barth moved to Bonn, he lectured at a conference in Eberfeld. He told the pastors and theology students gathered there: "There is much that I have constantly on my heart against the mode of speech of our present Evangelical Church; both in the pulpit, and, particularly, in the press. Are there not too many wrong notes in their melody, and far too many attempts to make people ignore the increasing impurities, by unchecked playing on, and to make up for these impurities by — playing fortissimo? I have in

over the Weimar years, he advances a critique of the church's discourse and calls the Protestant church in Germany to be a Protestant *church*, serving the ministry of the Word of God through self-criticism, prayer, and serious theological conversation.[126]

Perhaps the most dramatic example of this critique and summons comes in the context of Barth's 1930 essay "Quousque Tandem?" in which he quotes at length from an essay (by one Professor Schneider) featured in a widely distributed church yearbook, and then proceeds to examine its language, sometimes a word at a time, beginning with the following indictment:

> It is a glaring scandal to heaven, that the German Protestant church constantly speaks this language. . . . There is also a German Protestant church, who, drowned out by the constant scandal of this language, does not speak like this. But this is how their authoritative representative speaks. So we others, we, the *"Kirchenvolk,"* without being able to protest against it, must be represented outwardly before the workers, before the scholars, to those abroad, in this language. Professor Schneider speaks for dozens of our leaders and for hundreds and thousands of our pastors. I have nothing against him and those like him, but I have everything against the sort of language with which he and the army of those like him are leading this country astray. I am sick, too, of holding my peace. . . . For indirect theological objections these circles apparently have no time, no capacity and no will.[127]

---

mind those who are 'unsettled,' those who would like to be with their ministers in dead earnest, when I put the above question. But I often fear that many of the children of the world, who never enter a church nor read the church newspapers, know better than many of the clergy that here there is a point [to] this question." Barth, *Holy Spirit and the Christian Life*, pp. 57-58.

126. "For the particular wrong which makes theology a necessity, for the success with which heathen cleverness, heathen profundity, heathen (genuinely heathen) religion, introduced in ever new forms, gain control of the very place where God's honour should dwell, the whole Church is to blame and shares the responsibility for and the effects of the lack of discipline and the laziness of human thinking and speaking left to itself. . . . So likewise the reaction against it, the carefully considered call to the real centre, to discipline, to Christian strictness — and all this is in fact theology — must be given and carried fundamentally by the whole church." Karl Barth, "Church and Theology" (1925), in Karl Barth, *Theology and Church: Shorter Writings, 1920-1928* (New York: Harper & Row, 1962), p. 304.

127. Karl Barth, "Quousque Tandem?" in Karl Barth, *"Der Götze wackelt": Zeitkritische Aufsätze, Reden und Briefe von 1930 bis 1960*, ed. Karl Kupisch (Berlin: Käthe Vogt, 1961), p. 28.

What is significant about Barth's essay for our purposes here is the fact that his critique of the way the church communicates is an integral part of his larger critique regarding its neglect of its identity and vocation. He even takes up the question of ongoing Protestant self-promotion and aggrandizement, which, Barth notes, proceeds "heartlessly," "as if there was not homelessness and unemployment in Germany."[128] Is the church an advertising agency? Is the church just another competitor in the marketplace? It's not just *how* the church engages in self-promotion, but *that* the church does so that is "shocking." "The church cannot engage in propaganda — scandal and disgrace when the university begins to get into these ways! The church cannot want to build up itself, to praise itself like all others."[129]

What does Barth think is lost in all this self-promotion? The one thing the church should do and is able to do: preach the gospel. Instead it is desperate to win the youth and the worker, "brawling" with the Nazi and Catholic press, gazing with satisfaction on the deep-rooted spirituality of the German *"Volkseele."* Under such circumstances, Barth writes,

> When [the church] utters "Jesus Christ," even if it is uttered a thousand times, what one must and will hear is [the church's] own conceit and certainty, and one should not be astonished to discover that with all the utterances of "Jesus Christ" in the air, the real need of a real humanity is overlooked, [just] as God's Word is misheard, turning all caution, consolation, and teaching of the Bible and the Reformers into water for its own little mills. Therefore, because [the church] intends to clog and to poison her own well by an unhealthy *(heillose)* relevance, therefore one must speak against her with final anger . . . if one has love for her.[130]

For most Protestant church leaders at the time, Barth's advice made little sense. The idea that the Protestant church should abandon its efforts to increase its influence in public life, to turn its critical gaze from Bolsheviks, Catholics, November traitors, moral degenerates, "materialists," and so forth to itself, to commit itself to impractical "scholastic" theological work — what could be more counterintuitive? Why shouldn't

---

128. Barth, "Quousque Tandem?" p. 30.
129. Barth, "Quousque Tandem?" p. 31.
130. Barth, "Quousque Tandem?" p. 31.

the church speak the language of national renewal? Why shouldn't they borrow the rhetoric of German liberation? Their longing to be a part of the revival of the *Volk* and their continued fear for the German Protestant church's survival if the "unGerman" spirit prevailed made it difficult for Barth to get very far with the Protestant establishment. But could he gain a hearing among the next generation of church leaders?

"As If Nothing Had Happened"

As the reader is well aware by now, it was by no means the case that young Germans were indifferent to the political struggle all around them. On the contrary, they were at its very center, and the vast majority, inside and outside the Protestant church, identified with the vision, fear, and outrage of the nationalist right.[131] It seems very unlikely that these sorts of students would respond to someone like Barth in the early 1930s: a foreigner, a relentless critic of nationalism, a defender of Günther Dehn, a member of the Social Democratic Party, someone who was known to reject fascism, anti-Semitism, and militarism, someone who stressed the importance of theological thinking at a time when revolution was in the air.[132]

---

131. That this was often the case among Protestant students, even among relatively "free-thinking" young people, is evident in the series of questions put to Barth (and other theologians and church leaders) by the International Student Association in Berlin in June of 1932, the answers to be published in "Agni," the monthly newsletter of the organization. The International Student Association stated that it was not associated with any party, Weltanschauung, or religious group, but was a "free forum for spiritually-active youth." The questions put to Barth by the student editor include the following: "How do you explain the enormous disinterest in the Protestant church on the part of the general public?" "What do you consider the ideal interrelationship between the state and the church?" "What can be done in order that the Protestant church again becomes a concern of the *Volk?*" "From a religious perspective, what do you think of the youth of today?" "Do you consider Bolshevism a danger to the Protestant church, and with what means is it to be confronted?" These are many of the same questions that occupied the Protestant establishment during the Weimar years. Barth's response to them will not come as a surprise. Among other things, he urged the Protestant church to abandon "the ideology from which it now largely lives," to "return to its Christian theme and to its Protestant language *(Sprache),*" and not to see Bolshevism as "especially tragic." The church "does not have to confront it [Bolshevism] in the form of direct combat, but rather it should battle against the anti-Christ within its own walls." That is where the real danger lies. Barth, *Gesamtausgabe* V.35, pp. 231-33.

132. With regard to anti-Semitism, readers are reminded that Barth joined twelve others in endorsing Lamparter's book, which denounced anti-Semitism in the Protestant

Theological Existence and the Rhetoric of Weimar

In spite of all this, Barth had managed not only to "pack the house" in Bonn but also to inspire substantive debate and thoughtful inquiry among his students, even as the helmets and sashes of *Stahlhelm* and SS students hung on the walls of his Bonn lecture hall.[133] There in that classroom, as Barth would write in 1933, they did theology "as if nothing had happened."[134]

Although it involves something of a leap ahead, a brief word must be said here regarding this, Barth's most famous statement of his intentions as a theologian and teacher in relation to the political climate of 1932-33. When Barth wrote that statement in June of 1933, something had indeed happened. Hitler had seized control of the state. There would be no more free elections. The process of *Gleichschaltung* (coordination) had begun. All of this we will examine more closely as these events unfold in the course of the *Predigtvorbereitung* sessions.

What must be recognized at this point is that Barth's commitment to

---

church, in 1928. See Klaus Scholder, *The Churches and the Third Reich*, vol. 1 (Philadelphia: Fortress, 1988), p. 116.

133. In March of 1932, only days before the hotly contested presidential election, Charlotte von Kirschbaum, Barth's secretary and confidant, wrote that Barth was able to maintain good relationships with students across the political spectrum, in spite of the efforts of nationalist students elsewhere to incite campaigns against him. "We wait with anxiety for Sunday, which will lead us all to the ballot box. How may it end? Here one is now completely consumed by these political procedures. Karl's students parted in a friendly way toward him without exception. They were all against this answer in the *Westdeutschen Beobachter*, even the National Socialists." See Charlotte von Kirschbaum to Eduard Thurneysen, March 8, 1932, in Barth, *Gesamtausgabe* V.34, p. 211. Von Kirschbaum's reference to the *Westdeutschen Beobachter* concerns an article written by National Socialist students in Halle who questioned Barth's claim that his lectures proceeded peacefully in Bonn in spite of the many nationalist students in his classroom, mocked the praise Barth received from a "Jewish" newspaper, and called on the nationalist students in Bonn to disrupt Barth's lectures in the future: "If you . . . have come to the fallacy that because your colleagues have so far carried on without riotous scenes, the Bonn student body adores you, this is unfortunately a mistaken assumption. With utmost satisfaction we find your 'avowal,' that 'even' the National Socialist students (which you appear to know well!) have never conducted themselves 'unacademically'(!). . . . But we doubt this remarkable peace has been especially promoted by your 'courageous and chivalrous' little article in *Jewish partisan newspapers*, and we would like to regret it from the heart if [our] fellow students by their gracious participation, who are not maintained by the strong discipline of nationalist organizations, let themselves be carried away to this end: to disrupt what seems to you the remarkably peaceful progress of your lectures." *Westdeutscher Beobachter* 45, February 1932. Quoted in Barth, *Gesamtausgabe* V.35, p. 178.

134. Karl Barth, *Theological Existence Today! A Plea for Theological Freedom*, trans. R. Birch Hoyle (London: Hodder & Stoughton, 1933), p. 9.

do theology "as if nothing had happened" was not a claim to be "above parties" in the German Protestant sense, nor was it an apolitical stance, nor was it a form of the "inner immigration" later invoked by many disillusioned Germans.[135] Doing theology "as if nothing had happened" in a context where Hitler's accession was widely seen as a gift from God for the salvation of the German *Volk* was, for Barth, the only form that real, enduring resistance to fascism could take. It was not the mere partisan resistance of a good Social Democrat, but a resistance grounded in something universal and indubitable: the Godness (grace!) of God. To carry on "as if nothing had happened" in 1932-33 meant to deprive the brownshirts and their *Führer* of their pathos. As such, the theological existence Barth championed in Bonn was inevitably political, and Barth was confident that his students knew it. As he wrote in *Theologische Existenz heute!*:

> I regard the pursuit of theology as the proper attitude to adopt: at any rate it is one befitting church-politics, and, indirectly, even politics. And I expect that this communication, without "particular messages," will be heard and interpreted by the students committed to my charge, as well as may be, amidst the stirring happenings of our time.[136]

Barth's stated intention — to communicate *directly* to his students with regard to the theological heart of the matter and *indirectly* with regard to the church-political and broader political situation — provides a critical interpretive lens as we turn our attention to how he advises the rising generation of Protestant preachers.

Conclusion

The Great Depression mortally wounded the Weimar Republic. Soaring unemployment, homelessness, and violence in the streets were magnified

---

135. As Barth would later write in response to Brunner, "it is a legend without historical foundation that in 1933 I recommended a 'passive resistance' when I urged the Germans to fulfill their duties of Christian witness 'as if nothing had happened,' *i.e.* ignoring Adolf Hitler's alleged divine revelation. If they had consequently done so, they would have built up against National Socialism a political factor of the first order." Karl Barth, *Against the Stream: Shorter Post-War Writings, 1946-52*, trans. Ronald Gregor Smith (New York: Philosophical Library, 1954), p. 118.

136. Barth, *Theological Existence Today!* pp. 9-10.

to apocalyptic proportions by the partisan press. The year 1932 featured an unprecedented number of national elections compounded by numerous hotly contested local races.[137] It was, in Julia Sneeringer's words, "a total war of political symbols, gestures, and rhetoric the likes of which Germany . . . had never seen. Groups across the political spectrum deemed 1932 the 'year of decision.' This staging of identities through a war of political symbolism took the place of real debate."[138]

What could anyone do to turn back the tide of revolution on the one hand and reaction on the other? How could anyone secure a place for rational discourse about politics amid the onslaught of posters, rallies, slogans, parades, insults, banners, visions, and threats?[139] The Protestant church, in spite of its avowed position "above parties," had not managed to resist the rhetoric of *Volk* and *Kampf,* and the election battles that dominated the public square had become a feature of the church's life as well. By the spring of 1932, when Karl Barth decided he had to take on the question of practical theology, many nationalist Protestants saw the "decision" of 1932 as the choice between Christianity and atheism. As former court preacher and politician Bruno Doehring told the *Deutschen Reichstag* on May 11, 1932:

> about one thing we must be entirely clear: the great decision in our nation is between Christianity and Antichristianity. . . . I want to say to you: the nascent national *Deutschland* that is awakening will be a Christian *Deutschland,* and your children (speaking to the Social Democrats) will thank us, that we have saved them from you.[140]

As far as many Protestants were concerned, the very existence of the German church was in peril. Only God could save the German Protestant

---

137. National elections that year included the presidential vote of March 15, the April 10 runoff, the July 31 Reichstag contest, and Weimar's last free election: November 6, 1932.

138. Sneeringer, *Winning Women's Votes,* pp. 219-20.

139. Corey Ross argues that a party such as the Social Democrats had three choices in the early 1930s: to remain aloof from the propaganda wars, to try to counter the emotionalism of the extreme parties with educational campaigns, or to take up the weapon of propaganda themselves. Eventually, desperate Social Democrats took the third option, deciding that they too must "bamboozle and seduce" the public for their own good. Given the limited effectiveness of such techniques, even in the hands of the Nazis, would it have been better for the Social Democrats if they had stuck to their principles in the 1930s and stayed with education and reason instead? Not necessarily, Ross concedes. "The point is rather that there was no workable solution in the circumstances." Ross, "Mass Politics," p. 297.

140. Bruno Doehring, quoted in Nowak, *Evangelische Kirche,* p. 213.

church, and, fortunately, it appeared that God had indeed sent a *Führer* with the will to protect the *Volk* from its unGerman, unChristian enemies, within and without.[141]

Karl Barth also thought the German Protestant church was in danger. In its rush to advance its institutional interests, it had become all too willing to heed the voice of a stranger. In his Bonn classroom, Barth called his young students to do theology "as if nothing had happened," depriving that stranger of his pathos. And with propaganda campaigns raging not only without but within the walls of many a German university, it is no coincidence that Barth's efforts in that regard include his "emergency" attention to rhetoric of a different sort, a rhetoric, as we shall see, that proceeds entirely without weapons, the ground zero of resistance to every ideology.

But to see how and why resistance to ideological captivity — namely, the Godness of God — is at the heart of Barth's teaching in the *Predigtvorbereitung* sessions, we must add one final layer to the many we have already considered. Barth took up the question of the "what" and the "how" of preaching the Word of God in the context of the long history of German homiletics, the practice of preaching in the Protestant church in the Weimar period, and his own experience as one who had been and continued to be a practicing preacher.

How did Barth's understanding of the doctrine of the Word of God situate him in the broad sweep of the German homiletical tradition? What did the preaching of the gospel sound like in the Protestant churches of Weimar, and how did the inherited homiletical forms and methods encourage those practices? What were the consequences of Barth's theological existence with regard to the practical questions of preaching the gospel in a time of political and church-political agitation?

To such questions we now turn.

---

141. That Hitler was neither a German national nor a Protestant himself was not a concern for church leaders by this time. Hitler was certainly considered German as the *völkisch* understood the term, and Protestant leaders were comfortable with his neutral stance with regard to confessional differences and his (calculated) enthusiasm for "Positive Christianity."

CHAPTER FOUR

Theological Existence and Protestant Proclamation in Weimar

It was found in the files of the Old Prussian Church in Berlin, a sermon preached in Solingen, an industrial city south of the Ruhr region — a sermon for Christmas, 1936. By that time, Hitler reigned as dictator of Germany, *Gleichschaltung* (nazification) of institutions had been largely successful, and democracy was over. Opponents of the regime had been killed, imprisoned, marginalized, expelled, or forced underground. The National Socialist government claimed full responsibility for falling unemployment rates, a renewed national *Gemeinschaft,* and a recovering economy. For many Germans, the future looked full of promise.

The unnamed pastor of the church in Solingen was clearly attuned to the tenor of his times. What is the good news of Christmas — the "miracle" he proclaimed from the pulpit that year?

> Germany, after the Great War, was threatened with collapse. But then he came who, despite the great darkness in so many German hearts, spoke of light and showed them the way to the light. His appeal found an echo in thousands and hundreds of thousands of German souls, who carried the appeal further. It swelled out like a sweeping cloud and then happened that greatest miracle: Germany awoke and followed the sign of light, the Swastika.
>
> The darkness is now conquered, now suffering is over, which so long gripped our people. The Sun is rising ever higher, with our ancient German symbol, the Swastika, and its warmth surrounds the whole German people, melts our hearts together into one great German community. No one is left out, no one needs to hunger or freeze,

despite the deep night and snow and ice because the warmth from the hearts of the whole people pours out, in the emblems of the National Socialist Welfare program and the Winter Help work and carries the German Christmas in the most forsaken German heart.

In this hour, Adolf Hitler is our benefactor, who has overcome the winter night with its terrors for the whole people and has led us under the Swastika to a new light and a new day.[1]

In *völkisch* sermons like this one, the confusion of the Christian gospel and political propaganda so characteristic of Protestant discourse in late Weimar reached a new synthesis. Gospel and propaganda were no longer distinguishable, merged into a new holy history, a salvation story with a distinctly German cross and a radiant political messiah.

Beyond the multiplicity of factors in German society, church, academy, and public discourse that we have considered, one final context remains unexplored: How, exactly, did the preaching of the Christian church come to this? What was it about the dominant understanding of the nature and purpose of preaching that left room for sermons like the Christmas monstrosity from Solingen? Where did the preachers who welcomed National Socialism from the pulpit seek and claim the revelation of God, and what was the homiletical ground beneath their feet?

In addition to the many overlapping contexts we have already surveyed, we cannot understand the *Predigtvorbereitung* without finally situating it in relation to these questions, first within the broad sweep of the German homiletical tradition and the inherited practices of preaching that shaped sermons in the Weimar period, and then in relation to Barth's own existence as one who wrestled extensively with the question of proclamation, both as a dogmatic theologian and as a practicing preacher.

The tasks of this chapter unfold as follows: first, an orientation to German homiletics and preaching praxis from the nineteenth to the early twentieth centuries; second, an account of the effect of the Great War on German Protestant preaching; third, a description of the modern "theme" sermon and its function in the last years of Weimar, with particular attention to the sermons of Barth's nemesis in Bonn, the practical theologian Emil Pfennigsdorf; fourth, a brief overview of Barth's own background, development, and praxis as a preacher, culminating in a discussion of

---

1. Quoted in John S. Conway, *The Nazi Persecution of the Churches, 1933-45* (New York: Basic Books, 1968), pp. 364-65.

Barth's reaction to the homiletical debates and practices of the Weimar period; and finally, a return to the question of Barth's pedagogical aims as he began his emergency "sermon exercises" in response to the homiletical context at the end of the Weimar Republic.

The German Homiletical Inheritance

Germans of the nineteenth and early twentieth centuries thought, wrote, and argued about the task of preaching a great deal, and they produced, published, and consumed numerous volumes of sermons and homiletical treatises. Of this rich material we can only trace the broad dynamics, highlight the most influential debates, and make particular reference to the issues that will play a significant role in interpreting the *Predigtvorbereitung* artifacts. Among these must be included the task of the discipline of homiletics itself; the nature and function of Christian preaching; the relationship of the sermon to the Scriptures of the Old and New Testaments; the relationship of preaching to its congregational, political, and ecclesiastical contexts; and the changing fortunes of the discipline of rhetoric in German homiletics over the course of the period in question.

We could, of course, begin our survey of the German Protestant homiletical tradition with the theology and preaching of Luther — his recovery of the sermon as *Deus loquens*, his attention to the Bible in preaching, his law and gospel hermeneutic — for no doubt these emphases form the deep background for the developments that follow. That being said, for our purposes it is fitting to begin the story of modern German homiletics where Barth and so many others have — with the contribution of Schleiermacher.

Schleiermacher and His Legacy

In Schleiermacher's work, traditional Protestant orthodoxy, the romantic ethos of pietism, and the scientific spirit of the Enlightenment met and flowered — not only in a compelling theological vision, but also in practical proposals designed to strengthen clergy for their task. Schleiermacher's ideas proved foundational for German homiletics in particular in at least two distinct ways. The first was his understanding of the discipline of homiletics in relation to the broader theological encyclopedia and the second his "theory" and practice of preaching itself. Because most subsequent German practical theologians consciously adopted, adapted, or rejected Schleiermacher's insights, both warrant further comment.

In his *Brief Outline of Theology as a Field of Study* (1811, revised 1830) Schleiermacher argued that theology — like medicine or law — was a *positive* science, that is, it *produced* something beyond knowledge itself, namely, leaders for the Christian church. Theology belonged among the other sciences at the public university, Schleiermacher insisted, because the state had an interest in the education of the nation's clergy. The church played a crucial role in modern society, and the state needed it to remain strong and stable.[2] The whole theological enterprise was carried on with this particular practical *telos* in mind.

Schleiermacher organized the theological disciplines accordingly, with what he deemed "philosophical theology," and "historical theology" culminating in "practical theology," the "crown" of the theological sciences.[3] Prior to Schleiermacher's *Outline* there was no widespread consensus regarding exactly what subdisciplines were included in practical theology and how it related to the other theological disciplines. In Schleiermacher's schema, however, practical theology is a creative enterprise with a clear mission. The practical theologian is charged with generating the principles and *Kunstregeln* (rules of art) which guide the clergy in their tasks of preaching, care of souls, liturgics, catechetics, and church governance. Practical theologians generate theories of practice. Homiletics, as one of the distinct subdisciplines of practical theology, seeks to identify methods for effective mediation of the essence of Christianity through preaching, and it does so in relation to the insights of both philosophical and historical theology.

---

2. In this Schleiermacher sets forth an argument that will be amplified by the Protestant church in Weimar and the Third Reich.

3. In Schleiermacher's roadmap, *philosophical* theology inquires about the essence of Christianity through the investigation of the consciousness of existing church communities. Philosophical theology seeks to understand what makes a Christian church a Christian church both by comparing it to the consciousness of other religious communities (apologetics) and by examining the church's own internal conflicts and contradictions (polemics). For Schleiermacher, *historical* theology, on the other hand, investigates how the definition of the essence of Christianity has changed over time in the consciousness of Christian communities. This investigation takes place under the auspices of exegetical (biblical) theology, church history, and dogmatics. For further discussion of the *Brief Outline*, see Richard Crouter, "Shaping an Academic Discipline: The *Brief Outline on the Study of Theology*," in *The Cambridge Companion to Friedrich Schleiermacher*, ed. Jacqueline Mariña (Cambridge: Cambridge University Press, 2005).

The degree to which practical theology in Schleiermacher's system is merely "application" of the content generated by the critical (philosophical) and empirical (historical) branches of theology has been widely disparaged. But Schleiermacher's treatment of practical theology, and more specifically homiletics, was seen by many German practical theologians in the nineteenth century as a significant and liberating advance for the discipline. Most German homiletical textbooks in Schleiermacher's day (as earlier) treated homiletics as a species of rhetoric and proceeded to discuss everything from the "invention" of the sermon to its language and its structure in terms of (increasingly elaborate) rules and divisions imported from classical rhetorical textbooks. Homiletics as such was neither "theological" nor a "science"; it was merely "applying" the principles and rules and techniques of rhetoric to the established "content" generated by theology proper — it did not "invent" its own principles, rules, or techniques or reflect on the nature and content of preaching itself. It was in this sense that many German practical theologians praised Schleiermacher as the one who freed homiletics from what they understood as its *captivitas rhetorica*.[4] Although Schleiermacher's threefold encyclopedia would never be adopted, in his wake practical theology and thus homiletics claimed a place among the theological sciences at the German university with new clarity of purpose.

In addition to this elevation of the discipline of homiletics, Schleiermacher's own "homiletic," as evidenced variously in his writing, teaching, and preaching, also marked a new beginning in the history of homiletics in Germany. To understand how, we must scan the homiletical terrain at the time Schleiermacher began his work. Protestant preaching (and thinking about preaching) in Germany at the beginning of the nineteenth century can best be understood with reference to three longstanding traditions: Enlightenment rationalism, Lutheran orthodoxy (or, as it is sometimes called in relation to rationalism, "supernaturalism"), and pietism.

Rationalist preaching was designed to mediate between Christianity and modern culture, specifically the culture transformed by the philosophical and scientific discoveries of the Enlightenment. In such a context, the Bible and the Christian tradition were problematized, and liberal rationalist preachers responded by abandoning the "supernatural" elements of faith, appealing to reason and experience, and demonstrating the con-

---

4. Classical rhetoric and its rules did not by any means disappear from the homiletical textbooks of the post-Schleiermacher generation, but generally speaking rhetoric plays a more modest role, or at least is greatly supplemented, as we shall see.

tinuing relevance of the Christian religion in the face of growing secularization, largely through an emphasis on education and morality. The goal of such preaching was the enlightenment of the hearer; the preacher is the teacher and wise counselor of the *Gemeinde*. The desire to be "useful" and interesting led in some cases to "topical" sermons that seemed to have little relation to matters of faith. Niebergall famously told of a Christmas sermon on the advantages of feeding livestock in the stable and not in the field, an Easter sermon extolling the benefits of regular outdoor exercise, and a Good Friday sermon on the dangers of being buried alive.[5]

On the other end of the spectrum, Lutheran orthodox preachers refused to cede the field to the rationalists, defending the doctrine of verbal inspiration and insisting that God could and did intervene in the world in supernatural ways, the new science notwithstanding. Because lectionary preaching was the rule, orthodox preachers had the particular homiletical challenge of preaching the same texts year after year, and numerous sermon "helps" and resources were created to address this situation.[6] While orthodox preachers valued the exegesis of the text, it would be a mistake to think the resulting sermons were simply reports of the preacher's exegetical findings — most "supernaturalists" were concerned that their preaching remain "close to life," holding together the imperative of "true belief" with the importance of "right living." Both Lutheran orthodox and rationalist homiletics largely preserved the traditional and central role of classical rhetorical principles and rules.

Pietistic preaching in Germany as elsewhere aimed for the awakening and conversion of the individual. As a movement within Lutheranism, pietist preaching was consciously "biblical," regularly referring to passages of Scripture, and typically simple, emotional, and concrete, pressing hearers to make a decision and calling them to lead holy lives. Though certain influential pietists (most famously Philipp Jakob Spener) challenged some of the formalism bequeathed to German homiletics by the legacy of classical rhetoric, this only resulted in a relaxation and supplementation of rhetorical strictures in pietist homiletical treatises, not their abandonment.[7]

---

5. Quoted in Gerhard Krause, Gerhard Müller, and Siegfried Schwertner, eds., *Theologische Realenzyklopädie* (Berlin: W. de Gruyter, 1977), vol. 27, p. 307.

6. These included handbooks that "amplified" the pericopes, books of homilies, surveys of sermon forms, and collections of anecdotes, examples, parables, and quotations. Krause, Müller, and Schwertner, eds., *Theologische Realenzyklopädie*, vol. 27, p. 300.

7. "Admittedly the homiletical rules were no longer considered as an iron yoke for the preacher, but as beneficial laws, especially for beginners, but there still remained all too

Into this homiletical landscape Schleiermacher forged his own path. For Schleiermacher, the sermon was not a religious ritual or a moral exhortation or an educational talk but the coming-to-speech of the collective consciousness of the redeemed congregation. It was a *darstellendes Handeln* (representative act). Schleiermacher assumed that preaching takes place among Christian believers, and one of the results of this assumption was the exclusion of so-called "missionary" or "apologetic" preaching from many of the homiletic theories of the nineteenth century that followed in his wake.[8] The goal of such *Gemeinde* preaching is the animation, edification, and enlivenment of this collective consciousness through its representation in and through the preacher's inner life in the sermon. This representation takes place in a dynamic dialogue that occurs between the preacher and the Bible on the one hand and the preacher and the *Gemeinde* on the other. The preacher occupies a unique position in this dialogue, both representing the essence of the Christian faith to the congregation and representing the congregation in engaging the tradition, inviting the *Gemeinde* to participate in the questioning, deepening, and clarifying of the faith. The subject of the sermon is not God directly but the representative God-consciousness of the preacher, as it is "purified" through its encounter with Scripture and the Christian tradition. It sounds like a daunting task to navigate such a dialogue, and indeed, Schleiermacher understood the ideal preacher as a species of virtuoso, akin to an artist or a poet. Schleiermacher's own sermons offered models of this skillful navigation, and in published form they enjoyed long-lasting popularity, especially his patriotic and "household" sermons.

The Response to Schleiermacher's Vision

Schleiermacher's ideas had a wide-ranging influence in German homiletics and preaching in the nineteenth century. This did not mean that the power-

---

much of the old apparatus in traditional homiletics. For the most part these presentations are locked in rhetorical formalism, amended by a pietistic point of view, but not really broken through; it remains the old *genera dicendi*, the *loci* and *porismata*, only moderated by a greater freedom, rejection of all affectation, the elimination of alien material from the sermon, and the accent on comprehensibility and clarity in the speech." Werner Schütz, *Geschichte der christlichen Predigt* (Berlin: De Gruyter, 1972), p. 147.

8. Krause, Müller, and Schwertner, eds., *Theologische Realenzyklopädie*, vol. 15, p. 538. It was Schleiermacher's efforts to convert the cultured despisers of his day, not his focus on congregational preaching, that would resonate with Protestant homiletics by the end of the nineteenth century, given the renewed interest in apologetics.

ful streams of pietism, rationalism, and orthodoxy disappeared. Rather, each of these traditions grappled with the implications of Schleiermacher's proposals in its own way — some would celebrate, extend, and revise them; others would challenge them. Alongside and intermingled with these traditions was another tradition with roots reaching back to antiquity: classical rhetoric. Its fingerprints are evident in nearly every corner of nineteenth-century homiletics and preaching.

Of the many formal homiletical proposals that emerged in the nineteenth century, several foundational figures merit further exploration here, particularly with regard to the key issues of the nature of the discipline of homiletics, the definition and purpose of Christian preaching, the role of Scripture, and attention to the preacher's context.[9]

In what follows we will map the responses to Schleiermacher's work in the contexts of mediating theology, Lutheran orthodoxy, pietism, and finally, rhetoric.

"Mediating" Homiletics

Schleiermacher's influence led to the formation of a school among the rationalists/liberals known as "mediating theology" *(Vermittelungstheologie)*, which flourished in the nineteenth century.[10] This school also had its representatives in the field of homiletics, among them Alexander Schweitzer (1808-1888), professor of practical theology at the University of Zürich. Schweitzer agreed with Schleiermacher's basic conviction that preaching was an act of representation that takes place among believers, a practice which aims to edify its hearers.

Although Schweitzer was undoubtedly a Schleiermachian, he was not

---

9. It must be acknowledged that the Protestant preaching of the period was shaped not only by formal homiletical theories but also by admired preachers. Indeed, the line between academy and pulpit was often blurred. Many of the most-read homiletics texts were written by individuals who were also celebrated preachers themselves, and it was not unusual to have a pastor write a homiletic.

10. *Vermittelungstheologie* was a school in the tradition of Schleiermacher that sought to mediate between the Enlightenment and the Christian tradition. Major representatives include August Tholuck, Julius Müller, Richard Rothe, I. A. Dorner, Karl Hase, and F. C. Baur. The name comes from the stated agenda of the *Zeitschrift theologische Studien und Kritiken* (1828). Hans Martin Müller, *Homiletik: Eine evangelische Predigtlehre* (Berlin: W. de Gruyter, 1996), p. 109.

Theological Existence and Protestant Proclamation in Weimar

satisfied with Schleiermacher's treatment of the field of homiletics as a purely technical discipline, limited to generating theories of praxis. Instead, Schweitzer wanted to include as a part of the task of homiletics the consideration of basic substantive questions like the nature, definition, and purpose of preaching (general prolegomena to *Predigtlehre*) and the question of the *content* of the representation enacted in a given sermon (the religious consciousness as "purified" and "clarified" by Scripture and tradition).[11] To allow for such expansion, Schweitzer proposed a three-part division of the homiletical task: the *principle*, the *material*, and the *formal*. A *principle* homiletic established the basis, nature, and purpose of Christian preaching, the *material* homiletic considered the question of the content of preaching, and the *formal* homiletic dealt with the practical questions of preparation, form, delivery, and so on. Many subsequent German homiletical textbooks have been organized with reference to Schweitzer's scheme, and the language of principle, material, and formal homiletics continued well into the twentieth century.[12]

Schweitzer's material homiletic stresses the significance of Scripture and doctrine perhaps more strongly than Schleiermacher, though this is by no means "pure doctrine," but doctrine tempered "objectively" by the needs of the congregation and "subjectively" by the personality of the preacher.[13] Schweitzer's formal homiletic is dominated by the rules of classical rhetoric, though he does advance an argument that would later gain adherents: that the *Stoff* (content) of the sermon should create its *own* rhetorical form.

Another influential member of the *Vermittelungstheologie* school was C. I. Nitzsch (1787-1868), professor of practical theology at Bonn and later Berlin. Nitzsch called practical theology "the science of church life," and his two-volume *Praktische Theologie* was the first major presentation of the newly defined discipline.[14] Amid much agreement, Nitzsch departed from Schleiermacher in several significant ways. Contra Schleiermacher,

---

11. For Schleiermacher, these questions were considered *not* within the discipline of practical theology but within doctrinal theology.

12. Friedrich Wintzer, *Die Homiletik seit Schleiermacher bis in die Anfänge der dialektischen Theologie* (Göttingen: Habilitationsschrift, 1969), p. 24. The tradition of dividing the homiletical task into these categories will be important when we consider the nature and structure of Barth's sermon exercises in 1932-33.

13. Krause, Müller, and Schwertner, eds., *Theologische Realenzyklopädie*, vol. 15, p. 539.

14. Carl Immanuel Nitzsch, *Praktische Theologie*, 2 vols. (Bonn: Adolph Marcus, 1847).

he emphasized the sermon as "service to the Word" *(ministerium verbi)*.[15] As with Schleiermacher, the Christian consciousness/personality of the preacher mediates between God's Word (as *it* is mediated through Holy Scripture) and the congregation, but with Nitzsch there is a "something more" than just representation of Christian consciousness — something *new* is actually proclaimed. Thus Schleiermacher's boundary between congregational and mission preaching is blurred in Niztsch's revision.

Because Nitzsch considered the goal of preaching the "transformation and renewal of the self-consciousness of the people," the preacher employs the insights of psychology and the art of rhetoric to shape perception and influence the will of the hearer.[16] Niztsch advocated the preaching of ethical and dogmatic themes, which were in turn in agreement with the basic thought of the biblical text. But this was in no way a mere intellectual exercise — Nitztsch argued that even a "doctrinal" sermon must be forged in the meeting of Scripture and "life."

Lutheran Orthodox Mediation

Theodosius Harnack was another influential figure who took up Schleiermacher's proposals (largely via Nitzsch), but on his own Lutheran confessional ground.[17] Harnack (following Luther) considered preaching to be a sacramental act properly understood in the broader context of worship *(Kultus)*. For Harnack, worship is the *subjective* representation of faith;

---

15. Müller, *Homiletik*, p. 111. In this Nitzsch departs from Schweizer, who did not see preaching in the domain of "service to the Word" (along with catechesis), but in the domain of liturgy *(Kultus)*. The question of which ecclesiastical *context* ("Word" or liturgy) should encompass the practice of preaching remained something of a contested issue in German homiletics, though by the end of the nineteenth century the designation of preaching as an element of liturgy was increasingly common — so much so that the label *"Kultpredigt"* was regularly invoked. *"Kultpredigt"* meant more than the idea that the normal venue for Christian preaching was a Christian congregation at worship. It included the conviction that the purpose of preaching was *edification,* in contrast to instruction or moral exhortation. See Wintzer, *Die Homiletik seit Schleiermacher*, pp. 66-69.

16. Nitzsch was convinced that classical rhetoric was *inherently* Christian, arguing that there was "no present rule in antique rhetoric which is not exemplified by the prophets and apostles." Quoted in Wintzer, *Die Homiletik seit Schleiermacher*, p. 34.

17. Theodosius Harnack (1817-1889) was professor of practical theology, and later systematics, at the University of Tartu (Estonia). In his later years he taught at Erlangen and finally Dorpat. He was the father of theologian Adolf von Harnack.

Theological Existence and Protestant Proclamation in Weimar

Jesus Christ is its *objective* ground. In his homiletic, Harnack differentiated between "direct" and "indirect" subject matter in preaching — the "direct" content is the proclamation of justification; the "indirect" content he understands to be general religious themes and helpful guidance on subjects such as family, school, the state, history, nature, and so forth.[18] Both types come to expression in the sermon — justification is the "fixed" aspect, the general themes and "helps" are the variable. Not surprisingly, the Lutheran Harnack considered the preaching of the law a necessary prelude to the preaching of the gospel.

Harnack also took up Schweitzer's argument regarding the need for greater correlation between the content and form of the sermon, lamenting that creativity with regard to form remained stifled by the continued adherence to classical rhetorical rules.[19]

Schleiermacher also had a dramatic effect on the famed Lutheran preacher Claus Harms.[20] Harms started out as a devotee of rationalist theology, but as a result of Schleiermacher's *Speeches* he discovered "the impulse to an everlasting movement" and became increasingly focused on the life of the spirit and the holiness of God. Harms called reason "the pope of our time" in his own version of Luther's 95 *Theses*, a manifesto that included several theses directed specifically at rationalist preachers.[21] Harms demanded a "believing" preacher and a "biblical" sermon, though he did not understand this as preaching a biblical text as much as preaching "a present Word of God."[22] Following Schleiermacher, Harms argued that the preacher "should not be a slave to the text."[23]

Although he is considered here as a Lutheran orthodox preacher, Harms also garnered much praise from revivalists. He spoke against a sterile orthodoxy and stressed the involvement of the Holy Spirit in his sermons and other writings. Harms was known for the rough, earthy, and

---

18. Wintzer, *Die Homiletik seit Schleiermacher*, p. 44.

19. Wintzer, *Die Homiletik seit Schleiermacher*, p. 45, n. 66. In this Harnack anticipated an argument that would gain more traction in the early twentieth century — that there were negative consequences to rhetorical dogmatism.

20. Superintendent at St. Nicholas Church in Keil.

21. Johann Jakob Herzog et al., *The New Schaff-Herzog Encyclopedia of Religious Knowledge: Embracing Biblical, Historical, Doctrinal, and Practical Theology and Biblical, Theological, and Ecclesiastical Biography from the Earliest Times to the Present Day* (New York: Funk and Wagnalls, 1908), p. 156.

22. Müller, *Homiletik*, p. 114.

23. Otto Haendler, *Die Predigt: Tiefenpsychologische Grundlagen und Grundfragen* (Berlin: A. Töpelmann, 1949), p. 214.

even crude language of his preaching — "he did not want to speak the language of books but the language of life."[24]

Pietist-Revivalist Iterations

Friedrich August Gottreu Tholuck (1799-1877) was a key representative of the awakening that took place in Germany in the mid-nineteenth century.[25] While Tholuck's Schleiermachian orientation is certainly evident in his definition of religion as the "felt connection between God and life, the feeling of the dependency of the mortal spirit on the immortal," Tholuck combined his passionate emphasis on the experiential aspects of faith with a basically orthodox Lutheran understanding of central Christian doctrines.[26] Tholuck's sermons and addresses were wildly popular as devotional books, and his sermons were psychologically sophisticated, emotional, and imaginative meditations on biblical texts.[27] Tholuck was one of the rare preachers of the period who was not particularly attentive to the traditional rhetorical rules.[28]

Christian Palmer represents another pietist transformation of the insights of Schleiermacher, this time in relation to the rhetorical approach of Alexandre Vinet.[29] Palmer was more confessionally oriented than Schleiermacher, and he also exhibited the revivalist understanding of the sermon

---

24. Krause, Müller, and Schwertner, eds., *Theologische Realenzyklopädie*, vol. 27, p. 312.

25. Friedrich August Gottreu Tholuck (1799-1877), professor of theology first at Berlin, later at Halle.

26. August Tholuck, *Gespräche über die vornehmsten Glaubensfragen der Zeit: Zunächst für nachdenkende Laien, welche Verständigung suchen*, 2nd ed. (Gotha: Friedrich Andreas Perthes, 1867), p. 60. Quoted in David Crowner and Gerald Christianson, *The Spirituality of the German Awakening*, Classics of Western Spirituality (New York: Paulist Press, 2003), p. 48.

27. Krause, Müller, and Schwertner, eds., *Theologische Realenzyklopädie*, vol. 27, p. 313.

28. This was much to the chagrin of the editors who presented some of Tholuck's sermons to English readers in the nineteenth century. They write: "If a critic wishes to illustrate certain infelicities of style, he will find undoubted specimens of them in the sermons of Prof. Tholuck. These sermons were not designed to be models of fine writing, but to do good to the men who heard them. Had their author adhered more closely to the canons of true rhetoric, he had done more wisely, but then he would not have been Tholuck; and, as it is, we are disposed to derive as much pleasure as we can from his excellences, and to apologize, as far as candor will allow, for his faults." Bela B. Edwards and Edward Amasa Park, eds., *Selections from German Literature* (Andover: Gould, Newman, and Saxton, 1839), pp. 18-19.

29. Christian Palmer (1811-1875), professor of theology at the University of Tübingen.

as that which awakens or assures the hearer. Like some of the mediating homiletical theorists, he believed that preaching must involve something beyond representation. A Christian *Gemeinde* is never *finished*, according to Palmer; rather, there must always be a missionary and didactic element to the sermon. The content of preaching is the Word of God, not directly identified with the Scriptures, but with the revelation that "God is in Christ." This revelation continues in the word of testimony in the present, though Palmer insisted that it must make constant reference to its source, the "biblical presentation of the history of Jesus."[30] Palmer therefore placed great emphasis on biblical exegesis in his homiletic, but in keeping with pietist hermeneutics this exegesis is consciously practical, not technical. Such preaching aims to form and strengthen the pious personality of preacher and *Gemeinde* alike.

The approach of Paul Kleinert (1837-1920) bears some similarities to that of Palmer.[31] Kleinert also extended Schleiermacher's understanding of congregational preaching to include a sort of missionary preaching, because, Kleinert argued, "heathenism" lives even in the hearts of Christians.[32] Kleinert retained Schleiermacher's understanding of the sermon as representation of the congregational consciousness, not literally, but ideally. In addressing the hearer, the preacher will draw on both psychology and rhetoric, bringing the interests, dangers, fears, and hopes of practical life into the light of the Word. Kleinert did not equate the Word of God directly with Scripture. Instead, "the divine Word" is Scripture as interpreted in relation to the life of the *Gemeinde*.

Finally, worthy of mention is Johann Hinrich Wichern (1808-1881), best known as the founder of the "inner mission" of the German Protestant church. Wichern developed the concept of "inner mission" based on his interpretation of the German Revolution of 1848, which he saw as a sign of the failure of the church's preaching and pastoral care. Wichern thought Christianity in general and preachers in particular needed to take a more active role in influencing society, family, schools, and commerce, and he argued that the church needed to address "the social question," that is, the social unrest wrought by rapid industrialization.[33] His overarching

---

30. Christian Palmer, *Evangelische Homiletik*, 6th ed. (Stuttgart: Steinkopf, 1887), p. 68.

31. Paul Kleinert (1837-1920) was professor of Old Testament and practical theology at the University of Berlin.

32. Müller, *Homiletik*, p. 121.

33. Crowner and Christianson, *Spirituality of the German Awakening*, p. 230.

vision of a German Protestant church mobilized to protect its interest would gain new significance in the context of the Weimar Republic.[34]

The Rhetorical Tradition, Continued

The Swiss Alexandre Vinet (1797-1847) was a towering figure in French-speaking Protestantism — he has even been described as the French Schleiermacher.[35] Vinet's homiletics lectures did not appear in Germany until after his death, but when they did they were enormously influential among German Protestants, just as they had been among the Reformed in Switzerland.

Vinet considered homiletics a species of rhetoric and the sermon primarily a form of instruction: "The preacher is a teacher under the form of an orator."[36] The preacher transmits Christian truth to those who do not yet believe, and explains and applies that truth for those who already do. The preacher's eloquence proceeds, Vinet explained, on the basis of a "document," namely, Christ himself, the Word, making the sermon "second-hand," a "word about a word," "a preaching on a preaching." As such, preachers are "dispensers of the mysteries of God," and "heralds or messengers of justice."[37]

But it is important to recognize that while Vinet insisted on the "second-hand" nature of a Christian sermon, he also insisted that it is based on *Christ* as the Word, not *necessarily* on a biblical text: "What gives a Christian character to a sermon is not the use of a text, but the spirit of the preacher. A sermon may be Christian, edifying, and instructive without containing even one passage of Holy Scripture."[38] Vinet was troubled by preachers who used the biblical text as a pretext to say whatever they pleased. In this "we have witnessed a formal immolation of the Divine Word."[39] Texts should not be forced to say what they do not, and surely sermon subjects will arise for which there is no suitable biblical reference.

---

34. Wintzer, *Die Homiletik seit Schleiermacher*, p. 85.
35. Krause, Müller, and Schwertner, eds., *Theologische Realenzyklopädie*, vol. 15, p. 541.
36. Alexandre Rodolphe Vinet, *Homiletics; or, the Theory of Preaching*, trans. Thomas Harvey Skinner, 2nd ed. (New York: Ivison & Phinney, 1854), p. 29.
37. Alexandre Rodolphe Vinet and Thomas Harvey Skinner, *Pastoral Theology; or, the Theory of the Evangelical Ministry*, 2nd ed. (New York: Ivison & Phinney, 1856), p. 176.
38. Vinet, *Homiletics*, p. 96.
39. Vinet, *Homiletics*, p. 96.

In such a case, Vinet argued, "experience is also a book; experience also produces texts."[40] The pulpit is there to "treat all things in a Christian manner"; it must "introduce the Christian idea into life." The criteria for what is or is not an acceptable subject or "theme" for a sermon is whether it "forms Christ" within the hearer, whether or not it tends toward "edification," whether or not "an ordinary hearer" can convert what is said into "the bread of life."[41]

In greater independence from Schleiermacher, Heinrich August Schott (1780-1835) also treated homiletics as a special case of rhetoric, distinguishable from all other cases by its content (religious devotion and moral aspiration) and its goal (assurance and purification).[42] The preacher is not primarily a teacher, but a *"Geistlicher"* — a priest. As in pietism and some strands of ancient rhetoric, much is made of the piety and exemplary virtue *(ethos)* of the preacher. For Schott the content of preaching is Christian doctrine and morality, though doctrine only insofar as it has practical relevance and morality only as it is organically related to doctrine.[43] Schott was a mediator between rationalism and a mild supernaturalism. It proved to be an appealing combination: Schott's theory of *"Geistlichen Beredsamkeit"* (spiritual eloquence) was popular in practical theological circles, and his sermon collections were widely read.[44]

Based on this long view of preaching in the nineteenth century, we might make the general observation that, in the wake of Schleiermacher, there is a lot of "mediating" going on — not just among the representatives of the *Vermittlungstheologie,* but also among the pietists, the confessional Lutherans, and the more rhetorically oriented theorists. There is mediation between the experiential and the rational, between the exegetical and the psychological, between the rhetorical and the theological, between the doctrinal and the practical. Of course, a survey of influential theories and popular preachers cannot tell us everything. They cannot tell us exactly

---

40. Vinet, *Homiletics,* p. 98.

41. Vinet, *Homiletics,* p. 72.

42. Krause, Müller, and Schwertner, eds., *Theologische Realenzyklopädie,* vol. 15, p. 540.

43. Heinrich August Schott, *Die Theorie der Beredsamkeit mit besonderer Anwendung auf die geistliche Beredsamkeit in ihrem ganzen Umfange dargestellt,* 2nd ed. (Leipzig: Johann Ambrosius Barth, 1828), p. 18. Likewise Vinet, *Homiletics,* p. 74.

44. Franz Theremin (Reformed) also focused significant attention on preaching as a moral act by a virtuous speaker. See Franz Theremin, *Eloquence a Virtue; or, Outlines of a Systematic Rhetoric,* trans. William Greenough Thayer Shedd (Andover: W. F. Draper, 1860).

what was going on in the average pulpit. No doubt there were pockets of preaching that remained relatively untouched by the practical implications of Schleiermacher's revolution. But the next homiletical reformation was harder to ignore.

Reform and Renewal at the Turn of the Century

By the end of the nineteenth century, there was a new and persistent call for preaching reform. The reasons for this are rooted in the changing fortunes of the Protestant *Landeskirchen* in an Enlightened age, when industrialization was turning everything upside down, and when church leaders were faced with a growing labor movement that had little use for a theologically liberal but politically conservative church. All of these factors further eroded what was already lackluster church attendance. The numbers of people opting out of church membership and its unwelcome taxation were also on the rise. Meanwhile, industrialization had also changed the sociological complexion of many congregations, especially in and near the cities. As Wintzer observes, "Preaching was in multiple respects confronted with the phenomenon of pluralism."[45]

In addition, there was an ominous sense that the church and specifically the sermon were facing unprecedented competition from things like art and music and literature — aesthetic passions that seemed to take hold like a substitute religion. The "cultured despisers" of Schleiermacher's day were out again in force, and were sometimes openly contemptuous of the lowly sermon.[46] It was clear that discoveries in the natural sciences, too, in their simplified and popular forms, were attentively, even reverently, observed by the general public. Meanwhile, Protestant pastors could not ignore the enthusiasm for political oratory and the proliferation of newspa-

---

45. Wintzer, *Die Homiletik seit Schleiermacher*, p. 125.

46. Theologian David Friedrich Strauss summed up the general sentiment: "As if one only gathers in a church, as if one can only be edified by a sermon! In a time and with an intellectual environment where so many other and more fruitful sources of spiritual encouragement and moral invigoration flow, why hold firm to an antiquated, outlived form?" David Friedrich Strauss, *Der alte und der neue Glaube: Ein Bekenntniss* (Leipzig: S. Hirzel, 1872), p. 297. Quoted in Wintzer, *Die Homiletik seit Schleiermacher*, p. 124. For different reasons the liturgical movement in German Protestantism also called for the gradual abandonment of the sermon during this period, or at the very least that its role in worship be greatly minimized. Krause, Müller, and Schwertner, eds., *Theologische Realenzyklopädie*, vol. 15, p. 542.

pers and other printed materials. The increasing emancipation of the culture from the church was undeniable.[47] What was responsible for this state of affairs? And what could be done to change it?

Among the suggestions, one of the more persistent was the charge that the preaching style of Protestant clergy was no longer adequate for the changed circumstances. No longer would it be enough to "represent" a collective Christian consciousness when it was clear that such consciousness was threatened on any number of fronts. Although, as we have seen, the nineteenth-century ideal included the maxim that preaching be "close to life," critics complained that it was not nearly close enough. Preaching was simply too introverted — not only did it not speak directly to those alienated from the church, but it spoke too much of the life of the soul and not enough about moral and social questions, even for the "regulars."[48] The use of fixed rhetorical forms also came under fire in some quarters; it was argued that the predictable progression of exordium (introduction), exposition, theme(s), and divisions confined and paralyzed preacher and hearer alike.[49] The accusation was repeated again and again: *preaching had lost contact with the hearers of the time.*[50]

Treatises and articles from a number of theological perspectives began to appear which emphasized the seriousness of the problem and proposed various solutions. One early and representative text was William Wredes's 1892 essay "Der Prediger und seine Zuhörer," in which he argues that Christianity should "influence life" and the sermon should speak to the hearer about her "real life," acknowledging not only her *faith* but also her *doubts*.[51] Over the next several years, others joined Wredes in calling for change, though the kind of change invoked varied. Some wanted preaching to be more "psychological," others saw the need for revivalistic or apologetic preaching, others stressed the importance of education, others wanted more discussion of social questions, others advocated new creativity with regard to form, still others thought preaching needed to be more *volkstümlich* (popular, folksy), and some just thought sermons needed to be a lot shorter.[52] Some more scholarly treatments looked back

---

47. Wintzer, *Die Homiletik seit Schleiermacher*, p. 127.
48. Wintzer, *Die Homiletik seit Schleiermacher*, p. 119.
49. Wintzer, *Die Homiletik seit Schleiermacher*, pp. 120-21.
50. Krause, Müller, and Schwertner, eds., *Theologische Realenzyklopädie*, vol. 15, p. 542.
51. Wintzer, *Die Homiletik seit Schleiermacher*, p. 120. Wredes's essay can be found in *Zeitschrift für practische Theologie* 14 (1892): 16-50.
52. "If the preacher would be forced once to listen to his own sermons, they would get

to Enlightenment preaching, separating the wheat from the chaff so to speak, and recovering what they deemed its strengths: closeness to life, psychological sophistication, and *Gemeindemässigkeit*.[53]

What emerged from all of this ferment was a consensus of sorts around a kind of preaching that became known as "modern." The label comes from a question famously formulated by Friedrich Niebergall, an important representative of this particular homiletical reformation: "How do we preach to modern people?"[54] This was the question that unified the various voices into one choir. While the previous generation strove to connect with hearers, modern preachers were trying to understand more systematically who modern people were — their interests, their desires, their overall mood. To find out they turned to psychology, philosophy, and the culture around them.

Who were the pioneers of the new direction?

The braintrust of the movement was perhaps the group of liberal Protestant theologians associated with the publication *Die Christlische Welt*. Wintzer highlights Johannes Bauer, Otto Baumgarten, Paul Drews, Martin Schian, Ernst Christian Achelis, Heinrich Bassermann, Otto Frommel, Johannes Gottschick, Theodor Häring, Alfred Uckeley, and Paul Wuster as key figures in the overall modern preaching movement.[55] Is it possible to identify common characteristics of this "new" species of preaching in spite of some theological variations among its architects?

First, there is a widespread recognition of the need to identify with the modern person and even for the preacher to take up the modern *Weltanschauung* in a kind of solidarity. To speak to those alienated from the

---

shorter and shorter, shortened, in that the many obvious things would be let go: the religious and Christian trivialities, the potpourri of all kinds of histories and moralities, and aspire to the surely superior goal of clear groups of thoughts, short and precise." J. Bauer, "Die Kultuspredigt," in *Grundfragen des evangelischen Kultus*, Neue Folge von "Kultus und Kunst," ed. Curt Horn (Berlin: Furche-Kunstverlag, 1927). Quoted in Wintzer, *Die Homiletik seit Schleiermacher*, pp. 121-22.

53. *Gemeindemässigkeit* is very difficult to translate, but it will be important later in this study. It means that the sermon should be "measured" by the congregation, that is, "tempered" by it, or we might say, the sermon should be appropriate for it, though this loses the sense of congregational agency the term implies.

54. Friedrich Niebergall, *Wie predigen wir dem modernen Menschen?*, 3rd ed. (Tübingen: J. C. B. Mohr, 1909). Friedrich Niebergall (1866-1932) was professor of practical theology at the University of Marburg.

55. Wintzer notes that one should not overlook the fact that the theology of Albrecht Ritschl hovers in the background. Wintzer, *Die Homiletik seit Schleiermacher*, p. 123.

church, the sermon must be the personal witness of the preacher. Honesty, both intellectual and otherwise, was thought to be the only way to persuade those standing at a distance from the church to reconnect. Preachers should use traditional Christian words such as "sin" or "grace" or "justification" in moderation, and certainly not without explaining them clearly and demonstrating their relevance to regular life. The content of preaching should not be "theology" or "doctrine" but "religion," that is, "a practical affair of the spirit," "lived" Christianity.[56]

A biblical text was almost always involved in the modern sermon in some way. But the modern theorists were well aware that in their context the Bible had been problematized by historical-critical research and the new findings by scholars of comparative religions. The result was often the use of shorter texts in the Sunday sermon and less attention to the exegetical there and then. Instead, what was most important was what the text could say about "life" here and now. There was a resounding call for *Zeitpredigt*, that is, preaching that attends to the events and experiences and feelings of the time. Given these tendencies, it is not surprising that the use of the lectionary was relaxed in some areas and that in extreme cases the biblical text was abandoned altogether as a source for the sermon.[57]

Modern preachers challenged the assumption that the congregation gathered for worship should be addressed as a believing community, often arguing instead that the audience for the preaching of the church was the empirical *Volkskirche*, to whom "true" faith could not be ascribed. This recognition of the chaff mingling with the wheat led to a new interest in translating the "inner kernel" of the gospel for the unbelievers in their midst.[58] In general, there was also a continuation of the dissatisfaction with some of the strictures of the older rhetoric. In its place, modern preachers sought out tools that would help them tap into the moods, in-

---

56. Wintzer, *Die Homiletik seit Schleiermacher*, p. 131.

57. Wintzer, *Die Homiletik seit Schleiermacher*, p. 161. Emil Pfennigsdorf reported that in its most extreme form "modern preaching" exchanged biblical texts for literary ones: "The specific 'modern' sermon, especially as it is represented by the Bremen preachers Kalthoff, Burggraf, and Maurice with their Zarathustra, Schiller, and Goethe sermons, desists from a connection to the Bible and seeks to develop the meaning of religious things through an adoption of the ideas of modern literature." Emil Pfennigsdorf, *Praktische Theologie: Ein Handbuch für die Gegenwart*, 2 vols. (Gütersloh: C. Bertelsmann, 1929), p. 487. Friedrich Niebergall called this Bible-less preaching "the Bremen style." Friedrich Niebergall, *Die Moderne Predigt: Kulturgeschichtliche und theologische Grundlage; Geschichte und Ertrag* (Tübingen: J. C. B. Mohr, 1929), p. 212.

58. Wintzer, *Die Homiletik seit Schleiermacher*, p. 130.

terests, and longings of the modern person: psychology, *Volkskunde,* and philosophy.

There was also a widespread demand for something called "special" or *"kasual"* preaching — a term that can refer either to preaching on specific topics or to sermons designed for particular types of hearers. "Special" preaching in the first sense should be seen in contrast to the practice common by the late nineteenth century of preaching on general themes like "love" or "faith." Professor of Practical Theology Paul Drews argued that the constant repetition of these kinds of general religious themes and topics was tedious for hearers, and that a new balance between "general" and what he called "special" themes was needed. What constituted a "special" theme? Things like "Factories," "Lost Springtime," "The Housing Question," "Friendship," "Rainy Weather," and "Man and the Sea."[59]

As noted above, this plea for "special" themes was coupled with a concern to target specific groups of hearers. Drews explained,

> We no longer believe that preaching is preaching, whether it takes place in city or village, whether it happens today or tomorrow. We do not believe that God has released us from the duty, which once the greatest apostle perceived so deeply, to be a Jew to the Jews and a Greek to the Greeks. So preaching will have a local color, a contemporary garb.[60]

Hence collections of model sermons appeared designed for particular audiences, featuring designations like "apologetic sermons," "sermons to workers," and "academic sermons."[61]

At the beginning of the twentieth century, then, there was a preoccupation with the "how" question in German homiletics, not just how to preach, but how to preach in a way that would help the *Landeskirchen* to

---

59. These sermons and others can be found in *Die Welt Gottes,* a 1911 collection of sermons by the modern preacher Bernhard Dörries. Bernhard Dörries, *Die Welt Gottes: Ein neuer Jahrgang Predigten* (Göttingen: Vandenhoeck & Ruprecht, 1911).

60. Paul Drews, *Die Predigt im 19. Jahrhundert; Kritische Bemerkungen und praktische Winke,* Vorträge der theologischen Konferenz zu Giessen (Giessen: J. Ricker, 1903), p. 58. Quoted in Wintzer, *Die Homiletik seit Schleiermacher,* p. 140.

61. Friedrich Julius Winter, ed., *Apologetische Predigten, Die Predigt der Kirche: Prediger der Gegenwart* (Dresden: C. L. Ungelenk, 1905); Friedrich Julius Winter, ed., *Arbeiterpredigten: Die evangelische Predigt an der Schwelle des 20. Jahrhunderts* (Dresden: Fr. Richters Verlag, 1904); Friedrich Loofs, *Akademische Predigten, Die Predigt der Kirche: Prediger der Gegenwart* (Dresden: C. L. Ungelenk, 1908).

regain lost ground — in numbers and in influence. This was not just the preoccupation of the liberal ("culture Protestant") majority, but of many orthodox Lutheran and pietist pastors as well. Protestants continued experimenting with elements of the new style as the second decade of the new century unfolded.

But what happened when all that concern to connect with the *Weltanschauung* of the "modern" hearer, the relative eclipse of doctrine and the Bible, the longing for "relevance," and an apologetic stance met the "Spirit of 1914"?[62]

If God Be for Us, Who Can Be Against Us?

In August 1914, something Protestant preachers longed to see had finally come to pass. For the first time in a long time, their churches were full. And they were not just full; they were full of people who hung on every word. Kaiser Wilhelm II himself made it clear that the church was where Germans ought to be at such a time as this: "So now I commend you to God. Go into your churches, kneel before God, and implore his help for our brave army."[63] As we have seen, this period of patriotic devotion, euphoria, and spiritual renewal that accompanied the outbreak of war would haunt the Protestant imagination for many years.[64]

In his extensive study of German Protestant preaching in the Great War period, Wilhelm Pressel concludes that the designation "war sermon" must be applied not only to the "special" topical sermons devoted to the subject of the war, but to much of the preaching that went on during the

---

62. The *Theologische Realenzyklopädie*, which in its entry on *"Predigt"* hardly mentions preaching during the Great War (or the Weimar Republic, or the Third Reich, for that matter) concedes in a passing comment that in light of all that transpired, "In theological respects the modern sermon was enfeebled, because in it the contrast between God and world was partially relativized." Krause, Müller, and Schwertner, eds., *Theologische Realenzyklopädie*, vol. 27, p. 321.

63. Kaiser Wilhelm II, from the balcony of the Royal Palace, July 31, 1914. Quoted in Arlie J. Hoover, *The Gospel of Nationalism: German Patriotic Preaching from Napoleon to Versailles* (Stuttgart: F. Steiner Wiesbaden, 1986), p. 45.

64. Their memory of how glorious or unanimous the "spirit" was may well have been something of a fantasy. Nonetheless, the nostalgia for those days was powerful enough that the "Spirit of 1914" was evoked repeatedly in Protestant sermons. See Jeffrey Todd Verhey, *The "Spirit of 1914": The Myth of Enthusiasm and the Rhetoric of Unity in World War I Germany* (Berkeley: University of California Press, 1992).

course of the conflict. Overall, he argues, it was *"Zeitpredigt"* of the sort widely encouraged since the late nineteenth century, and very few of the German Protestant sermons published from this period do not refer in some way to the context of the war.[65]

Based on Pressel's comparative analysis of Protestant sermons from 1914 to 1918, a few characteristic features emerge, many of which would endure in the preaching of the Weimar period and beyond. Most relevant to the present study are the relation of preaching to the biblical text and the form of the sermon, and the understanding of the purpose and *Stoff* (content) of preaching more broadly. Because these will become flashpoints for Barth in the late Weimar period as well, we will explore each in turn.

The "Text" in Wartime

The strict use of a lectionary or *Reihe* in Sunday preaching had been gradually relaxing in the German Protestant church since the time of Schleiermacher, and, as noted above, the advent of the "modern" sermon chipped away at its dominance still further.[66] In some *Landeskirchen*, however, the practice of preaching on a fixed order of texts was still firmly in place in the period before the war, and this generally continued. Additionally, some *Landeskirchen* generated their own series of fixed texts (lectionaries) specifically to be followed by local preachers during the war period *(Kriegs-Textreihen)*.[67]

But the question of whether to preach on a "fixed" text, or on a biblical text at all, was hotly debated during these years. Paul Althaus spoke for many others in claiming that extraordinary times (like the war years) called for "free text choice." Preaching the lectionary in wartime, he thought, resulted in the "paralysis" of the sermon.[68] And for Althaus (and others) the critical issue was not only a question of whether one should use a prescribed text or "free text choice"; it was the relationship between the

---

65. Wilhelm Pressel, *Die Kriegspredigt 1914-1918 in der evangelischen Kirche Deutschlands*, Arbeiten zur Pastoraltheologie (Göttingen: Vandenhoeck & Ruprecht, 1967), p. 30.

66. In 1897 Martin Schian wrote a book arguing that, given the waning influence of the Protestant church in Germany, confining preachers to lectionary texts was "evil." The practice "hindered" the preacher's work, for the "active force" of "direct witness" was lost. Martin Schian, *Wider die Perikopen* (Leipzig: J. C. B. Mohr, 1897), p. 16.

67. Pressel, *Kriegspredigt*, p. 32.

68. Pressel, *Kriegspredigt*, p. 32.

biblical pericope and the content of the sermon altogether. For some, even if a biblical text is somehow involved, in a time of national crisis preaching should not be *text* preaching — if the word "text" refers to the Scriptures. "God has given us a new text," Johannes Müller wrote in 1916, "the clear Word of God, which today is living in our souls."[69] Althaus made the similar point that in "stormy times" in which the life of the *Volk* is unsettled in its depths, the subject matter of the sermon no longer rises from the text. Rather, it comes "through the events of the week, through the observation of *Volk* life."[70] As Pressel observes of this phenomenon,

> The text as God's Word was no longer authoritative. In the war it no longer goes from text to life but from life to the text. It was no longer exegesis of the text but the text serves as a commentary on handling life. Neither the *"Sitz im Leben"* nor the situation nor the theological scope of the text still played a role here. The individual text was nearly opened-endedly adaptable. It was enough if the sermon somehow exhibited the possibility of formal contact to it.[71]

The degree of consensus among Protestant preachers on this point explains why the use of very short biblical texts devoid of surrounding context is so common among the "free text" sermons published during the war.[72] There were, of course, exceptions to this rule, but the practice demonstrates that even when the Bible was included as a "text" for the sermon, the real "text" might well be unapologetically elsewhere.

The Purpose and Stoff *of Protestant Preaching, 1914-18*

The emphasis on preaching to modern people, the desire to preach in a way that was connected to "real life," and the efforts to address the needs and questions of the hearer in the years leading up to the war — all these concerns for individuals or particular groups of individuals (workers, city

---

69. Pressel, *Kriegspredigt*, p. 33.
70. Paul Althaus, "Wie sollen wir den Männer predigen? — Kriegspredigten für unsere Wortverkündigung," *Neue Kirchliche Zeitschrift* 29 (1918): 603. Quoted in Pressel, *Kriegspredigt*, p. 36.
71. Pressel, *Kriegspredigt*, p. 36.
72. Pressel supplies numerous examples of the minimal relationship between text and content in such sermons. Pressel, *Kriegspredigt*, pp. 37-39.

dwellers, etc.) broadened in the Great War period to include passionate concern for the mystical collective: the German *Volk*. The social divisions and secularization that troubled many church leaders in the prewar years seemed almost to melt away in the heat of August 1914. The orientation toward "real life" remained, but now it was concentrated on the war and all that the war represented. The attention to the hearer remained, but now it was not so much individuals or "special" groups that preoccupied Protestant preachers but the *Volk* as a whole, the *Volksgemeinde*, the *Volkskirche*. That was who preachers saw sitting in the pews before them.

What did German preachers understand as their homiletical mission to this *Volk* during the course of the war? Did it complement or depart from their prewar understanding of what preaching should be and do? What was the *Sache*, the subject matter, of the wartime sermon in relation to this goal?

To some extent the answer to these questions varied over the course of the conflict. In the beginning, many saw the preachers' role as a form of pastoral care — they were there to reassure the *Volksgemeinde* that Germany was the innocent victim of its neighbors and that God was on their side.[73] Thus Protestant preachers saw this work — fortifying the spirit of the *Volk*, urging them to sacrifice for the nation, and calming their fears — as a significant contribution that their preaching could make to the war effort. Paul Wurster, professor of practical theology and ethics at Tübingen, argued that the sermon should seek to sharpen the patriotism of the hearers so that the "God-willed love of *Vaterland*" could come to expression.[74]

---

73. That even the most reasonable of liberal churchmen saw this as their duty is obvious from these words from Martin Rade in 1915: "I am of the opinion, that the church has done its part. It has understood the calling for our *Volk* which the outbreak of war shows it . . . the church is from the beginning of the war to stand wholeheartedly and essentially on the side of the struggling *Volk*. For the church authorities — as state authorities — that was necessary. . . . Christianity rises up in Germanness. . . . We all become [battle]field preachers, not only confident with Luther, 'that military people also are able to be in a blessed state,' but even our Kaiser is confident: 'with pure conscience and pure hand we grasp the sword.'" Martin Rade, *Die Chronik die Christliche Welt* (1915). Quoted in Karl Hammer, *Deutsche Kriegstheologie (1870-1918)* (Munich: Kösel-Verlag, 1971), p. 51.

74. Paul Wurster, "Die Predigt und der Krieg," *Monatsschrift für Pastoraltheologie* 11 (1915): 36. Quoted in Pressel, *Kriegspredigt*, p. 69. Wurster considered both Schleiermacher's sermons during the Napoleonic invasions and the war sermon tradition that flourished in German pulpits during the Franco-Prussian War of 1870-71 as exemplary in this regard. Wurster also denounced what he called the "private Christianity" of Harnack, which was too exclusively a matter of "God and the soul of the individual."

Theological Existence and Protestant Proclamation in Weimar

Especially in this early period, war sermons frequently presented or represented the experience of the war toward this end of stirring up greater devotion to the German nation. The word "miracle" was used in the pulpit to describe not only the early victories on the battlefield but also the way the war had unified and spiritually awakened the soul of the *Volk*.[75] German heroes such as Luther, Fredrick the Great, Bismarck, and Kaiser Wilhelm II were evoked again and again as preachers told the story of God's providence in history that would surely not fail them in this, another hour of national need.[76]

But even in these early days another thread was already present *in nuce* — one that would come into its own as the early successes faded and the months and years dragged on. This second thread is related to the widely held and longstanding conviction on the part of Protestant academics and clerics alike that the church should be the moral/ethical conscience of the society — that this was their God-appointed task. As noted above, part of the anxiety on the part of most church leaders prior to the war stemmed from their perception that Christianity did not exercise the influence it once had in German cultural life. It found itself on the defensive. The modern preaching project was, among other things, the demonstration to skeptical hearers that Christian morality was not only the solution to their personal problems but also the remedy for the divisions, social struggles, and vices evident in contemporary society.

Once the initial shock of the war subsided, many preachers found the new situation a perfect opportunity to reassert this claim. The basic shape of the argument went something like this: God gave Germany a tremendous opportunity in 1871 when he sent Bismarck to unify the nation, but Germany had not lived into its destiny. It had been corrupted by the ways of the West: materialism, secularism, individualism, factionalism, selfish-

---

75. See, for example, the way these themes come together in this sermon from 1915: "As long as there are people, the year 1914 will live on in their memory and will be the most meaningful. Our most distant progeny will sing and say of these years of this most dreadful *Völkerkampfes* which has ever raged on earth, of the attack of half the world on peaceful Germany, on the German unity and joyfulness in sacrifice, of German power and German heroism, of never suspected victories of German weapons and of the tenacious, stirring struggles in the East and in the West, in the sea and in the air. Blood-red is the crown, in whose adornment the year 1914 is sunk in the sea of the times; but it is a crown, which will show all coming generations the way to German greatness." Pastor E. Le Seur, *Neujahrspredigt* (1915), quoted in Hammer, *Kriegstheologie*, p. 50.

76. For a discussion of this dynamic, see Hoover, *Gospel of Nationalism*, pp. 52-55; and Pressel, *Kriegspredigt*, pp. 80-106.

ness. Deep down, the soul of Germany — the strength of its *Geist* — was still there, but it could achieve its true greatness only if it returned as a *Volk* to its Christian roots and the moral code that went with it.

The kind of preaching that delivered such a message can be called *"seelsorgerlich"* — a complex term that can mean simply "pastoral" but often, as Wesley Smith explains, also included this moral component.[77] Many Protestant preachers understood their work as *Volkseelsorge*. They saw themselves as the moral guardians, not just of the soul of the individuals entrusted to their care or even of the Christian *Gemeinde*, but of the entire German *Volk*.

In the final phase of the war, as the bad news outweighed the good, Protestant pastors stressed the importance of staying strong *(Durchhalten)* in spite of the ambiguous news from the front. The will of the *Volk* must prevail.[78] When it was finally over, many pastors were as stunned as their parishioners. Preachers and theologians alike struggled to make theological sense of defeat, of the outrage of Versailles, and of the domestic upheaval that came with the advent of the Weimar Republic.

How could the God who had drawn them together so powerfully at the beginning of the war allow the conflict to end in this way? Uncoupling holy history from human history was unthinkable. The only coherent explanation for events was that the *Volk* had brought this upon themselves. They had failed to live up to their high destiny, and now it was clear what their neglect of their Christian identity had wrought. In this way, and with fresh urgency, church leaders reasserted the importance of the Protestant church as a moral compass for the nation in the aftermath of the war, even as, in the new democratic state, its status seemed more precarious than ever.[79]

Though this was the common theological explanation for the turn of events, it did not in any way represent a rejection or even questioning of

---

77. B. Wesley Warren Smith, "'Pastoral Care to the Soul of the Nation': Ludwig Ihmels and Germany's Domestic Crises, 1902-1933" (Ph.D. dissertation, Princeton Theological Seminary, 1998), p. 6.

78. Daniel R. Borg, *The Old Prussian Church and the Weimar Republic: A Study in Political Adjustment, 1917-1927* (Hanover, NH: University Press of New England, 1984), p. 37.

79. The notorious "stab-in-the-back" explanation for Germany's defeat may be seen as a part of this larger dynamic (Germany had somehow betrayed itself), and indeed, it was a Protestant preacher, Bruno Doehring, who first publicly made the charge in a sermon in February of 1918. The *Lutheran Evangelische Kirchen-Zeitung* confirmed the rumor a few months later. Borg, *Old Prussian Church*, pp. 54-55.

the appropriateness of the convergence between Christianity and patriotism. Germans had things to repent of after the war (materialism, secularism, selfishness, lack of will, disunity), but not their devotion to the *Vaterland*.[80]

As the new Republic began, a few did question the content of the church's proclamation during the war. Some church leaders wondered quietly if they had lost their way. A voice from a valley in Switzerland denouncing every conflation of the human with the divine began to gain a hearing. And, most maddeningly, a scathing assessment of Protestant preaching came from the newly emboldened political left in Germany, who criticized the way the preachers told their *Gemeinden* to stay strong and promised victory in the name of God even when it was clear that no such victory was likely. Not surprisingly, theologians and clergy responded defensively to such attacks from the likes of Social Democrats. The most formal rebuttal finally came from Giessen professor Martin Schian in his two-volume *Die deutsche evangelische Kirche im Weltkriege*, published in the 1920s. Schian conceded that there had been some excesses in the war sermons, but he insisted that those were aberrations and that it was a preacher's duty to "bolster the will to victory insofar as victory seemed possible."[81] But Pressel demonstrates conclusively that the "excesses" Schian describes were not the exception but the rule. Overall, Protestant preachers did not engage in rigorous self-examination after the war, perhaps because a fresh crisis was upon them. They forged ahead armed with a homiletical sensibility shaped by four years of war to face the challenge of the uneasy peace of Weimar.

The Modern "Theme" Sermon and the End of Weimar

In light of the extensive amount of material written about the Weimar period and about many different aspects of the German Protestant church at the time, it is strange that so little has been written about German preaching during the Weimar Republic.[82] Even texts devoted to the history of preaching and homiletics in Germany pass over this period with hardly a

---

80. As Hammer observes, "the patriotic tone" in Protestant preaching continued "even in the height of 1919." Hammer, *Kriegstheologie*, p. 59.
81. Martin Schian, quoted in Borg, *Old Prussian Church*, p. 37.
82. This is also true of the National Socialist period.

mention.[83] While a study like Wilhelm Pressel's of the war years would be invaluable, more than sixty-five years after World War II ended no such study of the Weimar period has appeared. What could explain this?

One can only speculate that the reason is at least twofold. One reason could well be the relative lack of source material. Given the tumultuous nature of the period, fewer sermon collections were published in the years leading up to the *Machtergreifung* of 1933.[84] There was certainly little incentive after the Second World War to keep sermon manuscripts that criticized the Weimar Republic and/or championed nationalist or *völkisch* renewal.

But a second reason for the lacuna might be part and parcel of the German *Vergangenheitsbewältigung*. For those who wanted to move Germany forward and put the past behind, an investigation into the role of the Protestant pulpit in facilitating the events of the early 1930s would not be particularly appealing. In the absence of studies and with the limited number of published sermons and other source materials, it is indeed a challenge to describe what happened to the Protestant sermon in the 1920s and early 1930s to make that Christmas sermon from Solingen in 1936 possible.

Nonetheless, much about the general landscape of preaching in Weimar can be discerned, some of it indirectly. Protestant *Kriegspredigten* pried open a door that was hard to close again in the decades that followed. Perhaps in less tumultuous times there would have been more introspection and a return to a more balanced relationship between local needs and the larger Christian horizon and its witness. But at the beginning of

---

83. Most texts jump from "modern" preaching to dialectical theology. While dialectical theology presented a challenge to the inherited homiletic that Protestant practical theologians could not ignore, none of the dialectical theologians nor any of their disciples produced a "homiletic" proper during the Weimar period. Though the various representatives of dialectical theology had a following, especially among theology students and younger pastors, the dominant preaching of the Weimar years was the inherited "modern" sermon, in some cases radicalized by the Great War and the survivalist mentality of the Protestant *Volkskirche* in the Republic that followed. Michael B. Aune (using the study by Matthias Wolfes) joins others in emphasizing that the theological tradition known as "liberalism" did not fade away after the Great War. Neither did its homiletical practice. Michael B. Aune, "Discarding the Barthian Spectacles, Part III: Rewriting the History of Protestant Theology in the 1920s," *Dialog* 45, no. 4 (2006): 389-405.

84. Published sermon collections of the Weimar period include: Karl Bernhard Ritter, *Von Dem Der Da Kommt* (Schwerin: Fredrich Bahn, 1925); Paul Althaus, *Der Lebendige: Rostocker Predigten* (Gütersloh: C. Bertelsmann, 1926); D. Carl Stange, *Unser Glaube: Predigten* (Gütersloh: C. Bertelsmann, 1926); and Karl Fezer, *Der Herr und seine Gemeinde* (Stuttgart: Calwer Vereinsbuchhandlung, 1930).

Weimar there were plenty of problems, concerns, and fears that could more than fill the homiletical template left by the war.

The 1920s began with a Protestant church in crisis. More than ever it needed to assert its relevance, slow the tide of church defections, and preach Christian values to the nation even as it worked to bind up the wounds of those mourning fallen sons, the lost monarchy, and the now distant "Spirit of 1914." Many Protestant preachers undertook these tasks using the homiletical ethos that came with "modern" preaching after its wartime transformation. Indeed, in many ways it was well suited to the needs of the day. The apologetic stance, the *seelsorgerlich* critique of society, and the drive to connect the Christian message to "real life" and current events (*Zeitgemäß*) — all these impulses felt natural under the circumstances.[85]

Two Awakenings

Formally speaking, there were no dramatic new proposals in homiletics proper during the Weimar years. Karl Fezer did publish a protest homiletic of sorts in 1925 in which he criticized Protestant preaching during the war and argued that the homiletics of his day fell into one of two categories: the "missionary-pedagogical-*seelsorgerlichen*" and the "artistic-representational sermon."[86] In the former, according to Fezer, the *Gemeinde* is seen as the *object* of the preacher — the preacher must fix its defects. In the latter, the preacher becomes the *mouthpiece* of the *Gemeinde*, mirroring its faith-consciousness back to it. Fezer charged that both kinds of preaching are primarily concerned with the *Gemeinde* and not the presence of God. Instead, true preaching must express the "spiritual reality" of God in a way that can

---

85. This is certainly not to claim that there were no preachers, even "modern" ones, who preached responsibly and faithfully during the Weimar years. What was being said in even a fraction of local Protestant pulpits on any given Sunday, much less all of them, is impossible to determine. It would be difficult in any time and place, but it is particularly challenging in this situation, where in many cases records of what took place were deliberately destroyed. What we do know is how the majority of Protestant clergy felt about things like their nation, their *Volk*, the war, the Weimar government, church membership numbers, Marxism, etc. It would be strange if these views did not find their way into the pulpit, especially given the popularity of the "modern" style and its apologetic, *seelsorgerlich* ethos.

86. Karl Fezer, *Das Wort Gottes und die Predigt: Eine Weiterführung der Prinzipiellen Homiletik auf Grund der Ergebnisse der neuen Religionspsychologischen und systematischen Forschung* (Stuttgart: Calwer, 1925), p. 28. Quoted in Wintzer, *Die Homiletik seit Schleiermacher*, p. 201.

be "sensed." Fezer thought the Bible testified to just such experiences of the *"Versinnlichkeit"* (sensualization) of God, and that the sermon should offer the experience of *Versinnlichkeit* here and now by placing the *Gemeinde* before the past *Versinnlichtkeit* of God that is "behind" the biblical text.

While Fezer's critique of "modern" preaching did generate much discussion among practical theologians and others, Fezer's constructive proposal never gained a following even among those who agreed with his analysis of the weakness of the modern sermon, because it failed to offer a coherent account of what exactly this *Versinnlichkeit* was. In spite of the linguistic overlap with dialectical theology, Fezer's vague understanding of the "Word of God" became the focus of a dialectical critique, most thoroughly in a review of the book by Thurneysen.[87]

Friedrich Niebergall also produced a noteworthy volume, *Die Modern Predigt*, toward the end of the 1920s. As noted above, Niebergall played a role in the development of the modern preaching movement, but as Wintzer argues, his 1929 work represents something of a "second-phase" in its development. The later Niebergall still considered it the preacher's task to offer modern hearers religious education, ethical guidance, and help for coping with life, but now he more vigorously advocated the use of scientific tools to help the preacher be more effective in this task, particularly the tools of *"Völkerkunde"* (ethnology) and psychology.[88] Wintzer also detects a certain pessimism about the fate of the sermon in the Niebergall of 1929, quoting his lament that "we must do without the masses; no preaching will attract these again. Perhaps the time of the territorial and locally constructed church actually is past, at least in the cities."[89]

Though they produced perhaps the most discussed homiletic texts in late Weimar, neither Fezer nor Niebergall prompted a change of course. But there were two developments in the 1920s that claimed the attention of practical theologians, because they had something to say about the nature

---

87. Eduard Thurneysen, "Das Wort Gottes und die Predigt: Im Anschluß an Karl Fezers gleichnamiges Buch," *Theologische Blätter* 5 (1926): 197-203. For an assessment of Thurneysen's review, see Wintzer, *Die Homiletik seit Schleiermacher*, pp. 201-3.

88. In the 1929 text, Niebergall identifies what he considers exemplary modern preachers: Robertson, Bitzius, J. Bauer, Drews, Bornemann, Kaftan, Dörries, Kutter, Ragaz, Baumgarten, Geyer, Rittelmeyer, and Hesselbacher. Barth and Thurneysen, on the other hand, Niebergall describes as "post-modern" preachers. Wintzer, *Die Homiletik seit Schleiermacher*, p. 177.

89. Niebergall, *Moderne Predigt*, p. 232. Quoted in Wintzer, *Die Homiletik seit Schleiermacher*, p. 179.

and purpose of preaching. One was dialectical theology, which entered the scene with something of a unified voice early in the decade and then dispersed. We do not need to revisit those contributions here. Suffice it to say the movement as a whole was largely perceived by practical theologians as a critique of the preaching that culminated in the war sermon, and in this they were certainly correct.

But, as Hans Martin Müller argues, dialectical theology did not have much direct effect on practical theology in the 1920s.[90] What the various representatives of the group did do was force the practical theologians to respond to their principle and material critique, which many of them did either directly or tacitly. But none of the dialectical theologians nor their disciples produced a "homiletic" during the Weimar period. There were pastors and theology students who were influenced in their preaching praxis by Barth's early essays on the problem of preaching, for example, or the sermons of Barth and Thurneysen, or some of the later proposals by Brunner and Gogarten.[91] But there is no evidence to suggest that "dialectical theology" as a whole or in its members unseated the inherited "modern" homiletic broadly speaking. The traction that Barth and his compatriots did get in the early postwar years among younger theologians and pastors was partly due to the sense that something *had* in fact been wrong with the way German Protestants had preached during the war.

But dialectical theology was not the only bright new movement causing a stir in the Weimar years, and it was not the only movement with an interest in the church's proclamation.

The nationalist "Political Theologians" discussed in Chapter Two of this study came into their own in the mid to late 1920s. Emanuel Hirsch and Paul Althaus, progeny of the *Lutherrennaisance* emanating from Erlangen, made their presence felt well beyond academic theological circles. The *Theologische Realenzyklopädie* even credits Althaus and Hirsch and their

---

90. Müller, *Homiletik*, pp. 135-36. If anything, what unified practical theological proposals more broadly during the 1920s was their intention to use "psychological, sociological, *volks-* and *volkstumkundlich, volkswirtschaftlicher,* pedagogical, worldview and lifeview" resources to accomplish their practical goals. See Horst Stephan and Martin Schmidt, *Geschichte der Evangelischen Theologie in Deutschland seit dem Idealismus,* vol. 3 (Berlin: de Gruyter, 1973), p. 416.

91. We might also include Thurneysen's 1921 essay "Die Aufgabe der Predigt," *Pastoralblätter für Predigt, Seelsorge und kirchliche Unterweisung* 63 (1921): 209-19. Reprinted in Hummel, ed., *Aufgabe der Predigt* (Darmstadt: Wissenschaftliche Buchgesellschaft, 1935), pp. 105-18.

comrade Otto Dibelius with a "renewal of preaching" after the war, noting the "theological depth" and "sharpened cultural critique" of the movement.[92] The leading nationalist Political Theologians published collections of sermons in the 1920s, but more importantly, they offered a theological foundation that would allow for the increasingly blurred boundaries between the language of the pulpit and the language of political propaganda.[93] What did the Political Theologians have to say that would shape the church's proclamation in the last years of the Weimar Republic?

Hirsch, Althaus, and Dibelius shared the majority perspective that democracy placed the German Protestant church and thus the collective German *Volk* in grave peril. The church must do something about such threats as communism, socialism, materialism, cosmopolitanism, and "the Jewish spirit." It must preach the gospel in solidarity with their embattled *Volk*. Not surprisingly, then, for the Political Theologians the preacher has two tasks. One is *Seelsorge*, to offer moral guidance to the *Volksgemeinde* in the face of the immorality and materialism of modern society. The second is apologetic in character: to persuade hearers that the *Volk* cannot survive and thrive without the Protestant faith. Individuals need Christianity, true, but the church must also have the power and influence to shape the values of the whole *Volk*. In 1927 Paul Althaus addressed the *Königsberger Kirchentag* with the following summons:

> The churches are never allowed to forget they have to put not only the life of the individual, the life of the family, and the life of the *Gemeinde* in the light of the Word of God in their proclamation, [but] that the gospel is directed to the entire *Volks'* life. The churches have the idea of *Volkheit* to proclaim, they should witness to the holiness of the bond to *Volk* life, they must seek to interpret their history to the people with prophetic *Geist*, vicariously struggling for the knowledge of the always new will of God. [The church] is not permitted to ignore the questions and sins of the people as a whole, their public and their hidden life — the pulpit and the Christian press have here their great, pressing tasks. Here are only two examples. Our *Volk* expect today a clear word of *Seelsorge* to the burning marriage question, to the sixth commandment, a clear word publicly and in personal *Seelsorge*. What has hap-

---

92. Krause, Müller, and Schwertner, eds., *Theologische Realenzyklopädie*, vol. 27, p. 324.

93. Emanuel Hirsch, *Das Evangelium: Predigten* (Gütersloh: C. Bertelsmann, 1929).

pened there up until now is not enough! The hour is short! There is another: the churches must have an eye and a word for the Jewish menace to our *Volkstum*.[94]

The preaching Althaus has in mind, then, is a species of modern preaching in its postwar transformation: *zeitgemäß*, close to *(Volk)* life, ethically oriented, apologetic, relevant.[95] The Bible, its words, its images are certainly involved in such preaching, mixed up with the language of *Kampf, Geist,* and *Volkstum* — to the degree that the Bible is helpful. It is "theme" preaching in the following sense: Althaus has his goals already firmly in mind. Preaching any particular sermon is one means to accomplish that greater end. And indeed, Althaus's own practice in the period lives up to his theory.[96]

Göttingen professor Emanuel Hirsch shared Althaus's apologetic and *seelsorgerlich* understanding of preaching.[97] Like Althaus, he was con-

---

94. Hans-Walter Krumwiede, *Evangelische Kirche und Theologie in der Weimarer Republik*, Grundtexte zur Kirchen- und Theologiegeschichte (Neukirchen-Vluyn: Neukirchener Verlag, 1990), pp. 198-99.

95. Althaus discusses this in the foreword to his 1926 volume of sermons, *Der Lebendige*: "The sermons are, apart from the self-evident freedom of speech, printed as they were given. Many of them bear the traces of the day. Preaching, which should attend to the day, must be in accordance with eternity. But preaching is only in accordance with eternity when it is not 'timeless,' but rather is spoken to the special need of the hour. To me and no doubt to my hearers the worries about the *Vaterland* and questions of the last years have been a lot to cope with. The sermons cannot be silent about it. Everything that we have experienced lingers in them, and not always only in the introductions. So much in them is dated and past. However, I have not wanted to delete these traces of the day and the past. Not only because the sermons in their original form give again a piece of our inner history in the last difficult years, but above all, because the final seriousness and the full joy of the life with God then first develops, when we dare to interpret the entire concrete situation and need out of it. The living spirit always deals entirely concretely with us. And if his light will break even through the particularity of every day, it remains still his eternal light." Paul Althaus, *Der Lebendige: Rostocker Predigten*, 2nd ed. (Gütersloh: C. Bertelsmann, 1926), p. 5. Notice that Althaus assumes that sermon *introductions* are the logical place where national experiences are evoked. This is important to keep in mind as we consider Barth's attitude toward the sermon "introduction" in the *Predigtvorbereitung* sessions.

96. See for example his sermon of May 1932, *"Kirchgang"* (Going to Church), and May 1933, *"Lebendige Kirche?"* (Living Church?), both found in Paul Althaus, *Der Herr der Kirche*, vol. 1: *Von der Kirche* (Gütersloh: Bertelsmann, 1934).

97. Hirsch also held homiletics seminars in Göttingen. See Wolfgang Trillhaas, "Die Wirkliche Predigt," in *Wahrheit und Glaube: Festschrift für Emanuel Hirsch zu seinem 75. Geburtstag*, ed. Hayo Gerdes (Itsehoe: Verlag "Die Spur," 1963). For a discussion of Hirsch

cerned about the church's loss of influence in German society and wanted to insure that the church did not get left behind once it was clear National Socialist enthusiasm was unstoppable. The church must not remain aloof from the *Volk*, Hirsch argued in 1933, or it would hurt its interests, "for the bulk of the German people will interpret such a stance as at least irrelevant, and possibly hostile, to the excitement and meaning they find in the German revolution."[98]

Later, it was this concern for securing the "relevance" of the Protestant church in a new Reich that led Hirsch to affirm the Aryan paragraph, which removed pastors of Jewish descent, for though "the message of the gospel reaches an individual through the mystery of the Holy Spirit, the message-bearer can get in the way if he appears strange, foreign, or offensive in some way to the hearer. So the best foundation for an effective proclamation of the gospel is a common blood, nationality, and culture."[99] The message of the Political Theologians to German preachers, then, was "effectiveness," no matter the cost.

As the political frenzy of the early 1930s made its way into the church, we know from records kept of the complaints made in various *Landeskirchen* that there was a corresponding increase of overtly "political" preaching. Richard Karwehl observed in 1931, "The prophecy of the church is so fully extinguished that even Protestant preachers exchange the legitimate eschatology of church proclamation with the secular eschatology of the *völkisch* movement."[100] Even in less rabidly *völkisch* settings, Hirsch and Althaus provided the necessary theological rationale for nationalist Protestants to blur the lines between faith and ideology, given all they felt was at stake.

By the early 1930s, Protestant preachers were steeped in a homiletic and a theology that facilitated the conflation of Christianity and Germanness. As we prepare to hear Barth's response to this development in his ser-

---

and preaching, particularly after the Second World War, see Wilhelm Gräb, *Predigt als Mitteilung des Glaubens: Studien zu einer prinzipiellen Homiletik in praktischer Absicht* (Gütersloh: G. Mohn, 1988), pp. 115-67.

98. Robert P. Ericksen, *Theologians under Hitler: Gerhard Kittel, Paul Althaus, and Emanuel Hirsch* (New Haven: Yale University Press, 1985), p. 147.

99. Ericksen, *Theologians under Hitler*, p. 147.

100. Richard Karwehl, "Politisches Messiastum," *Zwischen den Zeiten* 9 (1931): 542. Quoted in Kurt Nowak, *Evangelische Kirche und Weimarer Republik: Zum politischen Weg des deutschen Protestantismus zwischen 1918 und 1932* (Göttingen: Vandenhoeck & Ruprecht, 1981), pp. 211-12.

mon exercises, it is critical to note that this was not a dynamic that he merely observed from a distance. Right there at the University of Bonn, it was a constant presence. It is fortunate for the purposes of this study that some of the relatively few sermons in print come from the one person of all people who is most helpful in understanding exactly what Barth is taking on when he volunteers to hold his exercises: Bonn's practical theologian and university preacher, Emil Pfennigsdorf.

The Theme Preaching of Emil Pfennigsdorf

Ludwig Friedrich Emil Pfennigsdorf was the son of a Lutheran pastor and served some twenty years as a Lutheran pastor himself before he was appointed professor of practical theology at the University of Bonn in 1913. Though Pfennigsdorf's legacy is a modest one in the context of the history of German practical theology, in his day he was quite influential. His writings on apologetics, psychology, religious education, practical theology, and the "modern" person were well received. Theologically he was sympathetic to thinkers like Hirsch and Althaus, and politically he was a passionate conservative nationalist. He argued for a "lively *(lebensvoll)* synthesis between Christianity and love of the Fatherland," and he considered Kaiser Wilhelm I, Bismarck, Hindenburg, and, above all, Luther to be the embodiments of this ideal.[101] Not surprisingly, Pfennigsdorf did not get along with Barth.

As university preacher, Pfennigsdorf preached regularly to students and community members at the *Schlosskirche* in Bonn. Some of the sermons he delivered there are published in the journal he edited during those years, the title of which announces its political sympathies: *Der Geisteskampf der Gegenwart* (The Spiritual Struggle of the Present).[102]

---

101. Emil Pfennigsdorf, *Wie Lehren wir Evangelium? Ein Methodenbuch auf psychologischer Grundlage für die Praxis des Religionsunterrichts in Schule und Kirche*, 2nd ed. (Leipzig: A. Deichertsche Verlagsbuchhandlung, 1925), p. 136. Quoted in Albrecht Geck, *Kirchengeschichte im Religionsunterricht — Wie und Warum?* (Göttingen: Vandenhoeck & Ruprecht, 2010), p. 17.

102. Pfennigsdorf became editor of the renamed journal in 1909. For the specific political connotations of the term *"Geisteskampf,"* see Matthias Pöhlmann, "Weltbildwandel im Spiegel symptomatischer Leitbegriff: Verbandsprotestantische Krisenbewältigung zwischen 'Geisteskampf' und 'Diest am Volksganzen' von 1900-1932," in *Nationalprotestantische Mentalitäten: Konturen, Entwicklungslinien und Umbrüche eines Weltbildes*, ed. Hartmut Lehmann and Manfred Gailus (Göttingen: Vandenhoeck & Ruprecht, 2005), p. 89. Pfennigsdorf's church-political opponents, student and otherwise, jokingly referred to the journal as

What were Pfennigsdorf's sermons like?

In general, they were a species of the modern "theme" sermon. They were ostensibly based on a biblical text, usually a short one — sometimes only a single verse. Often the "theme" was stated after an introduction and then the remainder of the sermon consisted of two divisions or points related to the theme.[103] Most significantly, Pfennigsdorf's sermons nearly always began with the "framing" of the situation in light of the needs of the hearers, or, to be more specific, in light of the goals of a worried German Protestant church in the early 1930s. The language of the biblical text and/or theological language occurred regularly in the sermons, though it was frequently wedded to the political rhetoric characteristic of the end of Weimar. The sermons were *seelsorgerliche* and apologetic, offering both cultural critique and an appeal for the importance of Christianity for individual salvation as well as the salvation of the German *Volk*.

The quintessential example of the vulnerabilities of Pfennigsdorf's approach to the task of preaching can be found in a sermon from the spring semester of 1933, given in the University Chapel not long after Hitler became chancellor of Germany.[104] The sermon is called "Gottes Botschaft zum nationalen Aufbruch unseres Volkes" (God's Message in the National Dawn of our *Volk*).[105] The text is Ezekiel 31:34: "You shall be the sheep of my pasture, and I shall be your God, says the Lord God." To understand what drove Barth to offer an alternative to the homiletic of Pfennigsdorf, it is helpful to consider the sermon at length. Pfennigsdorf begins:

> We have in the last weeks and months experienced a movement about whose meaning we today, still in the middle of it, are barely able to make a correct conception. Like a spring storm it comes over us,

---

"Geistes*krampf* der Gegenwart." *Krampf* means "cramp" or "spasm." Heiner Faulenbach, ed., *Das Album Professorum der evangelisch-theologischen Fakultät der rheinischen Friedrich-Wilhelms-Universität Bonn: 1818-1933*, Academica Bonnensia (Bonn: Bouvier, 1995), p. 230, n. 16.

103. In his two-volume *Praktische Theologie*, published in 1929, Pfennigsdorf explains that the *"Stoff"* of the sermon comes from "the Bible, the experience of the preacher, finally also from the experience and history of the *Gemeinde* and church." Emil Pfennigsdorf, *Praktische Theologie: Ein Handbuch für die Gegenwart*, 2 vols. (Gütersloh: C. Bertelsmann, 1929), p. 537.

104. Barth was holding his sermon exercises during this period.

105. Emil Pfennigsdorf, "Gottes Botschaft zum nationalen Aufbruch unseres Volkes," *Der Geisteskampf der Gegenwart: Monatschrift für christliche Bildung und Weltanschauung* 6 (1933). Henceforth cited as PF.

throwing down all the walls and bricks, which stood in the way of German unity, and laying the basis for a new *Reich*. An event so great, so transforming and pressing forward, that in the time to come it will be sung and spoken of as the dawn of a new period in our history. (PF201)

Pfennigsdorf then turns his attention to the church. This political transformation will also be a religious one, he argues. The Protestant *Landeskirchen* shall become one German church, where all Protestants, regardless of confession, will be as brothers. There will be resistance to this, Pfennigsdorf continues, but it will turn out well. The political renewal and the church renewal are inwardly bound together. The German *Volk* seek unity "in this fateful hour." And the church has a necessary task for the sake of the *Volk*, just like Ezekiel did for his *Volk*:

> For an agonizing, struggling *Volk* needs its wants and life to have final meaning. It wants and must know why it is actually there, for what purpose it exerts its power and brings its sacrifices. It wants and must know where at last and most deeply its longing and seeking, its hope and faith is directed. (PF202)

And the answer to the question the *Volk* ask? "You *Volk* should be the sheep of my pasture, and I will be your God." That is the message of God given in the national dawn of our *Volkes*, Pfennigdorf says, thus announcing the theme.

Pfennigsdorf explains that as a shepherd rules the sheep, the will of God rules over the *Volkerwelt*. In each *Volk* individuals are drawn together "with the mystical power of blood, language, and history." God determines how long they will endure and how far and wide their land will stretch. God protects them in need and danger "so they do not decay before their time." God is their shepherd, but also their Lord. No *Volk* lives by itself and belongs to itself. It can only fulfill its destiny if it follows God's guidance. "Where that is forgotten, in the end order must turn into dissolution, wealth into poverty, blessing into curse" (PF202).

The age is behind us, Pfennigsdorf says, when Germany enjoyed a "brilliant ascension."

> We have learned to use the power of nature in unheard of ways: We bore through mountains, led with the *Blitz*, and lifted ourselves in the

ocean to the air. We have assembled an economy which carried its products as far as to the farthest lands and showered our *Volk* with riches and goods. One had expected the highest of this culture, a new world happiness, a new humanity, that would lie strong and secure in itself, resting on the basis of one eternal peace of humanity. But this shiny culture had a heavy flaw. (PF202-3)

The flaw? We put our faith in human beings. We were the goal of creation, the lord of the world, the master of destiny. And then the war came. And then the revolution. With the revolution it was "obvious that this entire culture had become rotten and foul as far as the core." It had no reverence before the highest thing, the Lord of history. The period lying behind Germany was a period of selfishness, of self- and world-worship, and Germans lost the meaning of life that came with the mysteries of "marriage, *Volk,* and state" (PF203). Germans did not conform to God's will.

But now that time is over. A "dawn" of national and political movements has come. The *Volk* have remembered that "*Volk,* Nation and state are not built by contractual conditions between individuals." What is happening today, the rising up of the authority of the state, is the move from the "I" to the "we." This is what the youth have long desired. "The strong will to be one's own *Volk* . . . through blood and soul bound together," this will "became a power in the youth" (PF203). This national dawn is not only a political happening but "a new breakthrough of the divine will":

> Again God has restored our *Volk* from the brink of Bolshevism, placed it again before a great historical mission. And now everything depends on this, that this will of God is clearly known and that every individual makes it the rule of his own life. Faith in humanity, faith in the here and now has made us weak, unhappy and without honor. As Hitler expressed it on the 21st of March in his great inaugural address, we will return to "a truly deep contemplation of religious life." (PF204)

But for this to happen we must be still before God, before whom we are guilty. We must thank God for the mercy, for the certain faith that "everything that is said and is planned against him is futile and will lead the *Volk* like the *Vaterland* in new disaster." This transformation is the main thing, the eternal meaning of these events. "The kingdom of God will again achieve form in the German *Volk*" (PF204).

Here begins the task of the church. If the church shall do its service to the *Volk*, then it must remain the church, for it must carry the entirety of the message entrusted to it with pure hands and in all circumstances to the life of the *Volk*. The church, Pfennigsdorf explains, is "the bearer of the message of God." The message is this, Pfennigsdorf says, quoting from the catechism: "I believe that Jesus Christ, born of the Father in eternity and also truest man born of the Virgin Mary, is my Lord, who has redeemed my lost and condemned people" (PF204-5).

All Protestants agree with this, and in this time of need the church should not be concerned with the details of other confessions, which are historically conditioned. Confessional differences must recede into the background and a new unity take hold: "You shall be the sheep of my flock."

Pfennigsdorf makes his final point: in spiritual things, the church must be free from the state. The church in early times was so closely bound to the state that this close association hindered the church's message. Rather, the church must place everything "in the light of the divine Word."

> That is their political mission. They do not intervene directly in the political things. They do not have to carry on party politics. But they must place all levels, classes, and directions under the Lordship of God, that they ultimately and most deeply know themselves to be responsible before God and in spite of all separations in a *Gemeinde* bound to God. With such service the church proves itself as the heart of the *Volk*, as the conscience of the nation. With such work they serve the new *Deutschland*, to help it. (PF205)

Did Barth hear Pfennigsdorf deliver this particular sermon to the Bonn University community in 1933? There is no evidence one way or the other. But even if he wasn't present on this particular Sunday, surely Barth heard Pfennigsdorf preach on occasion. Surely his students would have told him something about Pfennigsdorf's preaching classes. At any rate, Pfennigsdorf's Bonn sermons were readily accessible thanks to their regular publication in *Der Geisteskampf der Gegenwart*. Pfennigsdorf's homiletic, like his political sympathies, was no secret.

Karl Barth was not technically a practical theologian himself, but, as we will see in the remainder of this chapter, he was not without a homiletic of his own as he embarked on his rescue mission into Pfennigsdorf's territory in the fall of 1932. We begin with the broad outlines of Barth's development as a preacher and then turn to his theoretical and practical engagement with the homiletic of Weimar.

Karl Barth and the Modern Sermon

Early Influences

Karl Barth grew up listening to his father preach. Fritz Barth was a moderate pietist, thoughtful, and not uncritical of the pietist tradition. He valued its emphasis on Christian experience as an antidote to the dangers of a paralyzing orthodoxy.[106] Barth wrote of his father's time as pastor of Reitnau, "People there did not easily forget the earnestness of his preaching, his outspokenness for the truth and his personal humility."[107] As a teenager, Barth once compared going to the theatre as a kind of worship and dubbed Wagner's opera Tannhäuser as "powerful preaching."[108] And around the time of his confirmation, he reports that his decision to become a minister was influenced by the confirmation classes he attended given by a popular preacher in Berne, Robert Aeschbacher. Fritz Barth described Aeschbacher as someone who

> refused to evade the problems of theological thought . . . even if this seemed to undermine much of the tradition. . . . But he never regarded the question of Christian thought as a purely theoretical one; it concerned real life. . . . Through severe inner struggles he arrived at the assurance that all man's salvation is to be found only in Jesus, and it was now his joy in life to proclaim this good news. However, he proclaimed it like a shepherd, going out after those who are lost. . . . He applied the demands of the gospel to social life with such decisiveness that many anxious people who could not understand him called him a socialist.[109]

Barth would later describe hearing Aeschbacher's sermons in the crowded church: "I shall never forget a series on Romans 1:16 and another on Psalm 23:1" — "I was completely wrapped up in them."[110]

The details of Barth's formal education as a preacher remain somewhat lost to us. He did take the required seminar on homiletics while at

---

106. Eberhard Busch, *Karl Barth and the Pietists: The Young Karl Barth's Critique of Pietism and Its Response* (Downers Grove: InterVarsity Press, 2004), pp. 11-12.
107. Eberhard Busch, *Karl Barth: His Life from Letters and Autobiographical Texts* (Philadelphia: Fortress, 1976), p. 3.
108. Busch, *Karl Barth*, p. 30.
109. Busch, *Karl Barth*, pp. 30-31.
110. Busch, *Karl Barth*, p. 32.

Theological Existence and Protestant Proclamation in Weimar

Berne and would preach for the first time for a congregation in 1907. His first sermon as assistant pastor in Meiringen was on Psalm 121, and one gets a sense of his romantic sensibilities by his rhapsody on the local enviroment: "When the tones of the organ resound through God's house and the streams rush down as always, from above, and the high snows give their greeting with eternal purity, who would not feel that 'the prospect gives the angels strength' . . . ?"[111]

Barth later attended a homiletics seminar at the University of Marburg, most likely with Ernst Christian Achelis, who was professor of practical theology at the time. The liberal Achelis was something of a "mediating" practical theologian, forging a connection between the Reformed view of preaching and the emerging modern preaching tradition.[112]

Barth would not preach again regularly until he became assistant pastor in Geneva in 1909. He would later describe his Geneva sermons as "very academic" and "very liberal."[113] It was around this time that Barth first read the sermons of Schleiermacher, to which he would return again and again. Not long afterward, he was called to the congregation of Safenwil.

Safenwil

Barth preached some five hundred sermons during his time at Safenwil, and it is clear that he took the task very seriously.[114] As Eberhard Busch reports,

> More than once the Sunday sermon "was forced out with terrible birth-pangs." On occasions he had to spend two whole days on it; "had to begin again five times"; or only finished preparing it on the Sunday morning. "He did not read out these sermons on Sunday, but delivered them to his congregation freely, in a most impressive way."[115]

What were Barth's Safenwil sermons like?

---

111. Busch, *Karl Barth*, p. 42.
112. Wintzer, *Die Homiletik seit Schleiermacher*, pp. 166-67, n. 7.
113. Busch, *Karl Barth*, p. 35. Busch writes that Barth's sermon on Reformation Day 1910 consisted of an analysis of Melanchthon's *Loci Communes*.
114. A selection of these sermons in English may be found in Karl Barth and William H. Willimon, *The Early Preaching of Karl Barth: Fourteen Sermons with Commentary by William H. Willimon*, trans. John Elbert Wilson (Louisville: Westminster John Knox, 2009).
115. Busch, *Karl Barth*, p. 61.

In the early years they were excellent examples of the modern preaching style, as Barth himself readily acknowledged. It is true that even then the Reformed Barth did not question the "fine old custom" that a sermon should be based on a biblical text, but this was not unheard of among champions of the modern homiletic. What made Barth's preaching "modern," in addition to its content, was his way with the text. Barth often preached on "themes" in Safenwil: prayer, the Reformation, pride, mission, springtime, "the life of William Booth," and, of course, his notorious sermon on the sinking of the *Titanic* in 1912.[116] Barth's early sermons, in keeping with the modern ideal, stay "close to life," regularly referring to events and problems of the day, and offering opinions and advice even on controversial issues. Likewise, Barth made obvious efforts to be honest and authentic with his *Gemeinde*, sharing his doubts and enthusiasms as the proponents of the modern sermon recommended. In spite of these efforts, Barth did not feel his sermons were "successful" in Safenwil, even at the time.[117] Part of this was no doubt owing to his burgeoning socialist activism and the discomfort it created between congregation and pastor.

Meanwhile, Barth's friendship with the neighboring pastor Eduard Thurneysen led to his first encounters with socialists Herrmann Kutter and Leonhard Ragaz. Kutter in particular impressed Barth with his preaching, by the "molten lava of his eloquence," "like an uncanny volcano." Barth remembered, "from Kutter I simply learned to speak the great word 'God' seriously, responsibly, and with a sense of its importance." "When he preached, and indeed in private conversation, he could impress on one that this was a deadly serious matter, which could not be taken lightly."[118] Barth preached two extensive sermon series during 1914 on the revolutionary implication of the word "God," and returned repeatedly to "the social question."[119] And then the war broke out, not just in Europe,

---

116. Busch, *Karl Barth*, p. 61. For the sermon on the sinking of the *Titanic*, see Karl Barth et al., *The Word in This World: Two Sermons* (Vancouver: Regent College, 2007), pp. 31-42.

117. On a visit to Safenwil in 1935, Barth addressed the congregation: "I can see now that I did not preach the gospel clearly enough to you during the time when I was your pastor. Since then I have often thought with some trepidation of those who were perhaps led astray or scandalized by what I said at that time, or of the dead who have passed on and did not hear, at any rate from me, what by human reckoning they ought to have heard." Busch, *Karl Barth*, p. 64.

118. Busch, *Karl Barth*, p. 76.

119. Busch, *Karl Barth*, p. 80. The texts for the series were Romans 1:16 and Matthew 6:33.

but also in Barth's sermons. It was only after a distressed woman in the congregation begged him to preach on something else that Barth's opposition to the war "did not appear so directly" in the sermons.[120]

In the period of disillusionment that followed the war-enthusiasm of his teachers, Barth questioned not only the theology, ethics, and exegesis he had imbibed from them, but also the homiletic. The way forward seemed to come in the eschatological hope he heard from the Blumhardts:

> The need for me to preach proved a very healthy corrective and stimulus in the development of my ideas. . . . Above all, it has become increasingly clear to me that what we need is something beyond all morality and politics and ethics. This is true even of so-called Christian morality and so-called socialist politics.[121]

By 1916 Barth was increasingly focused on the "limitless problem" of preaching, which became the epicenter for his struggles to rethink how God is known by human beings at all. The impossibility of preaching weighed heavily on him and the problem itself began to infiltrate his sermons.[122] Barth struggled to retain the concern for the hearer he inherited from modern preaching while attending with new seriousness to the Bible:

> As a pastor I wanted to speak to people in the extraordinary contradiction of their lives, but to speak the no less extraordinary message of the Bible, which was as much of a riddle as life. These two factors, life and the Bible, have risen before me like Scylla and Charybdis: if these are the source and the destination of Christian preaching, who should, who can, be a pastor and preach?[123]

It is important to recognize that, even at this early stage, Barth already exhibited what would be a characteristic focus on principle and material homiletics: "Thus the predicament in which Barth found himself when preaching was not primarily a technical and practical matter (*how do I say it?*), but a problem which concerned the basic content of preaching

---

120. Busch, *Karl Barth*, p. 81.
121. Busch, *Karl Barth*, p. 84.
122. See for example his famous sermon on Ezekiel 13, or the 1916 series on 1 John.
123. Busch, *Karl Barth*, p. 90.

(*can* I, *may* I, speak of God at all?)."[124] Meanwhile, he had begun to grapple with the book of Romans, and the commentaries that emerged would include, among other things, a challenge to the basic program of the German Protestant "inner mission" (apologetics, *Seelsorge*, and social work) and the preaching that went along with it.[125]

Karl Barth and the Homiletic of Weimar

By the time Barth arrived in Göttingen, his first Romans commentary had garnered him both admirers and critics. Over the next few years several of Barth's addresses and essays were published that in some way addressed the problem of preaching. These writings caused a stir in German theology in general and practical theology in particular. Of course, the idea that preaching was a "problem" was nothing new. But Barth problematized modern preaching's idea of what exactly constituted the "problem." In *The Word of God as the Task of the Ministry* (1922) Barth told a group of ministers that the problem is not that ministers are no longer held in high esteem or that in "the new Germany" there had been a discussion about whether the church "was really needed or not." Rather, it is the paradox that ministers must talk about God; yet this they cannot do. And this "perplexity" will not, and should not, go away.[126] With regard to the *seelsorgerlich* tasks of the dominant Weimar homiletic, Barth is not very encouraging:

> Obviously the people have *no* real need of *our* observations upon morality and culture, or even of our disquisitions upon religion, worship, and the possible existence of other worlds. . . . We may possibly be able

---

124. Busch, *Karl Barth*, p. 91. On the concept of "principle" and "material" (vs. "formal") homiletics in the German tradition, see above, p. 145.

125. Speaking of the unconverted masses, Barth writes: "They do not give attention to our Word of God, because they have heard it long ago apart from us, and have long ago proclaimed it. The unholy and unbelieving children of the world are — in spite of their quite naked misery and in spite, maybe, of their merry freedom — not 'objects' of our preaching and pastoral care, of our evangelistic, missionary, and apologetic activities, or our busy efforts for their salvation; they are not objects of our 'love' — for, long before we appeared upon the scene to have mercy on them, they had sought and found the mercy of God." Karl Barth, *The Epistle to the Romans*, 6th ed., trans. Edwyn Clement Hoskyns (London: Oxford University Press, 1968), p. 364.

126. Karl Barth, "The Word of God and the Task of the Ministry," in *The Word of God and the Word of Man* (Boston: Pilgrim, 1928), pp. 185-86.

to give pleasure or help to this man or that, or perhaps even to hundreds, by our more or less stimulating preaching and satisfying teaching in regard to these troublesome questions. And I suppose there is no reason why we should not. But let us *not* think that by doing so we face the questions which really bring the people to us; or that we discharge our duty as minsters of the Gospel by making dexterous answers, or otherwise performing useful ministries. . . . When they come to us for help they do not really want to learn more about *living*: they want to learn more about what is on the farther edge of living — God.[127]

What is critical to observe at this point is that Barth is not dismissing the defining component of the modern preaching movement out of hand — he does not reject the significance of the hearer of the Word, and even in the midst of the *Predigtvorbereitung* lectures he never will. But he does consistently place that concern in the widest possible horizon. The "problem" of preaching is framed in a completely different way. There is still attention to the needs of the hearer, but now those needs are seen in relation — not to "modernity" or to the degeneracies and dangers of Weimar culture or to the Protestant church's future vitality — but to the Godness of God. A horizon infinitely bigger than the German *Volk* is evoked again and again.

In Barth's two dogmatic efforts, which emanated from Göttingen and Münster respectively in the 1920s, there is also a marked concern to consider the needs, questions, and longings of the hearer in the discussion of the dilemma of proclamation. But again, it is not an exposition of the needs, questions, and longings projected by German nationalists in the Weimar Republic, but a consideration of the needs, questions, and longings of the human being as one already addressed by the gracious God. Barth explains that

> modern preaching is only too heavily directed to people, only too emphatically aimed at the public. But the fact that preachers pay attention to the needs, interests, situation, and capacity of the public is no guarantee that they are really addressing man, for in no case is the man who ought to be addressed and waits to be addressed the public. He is arcane, secret, hidden. Sermons which should stir and edify and move

127. Barth, "The Word of God and the Task," pp. 188-89.

him will probably leave this man cold and empty and untouched. . . . But what sermons aim at is the *human* in people: not their morality that needs confirming and strengthening, not their devotion that needs to be piously nurtured, not their culture that needs religious underpinnings, not their nationality and its peculiar values that need to be conserved, not the bourgeois element in them that longs for peace and order, and naturally not the proletarian element in them that seeks justification for its dissatisfaction and rebelliousness. People are all these things, but not the *human* in them. . . . If preaching does not press on through all those things — through them indeed, but still *through* them — to the fortress which is the seat of man . . . if it does not see their relativity even in human terms but remains stuck in them; if it does not begin with the presupposition that man wants to be taken more seriously by it than he takes himself, namely, with *total* seriousness, then it is setting its sights too low, and its effort is meaningless no matter how great its sound and fury.[128]

By the time Barth returned to the same territory in Münster in 1927, the critique of the orientation of the modern sermon was even more pointed. Barth argued that a homiletic that aims only at "the public" may well pay great attention to the different types of hearers: "German or French, middle class or proletariat, educated or uneducated, pious and impious, moral and immoral, to interested and uninterested, to pious and unpious, moral and immoral, to the so-called '*Männerwelt*' or to '*die Frau*' or to the not-taken-seriously-enough 'youth.'"[129]

But if preaching is really a matter of "speech about God and the people in their relationship to God," then it simply cannot be addressed to Germans, to pious people, to the educated, to "women" or to "young men" *as such*. To reduce human beings to "certain observable categories" is to assume they cannot and do not want to hear of God. To pursue this constant reduction of people to categories ends at a kind of idolatry. It ends in "German theology," "proletarian theology," "youth theology," and thus finally "polytheism."[130] The preacher who wants to speak of God must be "entirely hard-hearted" on this point, Barth insisted. The person addressed by the

---

128. Karl Barth, *The Göttingen Dogmatics: Instruction in the Christian Religion*, vol. 1, ed. Hannelotte Reiffen, trans. Geoffrey W. Bromiley (Grand Rapids: Eerdmans, 1991), p. 70.

129. Karl Barth, *Gesamtausgabe*, ed. Hinrich Stoevesandt and Hans Anton Drewes (Zürich: Theologischer Verlag, 1971), II.14, p. 91.

130. Barth, *Gesamtausgabe* II.14, p. 92.

Word of God is that person hidden in humanity, "absolutely independent of *Volkstum*, gender, age, class, culture," the person as an individual who is not just an "abstraction, a "case" who falls under a "category," but "potentially and actually" "a member of the church," and here in the church there is "neither Jew and Greek, here is neither slave nor free, here is neither male nor female" (Gal. 3:28).[131] The preacher turns to people specifically and concretely in their relationship to *God*, in "the center of their humanity," in their "naked humanness," in their "full loneliness before God."[132]

But Barth's problem with the modern approach was not only the tendency to reduce hearers to categories; it was also the purpose for which preachers performed this reduction. Broadly speaking, Protestant preachers in Weimar directly or indirectly used the pulpit to influence public life — morally, ethically, and politically — and/or they tried to persuade hearers that the Protestant church and its gospel were necessary for the safety, recovery, and well-being of the German *Volk*. The latter concern included an apologetic effort — to convert or at least "revive" modern individuals who were perhaps thinking about leaving the church. By the early 1930s, the desire to convert or revive reached a fever pitch. After all, conversions of the political sort were impossible to ignore. There was a nagging feeling that the "spirit" so evident on the streets was marching right past the Protestant church. It was time to catch the wave.

Preaching, then, had become a way to accomplish certain apologetic, *seelsorgerlich*, and church-political goals. The attention to the demographic and existential situation of the hearer, a task that was often pursued in Weimar homiletics with the aid of psychology, *Volkstum*, or philosophy, was an effort to help the preacher be more effective in persuading hearers with regard to the nationalist Protestant agenda.[133] It is this instrumental understanding of the sermon — that preachers can wield the Word of God like a weapon to prevail in the *Kampf* of the moment — which made Barth increasingly uneasy as the 1920s drew to a close.

---

131. Barth, *Gesamtausgabe* II.14, p. 92.
132. Barth, *Gesamtausgabe* II.14, p. 92.
133. The discipline of "rhetoric" (as Germans understood it) had largely, but not entirely, been trumped in German homiletical theory by the new and exciting insights from psychology, *Volkstum*, and philosophy. "Rhetoric" in the context of Weimar homiletics often meant rigidity, predictability, and dogmatism with regard to form. But it is clear that the tools of psychology, *Volkstum*, and philosophy were regularly used as means of persuasion. Weimar homiletical theories were not anti-rhetorical; indeed, they were full of rhetorical concerns. They just engaged in rhetorical reflection under another name.

In his "Quousque Tandem?" of 1930, Barth lamented the way Protestant preachers were trying to win over the youth and the workers and arguing with political enemies rather than "honestly and genuinely preaching the gospel."[134] When the church is busy asserting its usefulness and its relevance, Barth argues,

> no word in its Christmas and Easter and Sunday preaching is believable. When she utters "Jesus Christ," even if uttered a thousand times, what one must and will hear is one's own conceit and certainty and one should not be astonished to discover that with all the utterances of "Jesus Christ" in the air, the real need of a real humanity is overlooked, [just] as God's Word is misheard, turning all caution, consolation, and teaching of the Bible and the Reformers into water for their own little mills.[135]

It was around this time that Emil Brunner announced from Switzerland that there was "another task of theology."[136] It could not have come at a worse moment.

Brunner's "other task" concerns us at this point because it was intimately related to the practice of preaching. Specifically, Brunner thought theology needed to serve the church's proclamation by turning its attention to the "situation" of the hearer. This would result in information that would help preachers prepare their unbelieving congregations to receive the Word of God. Without this information, a sermon could not establish "contact" with modern people, people who already had an understanding of "existence," and who would not relinquish it without a fight. The gospel, Brunner insisted, was polemical, and theology must arm preachers for the *Kampf* between the gospel and the arrogance of human reason.[137] Preachers must force unbelievers from their theoretical hiding places into an existential crisis.[138] Brunner called his new passion "eristics" and urged

---

134. Karl Barth, "Quousque Tandem?" in *"Der Götze wackelt": Zeitkritische Aufsätze, Reden und Briefe von 1930 bis 1960*, ed. Karl Kupisch (Berlin: Käthe Vogt, 1961), p. 31.

135. Barth, "Quousque Tandem?" p. 31.

136. Emil Brunner, "Die andere Aufgabe der Theologie," *Zwischen den Zeiten* 7 (1929): 255-76.

137. John W. Hart, *Karl Barth vs. Emil Brunner: The Formation and Dissolution of a Theological Alliance, 1916-1936* (New York: Peter Lang, 2001), p. 104.

138. For Brunner, the awareness of one's own spiritual bankruptcy is synonymous with asking "the question of God." And no one asks "the question of God" without knowing

Barth to abandon his "one-sidedness" and embrace the existential "bridge" to faith which God provided to contemporary preachers.[139]

Of course, this "other task" did not seem new to Barth. It was a version of the same sort of apologetic program he encountered all the time in late Weimar. Additional encouragement to incite and stoke existential angst in Weimar hearers who were already on the verge of hysteria was possibly the worst advice Brunner could have contributed to German homiletics in the early 1930s.[140] Brunner's admission of a *theologia naturalis* that did not firmly close the door on the "orders" of creation, which so animated the Political Theologians (and Friedrich Gogarten), and his conviction that "today anthropology must take center stage," were equally unwelcome developments as far as Barth was concerned.[141] By the

---

something of the answer already. It is only a trace, a hint, a whisper, but the answer is there. It is critical to understand that, in Brunner's formulation, knowledge of the "law" brings with it this answer, this little scrap of ("negative") knowledge of God, this faint inheritance of Eden. This, then, is the famous "point of contact" that will loom large in the "natural theology" debate of 1934. Barth's pursuit of "dogmatics" was fine in itself, Brunner asserts in his 1929 essay, but unless it began with the exploration of the existential situation of contemporary people, it was an ivory tower affair. Sometimes Brunner uses the language of "general" vs. "special" revelation to describe the situation, as in this text from *The Mediator* (1927): "It is impossible to believe in a Christian way in the unique revelation, in the Mediator, without believing also in a universal revelation of God in creation, in history, and especially in the human conscience." Emil Brunner, *The Mediator: A Study of the Central Doctrine of the Christian Faith*, trans. Olive Wyon (Philadelphia: Westminster, 1947), p. 32.

139. Hart, *Karl Barth vs. Emil Brunner*, p. 106.

140. Brunner's fundamental concern had become the question of how to speak effectively to his unbelieving neighbors. While he complained repeatedly that Barth was oblivious to the real situation "on the ground," it was actually Brunner, writing as he did from Switzerland, who was not paying attention to the escalating situation in Germany where his works would be read and distributed. The "German Christians" loved Brunner's book *Nature and Grace*, in which they found legitimation for their claims. John Hart concludes, "It is striking how oblivious Brunner was to the context into which he hurled *Nature and Grace*." Hart, *Karl Barth vs. Emil Brunner*, p. 168.

141. Hart, *Karl Barth vs. Emil Brunner*, p. 107. Gogarten laid out his own anthropological goals in his 1929 essay "The Problem of a Theological Anthropology," stressing (like Brunner) that theology must direct its attention to the task of exegeting the way "modern" (presumably German) people understand themselves in contrast to those of previous eras. Without this attention to the nuances of the reigning zeitgeist, Gogarten argues, real theology and preaching are not possible. See Friedrich Gogarten, "Das Problem einer theologischen Anthropologie," *Zwischen den Zeiten* 7 (1929): 493-511. It would be Gogarten's favorable assessment of certain *Deutsche Christen* themes in subsequent essays that would prompt Barth to distance himself publicly from his former dialectical colleague. See, for ex-

early 1930s, Barth argued that Brunner's "point of contact" was part of a powerful family of ideas that posit a revelatory dimension in some element of "natural" life: in the orders of creation, in the splendor of culture, in human consciousness, in existential anxiety, in the *analogia entis* affirmed in Roman Catholic theology.[142] By 1932, Barth feared the cumulative weight of these concessions left theology unable to unequivocally resist the identification of God's revelation in "the intoxication of Nordic blood" and the "political Führer."[143] Barth was not surprised that some German nationalist Protestants praised Brunner's proposals. The ensuing debate between Barth and Brunner over "natural theology" and the *Anknüpfungspunkt* (point of contact) is embedded in the larger contextual question of the content and function of Protestant preaching as Weimar tottered and finally collapsed, though the conflict would not end until the famous parting exchange of 1934.[144]

---

ample, Friedrich Gogarten, "Staat und Kirche," *Zwischen den Zeiten* 10 (1932): 390-410. Gogarten joined the German Christians in the summer of 1933 along with a group of theologians and church lawyers, within which he functioned as representative theologian. The "declaration" the group drafted to explain the reasons for their decision to join included the observation that the new order of the National Socialist state "had created 'a necessary precondition' for 'the unhindered proclamation of the risen Lord, crucified for our sins, to fall upon productive soil.'" In other words, National Socialism had become the necessary "point of contact." See "Erklärung der Jungreformatischen Bewegung Schlesiens," in *Die Bekennende Kirche in Schlesien 1933-1945: Geschichte und Dokumente*, ed. Ernst Hornig (Göttingen: Vandenhoeck & Ruprecht, 1977), p. 80. See also Klaus Scholder, *The Churches and the Third Reich*, vol. 1 (Philadelphia: Fortress, 1988), p. 424.

142. The *analogia entis*, a scholastic term famously formulated by Thomas Aquinas, means that God and human beings (and all of creation) are similar in that they all participate in something called "being." Hence, we can figure out what God is like by looking at the created order, because everything is connected to everything else in the great chain of being, which stretches all the way up to being itself (God). The human ability to know God, then, is a faculty guaranteed by virtue of the fact that we are created beings. We have this knowledge or capacity "naturally." It is "given" with human existence. For Barth, this *analogia entis* converted the dynamic that was revelation into a static revealedness. See Barth, "Fate and Idea in Theology," in *The Way of Theology in Karl Barth: Essays and Comments*, ed. Martin Rumscheidt (Allison Park: Pickwick Publications, 1986), pp. 25-61.

143. CD I/1, p. xiv.

144. The most detailed study devoted to the entirety of the Barth/Brunner relationship is Hart, *Karl Barth vs. Emil Brunner* — though it is not without its problems. Hart's claim (in contrast to Marquardt and Winzeler) that Barth's opposition to "natural theology" was for theological, not political, reasons, because it dates from 1929, misses the point entirely. Hart, *Karl Barth vs. Emil Brunner*, p. 2. Yes, Barth opposed what he meant at that time by "natural theology" for "theological" reasons. But given what "theological existence" meant for Barth

Theological Existence and Protestant Proclamation in Weimar

Barth first expressed his concerns to Brunner not long after "The Other Task of Theology" appeared in 1929, only to be told by Brunner that he was out of touch with his "timeless" dogmatics and that "precisely because eristics considers timeliness to be a great *bene*, it will put 'theological journalism' ahead of dogmatics."[145] Needless to say, the Protestant church in Weimar was all too happy to engage in "theological journalism," and "timeliness" was of course a hallmark of the modern "theme" sermon.

In the midst of the National Socialist surge of the early 1930s, Barth responded to Brunner and the question of the nature, function, and content of preaching in Weimar in a number of forums. While an analysis of Barth's own preaching over the course of the Weimar period is beyond the scope of this study, it must be noted that Barth's preaching praxis during these years may be seen as his enacted response to the homiletic of his day. While Barth's Weimar sermons are clearly directed to a particular congregation and do not lose sight of the "situation," overall they are more expository than his Safenwil efforts, that is, they exhibit a deeper and more consistent engagement with a particular biblical text and its "way," its trajectory. "Themes" and commentary on current events no longer take center stage, as was sometimes the case in Safenwil. Instead, there is a constant though often tacit interrogation regarding the witness of the text: What does this mean for us today? How does this particular Word call us and our assumptions into question?[146]

As the Weimar Republic limped toward its demise, Barth increasingly argued for the freedom of the Word against the *seelsorgerlich* and apologetic stance of the German Protestant preacher, so eager to secure a place in the Reich to come.[147] He rejected the confident German Protestant homiletic

---

(i.e., that it includes participation in the political realm) this does not mean that he did not take his position with reference to the political and cultural dynamics of the period. Hence he can affirm his own approach as "one-sided." Does Barth's rejection of "natural theology" actually date from 1929, or might we find it (perhaps by other names) in Barth's initial and subsequent reaction to the militant nationalism exhibited by Christian theologians with regard to World War I, and hence in everything he wrote from *Romans I* forward?

145. Hart, *Karl Barth vs. Emil Brunner*, p. 108.

146. Barth's sermons from this period (1921-35) may be found in Karl Barth, *Gesamtausgabe* I.31. The definitive contextual study of Barth's preaching in the Weimar years has yet to be written.

147. "Church proclamation, as regards its content, cannot let itself be questioned as to whether it is in harmony with the distinctive features and interests of a race, people, nation, or state. It cannot let itself be questioned as to its agreement with the demands of this or that scientific or aesthetic culture. It cannot let itself be questioned as to whether it is contribut-

with its holy agenda and self-conscious "relevance," and begged for a homiletic that would put down the weapons of propaganda and turn from the claustrophobic fixation on German fate to the wide, critical, and eschatological horizon the witness of the Scripture could provide.[148]

Barth pointed again and again to that widest horizon, even as much church discourse around him deteriorated into a messy synthesis of Christian rhetoric and the language of *Volk, Blut, Kampf,* and *Führer.* Barth regularly lamented the state of German practical theology and the *Predigerseminare* of the *Landeskirchen,* which trained young Protestants to craft the timely "theme sermons" so susceptible to ideological infiltration, as Pfennigsdorf demonstrated week by week.[149] Barth's *Predigtvorbereitung* sessions were an attempt to head this dominant pattern of homiletical formation off at the pass.

But how did Barth hope to accomplish such a feat? Especially with students who came to his exercises with a variety of political and church-political commitments?

---

ing what is needed to maintain or perhaps even to overthrow this or that form of society or economy. A proclamation which accepts responsibilities along these or similar lines spells treachery to the Church and to Christ Himself. It only gets its due if sooner or later its mouth is stopped by some refined or brutal ungodliness. Far better no proclamation at all than this kind." CD I/1, p. 72.

148. See, for example, Barth's extended discussion in the first part-volume of the *Church Dogmatics* (1932) of the criteria by which proclamation should be assessed. He explains that modern Protestantism measured its preaching by philosophical, psychological, ethical, and political norms derived from the surrounding culture or "the prevailing modern philosophy, or the most pressing practical needs and tasks, or the most eloquent forms of expression" because "it could see no further possibility of viewing the Word of God as an entity distinct from Church proclamation." There was no "Word of God" or "revelation" grounded in broader witness of the Bible that could function as transcultural critique, as the German Protestant enthusiasm for the war effort and its delight in the "Spirit of 1914" amply demonstrated. CD I/1, p. 251. For the larger discussion of criteria and proclamation see CD I/1, pp. 248-75.

149. As a rule, German theology students mostly studied principle and material homiletics at the university, taught by the resident professor of practical theology. The formal, more practical aspects of preaching were generally the focus in the homiletics portion of the *Predigerseminar.* The *Predigerseminar* was the practical supplement to the theoretical instruction students received at the university and was comprised of classes designed to help them in the transition to the parish. *Predigerseminare* were usually taught by experienced pastors and included practice preaching. For the history of the *Predigerseminar* see Krause, Müller, and Schwertner, eds., *Theologische Realenzyklopädie,* vol. 27, pp. 221-23. For a description in English of the late-twentieth-century *Predigerseminar,* see Richard Lischer, "Preparation for Preaching: A German Model," *Homiletic* 9, no. 1 (1984): 1-4.

The *Sermon Exercises* as Emergency Principle and Material Homiletic

What we know of Barth's intentions in offering the *Predigtvorbereitung* sessions has come to us mostly in scattered references in letters. It is clear from Barth's reports to Thurneysen, for example, that he considered the "theme sermon" to be the dominant homiletic his Bonn students had encountered and would encounter, and that he was determined to offer them an alternative, in spite of likely objections from church officials.[150]

But there is one exchange dating back to January of 1931 — some sixteen months before Barth informed Pfennigsdorf of his intention to hold his own sermon exercises — that offers clues to Barth's overall approach to the task in relation to his diagnoses of the problem. The reader will note that by this time the National Socialists were rapidly gaining ground.

In the winter of 1931, Scottish pastor John McConnachie wrote to Barth about a book he was preparing, to be entitled *Karl Barth and the Preacher*.[151] McConnachie had been an enthusiast for Barth's work for some time and had begun to publicize him in Great Britain beginning in 1927. He told Barth in his letter of 1931 that his new book is

> not meant to be a scientific treatment of your theology but rather your message to the Preacher. We are a practical people, and what people want to know is "Is this a preachable theology?" So much of our preaching is of the subjective psychological type and there is a sense of dissatisfaction and a desire for something objective and authoritative.[152]

McConnachie proceeded to ask Barth to write an introduction to the forthcoming volume and enclosed a brief outline of the project with titles

---

150. "Because I reject as completely impossible the theme sermon, which by the local *Predigerseminar* and examination authorities is considered as the only possibility, and embrace the necessity of the homily as almost an article of faith, I will become embroiled in who knows what kinds of struggles with those authorities (not to mention the local faculty representative Pfennigsdorf)." Karl Barth to Eduard Thurneysen, December 23, 1932. Barth, *Gesamtausgabe* V.34, p. 323.

151. John McConnachie (1876-1948), minister of St. John's Church, Dundee. For a detailed genetic account of McConnachie's early reception of Barth, see D. Densil Morgan, *Barth's Reception in Britain* (London: T&T Clark, 2010), pp. 29-33, 35-40, 43-47.

152. John McConnachie to Karl Barth, January 4, 1931, quoted in Barth, *Gesamtausgabe* V.35, p. 147.

and headings, concluding with a final section devoted to the question, "What difference would this make to my preaching?"

Barth wrote back to McConnachie a few days later, explaining why he did not want to write the proposed introduction.[153] He thanked the pastor for the letter and the forthcoming book, but said that to write what McConnachie desired would be "entirely contrary to both my principles and my existing praxis." McConnachie wanted to present him and his work to the English theological public as "practical," as "a preachable theology." Barth had no doubt in McConnachie's ability to do this "with care and caution." But this was a responsibility that McConnachie must take on himself. As for Barth, if he were to try and speak directly to the English and Scottish theologians — whom he did not presume to know or understand — he would not turn to the practical questions so quickly. That could come slowly "with a certain peace and love" only after serious theological work. "The praxis and the methods of praxis would then subsequently arise either in this generation or in a later one entirely by itself." At present, would it not be better for theologians and pastors to become "thoroughly disturbed and unsettled in their praxis," rather than charging immediately "from one magnificent and lively praxis to another"? "This is my own situation," Barth wrote to the Scottish preacher,

> and in this situation I would like to see in Germany . . . not a new confidence, but rather a new questioning and seeking. I am afraid when someone approaches me with the question, "what difference would this make to my preaching?" and hears nothing from me other than a circular answer to this question, he will not at all understand what I am saying. I do not know now, dear Herr pastor, whether you are not so much a very characteristically English theologian as to be able to make my point of view your own. I have much too much respect for the peculiarity of the spiritual situation in another country to judge offhand if another way is pursued there than in my own.[154]

Barth explains that he understands that McConnachie might have to proceed as he had planned, but for himself, he must "counteract the attempt

---

153. Karl Barth to John McConnachie, January 9, 1931, in Barth, *Gesamtausgabe* V.35, pp. 149-51.

154. Barth, *Gesamtausgabe* V.35, p. 150.

to make me practical as quickly as possible. Even if this attempt is made by such a well-known man as you!"[155]

Barth's response to McConnachie makes it clear that, given the situation in Germany in the early 1930s, one could only begin homiletics again from the beginning. No mere tinkering with techniques would be sufficient. Things were "magnificent" and "lively" enough in the pathos-laden sermons of Emil Pfennigsdorf and countless others like him. From this incidental account of Barth's homiletical state of mind in 1931, we can anticipate a rigorous, relentless return to basic questions in his conducting of the *Predigtvorbereitung* sessions — a principle and material homiletic that would "thoroughly disturb" and "unsettle" the preachers in his care.

Conclusion

By the time the *Predigtvorbereitung* commenced in 1932, Weimar was reeling from election to election, and the Protestant church was vacillating from intoxication with the spirit of the National Socialist revival to fear that the godless communists might prevail after all. In some places the church used its pulpits to shore up support for the nationalist cause, while the minority religious-socialist preachers often fought back with aggressive political sermons of their own.[156] The lines between church and state, gospel and politics, divinity and Germanness were blurred as the rhetoric of Weimar propaganda found a natural ally in a homiletic of "timeliness," "closeness to life," and "relevance." Because God was revealed in historical events and the "natural" orders of creation, there was nothing objective that could call the nationalist interpretation of these events and orders into question. It was a situation of increasing myopia. Political Theology, "political" preaching in such a situation, means narrowing, constriction, inwardness. This was the climate in Germany when Karl Barth decided to challenge the homiletic of the likes of Emil Pfennigsdorf. It was an emergency homiletic, forged in response to a Protestant pulpit that often ig-

---

155. Barth, *Gesamtausgabe* V.35, p. 151. After reading Barth's response, McConnachie asked if he could print part of the letter in the foreword to the book, in lieu of Barth's introduction. Barth agreed. Barth, *Gesamtausgabe* V.35, p. 148.

156. "The pastors in the election struggled against each other as agitation orators and the sermons one heard, infiltrated by political *Schlagworten* to an unprecedent degree, only demonstrated how far theological-religious and political acts could merge with each other." Nowak, *Evangelische Kirche*, p. 211.

nored the height and depth of the larger story of God's redemptive activity for all people in Jesus Christ — a story bound up with the witness of the Old and New Testaments. In a time of political narrowness Barth unfurled a homiletic of theological and eschatological breadth, one designed to disturb and unsettle the practitioners of a self-confident, instrumental, and "relevant" homiletic.

With the overlapping contexts of Weimar — politics, church, academy, rhetoric, and homiletics — now in view, we turn our attention to the artifacts of Barth's emergency homiletic themselves. What will they sound like when we read them in relation to the seismic shifts of the years 1932 and 1933?

CHAPTER FIVE

Karl Barth's Predigtvorbereitung *in Context: Winter Semester 1932-1933*

This chapter is the first of two to offer a close reading of the artifacts that constitute our only access to what Barth said to his students during the course of his *Predigtvorbereitung* meetings.[1] Strictly speaking, the notes interpreted here inevitably provide more insight into what was *heard* than into what was said.[2]

Every effort is made to read these notes not only as an account of a "text" — i.e., of the material Barth presented, with an inner logic of its own — but also in relation to the multifaceted situation in which Barth's comments were delivered and interpreted. The latter task is particularly challenging because none of the contexts explored in this study thus far — theological, political, ecclesiastical, academic, rhetorical, or homiletical —

---

1. Two documents serve as the primary source material for the interpretation presented in the next two chapters: (1) Charlotte von Kirschbaum's notes for the winter and summer semesters, cited as (K) and (KS), respectively; and (2) a transcript of the protocol-like notes generated by the students in the class, cited as (P). (A third document, the "free interpretation" of the material presented in the summer semester of 1933 by Werner Degeller [D], will be taken up in the following chapter.) When the material described below appears in only one of the source documents, the page number in the respective document will be noted. A description of these documents and the complex history of their origin, translation, redaction, and publication can be found in the Appendix to this study.

2. Some things do not get recorded because they seem too obvious to the one documenting the event, and so writing them down is not necessary. Others are omitted given the nature of a protocol, which aims to *summarize* what is said; thus some things are omitted because they seem too casual or tangential. Either way, it is likely that some things that were said in the course of the sermon exercises are not included in the artifacts available to us.

remained static over the course of what has turned out to be one of the most dramatic nine-month periods in German history.

To facilitate this contextual reading, Chapter Five moves chronologically through the winter semester of the *Predigtvorbereitung* sessions week by week. The accounts of the material covered in a given week are interspersed with sections that describe the changing context, both in terms of the broad dynamics of the German situation and with regard to Barth's own struggles and concerns. Of course, a full account of this nine-month period in German history cannot be attempted here. Instead, these context sections will provide readers with a basic orientation to the developments and issues that will offer the most insights into the *Predigtvorbereitung* lectures as they unfold. We begin with the period from the time Barth announced his intention to hold the exercises in preaching preparation until the class commenced some six months later.

May to November 8, 1932

Contextual Developments

A few weeks after Barth wrote to Pfennigsdorf in May 1932 of his plan to offer supplemental preaching exercises the following term, the series of political events that would lead to the end of democracy in Germany was already set in motion. After the Nazi electoral breakthrough in 1930, the Reichstag had descended into a virtual riot of shouting, chanting, and obstruction. By 1931 it was no longer functional as a governing body, and the locus of political decision-making was from then on constricted to the circle of bureaucrats around President Paul von Hindenburg.[3]

Though Hindenburg ultimately prevailed against Adolf Hitler in the presidential election in April 1932, it was clear that the Nazi leader was a serious threat. Henceforth, political decisions would be made in consideration of how the Nazis would react. Reich Chancellor Heinrich Brüning was forced out and replaced by the even more conservative Franz von Papen at the end of May 1932. Like Hindenburg, Papen was eager to bring an end to the parliamentary system of Weimar. New Reichstag elections, which Hitler demanded, were set for July 31, 1932; the existing Reichstag was dissolved.

---

3. Richard J. Evans, *The Coming of the Third Reich*, 1st American ed. (New York: Penguin Press, 2004), p. 276.

Karl Barth's Predigtvorbereitung in Context: Winter Semester 1932-1933

The months leading up to the Reichstag elections were marked by an increase in political violence. Approximately 105 were killed in Prussia alone in June and July, with hundreds more wounded.[4] The infamous "Bloody Sunday" battle between Nazis and Communists in Altona in Prussia on July 17 resulted in Reich Chancellor Papen's takeover of the state government, arguing that the Social Democratic (SPD) government had failed to maintain law and order. Richard Evans explains that it was this action by Papen that

> dealt a mortal blow to the Weimar Republic. It destroyed the federal principle and opened the way to the wholesale centralization of the state. Whatever happened now, it was unlikely to be a full restoration of parliamentary democracy. After 20 July 1932 the only realistic alternatives were a Nazi dictatorship or a conservative, authoritarian regime backed by the army.[5]

The outcome of the July Reichstag election revealed a polarized German population and resulted in a Reichstag composed largely of extremists on the right and the left with effectively no one in the center. Politically motivated violence escalated on the streets, owing in part to the fact that Papen banned all public political meetings on July 29. Without sanctioned public meetings to attend, there was all the more involvement in unsanctioned ones. In response to the ensuing mayhem Papen issued an emergency decree in August that imposed the death penalty on anyone who killed a political opponent.[6] Behind the scenes, Hindenburg, Papen, and Hitler argued about how the Nazis would be represented in the government. Hitler said he would only consider the position of Reich Chancellor.

When the Reichstag met in September, Papen tried to dissolve it, but the Communist bloc resisted, issuing a vote of no-confidence in the government. Yet another Reichstag election was scheduled for November.

Barth followed all these political developments closely, even while he was in Switzerland for the break after the summer semester. He writes to friends of his depression during this time:

> Why was I depressed? One cannot say in such cases, as is well known. One just is. . . . The manifest form of the evil was on the one hand an

---

4. Evans, *Coming of the Third Reich*, p. 270.
5. Evans, *Coming of the Third Reich*, p. 287.
6. Evans, *Coming of the Third Reich*, p. 296.

agonizing worry concerning the academic requirements of the coming winter, for which I have much too little coverage, on the other hand a heavily erupting anger about the German political scene: I have called the Papen people "the enemy of the human race" in my soliloquy.[7]

By September Barth was writing to Thurneysen of the "brutality and stupidity" that was on the rise in Germany, which reminded him of 1914.[8] "To *this* Germany," he wrote, "if it comes again, I have no relationship [other] than that of a fundamental objection."[9]

In addition to these political dynamics, there was a crucial church election in Prussia slated for November 1932.[10] The pro-Nazi "German Christian Faith Movement" *(Glaubensbewegung Deutsche Christen)* was officially launched in Berlin in May 1932. They issued their infamous "guidelines" on May 26, and by June they had at least some organized presence in most *Landeskirchen.* The Old Prussian church election was the first coordinated attempt of the *Deutsche Christen* to take over local church governments.[11]

By September even the SPD was urging its members to vote in the

---

7. The unpublished letter was written to Rudolph and Gerty Pestalozzi on September 23, 1932. An excerpt from the letter can be found in Karl Barth, *Gesamtausgabe,* ed. Hinrich Stoevesandt and Hans Anton Drewes (Zürich: Theologischer Verlag, 1971), V.34, p. 287, n. 4. Barth was feeling overwhelmed in a number of ways during this period, as he testified in a letter to Charlotte von Kirschbaum in the middle of September. He wrote: "[It] is right for me to tremble in the difficult and dangerous work in which I stand: due to the almost total loneliness in which I must see myself due to my bad memory, my insufficient knowledge, my low work intensity, due to the overall — one can say as well — hopeless absentmindedness of Protestantism to which I perhaps also still contribute, due to the hopeless relativity of all human action that steps so starkly in the world by the day, as well as in the theological thinking, speaking, wrestling, organizing, which I now have committed the days of my life. I approach the Cyclopic program of this winter so discouraged, Lollo." In the same letter, Barth also reports that the "long face" of Papen chases him from the pages of the newspapers into his dreams. Barth, *Gesamtausgabe* V.45, p. 246.

8. Karl Barth to Eduard Thurneysen, September 18, 1932, in Barth, *Gesamtausgabe* V.34, pp. 273-74.

9. Barth, *Gesamtausgabe* V.34, p. 275.

10. Bonn is located in the *Kirchenprovinz* Rheinland and thus is part of the enormous *Landeskirche* of the Old Prussian Union.

11. Ernst Christian Helmreich, *The German Churches under Hitler: Background, Struggle, and Epilogue* (Detroit: Wayne State University Press, 1979), p. 126. See also Kurt Meier, *Der evangelische Kirchenkampf,* 3 vols. (Göttingen: Vandenhoeck & Ruprecht, 1976), vol. 1, pp. 56-64.

church elections, while within the Prussian church proper the Religious Socialists and the conservative faction ("positives") launched campaigns of their own in an attempt to counteract the *Deutsche Christen* onslaught. There were hundreds of church election rallies in Prussia in September and October.[12] The pamphlets, flyers, editorials, and slogans emanating from the church "parties" joined and sometimes mirrored those of the secular political parties vying for votes in the Reichstag elections, also slated for November.[13] Among the Protestant leaders in Bonn and the surrounding regions, there was enough concern about the blurring of the lines between the political and church-political campaigns that an appeal was read from all pulpits on October 22, which warned Christians of the "danger that the church elections in our situation of intense political agitation be determined by other than church viewpoints."[14]

The *Übungen in der Predigtvorbereitung* had its first class meeting two days after the November Reichstag elections. The Nazis, though still the largest party represented in the Reichstag, actually lost some votes. The Communists saw modest gains. Both were poised to take down the Weimar "system." But their intent was now immaterial. With the Reichstag no longer a political player, all eyes were on Hindenburg and Papen. Governance now took the form of emergency decrees that bypassed the Reichstag altogether.

As the semester began, Barth faced a demanding teaching load. For the winter term he lectured on the theology of the nineteenth century, taught a seminar on Book III of Calvin's *Institutes*, and led a dogmatics "society" on Luther's Large Catechism. For the "open evenings" Barth hosted in his home, the topic was Brunner's recent volume on ethics. And, of course, there were the sermon exercises themselves, which drew approximately 110 participants, many of whom also attended at least some of Barth's other lectures.[15]

---

12. Klaus Scholder, *The Churches and the Third Reich*, vol. 1 (Philadelphia: Fortress, 1988), p. 215.

13. For a description of the campaigns in the 1932 Prussian Church elections, see Meier, *Der evangelische Kirchenkampf*, vol. 1, pp. 56-64.

14. Annette Hinz-Wessels, *Die evangelische Kirchengemeinde Bonn in der Zeit des Nationalsozialismus (1933-1945)* (Cologne: Rheinland-Verlag, 1996), p. 126.

15. Karl Barth to Eduard Thurneysen, December 23, 1932. Barth, *Gesamtausgabe* V.34, p. 322.

Session 1: November 8, 1932

Barth began the sermon exercises by giving an answer to an unspoken question: What is a theology professor doing teaching "sermon preparation"? The explanation he offered his students is rooted in the claim that all theology, as a science of the church, is in service to sermon preparation.[16] Systematic theology and exegesis no less than practical theology exist to prepare those who will preach the *verbi divini*, and as such the boundaries between these disciplines are and should remain porous and flexible (K1, P1). Given this intertwining relationship, why shouldn't a systematic theologian engage in practical theological reflection (K1)?

After addressing the matter of his cross-disciplinary venture, Barth turned to the task of the course. Three kinds of activities help to prepare preachers. First, there is the learning that comes from doing — the actual practice of preparing sermons. Second, there is the kind of learning that comes from listening and reading the sermons of others. And finally, there is the kind of learning that comes from theological reflection regarding the nature and purpose of preaching. The class would begin its work with this third activity, starting with the presentation and discussion of various definitions of preaching largely drawn from the past (K1, P1). What could they learn from the principle homiletic of others?[17]

The questions Barth posed to the various figures he would introduce over the course of the next several class sessions offer particular insight into his assessment of the strengths and weaknesses of the preaching of his own day. Already in these early sessions he was discouraging certain things and encouraging others by means of his running commentary about the homiletical proposals of others.

The first session was dominated by the discussion of two figures, Da-

---

16. Cf. CD I/1, p. 81: "the normal and central factum on which dogmatics focuses will always be quite simply the church's Sunday sermon of yesterday and tomorrow."

17. In the German homiletical tradition, a *principle* homiletic establishes the basis, nature, and purpose of Christian preaching, the *material* homiletic considers the question of the content of preaching, and the *formal* homiletic deals with the practical questions of preparation, form, delivery, etc. Generally speaking, homiletics in the university setting primarily dealt with principle and material questions, while the formal homiletic was the focus of the *Predigerseminare*, though there was certainly some overlap. This threefold division of homiletics originated in the nineteenth century in the work of Alexander Schweitzer. On Schweitzer and the threefold divisions, see Friedrich Wintzer, *Die Homiletik seit Schleiermacher bis in die Anfänge der dialektischen Theologie* (Göttingen: Habilitationsschrift, 1969), p. 24.

vid Hollaz and F. D. E. Schleiermacher. Barth offered an outline of their respective principle homiletic and introduced a smattering of quotations for discussion. Generally speaking, Barth used the contrasts between the two to establish right from the beginning a path of resistance in relation to the homiletics of both the theological right (Hollaz) and the theological left (Schleiermacher).

David Hollaz (1648-1713) was an orthodox Lutheran theologian, who, as such, was a staunch opponent of rationalism and who was ambivalent with regard to the pietism beginning to make inroads all around him. Not surprisingly, he subscribed to the doctrine of verbal inspiration and had an authoritarian understanding of the office of the preacher. It was this "top-down" understanding in particular that Barth called into question in the *Predigtvorbereitung*. According to Hollaz, the preacher must do two things: extract the "true sense of the Word of God" from a text of Scripture, and then apply that explanation to the *Gemeinde* in the form of instruction, condemnation, or comfort. Barth pointed out that the latter task includes the derivative problem of form: How can this "application" of the Word be expressed appropriately, gracefully, fittingly *(decenter)* for the *Gemeinde* (K1-2, P1-2)?

But what troubled Barth about Hollaz was the attitude of the preacher his theory assumed. Was it really the situation of the minister of the Word of God that he could so confidently "take possession" of what is written in the Bible, call it legitimate, and set off to "apply" it to the congregation? Shouldn't preachers be much less certain, much less complacent than Hollaz dreamed of in his orthodoxy (K2, P2)? These were, of course, the very questions Barth had for the German Protestant preachers of Weimar.

Barth insisted that the students would see that there was some progress with Schleiermacher's view of the matter, especially his later view. Schleiermacher's preacher comes out from the *Gemeinde* as their representative, and to the *Gemeinde* the preacher will return. This sense of movement — that the preacher's authority is bound up with the activity of preaching and not with a vested office or some prophetic delusion — might help to guard against arrogance, Barth suggested. There was even a dialectical or at least dialogical sense to Schleiermacher's understanding. The preacher represents not only the *Gemeinde*, but also the church that is beyond it. The preacher must not contradict the doctrines and practices that constitute the present unity of the church (K2, P3).

Nonetheless, dangers arise with Schleiermacher, Barth reminded his students. Another sort of confidence is at work, the confidence that God can be known in the depths of human feeling. Schleiermacher reveled in the great swelling wave of the *universum,* of the divine, of a reality that bears up the *Gemeinde* and to which the preacher bears witness. This *universum* is the same reality that animates the lyric poet and trembles out through the pipes of the organ. But is there really any place for a Word of God in this "immanent sea of feeling"? Is preaching — as in Hollaz — simply the expression of something already possessed? Is there any room in Schleiermacher's account for a preacher to be shocked by a law and a grace that break in from somewhere entirely *other,* another *world* (K3-4, P3-4)?

The first session returned repeatedly to this question of possession, confidence, and arrogance. The work of unsettling the next generation of preachers was already in motion.

November 8 to 29, 1932

Contextual Developments

The Prussian Church elections took place November 12-14, 1932. The story of the day was that the *Deutsche Christen* won an estimated one-third of the total seats in Prussia. Whether this was owing to their persuasive campaigning among the faithful or to the recruitment of National Socialist voters who did not normally participate in church elections is unclear, though there is some evidence for the latter.[18] In any case, it is clear that while the *Deutsche Christen* took a third of the seats in the Prussian *Landeskirche* overall, they did much better in the eastern part of the territory than in places (like Bonn) in the west.[19]

Meanwhile, Reich Chancellor Papen, unpopular with the public, lacking the crucial support of the army leadership, and unable to control the violence on the streets, was forced to resign on November 17.[20] Over the course of the next two weeks, Hindenburg and his advisors tried to negotiate their way to a new government, paying no attention to either election results or the legislature.

The political uncertainty was palpable throughout the country.

---

18. Scholder, *Churches and the Third Reich,* vol. 1, p. 215.

19. In the 1932 church elections in Bonn, *Deutsche Christen* candidates received only about 15 percent of the vote. This would change dramatically in the church elections of 1933. See Hinz-Wessels, *Kirchengemeinde Bonn,* pp. 132-33.

20. Evans, *Coming of the Third Reich,* p. 301.

Karl Barth's Predigtvorbereitung *in Context: Winter Semester 1932-1933*

Session 2: November 15, 1932

Barth opened the second session with a brief review of the definitions of preaching in Hollaz and Schleiermacher, again raising questions with regard to each (P6). The remainder of the session was dedicated to adding three additional, and well known, voices to the discussion: Alexandre Vinet, Christian Palmer, and C. I. Nitzsch.

In discussing the Welsh-Swiss Vinet, Barth acknowledged his ongoing influence in Germany and described him as a faithful student of Schleiermacher. Though Vinet did indeed consider homiletics to be a species of rhetoric, Barth explained that Vinet did not understand this to be a secularizing or paganizing of homiletics — it was more the reverse. Rhetoric in its truest, fullest form *is* homiletics, because the sea of faith and emotion that underlies all of natural life is itself already Christian if you swim down deep enough. The goal of preaching is to give expression to this deepest Christian being that wells up in the personality of the preacher and thus enables a connection between people. It is an ideal human speaking, Christian deep calling unto Christian deep. Naturally, a biblical text is not necessary for such speaking, though it may well be involved (K4-5, P6-7). Barth concluded his exposition of Vinet by pointing out a difference between Schleiermacher and Vinet, namely, that Vinet understood preaching to be necessary for both unbelievers (missionary preaching) and believers (*Gemeinde* preaching). Believers must constantly return to the truth that awakened them (K5, P7).

After his description of Vinet's homiletic, Barth turned his attention to another nineteenth-century figure influenced by Schleiermacher: Christian Palmer of Tübingen. Barth proceeded to parse Palmer's definition of preaching with the students: "Preaching is the offer of salvation by living witnesses in the name of God, a salvation which appeared and is now present for human beings in the person and work of Jesus Christ" (K5, P7). Barth pointed to the implied relationship in Palmer's definition between the objective fact of the appearance of Jesus Christ in history and the subjective "offer" of salvation that is made today. This offer is made by living personalities, since Jesus Christ appeared as a personality. Personality is thus the means by which salvation is presented, according to Palmer. The preacher, as representative of the *Gemeinde*, takes the Word already present in the spiritual personality of the *Gemeinde* and directs it to them, thus returning to them their original possession (K5, P7-8).

What did Hollaz, Schleiermacher, and Palmer have in common? The preacher is master of that which he proclaims. Barth was particularly troubled by the idea that, according to Palmer, the preacher can "offer" salvation. Is this not something like that which is offered in the altar sacrament in the Catholic Church? Does the Protestant preacher claim this ability? Barth told the students they should keep in mind that Palmer was a southern German and that the "power theology" of J. T. Beck was close by — a theology focused on action, not words. The preacher doesn't just *talk;* the preacher "offers" salvation. Here, Barth noted, "the Württemberg pietism rears its head" (K6, P8).[21]

But the most detailed analysis of the session came when Barth introduced the preaching definition formulated by C. I. Nitzsch: "A sermon is ongoing proclamation of the gospel for the edification *(Erbauung)* of the *Gemeinde* of the Lord, a proclamation of the Word of God mediated through texts of Holy Scripture, which happens in living connection to present conditions and by called witnesses" (K6, P8).

Barth led the class in a consideration of the key terms and phrases in Nitzsch's definition. "Ongoing proclamation" indicates Nitzsch's understanding that preaching is directed not only to those outside the faith but also to those "inside." The Word of God must be heard again and again. The church proclaims Christ *as Christ is mediated through Scripture;* preaching is not a matter of prophecy, but is biblically ordered speech. This biblically ordered speech is not indifferent to the situation of the hearer, however. The preacher's attention to the needs, circumstances, and longings of the hearer is an echo of the way God condescends to human beings. Only a preacher with a "full believing self-consciousness" — a born-again personality with an inner call to serve — can preach. The goal of preaching is *Erbauung,* the capturing and mobilization of people, the putting them to work, assembling them as stones that form a temple on the foundation that is Christ. *Erbauung* for Nitzsch was less a matter of knowledge or will or feeling than an attitude of love, an attitude that sustains hope and leads to repentance — that is, Christian self-consciousness (K6-7, P8-9).

As the session neared its conclusion, there was no time to press Nitzsch further, but it is clear by what Barth emphasized in Nitzsch that he found him particularly important for the students. Why? Nitzsch featured

---

21. Barth lectured on Beck in his "Protestant Theology in the Nineteenth Century" course, delivered in the winter semester of 1932-33 and continued in the summer semester of 1933. Because the course moved chronologically, Barth would not have talked about Beck until the summer session. See Karl Barth, *Protestant Theology in the Nineteenth Century: Its Background and History* (Grand Rapids: Eerdmans, 2002), pp. 602-10.

a preacher who is the servant of a *Gemeinde*, not its lord. He attends to the needs of the hearers, but not as a wise and triumphant prophet. Nitzsch assumed that preaching has to do with the Word of God, Jesus Christ, a Word that comes only indirectly as it is mediated by the Scriptures. On all these counts, Nitzsch offered a way forward as far as Barth was concerned. His critique would have to wait until the next session.

Session 3: November 22, 1932

The third session began with a return to Nitzsch's definition of preaching, this time in relation to those studied earlier in the course. What did Barth think Nitzsch had accomplished in relation to the other definitions? In contrast to Schleiermacher, Nitzsch recovered a difference between the Word of God and human words and the recognition that the preacher's task involves something beyond representation of the faith of the *Gemeinde*. In greater continuity with Schleiermacher, Nitzsch also offered an answer to the question left open in Hollaz: *Who* is able to rightly explicate and apply the Word of God in relation to concrete human situations? Nitzsch suggested that it is the *preacher* who possesses this ability — not by his office, but by virtue of his new being as a regenerated, born-again personality. A true believer. A "called witness" (K8, P11). What critique did Barth present to the students with regard to Nitzsch?

Barth's concerns with Nitzsch's formulation all have to do with the issue he raised from the beginning of the exercises: the question of the relationship between the preacher's identity, authority, and activity and the Godness of God.

First, Barth questioned Nitzsch's particular understanding of the preacher as "called witness." Is it true that the preacher can discern and wield the Word of God with confidence because of some divinely bestowed ontological purity? Is there any room for a Word of God that "presses" the preacher "to the ground"? Can the Word of God ever call the preacher and his preaching into question?

Second, Barth challenged Nitzsch's idea that the preacher, *like God*, can "condescend" to the people, diagnosing their circumstances with his superior knowledge of social, economic, and political issues and healing them with the medicine of the gospel. Does the preacher by virtue of his regenerated "being" really have this ability?

Third, Barth homed in on the goal that Nitzsch envisioned, the *Er-*

bauung (edification or building up) of the *Gemeinde*. Again, is the *preacher* able to build up the church — to know so confidently what the "building" should look and feel like and to cause such a construction with his explication and application (K9-10, P12-13)? Is this not what Barth thought Protestant preachers were claiming for themselves in the last years of Weimar — that they could construct a holy building with the stones of the German *Volk*? Even Nitzsch's description of the goal of *Erbauung* — "faith" — was abstracted from its basis in the concrete and ongoing relationship of human beings to God, Barth argued, and thus was reduced to psychological concepts (K11, P14).

Barth then led a discussion of the nature of Nitzsch's material homiletic, to the *Stoff* of the sermon, though it was not long before the problematic of the preacher's authority returned to center stage. Nitzsch claimed that the subject matter of preaching is the Word of God — but what did Nitzsch mean by "the Word of God"? He thought that the Word of God is something mediated *through* Holy Scripture, not Holy Scripture itself. But how, then, does the interpreter differentiate between the "husk" of the Bible and the Word of God mediated by it? Nitzsch's answer did not satisfy Barth. If the preacher possesses an inherent or infused ability to discern husk from kernel, wouldn't it put the preacher on the same level, "collegially," with the witness of the Scripture itself, deciding what is "Word of God" and what is not? Is it possible for such an interpreter — who has the "Word of God" already — to really listen to the witness of the prophets and apostles (K11, P13-14)?

Despite his recovery of key terms, Nitzsch invested the preacher and his (regenerated) personality with too much power, righteousness, and wisdom, Barth thought. It is hard to miss the indirect critique of Weimar proclamation in the aftermath of contentious church elections. Indeed, concerns regarding the identity, authority, and attitude of the preacher were the focus of nearly the entire session.

Session 4: November 29, 1932

The fourth class session was devoted to two more contemporary figures: Johannes Bauer, a representative of the "modern" preaching movement, and the Tübingen practical theologian Karl Fezer. Bauer's definition was presented to the students as a regression, Fezer's as instructive and full of potential. What factors led Barth to this conclusion?

In contrast to Nitzsch, Barth remarked to the students, Bauer was a "very lightly armed theologian" (K12). His theology of preaching was conceptually unclear, superficial, and verbose (K12, P15). This was so much the case, Barth observed, that it was difficult to find an actual definition of preaching in Bauer's writings. Rather, such a definition must be gleaned indirectly. Bauer was focused on the person of the preacher, his personality, his "life of faith." Such a preacher can and should influence the will of his hearers toward moral action and feeling by his "simple, convinced, inspired presentation of the life of faith itself" and with the faith that "radiates" from him. Bauer's preacher should engage the Bible because it "gives a certain security of witness and fruitfulness of thought" to his apologetic efforts. In all of this, Barth contended, Bauer represented a "catastrophic" regression (K12-13, P15-16). So much of what Nitzsch struggled to understand has disappeared from Bauer's homiletical landscape: the question of how to interpret the Bible, the relationship between explication and application, the basis of any of this in God's past, present, and promised activity (the *"Woher"* and the *"Wohin"*), the commission of the church — all were invisible to Bauer (K13, P17).

Barth wanted the students to know that Bauer was not an exception but was representative of his generation. Clarity and depth with regard to homiletics were not to be had in the prewar years, Barth explained, when systematic work was replaced by a passion for the soul of the individual, for experience, for "personality." The preacher and the preacher's plans and goals stand at the center of the enterprise, and it is not clear from Bauer whether anything objective stands behind this "overgrown subjectivity" (P16). Once again Barth marveled at the "astonishing confidence" that the preacher knows what is "beneficial" to his hearers, what they should "feel, imagine, and desire," and how "to bring it about." "Is that not an incredible claim?" Barth asked the students.

After this relentless critique of Bauer, Barth then put before his students an alternative to Bauer and the modern preaching movement with his introduction of the homiletic of Karl Fezer. Fezer's 1925 text *Das Wort Gottes und die Predigt* and his subsequent definition of preaching in *Die Religion in Geschichte und Gegenwart* (1930) constituted the basis of the discussion.[22] What did Barth praise in Fezer's definition of preaching?

---

22. The following quotations from Fezer are included in both sets of notes: "Preaching is the effort of a human being through free speech to cooperate, in order that the God who gives the Word of Scripture to his *Gemeinde* becomes corporately present in a cir-

First and foremost, Barth pointed out the way Fezer's definition decentered the person of the preacher. The preacher steps back. God is the one who acts, builds up, gives. The preacher simply tries to cooperate with — and, in the second, superior definition, obey — a God already at work through the power of the Holy Spirit, a divine work that involves not only the preacher but the *Gemeinde*. Instead of a preacher with plans and goals, Fezer described the preacher using the language of command and obedience. Instead of a prophet with a direct revelation to wield, Fezer recovered a witness who passes the (indirect) witness of the Scripture along to people here and now as a Word — an address — to and for them (P18).

In its decentering, dethroning, deweaponizing of the preacher, Barth argued, Fezer's definition was the "most excellent" of those they had considered (P19). Could even Fezer's strong definition be improved? That would be a question for the next session.

It was most likely in the course of this class meeting that Barth gave the students an assignment. They had parsed, tested, and debated a number of definitions of preaching. Now, Barth told them, they must write their own. He would refer to the definitions submitted by the students — all 110 of them — in the class meeting of December 6.[23]

---

cle of other people by the Holy Spirit" (K13, P17). "Preaching is the service commanded of the church to pass on the witness to revelation given to it in the Scriptures to the people of the present in obedience to the God acting with us in this Word of Scripture and in faith that this God in his grace and faithfulness in, with, and among their poor human words is present himself as the Living One and uses it to speak his own Word" (K13-14, P17).

23. Barth wrote to Thurneysen about his plan for the exercises, including the student definitions, as follows: "About my homiletic exercises Lollo has given you a preliminary report, and details will follow. The notes, which I was allowed to make from your notebook, were and are extremely valuable to me. But I have the concern to commit no plagiarism, to go about it somewhat otherwise: first an introduction to the entire problematic at hand [with] several examples from the older homiletics. (That has already its certain value. I should like to make you consider for example Nitzsch, with whom one can see, after all, how even the nineteenth century has grappled with the question which occupies us and is not simply begun with the names of Schleiermacher-Ritschl.) Subsequently then an investigation of the concept of preaching, which I allowed to be formulated by all 110 participants in writing, and not until and after discussion of the findings to bring forward my own concept (still somewhat different than in the new dogmatics, p. 56), whose nine constituent parts now form the basis for a homiletical axiomatic, which at the conclusion then the instructions to them: 'how does one make a sermon?' should follow." Karl Barth to Eduard Thurneysen, December 23, 1932, in Karl Barth, *Gesamtausgabe* V.34, pp. 322-23.

Karl Barth's Predigtvorbereitung *in Context: Winter Semester 1932-1933*

November 29, 1932, to January 24, 1933

Contextual Developments

In the days after Papen's resignation as chancellor, Hindenburg and his advisors tried again to persuade Hitler to accept a cabinet position, which they hoped would pull the country back from a civil war and harness the mass appeal of the Nazis for themselves. But Hitler would not cooperate, and cabinet member and Minister of Defense General Kurt von Schleicher was compelled to accept the position of chancellor himself on December 3.[24] He would not hold the position for long.

Meanwhile, Barth had long been troubled by the direction in which some of his dialectical associates were heading — especially Brunner and Gogarten — and his correspondence from this period demonstrates his escalating frustration with his *Zwischen den Zeiten* colleagues. Given the political situation, Barth felt increasing pressure to distance himself from the journal. In addition to his own misgivings about the direction his associates had taken, sometimes others urged him to make it clear where he stood. As Charlotte von Kirschbaum reported in a letter on January 3:

> Karl currently has difficult days in the thought of his theological friends: the echo between Brunner and Althaus (who yesterday also received a very renunciatory letter), the preoccupation with Gogarten's *Ethics*, everything makes him raw and in pain and shows him the isolation of his work and of his way. Yesterday evening Privatdozent Fuchs, a younger radical Württemberger, Schmidt's assistant, came over and objected to his [Barth's] present position, [saying] that going together (outwards!) with a Gogarten, a Brunner, yes, with the circle of authors of ZdZ was impossible and [could be] misunderstood in more dangerous ways.[25]

Brunner, in particular, fanned the flames still further with a second article on his "eristics" that appeared in December. Barth and Brunner ex-

---

24. The fact that Hitler refused to join the cabinet had actually become controversial within the National Socialist Party. Some in the party thought the Nazis should act immediately to secure a place in a coalition government. Hitler moved swiftly to remove Gregor Strasser, the leader of the dissenting group, and quash the rebellion. Evans, *Coming of the Third Reich,* pp. 302-3.

25. Charlotte von Kirschbaum to Eduard Thurneysen, January 3, 1933, in Barth, *Gesamtausgabe* V.34, p. 337.

changed tense letters during this period about Brunner's insistence that preachers must always begin by finding a "point-of-contact" in the "natural" existence of the hearer, among other things.[26]

On December 18, 1932, the fourth Sunday in Advent, Barth preached on Philippians 4:4-5 in the University *Schloßkirche*. That year there was no *"Schutz des inneren Friedens"* that called for a political "cease-fire" over the Christmas holidays as there had been in 1931. The political and church-political campaigning continued without mercy, and the street violence was unrelenting. This is surely the backdrop that Barth had in mind as he preached to the Bonn community:

> It is surely true: without joy in the Lord the old ritualistic dogmatism of everyone against everything undoubtedly remains, with that deadly seriousness with which the so-called good people embitter one another's lives still a good deal more than the so-called evil people and serves to make the world as [a] hell in the name of ideals, sometimes even Christian ideals, consciously or unconsciously controlled by a reciprocal war of extermination.[27]

Session 5: December 6, 1932

The session began with a return to Karl Fezer's definition of preaching. Barth moved phrase by phrase, raising a number of questions for the class to consider. Did Fezer's idea of "passing along" or "transmitting" the witness to revelation still imply that the church or the preacher has something "in hand," something it controls? Did Fezer need to be more specific when he refered to "Scripture" in relation to the sermon? Is it only Scripture "as a whole" the sermon engages, i.e., a sort of "general" revelation so characteristic of "theme preaching," or should a sermon engage a particular, concrete passage of Scripture even as it materially includes the "whole"? Had Fezer adequately distinguished the differences between preaching and the other forms of church proclamation (instruction and *Seelsorge*)? Had Fezer said enough with his description of the hearers as "people of the

---

26. See for example Emil Brunner to Karl Barth, December 13, 1932; Karl Barth to Emil Brunner, January 10, 1933; Emil Brunner to Karl Barth, January 16, 1933. The exchange may be found in Barth, *Gesamtausgabe* V.33, pp. 210-22.

27. Barth, *Gesamtausgabe* I.31, p. 282.

present"? Is one not primarily, primally made a hearer by *God's* acceptance, by *God's* placing one in the church rather than by virtue of one's context? Fezer distinguished between "God's Word" and our "poor human word," Barth observed, but perhaps a definition should not look back to the preposterous nature of human words, but forward (on the basis of God's justifying grace) to God's promise to speak in human words (K14, P20, 21).

At the end of this detailed dissection of Fezer's statements, Barth invited the students to think with him about what factors *should* be included in an adequate definition of preaching as they moved forward. He put forth nine possibilities, which he told them he had gleaned not only from the definitions discussed in the course thus far but also from the definitions *they* individually submitted. These were the issues that emerged again and again, he told them: revelation/Word of God, the church, the divine command, the office of the preacher, the nature of preaching as an "attempt," Scripture, the idea that preaching is "one's own speech," the *Gemeinde*, and the Holy Spirit (K14, P22).

In the final moments of the session, the class debated whether or not these nine things should always have a place in a definition of Christian preaching and if there were other critical factors not represented in the nine. As the student protocol stated, these questions "could not be resolved" in their discussion (P22).

In this session we see Barth's characteristic teaching style — the class moved inductively to these nine elements, and Barth had the students make their own attempt at a definition before advancing a possibility of his own. Even as he worked to unsettle them with regard to the homiletical dogma they had learned from, say, Pfennigsdorf, he did so without simply attempting an indoctrination of his own. He encouraged them to think for themselves and made a point of engaging their ideas.

Session 6: December 13, 1932

The sixth class meeting began with what seems to be a strange structural detour. Instead of proceeding with his own attempt at a definition and the subsequent exploration of the nine factors suggested at the end of the previous session, Barth turned instead to yet another preaching definition from a contemporary, this time Professor Leonhard Fendt of Berlin.[28] The

---

28. Leonhard Fendt (1881-1957) was professor of practical theology in Berlin. For

abrupt turn to Fendt is something of a mystery. Fendt was not as well known as Bauer and Fezer, and he had not published much directly related to the question at hand. So why would Barth pause to consider him at this point in the exercises? A clue can be found in Charlotte von Kirschbaum's notes on the session, in which she recorded that the meeting began with a discussion, perhaps initiated by the students, of the "guidelines for sermon evaluation" used in Prussian *Prediger* seminars, where most of the students would be examined. The existence of these particular (presumably superficial and problematic) "guidelines," Barth contended, was the reason they must concentrate on the "basic" questions of preaching in their time together. This was precisely what Barth told John McConnachie in his letter of January 1931.[29] As for Fendt, Kirschbaum's account suggests that the definition from Fendt may have been brought forward for consideration by a student as part of this less formal opening discussion.[30] But regardless of who initiated the discussion of Fendt's understanding of preaching, Barth was largely appreciative of his approach.[31] Fendt, like Fezer, was "standing on the ground of a theology that takes God seriously" (P22).

There were certainly problems with Fendt's formulation — the exclusion of the Old Testament, the "sloppy" rhetoric of making the kerygma "palatable" — but many of the key elements of a comprehensive definition were present. And as Barth returned to the question of the sufficiency of the nine constitutive factors put forth in the last meeting, he wondered aloud why the Protestant church in Germany in the 1930s had no authoritative word to say about the nature and basis of its preaching. There was no guide, no directive, no consensus from the church. It was "certainly a state

---

more information on Fendt, see Karl-Friedrich Wiggermann, "Leonhard Fendt als Lehrer der praktischen Theologie in Berlin," in *Zwischen Volk und Bekenntnis* (Leipzig: Evangelische Verlagsanstalt, 2000), pp. 151-66.

29. For an account of Barth's correspondence with McConnachie, see Chapter Four of this study.

30. According to Kirschbaum, the definition of Fendt was read out from a manuscript procured by a student (K15). The source of the definition is not named, something unusual for her.

31. Fendt's definition of preaching reads: "Protestant preaching is the form of Protestant worship in which a Christian, trained academically therefore and called by the *Gemeinde* thereto, makes the Christian kerygma, as it is presented in the New Testament, palatable to the people of his time in their manner, but without damage to the substance of the kerygma or to seek to make additions, not from pedagogical, aesthetic or other humanly meaningful reasons, but because the Christian kerygma is the Word, in which the promise is in force that the Holy Spirit will effect faith, where and when it pleases God" (K15, P22).

Karl Barth's Predigtvorbereitung in Context: Winter Semester 1932-1933

of emergency," Barth said (K16). Theologians and pastors had to figure this out for themselves, without guidance from the Protestant church. The church, Barth said, was like Nebuchadnezzar, who not only wanted his dream to be interpreted but also wanted to be told what he had dreamed in the first place.[32] In the absence of the starting place a Protestant doctrine of preaching would have provided, theologians were forced to start from scratch. And yet, Barth asked the students, could things be completely hopeless, even in this regard, when three Protestant theologians — Fezer, Fendt, and Barth himself — from such different "schools" of theology, could generate definitions of preaching with a high degree of common ground (K16, P23-24)? With this, Barth introduced his own "attempt" at a definition of preaching.

Barth's definition consists of two statements, neither of which is complete without the other. Each one describes the same activity, but from a different perspective. One begins from "above," the other from "below" (K17, P24). All nine "elements" are present in both. Barth's dialectical definition reads thus:

> a. Preaching is God's Word spoken by God's own Self, laying claim to a person called to do so in the church obedient to its commission, who proceeds in free speech to interpret a biblical text to the people of the present.
>
> b. Preaching is the attempt commanded of the church to serve the Word of God by a person called to do so, in which a biblical text is interpreted in free speech to the people of the present as directly concerning them, as an announcement of what they have to hear from God's own Self. (K17, P24)

The question of the nature and basis of preaching cannot be answered undialectically; indeed, it cannot really be *answered* at all, Barth explained to the students. A theologian can only circle around its center, erecting signposts, pointing fingers toward its reality. The Subject of preaching remains Subject. Alive. It cannot be contained in a concept (K17, P24-25).

Behind the two sentences of his definition, Barth argued, there lies a third, irreducible one, "the decisive sentence of the divinity and humanity

---

32. Barth made this same comparison in other contexts. See for example Karl Barth, *The Göttingen Dogmatics: Instruction in the Christian Religion*, vol. 1, ed. Hannelotte Reiffen, trans. Geoffrey W. Bromiley, 1st English ed. (Grand Rapids: Eerdmans, 1991), p. 40.

of Jesus Christ" (K17, P25). To define preaching places us before the same difficulty we face when speaking the name Jesus Christ: the question of the unity of the divine and the human. As such, for theologian and preacher alike, there can only be broken speaking — a knowing not-knowing or a not-knowing knowing (K18). The decentering continues.

Barth responded to a few comments and questions about his definition in the remainder of the session; he would begin to work his way through the nine constitutive elements beginning the following week.

Session 7: December 20, 1932

The seventh session was the first of two devoted to thinking through the consequences of the first of the nine "elements" introduced on December 6: the relationship between preaching and revelation. Sermons, Barth argued, must be tempered, shaped, *qualified* by God's Self-disclosure.[33]

What did this mean for these young preachers? Negatively, Barth told them, it means that preachers do *not* repeat or transmit the revelation of God in the sermon. Preachers are, in all circumstances, to recognize that God has revealed himself in Jesus Christ and will reveal Godself again — as the one that is to come. Here in this space between the first and second Advents, we do not conjure up Christ, who only arrives as God's action. Therefore, preachers do not try to mediate the truth of God by trying to *prove* God via an intellectual demonstration, or trying to paint an aesthetic picture of Jesus before the eyes of the hearers. Nor can a preacher aspire to create the *reality* of God: to convert or to build the Kingdom of God or to confront people with a decision or even to expose the existential situation of the hearer and hence place her before God[34] (K19, P26-27). Barth knew that to reject such intentions was swimming against the current. He referred to the well-known slogans of the modern preaching movement: preachers must progress from "mere word" to "reality," from doctrine to "life"; they must be "lively" and "convey an experience" (P27).

---

33. The English translation of the student notes in *Homiletics* (1991) renders *Offenbarungsmässigkeit* as "to conform to revelation." "Conformity" is perhaps too restrictive a term for *Mässigkeit*. *Mässigkeit* is literally "temperedness" in English. To be tempered by something is to be shaped, influenced, or qualified by something else, but not to be completely determined by it. See Karl Barth, *Homiletics*, trans. G. W. Bromiley and D. E. Daniels (Louisville: Westminster John Knox, 1991), p. 47.

34. This is clearly a reference to Brunner's program of "eristics."

Karl Barth's Predigtvorbereitung in Context: Winter Semester 1932-1933

But genuine hearing, experiencing, or awakening is something that only *God* can do, Barth argued. It may happen, it does happen, but not because a preacher set out with a plan, a system, a program to bring it about. If we believe that God is a living, acting God — that God is God — then there is no place for our "prophetic booming" (P27). All we can do is make an attempt, expecting God to speak. And preaching that grows out of this expectation is an interpretation of something beyond a preacher's plans and goals and programs: Holy Scripture. Such interpretation, Barth told the students, will not set out with a theme or *Skopus* in hand nor approach the task with the intent to produce a certain mood or action in the hearers. Preaching that is revelation-tempered is not talking *about* the Bible, not *using* it, but listening to its witness, pointing where it points, "speaking after"[35] it (K20).

The preacher, Barth insisted, must stand under the "constraint" of this *Offenbarungsmässigkeit*, coming to listen with empty hands (P27). What a contrast to the sermons many of these students would have heard week after week: sermons that confidently advanced a Protestant *seelsorgerlich* or nationalist agenda, engaging the Scriptures as a means to some predetermined, unquestioned end. Surely most would have encountered Protestant pastors who exploited their influence as opinion leaders of their *Gemeinden* — the "popes" that Barth railed against here (P28). This kind of approach, Barth told the class, is a concrete expression of the denial of the Godness of God.

Session 8: January 10, 1933

After a three-week Christmas hiatus, and in the midst of political uncertainty, the "sermon exercises" resumed, and Barth returned to the question of the *Offenbarungsmässigkeit* of preaching. In the last session they had primarily discussed how the Godness of God ruled out certain approaches to the task of preaching; now Barth wanted to explore what commitment to the *Offenbarungsmässigkeit* of preaching rules in, affirms, authorizes, and why.

---

35. In the English text published as Barth's *Homiletics* (1991), the word *"nachzusage"* is translated "to repeat," i.e., "to repeat" the witness of Scripture. But *nachzusage* does not exactly mean "repeat." To "speak after" something, as to "think after" something, allows for a degree of participation and creativity that is lacking in the term "repeat." Karl Barth, *Homiletics*, p. 49.

The fact that God has revealed and will reveal God's own self is not incidental but constitutive of the existence of a preacher, Barth explained (K20, P28). The preacher is called into being as a preacher by this happening (the Word became flesh) and the promise of it happening again (come, Lord Jesus). Preaching is a "speaking-after" the "yes" of Jesus Christ who came and will come again, a speaking *von Gott aus*. Two consequences flow from this existence between the first advent and the second.

First, though preachers are constantly tempted to proclaim the sins of people instead of the "yes" of God — the law severed from the gospel — preaching that is tempered by revelation always goes "downhill" *(Gefälle)* from "the Word became flesh." God *has* reconciled Godself to humanity in Christ. Preachers do not need to drag the hearers uphill to get to the gospel; there is no need for "tormented attempts" to bring the hearer to Christ (a likely reference to Brunner's laborious "eristics," among other things). Revelation-tempered preaching recognizes that Christ has already come near, that these sinners are already forgiven sinners (K21, P30). The recognition that preaching is "downhill" cannot be translated into yet another call for greater enthusiasm, piety, or honesty from the preacher (P31).

Second, the "downhill" *(Wohin)* takes place in the wide horizon of an eschatological *Woher*.[36] Preaching that begins on the mountain top of the affirmation "the Word became flesh" cannot rest there contentedly but leads forward expectantly, full of hope that what happened will happen again. Preaching between the *Wohin* of the Incarnation and the *Woher* of eschatology, like the Christian life itself, can "in no case mean a being-at-ease, a being-secure" but is in its assurance at the same time "the deepest un-security and un-ease," a "having" that is simultaneously a "full-fledged trembling not-having," a "wealth" that is "poverty" (K22). The Christian "strides" back and forth between the having and not having, "living in faith and not in sight." This longing for Jesus Christ as the coming one — the deepest unsecurity and unease — must be the "secret center" of Christian preaching. And this, Barth told his mostly Lutheran audience, is something that Lutheran preachers with their "overconfident insistence on the event that lies behind us" need to be reminded of again and again (P33, K22). We still "walk in darkness" though we have seen a great light (P33).

Offenbarungsmässigkeit as a criterion for preaching is the deep back-

---

36. *Wohin* and *Woher* are rather awkward to translate into contemporary English. Literally *Wohin* means "whither" (from where something came) and *Woher* means "whence" (to where something is going).

ground, the acknowledgment of the *Realdialektik*, the Godness of God, that grounds the rest of the nine elements and indeed everything that Barth would say for the remainder of the exercises. Barth would spend more class time on *Offenbarungsmässigkeit* than on any other element of the nine he compiled — and he would refer to it again and again.

Offenbarungsmässigkeit with its dialectical affirmation of the "downhill" and the "empty hands" offers resistance to *seelsorgerlich*, propagandistic, and nationalistic preaching on two fronts: first, the rejection of apologetics as integral to the task of preaching, especially the pursuit of a "point of contact" in some "natural" aspect of human existence, be it existential, psychological, historical, national, or *völkisch*; and second, the insistence that preachers do not "have" Jesus Christ, the gospel (nor the witness to it). God, gospel, Scripture, "Spirit" cannot be deployed as a means to some other end. With the acknowledgement of empty hands comes the humility, openness, and attentiveness that Barth found lacking among the Pfennigsdorfs of late Weimar.

Session 9: January 17, 1933

In the ninth (and part of the tenth) meeting of the *Predigtvorbereitung*, Barth moved to the second element that must be considered in a definition of preaching: its "where." If the activity of preaching begins from the fact and promise of revelation, then it is already "placed" in a particular situation, a concrete event, and that event is "church." The practice of preaching is not what it *is (Offenbarungsmässigkeit)* in relation to some other context — existence itself, one's "natural" or historical situation. The context of preaching is not established by some philosophy or worldview, nor is its location in the event "church" something preachers can create by a technique or ability. "It does not lie in our hands," Barth said. Preachers do not set out to decide the "where" of preaching by selecting from among philosophical, political, or aesthetic options. We "simply see ourselves inexorably led" to the "only place where we can still stand" — that is, church (K23, P34).

What is in this "space" God prepares? It is, according to Barth, an ontological togetherness, a being-in-Christ, that qualifies every other kind of commitment that people have on earth: family, marriage, *Volk*, race, and so forth.[37] In the church, these kinds of bonds "are unmasked as unpure, as

---

37. Barth called these "creation-tempered" (vs. revelation-tempered).

poisoned, as immersed in the sphere of the fall and judged as such" (K24, P34). The bond that is forged in the event "church" is "absolutely superior" to them. The damage that flows from such earthly commitments can only be healed by the word of reconciliation that constitutes church. Only then and there, in that being-reconciled-in-Christ-being, can created-being be recognized, and that only "insofar as the message of creation is included within the message of reconciliation" (K24, P34). The direct critique of the nationalist Protestant and *völkisch* theology is unmistakable. To describe commitment to the *Volk* as "unpure" and "poisoned" was unheard of — riots had erupted in other university classrooms for much less. But Barth pressed on.

How does "church" happen? When the Word of revelation is heard, there is church — the *kyrie ekklesia*, the congregation of those "called out by the Lord." In the calling and the hearing, we are planted in church. This is where the Word of double advent comes, and this "happening" is where preachers bear witness to the witnesses to this Word.

Barth then turned to the question of the relationship among preaching, *Offenbarungsmässigkeit*, church, and the sacraments, beginning with the claim of Article VII of the Augsburg Confession, that the church is where "the gospel is purely taught and the sacraments rightly administered." It was an extensive discussion that continued into the next class meeting, and we will only note here that Barth identified the sacraments as the signs of the first Advent (baptism) and the second (the Lord's Supper) and stressed that, contrary to the Protestant practice of the day, preaching and sacrament must not be separated. Preaching is itself both a sign (sacrament) and an interpretation of the signs baptism (the "downhill") and Lord's Supper ("Come, Lord Jesus") (K24-25, P37).[38]

In his explicit connection between baptism and the "downhill" (which requires no apologetic scheming) and between the Lord's Supper and the "empty hands" of eschatological longing, Barth made it clear that the sacraments are also *Offenbarungsmässigkeit*, and thus his discussion of them continued and deepened his relentless decentering of the Protestant preacher. The insistence that preaching can only happen in the event "church" must be read in contrast to the claims of the Political Theologians, i.e., that preaching should be directed to the *Volk* or the *Volksgemeinschaft*, not the "church" per se, especially not "church" defined in

---

38. Preaching, baptism (the "sacrament of grace"), and the Lord's Supper (the "sacrament of hope") all point to the same thing — but preaching points with *words* (K24, P36).

actualistic terms. Many Protestant leaders desperately wanted to speak to the soul of the *nation,* just as they had when the church pews were overflowing in the heady days of 1914. Given the political developments of the weeks after this class meeting, it looked like Protestant preachers would soon have that chance again.

Session 10: January 24, 1933

The session began with a return to the question of "church" as the context of preaching and the sacraments, with Barth adding to this constellation of elements Holy Scripture. If the sacraments point the church to the "that" of revelation (that it happened and will happen again), he told the students, then the Scripture of the Old and New Testaments points the church to the "what" of revelation. God reveals Godself in the middle of human life and history, not generally, but particularly. Therefore, Holy Scripture is required as witness to that particularity of revelation, and the church is founded on the basis of that witness, the witness of the prophets and apostles. Holy Scripture in its concreteness shows that the church does not live for itself or from itself; it does not possess its "own free life," but springs from the absolutely unique event of God's revealing. Israel and Christ are the focal points of revelation, what happened *happened,* once, uniquely. To acknowledge this is to acknowledge Holy Scripture, to embrace its "constriction" (K26-27, P38).

What is the alternative to revelation as the particularity Israel-Christ-Scripture-church? A conception of revelation that begins generally with God and humanity, God and "existence," God and creation, God and "history," God and "*Volk,*" Barth argued (K27, P39). But it is not a matter of choosing among such generalities, Barth told the students. Christians assume the church is the place "where the Bible is opened." We do not choose it; revelation chooses us, gives us a commission, a command, a witness. As such, the church's preachers testify to this revelation that constitutes "church" by attending to what has been given, by "speaking-after" the gift. How would it be possible for preachers to "emancipate themselves" from the Bible, any more than a father could emancipate himself from his children (K27-28, P38-39)? Thus, Barth summarized, preaching happens in the event "church," in the presence of the sacrament (that) and the Scripture (what).

With this, Barth moved to the discussion of the third of the nine constitutive elements of a preaching definition, namely, the way preaching is shaped by what he called "confession" *(Bekenntnismässigkeit)*. What he meant by this can best be understood by attention to his fairly extensive discussion of what it *(Bekenntnismässigkeit)* does *not* mean. It does not mean a church that engages in proclamation in order to accomplish some other goal, even the "best" goal. Preaching does not set out with a plan to educate, or to "prop up" the world, to promote "progress," to be an instrument for "old things" or "new things." Preaching is not "an ambulance on the battlefield of life," nor can it strive to establish an "ideal *Gemeinschaft*," whether this is understood as an intellectual, emotional, or spiritual community (P40). A church that preaches "cultural goals" has "forfeited" its true being (K28). Barth told the students that he understood the value of such things, and that because pastors and Christians are human beings in the world, they cannot help but desire its improvement. But these kinds of things cannot be the goal of the church's proclamation; and when they are, its sermons become superfluous. "That is especially clear today," Barth observed (P40). All the public tasks of culture, life, morality, the "soul," and the family have been addressed by "the children of the world" with their newspapers and radio broadcasts and politics. The church becomes one more dilettante on the public stage, a "fifth wheel on the wagon" (P40). The one thing Protestant leaders desperately wanted to establish — that the church (as the guardian of the soul of the nation) is essential for a strong, united Germany — is here utterly rejected.

Preaching that is shaped by confession, in contrast, means to respond to an imperative "which exists like the fact of our birth and our death" (K28, P40). That imperative is the command, the call. Barth quoted the apostle Paul: "Woe is me, if I do not proclaim the gospel." "He does not have a plan, but a task," Barth commented (P40). "Confession" in this sense is not the expression of what is inside us or what we might dream up looking at existence generally speaking, but it is the response to what is given in revelation, to the call, to the command. Preaching that is *Bekenntnismässigkeit* comes from listening, receiving, and being placed in the event "church" (P41).

Barth ends the session by exploring two practical consequences of confession-tempered preaching. First, while it does not mean literally preaching the church's creeds (e.g., Augsburg), preaching *is* a confession of the *church's* credo. Creeds, confessions, dogma are *symbols* that acknowledge and testify "we have heard"; as such, they are a limit and goal that the preacher should respect (K29).

Second, to grant preaching the character of confession has implications for the longstanding belief that preaching should edify or "build up" the congregation. Barth did not discourage this intention but radically qualified it. Whatever it means to say that people are "edified" by preaching, it cannot be something like the vision of *The Shepherd of Hermas*, in which the church is a tower rising higher and higher, consisting of the "stones" of the faithful believers (K29, P41).[39] Plenty of Protestant leaders at the time had visions of "building up" the church further and further: numerically, morally, and in its power and influence in German society.

In contrast, Barth reinterpreted the language of "edification" in actualistic terms. The church is built anew every time it hears and responds to revelation, and preachers are called to serve this hearing and responding. "Edifying" proclamation that includes things like education, helping others, and participating in culture may come by the grace of God, but only there in the space revelation creates again and again.[40] "Seek ye first the kingdom of God," Barth told the young preachers, "thus will everything else fall to you" (K30).

January 24 to February 21, 1933

Contextual Developments

The new Reich Chancellor Schleicher, like others around President Hindenburg, had every intention of dismantling Weimar democracy as soon as possible. Schleicher knew he did not have the parliamentary support necessary to put his plans in motion, so he asked the president to grant him the extra-constitutional powers he needed to establish an authoritarian state, put the army in charge, and suppress both the Nazis and the Communists.[41]

But Hindenburg balked. This left Schleicher's hands tied, and seeing no way forward, he resigned. Behind the scenes, those unhappy with Schleicher had been making the case for a Hitler chancellorship. These conspirators, conservatives but by no means National Socialists, thought

---

39. The *Shepherd* is a second-century apocalyptic Christian text. The author refers to himself as Hermas.
40. "In the shadows little huts may also be built" (P41).
41. Evans, *Coming of the Third Reich*, p. 306.

that by making Hitler chancellor (but surrounding him with a cabinet dominated by conservatives) they would effectively control him.[42] In this they were badly mistaken.

At eleven-thirty in the morning on January 30, 1933, Hitler took the oath and assumed the office of Reich Chancellor of Germany — an event that became known as the *Machtergreifung*.[43] Normally, such a governmental shift would not have attracted much attention; after all, the government changed all too regularly during the course of the Weimar Republic. But with Hitler's ascension to chancellor, celebrations broke out all over Germany, most notably in Berlin, which featured a torchlight parade with anywhere from 20,000 to 61,000 participants and many more observers.[44] There were also some scattered protests, especially by Communists and labor groups, though the police moved quickly to quell such activities. Some people were unsure exactly what Hitler's new position would mean, thinking (like many in the cabinet) that this move would serve to contain rather than unleash Hitler.[45]

But for countless German nationalists this turn of events evoked a euphoria they had not known since the first days of the Great War. Speaking on the radio, Hermann Göring declared that the mood on the streets "could only be compared with that of August 1914. . . . The Spirit of 1914 had been revived."[46]

What, if anything, changed in the weeks immediately after Hitler became chancellor? Hitler was indeed outnumbered by the conservatives in the cabinet. But the three particular cabinet positions the Nazis did hold (Chancellor, Reich Minster of the Interior, and Prussian Minister of the Interior) gave them a strategic advantage, especially in view of the next Reichstag election, slated for March 5. What Hitler had, from the end of January forward, was nearly unstoppable influence over the administration of "law and order" in Germany, and it was not long before he had managed to neutralize the army as well.

---

42. Evans, *Coming of the Third Reich*, p. 306.

43. *Machtergreifung* means "seizure of power." In reality, Hitler's ascension to the position of chancellor marked the beginning of an eight-week *process* in which a dictatorship was established in Germany, one that culminated in the Enabling Act of March 23, 1933.

44. The estimate from a pro-Nazi newspaper was a fantastical 700,000. Evans, *Coming of the Third Reich*, p. 310. There was also a torchlight procession in the streets of Bonn. See Hinz-Wessels, *Kirchengemeinde Bonn*, p. 65.

45. Evans, *Coming of the Third Reich*, p. 315.

46. Evans, *Coming of the Third Reich*, p. 311.

Karl Barth's Predigtvorbereitung in Context: Winter Semester 1932-1933

In practical terms this meant that the National Socialists were able to use violence and terror against their political enemies without fear of reprisal. Now Communists, Social Democrats, and sometimes members of the Centre Party found themselves facing formal bans on their public meetings, censorship of their newspapers, and raids of their party headquarters and private homes, not to mention all the "unofficial" violence and mayhem inflicted upon them by marauding brownshirts.[47]

Barth was sick in bed with the flu on the day Hitler became chancellor. He would later recall that on that day it was clear to him that the German people were "beginning to worship a false god."[48] He decided it was time he read *Mein Kampf*.

The day after the *Machtergreifung* Barth met with Albert Lempp, owner of Christian Kaiser Verlag, to try to put an end to *Zwischen den Zeiten*. Barth reluctantly agreed to continue for the time being on the condition that the names of the editors were removed. For the remainder of the journal's existence, Barth's name would appear only on his own articles.[49]

Session 11: February 7, 1933

Who is the preacher? In relation to others in the church, what distinguishes the individual who preaches? How can one know if the practice of an individual taking on the role "preacher" is "legitimate" or if a given preacher is "authentic" as such? These are the questions Barth explored the week after the *Machtergreifung*, and their answers comprise the fourth of the nine factors of a definition of preaching laid out in early December. First was the claim that preaching be "tempered" by the fact of revelation, then that it be "tempered" by "church" and "confession," and now Barth argued that preaching is somehow "tempered" by the "office" occupied by the preacher *(Amtsmässigkeit)*. What did Barth mean by "office" in this context?

In the space-event "church," an individual steps out as an expression of the church's response to its commission, Barth explained, and this individual steps out to "lay down a witness of the reconciliation and salvation

---

47. Evans, *Coming of the Third Reich*, pp. 317-20.
48. Eberhard Busch, *Karl Barth: His Life from Letters and Autobiographical Texts* (Philadelphia: Fortress, 1976), p. 223.
49. Busch, *Karl Barth*, pp. 223-24.

of people happening with God in Christ" (K31). What makes this "stepping out" by the preacher *legitimate?* That is what was discussed in the context of the "office-temperedness" of preaching.

Barth argued that the question of "office" cannot be separated from the question of the existence of the church and the apostles — both are "church," but one is "teaching church" *(ecclesia docens)* and the other "hearing church" *(ecclesia audiens).* Where "church" is, there will be an analogy to that first teaching and hearing, though Barth was quick to point out that this cannot be a "repetition," since the appointment of the apostles was a "unique event" (K31, P42). Yet there must be people in succession who do what the apostles did initially and uniquely. This pattern/ordering of teaching and hearing is lived out by preachers as office-bearers in a second-order way, doing in a particular *Gemeinde* what the apostles did for the whole church (K31, P42). Any questions about the nature and character of this office, Barth explained, can be asked only in light of the question that is put to the church again and again in every time and place: whether it is the church of Jesus Christ, that is, whether there exists in it "the relationship of speaking and hearing as a speaking and hearing of God's own self-speaking through the mouth of the office-bearer and a hearing of God's Word by the Holy Spirit" (K32, P43). Any other criteria we put forth to identify the *authenticity* of the office or office-bearer are thus rendered relative (K32, P43).

Having carefully noted their limitations, Barth proceeded to set out four of these "relative" criteria. First, the preacher should feel called to this task ("I can do no other!"), even though this "feeling" will be laced with doubts. Preachers must always wonder if the compulsion to be a preacher is not simply a disguised form of one's own wish rather than the calling of God. While the calling of God should be accompanied by an inner desire to preach, our feeling and "knowing" that we are called cannot itself be identified with God's calling (K32, P43). The implication is that preachers exist as preachers by faith, not by sight. It is another form of the "having" that is also, again and again, a "not-having."

Second, when the pastoral epistles discuss bishops and deacons, they include "Hellenistic catalogues of virtue" that make it clear that those who hold such offices should be respectable people who do not "incriminate" their office by defying prevalent customs and morals. Barth told his students that preachers should not participate "boisterously" in the "all-too-human" things of the world. To do so is to draw attention to the preacher in "unnecessary ways," thereby "distracting" others from "the goodness of the gospel." Barth was not specific about what "all-too-human" behaviors he had in mind, though it is illuminating to recall that there was plenty of "boisterous" participation by nationalist Protestant pastors in the political chest-pounding that marked the end of Weimar. What Barth did tell these students is that the bearer of the office "preacher" should be someone who lives life "in the light of God" and "before God," as one who is "claimed" by God. This of course can only be an "obedience" in disobedience; it can only be the obedience of one justified "in Christ" (K32-33, P43-44).

Third, the pastoral epistles designated office-bearers as *"didaktikoi"* (teachers), and therefore the church regularly requires that its preachers have academic training for their task. This is in no way a denial of the primary and essential role of the Holy Spirit as Teacher. Preachers "with all humility and seriousness" should "wrestle," doing the theological work in an effort to "direct the Word rightly," even as the preacher knows such right teaching can become a reality only by the power of the Holy Spirit (K33, P44).

Fourth, in contrast to the apostles, the preacher is called to a particular place by the will of a particular *Gemeinde*. The calling of the preacher by a *Gemeinde* is therefore one of the criteria of the office. Nonetheless, the call of a *Gemeinde* does not amount to the call of God (K33, P44).

After the discussion of these four criteria, Barth returned to the question of their relativity in relation to the call of God that constitutes the being of the preacher. Barth thought it important that these criteria be *relative* — this relativity has implications for these young preachers. The preacher, the office-bearer, is not to promote his own interests, his "appetites" and "opinions of his will"; he is not "to serve the ideas and movements of his time," but instead to respond to his commission by making the testimony "God has spoken and God will speak" visible (K33-34, P44).

In spite of the continuing and irremovable "questionableness" and "impossibility" of preaching, if it is shaped by the "office" in these ways, preacher and hearers can have a certain "confidence" that it has pleased God to speak in this way. A preacher can venture to do this work "in simple obedience," in the faith that God has commanded it. This kind of preaching can be marked by "simplicity and relevance," Barth said, but there can be no definitive characteristics. Even the ever-popular criterion of "success" — i.e., a movement or awakening occurring in a *Gemeinde* — cannot be a criterion of the office, he told the class. The only "success" that matters is the speaking and hearing of the Word of God, a happening that is not available for our assessment (K34, P45). What would this have sounded like in those days right after the *Machtergreifung*, when "the Spirit of 1914" was back in the air and emotions ran high?

Session 12: February 14, 1933

In the twelfth meeting of the *Predigtvorbereitung*, Barth continued to work his way through the nine elements. With the fifth of these, what he called the "provisionality" of preaching, Barth told the students that they were making a transition from those elements primarily viewed in the context of the *justification* of the practice of preaching (revelation, church, commission, office) to those primarily grappling with the question of its *sanctification*. The fifth element ("provisionality") inquires as to the meaning and implication of preaching understood as an *attempt* that the church is commanded to make. The idea of the human side of preaching as "provisional" and "an attempt" should be considered not only as something negative, a limit, but also as something *positive*. "Provisionality," he told the students, means that the preacher is "sent out ahead" of something else, that the preacher points to something that will follow. It is in this context, this positive sense, that Barth evoked the image of the herald *(keryx)*, who "runs ahead" of the monarch (K36, P47). What the herald says is "provisional" because the king is still on the way. Preaching, like the herald running ahead, is a human action, but one that is commanded, blessed, and given with a promise of something more. To inquire regarding the meaning of preaching *as a human action* is to turn to ethics, to a "law" of preaching, to the question of the "sanctification" of this human attempt, this "running ahead" in the promise that God will speak.

Not surprisingly, Barth began the discussion of preaching as a human action by underlining that human beings are themselves neither capable of this task nor worthy of God. The justification of the preacher's stepping out (considered under the loci revelation, church, commission, office) is not a transformation of the human, not some sort of endowment or "infusion" of a new nature. Justification is the light of God shining on the untransformed human being. The elimination of the "contradiction" of the old (untransformed) being and the new being in Christ will not take place until redemption; here and now we live by the promise of it. Preaching *as human action* remains under judgment. The preacher can rely on no human ability or virtue, Barth argued. It is only *von Gott aus*, from God who makes the dead alive, who calls the non-being into being —

only by the miracle of God's grace that human action is justified. It is in this way that the human attempt to preach can be understood as a "good work," insofar as it happens under God's command, blessing, and promise (K37, P47). God takes this inadequate (impossible!) human attempt *as good work*. The "law" of preaching can be read only in light of this, its gospel. "A pardoned sinner is called out to proclaim God's Word," Barth told the students (K37, P48).

The "goodness" of this action is not some virtue of the preacher, but the faith of an undeserving person who turns to the mercy and goodness of God (K37, P48). Sanctification means that our existence as the undeserving, turning-to-God-person is claimed, captivated, "imprisoned," and "confiscated." The question of "how" then to preach or with what attitude to preach is not really a question of how preaching can be a "good" attempt but how preaching can be a "claimed" attempt (K38).[50]

Barth began his response to the question of what "claimed" preaching is like by turning to the sixth of the nine constitutive elements of a definition of preaching: its intimate, inextricable relationship to the witness of the Bible. Why is this intimacy necessary? If we look again at the first four elements of preaching — at its justification — we find ourselves placed again before Holy Scripture, Barth observed: Scripture witnesses to *revelation*, it founds the *church*, it gives the *commission*, it issues the call to *office* (K39, P49-50).

The activity of human beings who exist in this justification can take place only in the context of listening and understanding and explaining and "speaking-after" Scripture, the concrete basis of the being "preacher." This means, Barth insisted, that preaching cannot be the presentation of the preacher's own "system," that is, what he knows about life or humanity or society or the state of the world. *It cannot be ideology* (P49).

Everyone, of course, has a "system," and we are not capable of dismantling them. Being influenced by our "system" is a "constant threat," Barth said (P36). But the more we are attached to the Bible, the more we accept the commission to pass on the voice we hear there, the less we will try to "spin definitive nets" of systems and ideologies, "the more we will be anxious to give it free space" (K39). This of course is a direct commentary on the state of Protestant preaching in the heady days after the *Machtergreifung*.

50. Barth identified Psalm 119, though it is "often pushed aside as late-Jewish and Hellenistic," as a text that illuminates this "peculiar situation" of the preacher. Over the course of the 176 verses of the psalm, Barth told the students, a human being is addressed by God and is made "right" and "glad" about it. This psalm, he argued, demonstrates an order, a way forward for the preacher (P49).

But at least some of these students would surely have protested explicitly or tacitly that preaching must speak about life and society and the state of the world, that Holy Scripture cannot provide the kind of answers modern people, suffering German *Volk*, seek. What is the difference between preaching as interpretation of Holy Scripture and preaching as an expression of a preacher's "system"? Barth offered the students five characteristics of preaching as interpretation of Scripture; he would have time only for the first two of these during this class meeting.

First, Barth contended that the attitude of the preacher as interpreter of Scripture must be one of trust. It is a confidence that obedient "speaking-after" the words of Scripture in and with human words is *sufficient* for the deepest need of human beings. To imagine that "practical life" needs a "something more," some independent addition to that to which the Bible points, is not to exist by faith (P50). Every pulpit excursion from the *Sache* to which the Scriptures witness is not only doomed and lost time, but also *impoverished* time (K39).

Second, Barth described the interpreter of Scripture as a person who has a sense of *respicere*, a sense of *regard* for it. This is a person who is not preoccupied with himself, neither with his "wealth" nor with his "poverty," but is so captivated by the object of regard that the self fades away. It is all-consuming. Barth offered an analogy: it is as if a great stone tablet with mysterious writing was placed before this person, difficult to decipher. The person studies it closely, struggles to discern its meaning and establish connections. Preaching as interpretation of Scripture is like that, like the lip movements of a person who is fully claimed by this task of discernment, of regard, of understanding. This lip movement has "nothing to do with the involuntary speaking" of a person, who must express what is inside *himself*, Barth insisted.[51] It is instead a being-caught-up in something other than the self and expressing that something other (K40).

Barth's point was not that the preacher is a passive conduit in the preaching moment, but that in the context of interpreting the Scriptures the preacher is not focused on himself. His attention is fixed on the something that claims him — that to which the Scripture points.[52]

---

51. A literal translation of the German reads: "[T]his lip movement has nothing to do with the involuntary speaking of a man who is full in the heart" (K40). Cf. Barth's sermon, "Das Evangelium von dem Reich" (1932), printed in *Gesamtausgabe* V.31, p. 266.

52. The English translation of this passage in *Homiletics* (1991) is problematic, suggesting that the sermon should be "like" involuntary lip movements. Barth, *Homiletics*, p. 76. On the contrary, Kirschbaum uses "involuntary" only to describe what "preaching as inter-

Karl Barth's Predigtvorbereitung in Context: Winter Semester 1932-1933

Session 13: February 21, 1933

At the beginning of the session, Barth picked up where he left off the previous week: with the third of five characteristics of a preaching that begins with the interpretation of Holy Scripture. This third quality Barth called "attention" or "attentiveness." At first glance, this seems redundant, considering the discussion of *respicere* (regard) described above. But Barth meant something different than the broader attitude of regard for Holy Scripture here. "Attention" means attention to a *particular* biblical text, looking closely at what is actually there. Scripture "from beginning to end" is saying the same thing, Barth told the students, but it says that one thing differently (K40, P50). Every page is unique. The Bible speaks as a historical document of a historical event that erupts amid the dynamism of human life. To be attentive to this particularity is to be *diligent,* to discern what is said in this text and no other (K40, P50).

This diligence will take the form of exegetical, philological, and historical study. But it cannot stop there. Beyond this exegetical work the preacher must also ask diligently what this text says to him and to the *Gemeinde.* To do these tasks well requires an ever-new *respicere,* a being-caught-up in the particular text. It is not easy to sustain such attentiveness, and Barth told the students that even pastors who are very industrious in other ways can be lazy on this crucial point. But it is not only the pastors who are responsible for the neglect of the work of exegesis and interpretation — church leaders must insist that preachers have the time to do this work (K40, P51a).[53]

The fourth characteristic of the preacher who interprets Holy Scripture is one we have already encountered in the course of the *Predigtvorbereitung:* humility. This time Barth discussed humility as something that inevitably comes along with *respicere* for, and attentiveness to, Scripture. To interpret Scripture is to be contradicted by it, to be pointed to

---

pretation of Scripture" should *not* be. The handwritten student notes literally read (in English translation): "His preaching [is] like the involuntary of the — lips — moving of a person, who reads something with the greatest effort, attention and surprise, more spelling than reading in the usual sense, all eyes, entirely taken in claim, in the consciousness: I have not written the text." The unusual dashes around the word "lips" may well indicate that something was missed by the student recorder that Kirschbaum did not miss, namely, that Barth used the term "involuntary" in a negative sense here, not an affirmative one.

53. The transcription of the student notes repeats page 51. Here they are indicated as "51a" and "51b" respectively.

one's limits, to be humbled. In the encounter with the witness of the prophets and the apostles, the preacher steps back, the preacher's "system" is dissolved, and a space opens up for the Word of God. The "security" that comes with the preacher's "most precious habits" and "best insights" must be abandoned in order to listen (P51a). "Again and again I must let myself be contradicted," Barth told the class; "I must let myself be decentralized again and again" (P51a). Even the theology we bring along can only be an "emergency ration," not to be held too tightly in order to hear again and again anew (K41).

In this regard, Barth argues, one must even approach Luther's preaching with caution. Humility, Barth says, was not always Luther's strength. Luther believed he already knew what he would find in the Bible; he knew the one thing — justification! — that moved him. Because of that he ignored whole constellations of meaning in the Bible, such as "law" and "reward" (P51b). How this critique of Luther would have sounded in a room packed with Lutherans, many of whom considered him not only a *theological* but a *national* hero, we can only imagine.

The final quality Barth attributed to biblical preaching is something he called "flexibility." The Bible, Barth explained, is not God's Word the way a civil law book records the order of civil contracts and relationships. Instead, it is a Word that *speaks* — it *becomes* God's Word. Our relationship to the Scripture must be a history, a series of events, a life story. Flexibility means placing oneself in this movement, giving oneself over to it, being led through the whole of Scripture with its many testimonies and layers (K41, P51b). The fact that there is a canon of Scripture simply says: the church knows these Scriptures as the place where it expects to hear the voice of God. To be a flexible preacher is not to hold tight to some doctrine of inspiration, but to expect God to speak in the encounter with Scripture (P51).

As Barth concluded this discussion of preaching and its intimacy with the Bible, he reminded his students of "three fatal possibilities" that are ruled out for the biblical preacher. First, the preacher who attends to Scripture cannot be a pope, "puffed up" with the consciousness of his mission or office or theology — someone all-too-determined to act as "the representative of the dear God" to the world. Where the Holy Scripture is heeded, Barth insisted, "no papacy can grow, because the preacher cannot be secure and at peace with himself" (P52). Second, the preacher who takes the witness of the Bible seriously cannot be a visionary or enthusiast or idealist who has good intentions and conjures up "great thoughts" of his own. And finally, the preacher who is caught up with the particularity and movement of the Bible will not be boring. Hearers are often bored by preaching, Barth said, because they have heard it all before. Let the Scripture be what it is: unsettling. Then the sermon will not be boring (P52).

Following this exhortation regarding these "fatal possibilities," and after taking some questions from the floor, Barth returned to his large list of the nine elements comprising a definition of preaching, beginning a discussion of the eighth, "originality" — a discussion that he would continue the following week.[54]

By using the term "originality" Barth was referring back to a clause in his dialectical definition of preaching, namely, that the preacher interprets a biblical text "in free speech" to contemporary people. The attitude of *respicere* toward the Bible does not mean that Scripture is a "covering" behind which the preacher disappears. There is no *gratia infusa* of words and ideas. As the human being *that he is*, the preacher is called to do this work, with all his characteristics, his history, and his situation (K42, P53). *This person steps out.*

Preachers, then, should not play a part — not Luther, not a "churchman," not a prophet, not a visionary, certainly not a biblical character. Preaching is a responsible word by this particular "unadorned" individual to the people of today (P54). Preaching is to be original, Barth insisted, in that it is "not mere exegesis" and "not at all mere recitation of the words of Scripture" (K42). The text breaks off here, to be continued in the next session.

February 21 to 28, 1933

Contextual Developments

The last week of February 1933 saw an event that would enable Hitler to transform himself from a chancellor with constitutionally limited powers

---

54. The questions concerned the relationship between the Old and New Testament, the interpretation of the Old Testament in its historical context, the "eligibility" of allegorical interpretation, and whether it is possible to preach a "contemporary" interpretation of a biblical text. Barth strongly affirmed the need for Old Testament preaching, arguing that it should be understood both in its historical context and as "an entirely and completely Jewish book" that *as such* points forward to Christ. Barth also spoke positively about the possibility of "contemporary" interpretation, stating that "preaching is not exegesis but interpretation" (P53).

to the dictator of the Third Reich. The event that opened up this possibility was an odd one. On February 27, 1933, a frustrated, visually impaired Dutch construction worker and Communist activist sneaked into the Reichstag building and set the curtains ablaze. Though he was caught immediately and was certainly working alone, the Nazi leadership pounced on the opportunity to play on the already raging fears that Germany was on the brink of a Russian-style revolution.

As the head of the Prussian political police, Rudolf Diels, later recalled, Hitler addressed the functionaries gathering in the aftermath of the fire, his face "flaming red with excitement," saying,

> There will be no more mercy now; anyone who stands in our way will be butchered. The German people won't have any understanding for leniency. Every Communist functionary will be shot where he is found. The Communist deputies must be hanged this very night. Everybody in league with the Communists is to be arrested. Against Social Democrats and Reichsbanner too, there will be no more mercy![55]

Within hours the police began arresting Communist leaders, and by the end of the next day both the cabinet and, subsequently, Hindenburg agreed to a decree that would suspend several sections of the Weimar constitution "until further notice," particularly those guaranteeing freedom of the press, expression, assembly, and association, and allowed the government to take control of the federated states "if public order was endangered."[56]

Barth, like many Social Democrats, believed the fire had been somehow orchestrated by the National Socialists as a pretext to suppress all opposition.[57] But for most Protestants, the nonstop propaganda emanating from both the government and the right-wing press merely confirmed what they believed already. The Communists were poised to strike. The very existence of the Christian church in Germany was threatened. They certainly had no love for the Weimar constitution that would give them pause as it was rendered obsolete.

In addition, in the early months of 1933, the Nazis were actively courting the Protestant church, and church leaders were thrilled to hear

---

55. Rudolf Diels, *Lucifer ante Portas: Zwischen Severing und Heydrich* (Zürich: Interverlag, 1949), pp. 194-95. Quoted in Evans, *Coming of the Third Reich*, pp. 330-31.
56. Evans, *Coming of the Third Reich*, pp. 332-33.
57. Busch, *Karl Barth*, p. 224.

Nazi leaders encouraging Germans to rejoin the churches for the good of the *Volk*.[58] As campaign fever gripped the nation once again in advance of the March 5 elections, the Reichstag fire added a fresh urgency to an already feverish environment both inside and outside the Protestant church.

Session 14: February 28, 1933

The final meeting of the semester was dedicated to the last three of the nine elements of a definition of preaching. Barth began by returning to the discussion of "originality" that was interrupted at the end of the previous session. What are the concrete implications of "originality" in preaching?

First of all, the preacher is first a hearer, one who has heard for himself a Word that is both law and grace, who is both repentant and thankful. If an individual cannot personally be both appalled and joyful in this hearing, that person cannot preach with originality (K42, P53).

Second, originality requires *courage*. It is a risk to pass on what one has heard *as address* to others. The preacher must become a witness on the basis of the words of the apostles — explication must become application. It takes courage not to get stuck in exegesis, Barth told the students (P53). This movement of explication/application is by no means sequential, but intertwined from the very beginning.

Third, the preacher must resist the temptation to imitate others, to borrow their manners and ways. This is difficult for young preachers, Barth acknowledged. But original preaching is *independent* in relation to the habitus of others. Likewise, preaching requires *honest language*, language of one's own. Caution is required with the language of the Bible, the hymnbook, and Luther as well as the "sonorous sounds" of borrowed rhetoric. Stick to your own linguistic "poverty," Barth exhorted the students.

And finally, Barth told them that a certain *simplicity* is necessary to be original. It is not a matter of some grand system of "Christian truth" but about a history that takes place *von Gott aus* and is happening right now, with this preacher and this *Gemeinde* hearing this Word of Scripture. Every sermon must be something *new* (K43, P53-54).

Barth concludes the discussion of originality with a warning: "originality," he observed, "is a dangerous word." It is not a return to the "free,

---

58. Victoria Barnett, *For the Soul of the People: Protestant Protest against Hitler* (New York: Oxford University Press, 1992), p. 32.

independent, converted, born again personality," Barth said, quoting C. I. Nitzsch from earlier in the course. Nor is "originality" code for an "existential attitude," for "in the phantom of existentialism the old Satan of personality is hidden in a new mask" (P54).[59] An "original" preacher is rather one who simply lives from the forgiveness of sins, and as such is immune from over-confidence, vanity, and half-heartedness (K43, P54).

In the ensuing discussion, the students asked about the relationship of originality to "nativeness" and "authenticity." "Nativeness" *may* have been a reference by a student to the preacher's identity as a member of the *Volk*, while "authenticity" was of course a preoccupation of the modern preaching movement. In both cases Barth responded that these are misunderstandings of "originality" — the free speech described here is free "only as truly bound" in the ways already described. Likewise, the pastor is not just a mouthpiece or megaphone of the *Gemeinde*. "Originality" involves the pastor himself *as a believer* (P54). Theological students are by no means excluded from this call to originality. Theological education is about learning from one's teachers how to interact with the Scriptures independently, that is, originally (P54).

After the discussion, Barth introduced the eighth element of a definition of preaching: its relationship to the *Gemeinde*. The *ecclesia* — the ones called out — are placed before the preacher *as God's people*. That is the assumption with every sermon. They are those for whom God has already acted, for whom Christ has died and was raised. They are the ones who already belong to God and are thus placed in the very situation to hear what God has to say to them. To say that preaching is tempered by the *Gemeinde* is to say that preachers speak to these people *as God's own*. God has received them and God will open their ears (K43-44, P55-56).

What are the signs that preaching is tempered by this deepest identity of the *Gemeinde*?

First, the preacher must love this *Gemeinde*; the preacher must know: I belong with them, I want to share with them what I have heard from God. Without this love, not even the "tongues of men and angels" can help.

In addition, the preacher must be open to the real situation of the *Gemeinde*, and third, to somehow include this situation in the sermon. A preacher must live with the *Gemeinde*, share a history with them, and not just disappear into the study room — or even the Bible! — but "with open

---

59. Barth may be thinking of Brunner and Gogarten here.

eyes and ears go his way," asking what are the sins, the hopes, and the needs of these particular people.

But this living-with and -for does not mean that the pastor becomes some kind of *Volk*-sage. The preacher should not just say what the people have "on their hearts." The danger of *Gemeinde*-tempered preaching, Barth warned, is that the pastor will simply pick up "the flow of life" from the *Gemeinde* and be their mouthpiece, instead of speaking *to* them. In the good sense, *Gemeinde*-tempered means a movement between the life of the *Gemeinde* and the word of Scripture. *Gemeinde*-tempered preaching also requires the preacher to be tactful. What should be said in this hour, in this place, to these people, and in what way (K44, P56)[60]? Likewise, *Gemeindemässigkeit* requires a certain (relative) *Kairos*-consciousness on the part of the preacher (K45, P56). What does this particular situation demand? I experience a history with this *Gemeinde*, I know them, and my preaching speaks to this relationship — not of things "that are no longer important" (P56). This is certainly not to be understood as a kind of "customer service!" Barth exclaimed (K45, P57).

If preaching is tempered and shaped by its relationship to the *Gemeinde*, Barth concluded, the preacher cannot be a tyrant, a sycophant, or a hermit (K45, P57).[61]

In the final moments of the winter semester, Barth turned to the last of his nine elements: the *spirituality* of preaching. In a way, it is a return to the first: *Offenbarungsmässigkeit*. Preaching "requires the personal God himself," namely, the Holy Spirit, Barth told the class (K45, P57). Preaching is to serve God's own Word, and even if everything they have talked about all semester were in perfect order, all would be for nothing if God did not "remember" preachers (P57). Preaching is an event that occurs between heaven and earth, God and human beings, God and a *Gemeinde*, a

---

60. A little later in the session, perhaps in response to a question, Barth said that even biblical criticism in the pulpit should be subject to the criterion of tactfulness. Such criticism can be used when it is of service, but should not be deployed under the compulsion of a "false ideal of truthfulness" (P57).

61. In describing a sycophantic pastor, Barth called such a pastor one "who makes it right to the people," i.e., a preacher who tells the congregation only what they want to hear. This phrase *"den Leuten recht macht"* echoes the title of a sermon Barth preached in Safenwil in 1916, *"Der Pfarrer der es den Leuten recht macht,"* on Ezekiel 13:1-16. The sermon can be found in Barth, *Gesamtausgabe* I.29, pp. 44-61. For an analysis of the sermon in its context, see Arthur Marvin Sutherland, "Christology and Discipleship in the Sermons of Karl Barth, 1913-1916" (Ph.D. dissertation, Princeton Theological Seminary, 2000), pp. 112-21.

preacher and a *Gemeinde*. That this event has occurred, does occur, and will occur is predestination; it happens in "the free will of God," Barth explained, citing Calvin (K45).

Owing to this fact, Barth says, we can only in all circumstances have an attitude of *humility*. Aware of our humanness and the "absolute secret of preaching," we can only proceed with *soberness*, without pretention. And, Barth concluded, we certainly cannot preach without *praying*. Preaching finally can only be caught up with God. Its words "must stand in the flow" of our constant calling on God, and we must call the *Gemeinde* into prayer also.

With this, Barth said to the students, we have reached the limit of what we humans can say. This is the place "where the Spirit herself" must act in our place "with inexpressible sighs" (P57).

Conclusion

The first semester of the sermon exercises took place against the backdrop of a grueling series of national and regional election campaigns, escalating physical violence, and tremendous anxiety about the future of Germany. A majority of Protestant church leaders were pleased that big changes were in the air, though they worried about the church's fate in whatever might emerge from this chaotic season. The unprecedented participation, nationalist rhetoric, and partisan character of the Prussian church election campaigns demonstrate the continued blurring of the boundaries between *German* politics and *church* politics.

The students sitting in Barth's lecture hall in the winter of 1932-33 had grown up in the shadow of a Protestant church lamenting its loss of numbers and influence. They were children when the Great War erupted, and they had come of age during the tumultuous social and economic upheavals of Weimar. Many heard sermons shaped by the ethos of the modern preaching movement and the war preaching tradition, sermons that sought to win back the modern skeptic, bind up German wounds, and assert the importance of the church as the guardian of the moral and spiritual soul of a great nation that had lost its way in Weimar. During that winter they likely heard the sermons of nationalists such as their practical theology professor Emil Pfennigsdorf, who would soon preach enthusiastically in the Bonn University chapel about "God's message" in the National Socialist ascension.

In this emergency homiletical situation, Barth took these students back to the fundamental questions about what preaching is and what it is for, and underneath it all, returned again and again to the affirmation of the Godness of God, the only ground of resistance to ideological captivity. This affirmation — that only God can and will reveal Godself — entails the constellation Word of God–church–Scripture that guided Barth over the course of the semester. Barth's interpretation of each of these three elements served to decenter the preacher and deinstrumentalize the practice of preaching.

First, the *Word of God* is not a possession the preacher has, controls, and wields. Indeed, Barth's talk of the Word of God soon became Christology proper, as the preacher is located in the space between the Word that became flesh *(Wohin)* and the Word that will come again *(Woher)*. In this place every having is always a not-having, every confidence (even in salvation) can only be an unsettled, striding forward, unassurance.

Second, the *church* is neither something the preacher builds nor a *Volk* the preacher sets out to convert. It is an event in which the preacher is inescapably placed. The plans and programs and campaigns of the Protestant church to fill its pews, secure its funding, and increase its public influence are replaced by the language of commission, command, and obedience. Those who participate in the event "church" already belong to God, and the preacher needs neither to hunt for keys to unlock the contradictions of their existence nor to fan the flames of their *völkisch* fears and passions. Preaching is the humble and courageous attempt to address people who, in the deepest sense, are already God's own.

Finally, Barth's insistence on the intimate and inseparable relationship between the *Bible* — both as a whole and in its parts — and the practice of preaching also served to dethrone the preacher and deweaponize the practice of preaching. The Scriptures of the Old and New Testaments move the preacher (and the hearer) from the narrowness of *Volk*, nation, and race to the wide horizon of God's story with humanity. God has chosen and will choose to reveal Godself through the particularity of these witnesses and not through the generality of human consciousness, human existence, the orders of creation, or contemporary historical events. Preachers are not prophets, apostles, village sages, Luthers, popes, politicians, personalities, moralists, or visionaries. They are witnesses to the witness of the prophets and apostles. This is the one thing preachers are charged to do: to listen well, with regard, again and again, to that which the prophets and apostles heard, and to pass along what they hear as address to

God's people here and now. How hard this would be to hear for these young German Protestant ministerial candidates, who probably embarked on a path to ministry in order to save the Protestant church and protect the moral soul of the *Volk*, an ethos they learned at the feet of their fathers.

How did Barth gain a hearing from these students, in spite of all the reasons they would have to reject his views, and the fact that some of the positions Barth was taking here would have provoked open protest in some other universities?

Barth's strategy from the very beginning of the *Predigtvorbereitung* was to appeal to a potential common ground between himself and even his most nationalist students: the Godness of God. It was not an affirmation that could simply be reduced to the ravings of a Social Democrat. If Barth could get these young people to agree on the Godness of God, then a conversation could begin. The recognition of the Godness of God brings with it the particular posture Barth advocated for preachers throughout the *Predigtvorbereitung* lectures: humility, soberness, regard, expectation, prayer. Barth invited these young Protestants to come to the task of preaching with open minds and empty hands.

The first semester of the sermon exercises was devoted to establishing the nature, basis, and content of Christian preaching — a principle and material homiletic. In the second semester Barth would turn his attention to the questions of a formal homiletic. What does the actual preparation of sermons look like in the Third Reich if one begins from the affirmation that God is God?

It would be two months before the *Predigtvorbereitung* reconvened. When classes began again, they would be in the same lecture hall. They would be in the same university.

But they would be in a very different Germany.

CHAPTER SIX

Karl Barth's Predigtvorbereitung *in Context:* Summer Semester 1933

This chapter, like its predecessor, offers a contextual interpretation of the artifacts of Barth's sermon exercises of 1932-1933. But as we turn our attention to the summer semester, there are two new factors this chapter must take into account.

First, in addition to the notes provided by Charlotte von Kirschbaum (KS) and the student protocols (P), there is a third artifact, the notes of Werner Deggeller (D), a student who joined the class in the summer semester. Owing to the nature of Deggeller's account — a "free interpretation" as he describes it — his comments will appear in the notes when they provide a divergent or more detailed description of what took place in the exercises.[1]

Second, the rate and degree of change in the political, ecclesiastical, and academic spheres greatly increased in the spring and summer of 1933. Over the course of these months, Germany was transformed into a totalitarian state and much of the German Protestant church was overcome by chaos and infighting. The two-month period "between the times" (March-April) will require significant attention as we begin.

---

1. For more information about Werner Deggeller and his interpretation of the *Predigtvorbereitung* sessions, see the Appendix.

February 28 to May 9, 1933

Contextual Developments

As we have seen, the Reichstag elections of November 1932 were a bitter disappointment to the National Socialist leadership. Coffers depleted from the relentless election cycles of the preceding months, the Nazis lacked the funds to mount a propaganda campaign on the scale of their earlier efforts. In the end, they lost some seats while the Communists saw something of an increase. Some of the voters who had defected to the Nazis from other right-wing parties in earlier election cycles returned home in November. Though it was still the largest party in the Reichstag, this attrition might have marked the beginning of the end of the National Socialist movement.

But the propaganda campaign for the Reichstag election of March 5 was another matter entirely. With his sudden elevation to Reich Chancellor on January 30, 1933, Hitler made full use of his ability to mobilize the police against his political enemies, particularly the Communists, while the army leadership agreed to look the other way. Many who initially assumed that Hitler's appointment to Reich Chancellor in a government dominated by conservatives but non-Nazis meant he was "contained" and "neutralized" now recognized their mistake. Eager to protect their interests in the new situation, leaders of business and industry began to rethink their relative indifference to the National Socialist cause. Unprecedented amounts of money flowed into the National Socialist treasury. With it, the Nazis were able to saturate the electorate with nonstop propaganda in February and early March of 1933, while the Communists, Social Democrats, and sometimes even the Centre Party faced relentless and unimpeded aggression from the brownshirts and the SS as they tried to win votes themselves. Communist, Social Democratic, and labor union leaders in particular were under constant police surveillance, their party offices were raided, their newspapers were frequently banned, their vehicles were confiscated, and their public meetings were disrupted, often resulting in casualties.

Although he made it clear that it was open season on Communist political organizations and individuals, Hitler did not ban the Communist party outright for fear that Communists would then vote en masse for the Social Democrats, returning them to prominence.[2] Instead, Hitler framed

---

2. Richard J. Evans, *The Third Reich in Power, 1933-1939* (New York: Penguin, 2005), p. 12.

the March 5 election as a referendum on "Marxism," skillfully stoking the fear of a left-wing revolution already long present in large portions of the German electorate. The Reichstag fire of February 27 served to further legitimate Hitler's use of violence and suppression.[3] Many believed that Germany was on the brink of a Communist bloodbath, and Hitler was the only one willing to use whatever means necessary to stop it.[4] On election day, the streets of many towns and cities were patrolled by rowdy hordes of armed brownshirts and SS. In some places opposition parties were forbidden to post or distribute campaign materials, and often local police were prominently stationed at railway stations, bridges, and other public places, ostensibly to protect them from Communist terrorist attacks. Voters went to the polls on March 5 in "an atmosphere of palpable terror."[5]

In spite of this, the National Socialists did not receive a majority of the votes on their own in the March Reichstag elections. But together with their coalition "partner," the conservative *Deutschnationale Volkspartei*, they could claim victory with 51.9 percent.[6] And that was all Hitler needed to make the Third Reich a reality. With this majority he had the votes to pass legislation that would effectively establish him as dictator of Germany. Even before this became official — with the passing of the *Ermächtigungsgesetz* (Enabling Act) on March 23, 1933 — Hitler set his plans for the Third Reich in motion.

First of all, Hitler systematically and steadily eliminated, subdued, or marginalized his political enemies. The Communist Party, already para-

---

3. Four thousand Communist politicians, organizers, and activists were arrested in the immediate aftermath of the Reichstag fire. By March 15 that number had risen to ten thousand. Richard J. Evans, *The Coming of the Third Reich*, 1st American ed. (New York: Penguin, 2004), p. 335.

4. Richard Evans explains that the Communists themselves thought the revolution would come, but not immediately. Instead, they expected to be forced underground until the inevitable collapse of the Hitler government and its "big business" allies; this temporary struggle with fascism would only serve to strengthen the will of the proletarian masses toward revolution. Given this confidence, the Communists saw no reason to act in early 1933. National Socialist leaders, on the other hand, were absolutely convinced that the Communists were preparing an armed insurrection and could not understand why it had not yet begun. There were constant rumors of an imminent Communist attack, and the Nazis seized every opportunity to respond to "Marxists" of all sorts with unrestrained violence. See Evans, *Coming of the Third Reich*, pp. 325-27.

5. Evans, *Coming of the Third Reich*, p. 339.

6. Considering the circumstances, it is remarkable that the Communists still claimed 12.3 percent of the vote. Social Democrats fell only slightly to 18.3 percent, while the Centre held firm at 11.2. Evans, *Coming of the Third Reich*, p. 340.

lyzed by incessant persecution, was formally banned the day after the Reichstag elections.[7] Social Democrats were also under constant siege, though the party would not be formally banned until July. Opposition newspapers were subject to back-to-back bans until they were outlawed altogether. Hitler's alarmist rhetoric about the "Marxist" threat was naturally interpreted by brownshirt organizations as encouragement to continue their assaults with impunity.[8] Communists and Social Democratic leaders, including the newly elected representatives to the Reichstag, were subject to looting, arson, abduction, torture, and murder by zealous Nazis in the weeks and months after the election. Existing prisons and police stations proved inadequate to meet the needs of the moment. In addition to the many small makeshift jails and torture cellars quietly cropping up across the country, on March 20, 1933, Heinrich Himmler, leader of the SS in Munich, announced the opening of the first concentration camp at nearby Dachau. The camp, he explained, would allow the National Socialist government to place Communist, Social Democratic, and other opposition officials in "protective custody."[9] Other camps were soon established elsewhere.[10] While the (now largely cowed) press reported little about the many individual acts of violence perpetrated by gangs of Nazis, the existence of the camps, with their patina of legality, was deliberately and widely publicized by the regime — though the beatings, torture, and ritual humiliation that took place in them was not. The message to Communists, Social Democrats, Jews, trade union activists, and indeed anyone with unwelcome political convictions or connections was clear: continued opposition to the new government would have serious consequences.[11]

---

7. Evans, *Coming of the Third Reich*, p. 336.

8. Likewise, the anti-Semitic diatribes of Hitler and other Nazi leaders encouraged rampaging brownshirts to express their longstanding hatred of "unGerman" Jews in acts of violence, humiliation, and vandalism during this period, especially after the elections of March 5. Though the Nazi authorities did take some formal steps to stop these vigilante acts, their efforts were constantly undermined by the incendiary rhetoric that spewed forth endlessly from Nazi leaders and Nazi and *völkisch* press organs alike. Evans, *Coming of the Third Reich*, p. 433.

9. Evans, *Coming of the Third Reich*, pp. 344-45.

10. Some seventy such camps were established in the early months of 1933, with approximately 45,000 inmates among them. Deaths in the camps over this period number in the several hundreds. The majority of these camps would be closed by early 1934 as the revolutionary period ended and all organized political opposition had been destroyed. Evans, *Third Reich in Power*, p. 81.

11. Evans, *Coming of the Third Reich*, p. 434.

Of course, even with the restrictions on the free press, the many atrocities committed by the Nazis against their domestic enemies during this period did not remain entirely secret. But the information that did circulate was anecdotal and incomplete; rumors passed from person to person. Naturally those most inclined to believe the rumors were already opposed to the regime. Meanwhile, some foreign correspondents in Germany began reporting any human rights violations they observed, and stories about Nazi violence, including the street violence targeting German Jews, appeared in British, French, and American newspapers. There were protests in several American cities, and a boycott of German goods was called for on April 1, 1933.

To nationalist Germans, the news that the foreign press was reporting German atrocities was reminiscent of the way they thought Germany had been libeled and demonized in the foreign press during the Great War; indeed, Hitler called the press reports "Jewish atrocity smears." Most nationalist Germans did not believe atrocities were in fact taking place and were confident that whatever measures Hitler authorized were justified by the undeniable threat of a bloody Communist revolution. The public reaction to such reports in 1933, therefore, was largely indignation.[12]

In response to what he considered an orchestrated effort by Jews internationally to defame the Third Reich, Hitler announced a boycott of Jewish businesses for April 1, 1933, though in the interests of economic stability the largest Jewish-owned businesses were exempt. To underscore the purported "law and order" character of the Third Reich in the face of foreign reports of brutality, the boycott was to be an orderly, disciplined action. Violence of any kind was strictly forbidden. They would keep up the boycott, Nazi leaders warned, until the international press stopped printing "lies" about Germany.

The German population as a whole was clearly ambivalent about the April 1 boycott of Jewish businesses. While only a few crossed the lines of brownshirts and police to enter the stores the day of the boycott, it was clear to the regime that there was next to no public enthusiasm for the measure. In some places, it wasn't implemented at all, and in others, shoppers simply made a point of buying extra goods from Jewish-owned shops the day before the boycott, and returned to the stores en masse once the boycott was over. In spite of his threats, Hitler quietly let the matter drop,

---

12. Klaus Scholder, *The Churches and the Third Reich*, vol. 1 (Philadelphia: Fortress, 1988), p. 261.

though the negative stories about the Third Reich continued to appear in the international press.

But there was another message communicated by the April 1933 boycott. As Richard Evans explains:

> A major purpose of the boycott had been to advertise to the Nazi rank-and-file that anti-Semitic policy had to be centrally coordinated and pursued, as Hitler had written many years before, in a "rational" manner rather than through spontaneous pogroms and acts of violence. The boycott thus prepared the way for Nazi policy toward the Jews to take on a legal, or quasi-legal, course, in pursuit of the Party Programme's statement that Jews could not be full German citizens and therefore, clearly, could not enjoy full civil rights.[13]

In the months following the passage of the Enabling Act on March 23, Hitler initiated the process known as *Gleichschaltung* (coordination) to purge those he deemed politically unreliable from just about every arena of public life. Among the most sweeping measures was the April 7 *Gesetz zur Wiederherstellung des Berufsbeamtentums* (Law for the Restoration of a Professional Civil Service). The law stated that all employees of the state, which included state and local government workers, teachers, judges, university professors, and others, could be dismissed or forced into retirement if their previous or present political affiliation rendered them unable to offer the new regime their wholehearted support. The law assumed that non-Aryans would be politically disloyal by definition, regardless of their political convictions. Only those Jews who had proven their commitment to Germany by serving on the front lines in the Great War or by losing a father or a son in the conflict were allowed to remain at their posts.[14]

But not all coordination happened by direct government intervention; in fact, much of it was voluntary. In a time of widespread unemployment, people were eager to demonstrate their loyalty to the Reich and thus protect their jobs and advance their careers. In the first four months of 1933, 1.6 million people made their allegiance clear by joining the National

---

13. Evans, *Coming of the Third Reich*, p. 437; for a detailed discussion of the April 1 boycott, see pp. 433-36.

14. The exemption for those with military service or those who had lost a family member in the Great War was at the insistence of President Hindenburg. With Hindenburg's death in 1934 the exemption was removed.

Socialist Party.¹⁵ Most organizations and professional guilds from the press to the arts to the legal profession scrambled to coordinate themselves, purging their ranks of the politically or racially untrustworthy.¹⁶

But by no means were these speedy conversions to the National Socialist cause or the zeal for self-coordination simply a survival strategy for the majority of Germans in these early months. The other side of Hitler's plan to establish the Third Reich, the carrot to the stick of persecution and coordination, was his systematic wooing of the general population via propaganda and spectacle.¹⁷ While rowdy, thuggish behavior of the storm troopers on the streets offended the sensibilities of many conservatives, their misgivings were quickly overshadowed by their appreciation for the disciplined splendor of the many public events staged by the regime in the spring and summer of 1933 — parades, marches, speeches, rallies, and ceremonies. Many Germans, even some of the initially skeptical, were swept up in the romance of the new beginning for Germany and felt tremendous gratitude toward Hitler personally that disaster had been averted.¹⁸ Hitler shrewdly recovered and highlighted beloved German symbols and traditions in these early months, paying homage to the past even as he employed the latest technological innovations, including radio broadcasting, in his campaign to win the German soul.

But Hitler was concerned that there was one domain in German life where the strategy of coordination and propaganda might fall short, one domain in which the demand for total allegiance to the new state might be resisted: the Christian churches. Given their historic importance, present influence, and international connections, the refusal of the Catholic

---

15. Evans, *Coming of the Third Reich*, p. 382.

16. Over this period a number of Germans, many of them prominent in their fields, simply chose to leave the country.

17. On March 13 the Reich Ministry for Popular Enlightenment and Propaganda was established. Evans, *Coming of the Third Reich*, p. 396.

18. For most Germans, the Reichstag fire was irrefutable evidence that the Communists were about to seize their property, raze their churches, and murder their relations. The Nazis used the fire to great effect in their propaganda campaigns of 1933. In his March 8 pastoral letter to the clergy in his jurisdiction, Otto Dibelius, General Superintendent of the Kurmark, wrote that while pastors should remain "above parties" and refrain from celebrating "the victory of a political movement" directly in the upcoming *Volksvertrauertag* services, they should certainly offer thanks and praise that the *Vaterland* had been rescued from the Communists, for "the Communist action plans (arson, poisoning, hostages, [using] women and children as shields) are facts." Karl Barth, *Briefe des Jahres 1933*, ed. Eberhard Busch (Zürich: Theologischer Verlag Zürich, 2004), p. 84.

and Protestant churches to support the Third Reich would have posed an enormous problem for the regime during this period of revolution and consolidation. Any aggressive action to bring them into line would surely result in an immediate outcry domestically and internationally. That being the case, Hitler proceeded with caution in his dealings with the churches in 1933, using religious rhetoric in his public addresses and announcements in an effort to reassure church leaders of his piety and support.[19] The atheistic materialism of Weimar democracy was over, Hitler proclaimed. He would build the new Reich on a "Positive Christianity" that transcended confessional differences and would resonate with the spirit of the German *Volk*. He promised both communions that they would enjoy the protection of the state, and indeed, there were developments in various quarters in early 1933 that delighted Christian leaders: defamation of religious institutions was deemed a punishable offense, religion was restored as a regular subject at vocational and continuation schools, and in Prussia some two hundred sixty-five secular schools were closed.[20] Hitler and other Nazi leaders even publicly encouraged Germans as a *Volk* to rejoin the church, and Protestants were elated that for the first time in a long time more people were joining the church than were leaving it.[21]

In his policy speech of March 23, the same day the Reichstag would pass the Enabling Act, Hitler explained that the new government

> perceives in the two Christian confessions most important factors in the preservation of our *Volkstum*. It will respect the treaties concluded between them and the *Länder*; their rights shall not be violated. Conversely, however, it expects and hopes that the work on the national

---

19. This rhetoric would eventually disappear altogether. But this is not to say that Hitler did not genuinely desire a vigorous (though coordinated) German Reich church in the early years. He did not set out to cultivate a post-Christian *völkisch* neo-pagan religion, though some Nazi leaders and supporters certainly did. For a thorough discussion of the nuances of Hitler's understanding of "Positive Christianity" and his position toward the churches in the early years of the Reich, see Richard Steigmann-Gall, *The Holy Reich: Nazi Conceptions of Christianity, 1919-1945* (Cambridge: Cambridge University Press, 2003), pp. 13-50, 114-89.

20. Ernst Christian Helmreich, *The German Churches under Hitler: Background, Struggle, and Epilogue* (Detroit: Wayne State University Press, 1979), p. 129.

21. "In 1932, 215,908 left the church and only 49,700 joined it. In 1933, 323,618 joined the church and only 56,849 left it." Victoria Barnett, *For the Soul of the People: Protestant Protest against Hitler* (New York: Oxford University Press, 1992), p. 32.

and moral elevation of our people which the government has made its task will equally be respected.²²

A careful parsing of Hitler's statement reveals the following sub-text: if the churches want to enjoy the protection of the National Socialist state, they need to support its particular vision of "national and moral elevation." But it was not a time for careful parsing, and, regardless, the "national and moral elevation" of the *Volk* was a goal vague and lofty enough that the vast majority of Protestant leaders could wholeheartedly embrace it in 1933. At the time Hitler made these remarks, Protestants, like other Germans, were still basking in the glow of the pageantry of the preceding days. Because the fire had damaged the parliamentary building, the opening ceremonies of the new Reichstag were held two days earlier on what Germans considered holy ground: the Garrison Church at Potsdam.²³

The day began with Catholic and Protestant services for *Reichstag* members at two nearby churches, and then continued with the inaugural service in the Garrison Church itself.²⁴ The events featured a masterful blending of homage to the monarchical past and celebration of the National Socialist future. Trappings of the Prussian military tradition were everywhere in evidence. The Kaiser's throne sat respectfully vacant in the Garrison Church as Hitler bowed to the elderly President Hindenburg, the latter in his Field-Marshall uniform. Church bells rang out. Wreaths were laid on the tombs of the Prussian kings. Endless parades followed.

The newspapers were full of descriptions of the proceedings in the following days, images and texts of the addresses were widely distributed, and the entire event was broadcast on the radio. Protestant leaders were pleased that the church was there, symbolically, at the center of it all. Roman Catholics were more ambivalent. Unlike Protestants, they had their own political party that was now threatened with extinction, a connection

---

22. *Verhandlungen des Reichstags, VIII. Wahlperiode 1933*, vol. 457 (Berlin, 1934), p. 28. Quoted in Scholder, *Churches and the Third Reich*, vol. 1, p. 226.

23. The site was the burial place of the Prussian monarchs. The date of the Potsdam event was also significant, March 21. On that day Otto von Bismarck had opened the first Reichstag of the Second Reich sixty-two years earlier.

24. The preacher for the Protestant service was Otto Dibelius, General Superintendent of the church of Brandenburg. Though a committed nationalist, one with whom Barth had argued fiercely over the nature and mission of the church in the early 1930s, Dibelius nonetheless contacted Barth prior to this event seeking advice regarding the inaugural sermon and other matters, as we shall see.

to other Catholics that transcended national loyalties, and Roman Catholic bishops who had openly condemned National Socialist ideology, in some cases denying Nazis the sacrament. On all counts Hitler considered German Catholics a problem, and he worked quickly to ensure they would not oppose the regime in the future.[25] It did not take long.[26]

Once it was clear that there would in fact be a Concordat between the Third Reich and Rome, Protestant leaders began to worry that this left them at a distinct disadvantage in the days to come. Fears that the Roman Catholic Church would have the ear of the *Führer* while they were shut out began to take hold. There had long been a desire for a unified Protestant church in Germany in some quarters, and the prospect of the Roman Concordat gave the issue fresh urgency among Protestant leaders. Hitler himself was clear that he wanted a single Reich church with a single leader with whom he could negotiate a church/state agreement and who would oversee the process of coordination.

But the obstacles to a Reich church were enormous. It was not only the fact that the German Protestant church was made up of twenty-eight separate *Landeskirchen,* each with its own government, elected representatives, constitution, and relationship to its respective *Land* government, but the fact that there were wide confessional differences represented among them.[27] The majority of the churches were Lutheran, some were Reformed, and still others represented a "union" of the two traditions.[28]

---

25. Though Hitler and Goebbels, as Roman Catholics, were expected at the Mass on the day of the opening of the Reichstag, they declined to attend in protest that there was not yet a treaty between the new German state and Rome.

26. Though the Concordat would not be official until July 20, 1933, already by March 28 the German Catholic Bishops were forced to issue a statement withdrawing their earlier objections to the National Socialist movement.

27. The *Landeskirchen* did have a connectional relationship to each other in the form of the *Deutscher Evangelischer Kirchenbund* (German Church Confederation) and its most powerful governing body, the *Kirchenausschuss,* which represented the church as a whole.

28. The demand for a single Reich "bishop" — which Barth and others saw as a baptized version of the *"Führerprinzip"* applied to the church — was unthinkable to Reformed churches on confessional grounds alone. The *Führerprinzip* (leadership principle) cherished in National Socialist ideology claimed that certain individuals are naturally gifted to lead, an idea that resonated with the ethos of social Darwinism. Organizations and societies were to be governed by hierarchies of such individuals, who would command absolute obedience from subordinates. Hitler, of course, occupied the position of supreme leader in the Nazi hierarchy and was thus answerable to no one. Many Lutheran leaders were also initially opposed to the establishment of a Reich church, on the grounds that it would necessarily compromise the purity of the Lutheran confession. Instead, they advocated a newly strengthened

Karl Barth's Predigtvorbereitung *in Context: Summer Semester 1933*

Nonetheless, the possibility of a Reich church and corresponding bishop was embraced by many Protestants in the early months of 1933, most passionately among the growing ranks of the *Deutsche Christen,* though there was continuing disagreement over how and to what degree such a church might be established. This period is dominated by largely internal battles — some public, some private — over what the Protestant church would look like in the Third Reich, on what basis it would define and organize itself, and who had the legitimate authority to decide its fate. Some voiced concerns that whatever decisions the church made should be based on existing confessions, others called for a new confession in the new circumstances, while the *Deutsche Christen* rejected the idea that historical confessional identity should play any role at all in the creation and organization of a new Reich church. Along with all the debate over the Reich church there were also numerous power struggles, as those with power in the church sought to hang onto it, and those with little saw the impending reorganization as an opportunity to get some. But for all the disagreements, Protestant leaders were largely united on one thing in the spring of 1933: something important, good, and even revelatory had happened with the birth of the Third Reich. Whatever reservations they might have about the details, whatever concerns some might have regarding the independence of the church in the new state, on this point there was widespread consensus.[29]

Hitler wanted to see a Reich church established quickly in 1933, but he had no desire to get directly involved in church disputes, and most of his occasional interventions were designed to restore order when the church conflict threatened to attract unwelcome attention, especially internationally. In April he appointed the relatively unknown army chaplain and East Prussian *Deutsche Christen* leader Ludwig Müller to be his official advisor on church affairs, giving Müller the explicit commission to "fur-

---

alliance of the various Protestant confessions and the formation of a small but powerful representative committee to lead it. See Scholder, *Churches and the Third Reich,* vol. 1, p. 238.

29. The largest of the Protestant *Landeskirchen,* Prussia, issued some 10,000 copies of the following "Easter message" to be read from the pulpit on Easter morning, 1933: "This year the Easter message of the risen Christ goes forth in Germany to a people to whom God has spoken by means of a great turning point in history. We know that we are at one with all Protestant fellow believers in joy at the awakening of the deepest powers of our nation to a patriotic consciousness, to a true community of the *Volk,* and to a religious renewal." The mailing also included instructions to commemorate Hitler's birthday in the prayers of intercession the following week. Evans, *Coming of the Third Reich,* p. 236.

ther all endeavors" to create a German Protestant Reich church.[30] Meanwhile, the *Kirchenausschuss* of the *Deutscher Evangelischer Kirchenbund* anxiously moved forward with their plan for reform, granting their president, Hermann Kapler, unusual authority and appointing two other church leaders — one Lutheran, one Reformed — to work with him on a new constitution, meeting for the first time on April 25.[31] They were known as the *"Dreimännerkollegium"* (Committee of Three). The statement they issued that day left little doubt that — for all their concern for the claims of the historic confessions — the assumptions of Political Theology had become mainstream:

> A powerful nationalist movement has seized and uplifted our German people.... To this turning point in history we say a grateful Yes. God has given us this. To him be the glory! Bound by God's Word, we recognize in the great events of our day a new commission given by our Lord to his church.[32]

Shortly thereafter the Committee of Three began their work — in close consultation with Hitler's advisor, Chaplain Müller. The *Deutsche Christen* and their national Führer, the ambitious Joachim Hossenfelder, were effectively shut out of the formal process at this point, but they continued with the reformation plans they had announced in spectacular fashion at their first national assembly held April 3-5 in Berlin. There they resolved to take down what they saw as the stodgy Protestant establishment, dispense with the *Landeskirchen*, establish a single Protestant church of the German Reich — "above confessions" and governed by the *Führer* principle — and to cultivate an intimate relationship with the Reich government and the NSDAP.[33] Revolutionary times, they argued, called for a revolutionary

---

30. Peter Matheson, *The Third Reich and the Christian Churches* (Edinburgh: T&T Clark, 1981), p. 12.

31. In addition to *Kirchenbund* President Hermann Kapler, this committee included Lutheran August Marahrens, *Land* bishop of the *Evangelisch-lutherischen Landeskirche* of Hanover, and the Reformed representative Hermann Hesse, director of the *Predigerseminar* in Wuppertal.

32. Quoted in Scholder, *Churches and the Third Reich*, vol. 1, p. 305.

33. Though the "honorary committee" named for the event included Reich ministers Wilhelm Frick and Hermann Göring and various NSDAP dignitaries, only Nazi official and *Deutsche Christen* Wilhelm Kube was in attendance. After the *Machtergreifung*, Kube had been named *Oberpräsidenten* of Brandenburg-Berlin, making him the highest public official in the province. Kube's speech at the assembly, in which he proclaimed that the NSDAP in

church. As Hossenfelder proclaimed at the April assembly, "true believers" have the right of revolution "over against a church administration that does not acknowledge the nationalist uprising without reservations. . . . The state of Adolf Hitler calls upon the church, the church must hear the call."[34] The *Deutsche Christen* and the representatives of the Protestant *Kirchenbund* were thus on a collision course. It would not be long before impact.

Barth followed these political and ecclesiastical developments closely during the inter-semester period, even though he was traveling a good bit of the time. His first public response to the unfolding situation in Germany was given in a lecture, *"Das erste Gebot als theologisches Axiom,"* delivered first in Copenhagen and then in Aarhus, Denmark, on March 10 and 12, respectively.[35] It would be published in *Zwischen den Zeiten* later in the summer.

The address is a direct critique of every effort to secure a basis for theology in the Word of God *and* something else: national identity, "existence," historical events, orders of creation. Such "natural" theologies, Barth argued, violate the First Commandment. Of course, every theology claims it honors God, he continues, but every theology must be questioned as to the true source of its pathos, what it fears, loves, and trusts.[36] Is the source of its pathos the God who redeems Israel, who is merciful in Jesus Christ, who is known by the church only in connection to the unique witness to this unique revelation which is, of all things, a lowly "text"? What is the real passion of the theologies of the Word of God "and" something else — is it God, or is it the something else? These days, Barth explained, the call comes "from every side" for revelation *and*: revelation and creation or revelation and "primordial" revelation, or revelation and "human existence," or revelation and "orders of creation."[37] To find the real basis of a

---

Prussia would make the cause of the *Deutsche Christen* movement its own, was a source of jubilation for the movement and cause for alarm among Prussian church officials, who saw it as a threat to the independence of the church.

34. Quoted in Scholder, *Churches and the Third Reich*, vol. 1, p. 291.

35. Karl Barth, "Das erste Gebot als theologisches Axiom," *Zwischen den Zeiten* 11 (1933): 297-314. An English translation of the essay may be found in Karl Barth, *The Way of Theology in Karl Barth: Essays and Comments*, ed. Martin Rumscheidt (Allison Park: Pickwick Publications, 1986), pp. 63-78.

36. Barth echoed the language of Luther's *Small Catechism*. The response to the question regarding the meaning of the First Commandment ("Thou shalt have no other gods") is "We should fear, love, and trust in God above all things."

37. Karl Barth, *Theologische Fragen und Antworten* (Zollikon: Evangelischer Verlag, 1957), p. 137.

theology, follow the pathos, Barth suggested, naming names.[38] The address concludes with the admission: every theology, every theologian worships other gods. Therefore theologians must relentlessly question one another; they must call one another to account — not in anger, but as forgiven sinners who know the promise of the Lord of the church: "Lo, I am with you always."[39]

As he had done in the course of the Dehn controversy, Barth again pleaded with his contemporaries for a substantive theological debate, knowing very well that it was precisely in the soil of theological assumptions about the locus of revelation that the political ideology spreading so rapidly in the German church in the spring of 1933 was nurtured and sustained.

A few days after the lectures Barth received a letter from General Superintendent of the Kurmark Otto Dibelius. This was the same Dibelius Barth debated in the early 1930s over his triumphalist, *seelsorgerlich* understanding of the nature and mission of the Protestant church.[40] Dibelius would soon give the sermon at the Protestant service at the opening of the Reichstag.[41] His purpose in writing was to send Barth a copy of a "confidential" letter he sent out to all the pastors under his jurisdiction after the contentious March 5 Reichstag election, asking Barth for his opinion of the document. While Dibelius assumed that the Kurmark pastors would (like himself) recognize with gratitude that the National Socialists had preserved Germany from a Communist revolution, he nonetheless urged them to remain "above parties" vis-à-vis the new state, forbidding them to display the Swastika at the upcoming *Volkstrauertag* (memorial day), and to remember that there might be some in their congregations who had a different perspective regarding the political situation. For all his enthusiasm for the new regime, Dibelius's letter is remarkable for its insistence that the church must resist the temptation to preach the Third Reich and its values and not the gospel:

> My dear brothers, we may have all sorts of different theological convictions. But we must and will agree that the gospel does not know the in-

---

38. Barth, *Theologische Fragen*, p. 138. Althaus, Holl, Hirsch, Brunner, Gogarten, and Bultmann are all mentioned.
39. Barth, *Theologische Fragen*, p. 143.
40. For a discussion of Barth's debate with Dibelius see Chapter Two.
41. Dibelius's sermon can be found in Günther van Norden, *Der deutsche Protestantismus im Jahr der nationalsozialistischen Machtergreifung* (Gütersloh: Gütersloher Verlagshaus Mohn, 1979), pp. 52-55.

dependent individual but rather the justified sinner; that it preaches love and not hate; and that it is not *Volkstum* but the kingdom of God that is the object of Protestant proclamation. . . . Politics may dig trenches; statesmen may speak of annihilation, extermination and suppression; messages of hate at mass rallies may earn applause that does not want to stop. We have received another spirit! . . . Where hatred is preached, and now even hatred against members of our own people, the Spirit of Jesus Christ is not present.[42]

In his response, Barth thanked Dibelius for his letter, and said he was "sincerely glad" about its "key content." But Barth went on to challenge Dibelius regarding his belief that the nation had been "saved" from a Communist "action plan," and wondered why Dibelius had nothing to say about the "astonishing terrors" perpetrated by those now in power. Barth then took the opportunity to urge Dibelius to think long and hard about his upcoming sermon before the opening of the Reichstag, reminding him that for many this was not a time of thanksgiving:

> You have, Herr General Superintendent, the extraordinarily difficult task before you of giving the opening sermon to the new Reichstag. I am confident that you will try also there [to speak] according to the word of the church. Perhaps you will also be conscious of those who must hear this word in a situation which for many millions of Germans clearly stands under the aspect of tyranny and oppression — who, when the bells sound and the flags wave in Potsdam, will remain apart, silent and averted.[43]

Unfortunately, Dibelius did not heed Barth's advice. His Potsdam sermon of March 21, ostensibly on Romans 8:31 — "If God be for us, who can be against us?" — was full of enthusiasm for the "new beginning" for Germany, and was clearly designed to convince the dignitaries and party members in attendance that the gospel was not foreign to the German character, but was the very thing that would enable them "to become German again."[44] Luther, Bismarck, Schiller, the war, and "the German fate" all made an appearance in the sermon. Dibelius expressed confi-

---

42. Quoted in Scholder, *Churches and the Third Reich*, vol. 1, p. 232.
43. Karl Barth to Otto Dibelius, March 17, 1933, in Barth, *Briefe 1933*, p. 85.
44. Norden, *Der deutsche Protestantismus*, p. 54.

dence that the Reich government would soon restore order and there would be no more need for extreme measures. The sermon was punctuated with the exuberant refrain, "one *Reich,* one *Volk,* one God!"[45] And readers should keep in mind that Dibelius must be considered a "moderate" in his context![46]

For all his admirable instructions to the pastors of his region, Dibelius could not see the degree to which Political Theology shaped his own proclamation. Such was the pervasiveness of these views among nationalist Protestants, even the relatively conscientious ones.

Barth's correspondence during this period reveals his dismay as he saw acquaintances and even friends caught up in the nationalist fervor of the moment. One painful example of this was his longtime friend Georg Merz, who advised Barth in mid-April that if he was going to participate in the German church during this time, he must "confess the German fate" and "not stand against things" that were now taking place. Barth responded:

> Dear Georg, I have not opposed religious socialism (at a time when you still thought to discern "religious beginnings" in socialism) for the purpose of finding myself now ready to confess that it is German fate to combine Christ and Caesar on the other side, because the holy stream of history so runs for the moment, and that concerning the church I will not be allowed to stand "opposed to" these "things" (for example, to those [things] which now befall the German Jews). I stand "opposed" to most all of the "things" which now happen in Germany, and if after as before it is not my task to make this point of view effective politically, so I energetically after as before will not allow that I

---

45. Norden, *Der deutsche Protestantismus,* p. 55.

46. Indeed, when his "confidential" letter was leaked, it was printed in various *Deutsche Christen* publications and criticized as tantamount to treason, most famously in Wilhelm Kube's speech at the national assembly of the *Deutschen Christen* in early April. Of Dibelius's sermon on the "Day of Potsdam," Günther Brakelmann observes: "In no way was the sermon of Dibelius a 'brown' [sermon], as the *Deutschen Christen* tended to give. It was a patriotic-Christian sermon, which combined the yes to the new state and its consequent actions with the warning of a lapse into an arbitrary dictatorship." Günther Brakelmann, "Hoffnungen und Illusionen evangelischer Prediger zu Beginn des 'Dritten Reiches': Gottesdienstlieche Feiern aus politischen Anlässen," in *Die Reihen fast geschlossen: Beiträge zur Geschichte des Alltags unterm Nationalsozialismus,* ed. Detlev Peukert, Jürgen Reulecke, and Adelheid Castell Rüdenhausen (Wuppertal: Hammer, 1981), pp. 144-45. Though a conservative nationalist and an anti-Semite in this period, Dibelius would eventually join the Confessing Church.

should in some sense show solidarity with these "things" for the sake of the "Christian church in Germany."[47]

Even before the civil service law was formally announced on April 7, Barth was aware that, as a member of the SPD, his academic position was precarious. His letters testify to his concern that political developments could mean the end of his work in Germany.[48] The leadership of the Social Democratic Party spread the word to party members that they should not sacrifice their civil service positions just to preserve their membership.[49] But Barth had no intention of withdrawing from the party, and he resolved to tackle the issue head on, by writing directly to the Reich official with jurisdiction over such matters in Prussia, the newly appointed *Kultusminister* Bernhard Rust.[50] In his letter of April 4 Barth declared his membership in

47. Karl Barth to Georg Merz, April 21, 1933, in *Briefe 1933*, p. 157.

48. From Switzerland Barth wrote to his daughter in Sweden: "Perhaps you have also heard several things from the Swedish papers of the strange fever-convulsion that now makes its way in Germany: boycott of Jews, formation of the centralized state and so forth. Also to that now belongs the senseless plan to simply fully eliminate not only the communists, but also the social democrats by external violence, an intention which is especially meant to be achieved through a drastic 'purification' of the entire civil service, in which also the university professors are expressly reckoned. And now according to everything one hears the question is not entirely far off that in the sweeping of impure elements could also belong your dear father." Karl Barth to Franziska Barth, April 11, 1933, in *Briefe 1933*, p. 131. Barth even wrote to his landlord on March 27, to tell him that owing to the political circumstances his situation had become "uncertain." *Briefe 1933*, p. 93.

49. The question of whether to withdraw from the SPD in the interest of continuing to teach was the subject of a correspondence between Barth and Paul Tillich in March and April. At that time, Tillich was considering leaving the party, while Barth argued that his membership was a "practical political decision" and "if the Prussian state who called me in 1921 no longer likes me in 1933, unless I become another person, then it may send me away in 1933. This state can do a lot. It can, for example, according to [its] discretion pension off and depose [me]. But it cannot do everything. It cannot, for example, compel a free man to become otherwise for its sake. I say that without heroic defiance and a desire for martyrdom." Karl Barth to Paul Tillich, April 2, 1933, in *Briefe 1933*, p. 109. Barth also counseled a distressed socialist pastor who wrote to him that the *Kirchenpräsidenten* of his region had issued a "declaration" demanding that all pastors resign from the SPD. Barth told the pastor that he rejected this demand unconditionally, and that a true church would forbid the very thing that this "church" asked of its clergy — that they refrain from practical political decisions. Karl Barth to Theodor Wilhelm Erhardt, April 16, 1933, in *Briefe 1933*, p. 143.

50. Bernhard Rust (1883-1945), secondary school teacher and National Socialist activist. He was elected to the Reichstag in 1930, then appointed *Kultusminister* of Prussia by Hitler in 1933. He would later become *Reichsminister für Wissenschaft, Erziehung und Volks-*

the SPD to the minister and ironically vowed that in his academic activities he would "preserve in relation to the new form of the state as a citizen the same loyalty which I saw preserved by my politically right-wing colleagues to the previously existing form of the state during the twelve years which I spent in the Prussian universities."[51]

By the time Barth returned to Bonn at the end of April the *Gleichschaltung* of the university administration and faculty was formally under way in Bonn, as elsewhere. New "special" elections for rector and deans of the respective faculties were held, with the explicit instruction that only candidates with the proper ancestry and who demonstrated the proper political attitude were eligible for office. In practical terms this meant that many office holders, including the rector of the University of Bonn, were ousted, to be replaced by enthusiasts for the new regime. The dean of the Protestant theological faculty, the besieged Karl Ludwig Schmidt, lost his position in the course of the faculty meeting on April 27, and was replaced by none other than a triumphant Emil Pfennigsdorf.[52] Barth was also "demoted" from his office as senator of the faculty (which designated him as future dean).[53]

Between the political turmoil, concerns about the Protestant church, and the specter of *Gleichschaltung*, these days brought with them flurries of letters and many discussions late into the night as friends and colleagues gathered at the Barth household. Rumors about who joined the party or the growing ranks of the *Deutschen Christen* were common topics of conversation. Everyone was talking about Heidegger's dramatic entrance into the National Socialist Party on May 1, for example, but it was the defection of friends that caused perhaps the most alarm.[54] Barth wrote to a friend in early May of the steady stream of converts:

---

bildung, and eventually supervised medical experiments on prisoners of war. He was indicted (posthumously) for war crimes.

51. Barth, *Briefe 1933*, p. 112. The colleagues in question, of course, expressed nothing but hostility toward the Weimar state.

52. Hans-Paul Höpfner, *Die Universität Bonn im Dritten Reich: Akademische Biographien unter Nationalsozialistischer Herrschaft*, Academica Bonnensia (Bonn: Bouvier, 1999), p. 148.

53. J. F. Gerhard Goeters, "Karl Barth in Bonn 1930-1935," *Evangelische Theologie* 47, no. 2 (1987): 143. Barth told Georg Merz of this demotion, saying that he was now "professor second class." Karl Barth to Georg Merz, April 30, 1933, in *Briefe 1933*, p. 178.

54. On April 21 Heidegger was elected Rector of the University of Freiburg. He gave his inaugural address — on the *Führerprinzip* — on May 27.

> At present in the domain of *"Gleichschaltung"* the greatest and most glorious miracle happens almost daily, in quantities so large that I would hardly be surprised if next our canary bird perhaps or even our turtle should also lift its little feet in the German greeting and its little voice in the corresponding *"Heil!"* one morning.[55]

A few days later Barth had to add of the unfortunate turtle in question that someone had broken into the garden and carved a swastika on its back.[56] Barth joked that perhaps now it, too, would want to join the *Deutsche Christen,* but it was an ominous sign.

During this period, there were increasing demands for public demonstrations of allegiance to the new regime. Their upstairs neighbor was warned by "a friendly SA man," for example, that their residence had better display the Reich flags on the May 1 National Worker's Day or "evil things" might occur. "What should we do?" Charlotte von Kirschbaum wrote. "We *have* no flags!!"[57] Once the university reconvened in May, Barth was careful to avoid all campus ceremonies and celebrations, so that he was not confronted "with the singing of that song of the 'brown battalions.'"[58]

Barth wondered whether he should make some comment on the political situation, and he was asked by some if he would publish something. His response in early May was that the only place he *could* publish something, on, say, the church and the injustices perpetrated by the regime, would be *Zwischen den Zeiten,* and then it would probably be banned.[59] But he also doubted that his opinion would have much effect on the people he needed to persuade. "As already happened earlier," he told one inquirer, "in wider circles" my opinion would be "invalidated from the outset," because

> I as a Swiss just could not understand the German fate and the German will.... For the present I think that what I can do in this, my work, [is] more important for a better church understanding, in a sense, [than] what I could bring into line with a public vote, whose resonance is so jeopardized a priori. The situation could turn out that the

---

55. Karl Barth to Karl Stoevesandt, May 2, 1933, in *Briefe 1933,* pp. 189-90.
56. Karl Barth to Karl Stoevesandt, May 2, 1933, in *Briefe 1933,* p. 193.
57. Charlotte von Kirschbaum to Helmut Traub, April 30, 1933, in *Briefe 1933,* p. 103.
58. Karl Barth to Georg Merz, April 30, 1933, in *Briefe 1933,* pp. 178-79.
59. Karl Barth to Elisabeth Schmitz, May 2, 1933, in *Briefe 1933,* p. 188.

relationship reverses itself, that thus the ship must be set on the sand. For that I am certainly holding myself open.[60]

As a result of Schmidt's abrupt "sabbatical," other Bonn faculty members stepped in to cover his courses. Barth volunteered to cover the lectures on the Gospel of John, with the consequence that he would be teaching a grueling fourteen hours a week in the summer semester, and for the first and only time teaching in all four theological disciplines simultaneously. In addition to the lectures on John and the sermon exercises, he continued his lectures on the history of Protestant theology, read Calvin's *Institutes* (Book III) in his systematic seminar, and discussed Luther's *Larger Catechism* in the *Sozietät*. About fifty new students joined the *Predigtvorbereitung* for the summer semester, bringing the weekly attendance there to about 150.

Just before classes began for the semester an announcement was posted on campus, signed by the *"Führer"* of the Bonn student body, Walter Schlevogt. It instructed the Bonn students "to completely shun" the lectures of Fritz Lieb, Emil Fuchs, Karl Ludwig Schmidt, and Karl Barth, because of their SPD membership.[61]

It is clear from the letters of both Barth and Kirschbaum that they worried there might be disruptions in the classroom as the first semester in the Third Reich began. Barth wrote to the Stoevesandts after the first day: "It may also be comforting to you to hear that today I could begin my two lectures before overflowing lecture halls entirely undisturbed. Somewhere and somehow I must and will form a reasonably uncorrupt intellectual atmosphere again, even after all the lies."[62]

Session 1: May 9, 1933

Owing to the many newcomers to the sermon exercises, the first class meeting was devoted to a review of the material covered in the winter semester. Barth indicated that this reminder was important for the "old members" as well (KS1). The meeting was an exposition and discussion of

---

60. Karl Barth to Elisabeth Schmitz, May 2, 1933, in *Briefe 1933*, p. 188.
61. *Briefe 1933*, p. 197, n. 1.
62. Karl Barth to the Stoevesandts, May 4, 1933, in *Briefe 1933*, p. 193. Cf. Charlotte von Kirschbaum to Anna Barth, May 4, 1933: "Today Karl gave his first lectures, both in overflowing lecture halls with many *Hakenkreuzstudenten*, without the least disruption. For that we are very thankful." *Briefe 1933*, p. 196.

the nine criteria of preaching — there was no mention of the historical survey material from the beginning of the course. How did Barth summarize each of the nine elements in the presence of these new students in the new situation of May 1933?[63]

Offenbarungsmässigkeit was described by Barth as the imperative that preachers must proclaim the revelation that has happened (Epiphany) and the revelation of God that is to come (Parousia) here between the times. This involves "ever new listening" to the Word (KS1).[64]

Kirchlichkeit, the second element, again indicates the "space" in which preaching occurs, the event "church," bounded by baptism (the sign of grace), the Lord's Supper (the sign of hope) and Scripture (the document of the truth that founds the church) (KS1). Students could not miss the stark contrast of this understanding with that so widely held at the time: that *Volk* and *Vaterland* constituted the proper context of preaching.[65]

The third element, *Bekenntnismässigkeit* (confession-tempered), had particular resonance given the debates about the church's "confession" raging in the Protestant church in the spring of 1933. Barth reminded the students: a confession is an acknowledgment by the church that it has heard its commission — the call — of its Lord. In this hearing and confessing, which it must do again and again, the church is built up *(erbauen)*. It cannot be built on anything else (KS21).

What would these students have heard in this talk of "confession" in the context of the Protestant debate? Certainly the *Deutschen Christen* vision of a church "above confession" was impossible, and so was a church that responded to a commission from elsewhere, a "commission" from the *state* to reform itself, for example. The church could only listen and acknowledge the call *of its Lord*. Of course, what constituted "the call of its

---

63. Both Charlotte von Kirschbaum's notes and the student protocols are quite terse for this session, probably because this was a review of material covered in great detail previously. It is likely that much more was said than their notes indicate, as evidenced by the much fuller account of this class meeting offered by Werner Deggeller. Deggeller, new to the exercises, would not have heard all this before.

64. Deggeller adds, "If preaching is harmonized on this keynote, then it is revelation-tempered, for it exists in right relation to that Word proclaimed to it, from which it takes its starting point and hurries again to the Word of God as something entirely new, constantly regenerated, always alive" (D1).

65. Cf. Deggeller: "The place of revelation is not an arbitrary one, which we perhaps capriciously are able to expand or contract" (D1).

Lord" was also up for debate in the spring of 1933, an issue addressed throughout the *Predigtvorbereitung* lectures.

The fourth criterion of preaching, *Amtsmässigkeit*, refers only secondarily to the church act of appointing human beings to the office of preacher. At best it can only point to God's own, secret, action of calling, which is finally what legitimates the preacher. All human criteria are thus relativized (KS1, P58).

This sounds straightforward enough. But in some quarters of the Protestant church there was already discussion of a new "criterion" to be applied to Protestant preachers — the "Aryan paragraph" — and it would not be many months before the issue took center stage. In his summary Barth did not discuss any human criteria at all, but stressed the fact that it is *God's* call to preach that is of decisive importance — not the judgment of human beings.

The element Barth called "provisionality" *(Vorläufigkeit)* in the winter semester he now discussed under the heading *"Heiligkeit"* (holiness). The holiness of preaching does not rest on the ability or even the good will of the preacher, but on the command and blessing of God. Preachers are and remain sinners — thus their preaching is always provisional.[66] But this always inadequate work takes place in relation to God's promise, under God's command and with God's blessing, thus it is also not without holiness (KS2, P58).

The *Biblizität* of preaching is its form and content as interpretation of Scripture.[67] The source of the sermon cannot be something that "swells up" from inside of the preacher, Barth reiterated (P58).

Under "originality" Barth again referred to the personal repentance and gratitude of the preacher, a "binding" which thus makes the preacher's words "free." The "saying-after" or repeating of the commission given to the church cannot be a "parroting" — it must be original, that is, *personal* (KS2, P59).[68]

The concrete situation of the sermon is also determined by the *Gemeinde* who hear it, Barth continued. The *Gemeindemässigkeit* (congrega-

---

66. Deggeller: "It is clear that preaching from the mouth of a sinful human can never make the claim of finality" (D3).

67. Deggeller adds: "Otherwise it is not Christian preaching" (D3).

68. Deggeller's text includes: "If a certain person received the task to carry forward the interpretation of Scripture, he must himself have heard the Scripture before[hand] and must hear it again and again and indeed, in increasingly personal repentance and thankfulness before God" (D3).

tion-temperedness) of the sermon is the fact that it is directed to particular people at this particular time and spoken in such a way that they might understand it. He reminded the students that this cannot be separated from the second element, *Kirchlichkeit*. These hearers are baptized or should be — they belong to God (K2). Preaching that is *Gemeindemässigkeit* says directly to these particular people: your life has its basis and hope in Jesus Christ (S59). Again, this was a great contrast to the message rung out from pulpits far and wide in 1933, that the basis and hope of the German *Volk* could be found in the national awakening and its divinely appointed *Führer*.

The final element of the nine criteria, *Geistlichkeit*, was a return to Barth's repeated theme from the winter semester: preaching can only happen in humility, soberness, and prayer. The preacher is without power, decentered, knowing that only by God's will and action can human words become God's own Word, "standing before the secret of the gracious will of God" (KS3, P59). We are not permitted to hide ourselves from this reality with "the triumphant closure" of a "high gothic pointed arch." We can only be secure, Barth told the students, when we are insecure before God, vulnerable to the "coming near" of heaven (KS3, P59).[69]

The remainder of the class meeting turned from the outline of this principle and material homiletic to offer an initial introduction to the focus of the semester: the practical situation of the preacher faced with the task of "sermon-making," that is, a formal homiletic. A preacher faced with this task of "making" a sermon might experience one of two things, Barth explained. On the one hand, the preacher might be bursting with thoughts and ideas, with things he intends to say in the next worship service "from his soul." On the other hand, the preacher might feel a great emptiness and stand embarrassed before the text, having no idea what to say on Sunday. Indeed, a preacher might experience both at once, Barth suggested, being confident of his general intentions but at a loss with regard to the particulars (P59).[70]

---

69. As Deggeller described it: "Thus no triumphant conclusion, no sureness of victory, confidence in the success of one's own doing, but rather a willing self-opening to above and a remaining-open to God, so that God now confronts the human being and gives him everything and abundantly" (D4).

70. Deggeller expounds at some length particularly about the experience of the theology student just after graduation who faces his first Sunday sermon, asking, "how will he fare in this situation?" Deggeller discusses the two dynamics — the wealth and the poverty of the preacher — sequentially: "Either an honest feeling of joy will course through his soul, because now the moment has come, where he can mete out to his assembled *Gemeinde*, with

Neither of these situations, Barth told the young preachers, should be taken too seriously, for there is a something else which relativizes the significance of both. The something else is the fact that what the preacher is to say is given to him in the Old and New Testaments.[71] For a preacher overflowing with his own agendas and plans, this fact "applies reins to him," it pushes back his "dear" ideas (KS3, P60). For the one miserable about his "poverty of thought," this "givenness" should be a comfort (KS3, P60).[72]

From this starting point Barth's specific instructions regarding "sermon-making" would grow in the weeks to come. These students, there at the beginning of the Third Reich, would not have missed the fact that Barth's opening claim — that what a preacher is to say is bound, constrained, given in the particular witness of the New and Old Testaments and there alone — was a direct rejection of every sermon that began with "God's message" in the "great turning point" of January 1933.[73]

May 9 to 16, 1933

Contextual Developments

On May 10, the day after the sermon exercises met for the first time in the new semester, students and faculty members at universities all over Ger-

---

full hands, from the great theological inventory of the long years of study. He feels that he has something to say, a complete series of better and best thoughts which have occurred to him in recent days, lying, so to speak, in the drawer in his brain, already finished and just waiting to be taken out. . . . But then comes the time, where the abundance bit by bit is depleted" (D5-6).

71. "There is only one thing to do," Deggeller writes, "open the eyes and look at the treasure which is spread out before us. . . . The first step in sermon preparation is thus the knowledge, that we have to seek the material for our sermon solely from the Old and New Testaments . . . the *Gemeinde* of Jesus Christ waits for this uniquely and solely, for the food of Holy Scripture and nothing else" (D6-7).

72. Deggeller writes that while this experience of poverty seems "like a catastrophe," it is more "fruitful and promising" than the preacher with much to say. "For preaching does not involve a speaking and proclaiming from human stockpiles and thoughts. A perilous disturbance can be produced with one such mistaken presumption, from which I must let myself be called to order without delay. It does not involve my abundance, my richness of thought, my more or less intellectually rich ideas" (D6).

73. Cf. Emil Pfennigsdorf's sermon of two days earlier (May 7, 1933): Emil Pfennigsdorf, "Gottes Botschaft zum nationalen Aufbruch unseres Volkes," *Der Geisteskampf der Gegenwart: Monatschrift für christlische Bildung und Weltanschauung* 6 (1933): 201-6.

many engaged in what was officially called an "act against the unGerman spirit." The event had been planned for weeks, initiated by National Socialist student organizations with assistance from sympathetic librarians. Alfred Rosenberg's *Kampfbund für Deutsche Kultur* provided its support and ultimately the Reich Propaganda Ministry itself embraced the student effort.[74] The plan called for a four-week propaganda campaign, encouraging students and citizens to gather *zersetzendes* (corrosive) books, including but not limited to Marxist and Jewish literature, from libraries, bookstores, and personal collections, culminating on May 10 with public demonstrations at all German universities, in the course of which representative books would be ceremonially burned.[75] The events were to share a common structure, with speeches, nationalistic songs, and a responsive "litany" to be intoned as the offending volumes were consigned to the flames.[76] As George Moose argues, the leading participants in the book burning interpreted the act in quasi-religious terms as a purification ritual, burning away the dross so that the new Germany could rise from the ashes, with allusions to the "Spirit of 1914."[77]

In Bonn large crowds gathered in the market square, in spite of a steady rain. The local paper called it "an impressive and imposing ceremony," with the speakers standing on the floodlit steps of the city hall, with NSDAP leaders, students, docents, and professors gathered around.[78]

The keynote speech was given by the illustrious Professor of German Literature Hans Naumann, who exhorted the Bonn students that it would

---

74. J. M. Ritchie, "The Nazi Book-Burning," *Modern Language Review* 83, no. 3 (1988): 627. Pfennigsdorf was an active member of the local chapter of this organization in Bonn.

75. Books might be deemed "unGerman" on the grounds that they were Jewish, communist, socialist, anti-militaristic, immoral, corrupted the German language, or were disrespectful to the "immortal German *Volksgeist*," among other things. See Ritchie, "Nazi Book-Burning," p. 638.

76. The litany consisted of nine parts, each with a particular denunciation and affirmation, followed by the names of representative authors: "*Against* class struggle and materialism. *For Volksgemeinschaft* and an idealistic life style. Marx, Kautsky," or "*Against* decadence and moral decay. *For* discipline and morals in family and state. Heinrich Mann, Ernst Glaeser, Erich Kästner," and so forth. The litany is reprinted (in German) in Ritchie, "Nazi Book-Burning," p. 638.

77. George L. Moose, "Bookburning and the Betrayal," *New German Critique* 31 (1984): 148.

78. Helmut Heyer and Karl Gutzmer, "Kultur in Bonn im Dritten Reich," in *Veröffentlichungen des Stadtarchivs Bonn* (Bonn: Stadtarchiv und Stadthistorische Bibliothek, 2002), pp. 21-22.

be better to burn too many books on this night than too few. Naumann argued that the literature they destroyed in the fire represented "racially and nationally alien sources" and that therefore its existence was virtually "a continuation of the war."[79] "We shake off an alien domination," Naumann proclaimed, "we abolish an occupation. From an occupation of the German *Geist* we want to free ourselves!"[80]

What was the phoenix Professor Naumann imagined would rise from these ashes?

> We want a literature in which family and home, *Volk* and *Blut*, the entire existence *(Dasein)* of the religious bond is holy again, which educates us for the social feeling and for the life of the *Gemeinschaft*, which educates us for the state and for the *Führertum* and for the ability to put up a fight *(Wehrhaftigkeit)*. . . . We want the saints and the heroes. We want boldness and *Geist*. . . . *Heil* then therefore the new German literature! *Heil* to the supreme *Führer*! *Heil Deutschland!*[81]

After Naumann's speech was over, songs were sung, a professor of art history, Dr. Eugen Lüthgen, led the crowd in the litany, and the book burning began. Author Ernst Glaeser, who saw the burning of his own books that night, later described the scene:

> In the Bonn *Marktplatz* the funeral pyre of books was constructed, and in the glow of flames students, professors, uniformed Hitler youth, and SA-people surrounded this cult act of the [National Socialist] spirit. Civilians scurried self-consciously by behind the crowd. The faces of the students appeared all very familiar to me. Swarming spirits with the scowling neurotic look amid the unformed boy-face, between hooligans with bullnecks, short-winded graduates with the smug smiles of secret sadists, then again others, whose glance sank self-consciously to the ground when the books flew into the fire.[82]

---

79. Heyer and Gutzmer, "Kultur in Bonn," p. 22.

80. Heyer and Gutzmer, "Kultur in Bonn," p. 22.

81. Heyer and Gutzmer, "Kultur in Bonn," p. 22. George Moose notes the tension in Naumann's speech between his calls for heroic passion and "the stormy impulse of youth," and the simultaneous insistence on chastened "bourgeois virtues" such as duty, respectability, home, and hearth. Moose, "Bookburning and the Betrayal," p. 144.

82. Quote from "Scheiterhaufen auf dem Marktplatz: Die Bücherverbreenung vor 30 Jahren," in *Bonner Rundschau*, October 5, 1963. Quoted in Heyer and Gutzmer, "Kultur in Bonn," p. 22.

The same day the fires blazed in market squares all over Germany, May 10, 1933, the Reich government seized all the assets and property of the Social Democratic Party, which effectively incinerated the party as well.[83]

It was Barth's birthday.

Student-led demonstrations like the book burning, which administrators and faculty members not only tolerated but endorsed, served as a warning to the remaining "politically unreliable" professors at Bonn as elsewhere that anything might happen in the classroom if something "unGerman" was said.

Barth understood this dynamic. Six days after the book burning the *Predigtvorbereitung* met again to discuss "text selection," which sounds innocuous enough. But it is clear from Charlotte von Kirschbaum's account of the session that day in a letter to a friend that by this time Barth was self-consciously engaging in the kind of indirect political critique he would write about in *Theologische Existenz heute!* a month later. Kirschbaum wrote:

> We are just come home from the *Predigtübungen*.... The sermon exercises a little while ago went over the problem of "text choice." With this opportunity it was only natural to raise *many things,* even the question of preaching and war. Karl disentangled himself virtually expertly in all dangerous situations and discussions, and today afterwards honestly we really had to laugh. This disentangling oneself is at base not any clever agility, but simply taking the *theological* problems seriously. But simply as a *Schauspiel* [play, spectacle] it is sometimes revitalizing.[84]

Barth managed to talk about these "many things" in the presence of Nazis and *Stahlhelmer* without talking about them directly. Clearly Barth and Kirschbaum took a certain delight in this transgression. Barth criticized the nationalistic *Geist* and the preaching that nurtured it by attacking it at its root and, *Gleichschaltung* notwithstanding, he got away with it.

Session 2: May 16, 1933

Barth began the session by considering what it meant to "choose" a text as the basis of a sermon. "Choosing" in general is something human beings

---

83. Evans, *Coming of the Third Reich*, p. 358.
84. Charlotte von Kirschbaum to Erica Küppers, May 16, 1933, in *Briefe 1933*, pp. 205-6.

do, Barth explained, something we carry out "from one moment to another." We are always deciding, "voting," all the time, and we live with the "shackles" of these decisions. "Choices" frame our life, Barth observed, something to which everyone in the room, in the aftermath of a decisive election, could testify (KS4).[85]

But when we speak of "choosing" a text in the course of sermon preparation, Barth continued, the first thing to remember is that the selection of a text happens *in the church*, and as such it is subordinated to the "law" of the church. The question for the preacher is: Is this choice of a particular text an answer to the call of God? Is it obedient? Is it a choice that corresponds to our *being* as those elected by God? Or is it a choice made on the basis of our desire to be masters, lords? Is it a choice rooted in our hearts, our feelings, our consciences? Is it a matter of caprice (KS4)?

The selection of a text cannot be a leafing through the Bible to "choose" this or that word on the basis of one's own intentions and insights, Barth argued. To simply choose what is "serviceable" is "to confront the Scripture in our own freedom and absolute power" (P60). To do this, Barth warned, is to begin sermon preparation with an act of disobedience. The Holy Scripture cannot serve that "theme" which already "lies in our hearts" — here Kirschbaum put in parentheses: "the word, which 'underlies' our preaching today!!!" — no doubt a reference to the incessant sermonic endorsement of the Political Theology of *Volk, Blut,* and *Führer* (KS4).

The text is not to serve us, but we are to serve it, Barth told the young preachers. To prevent ourselves from going "astray" in this regard, Barth suggested, there are four practical safeguards.

First, it is advisable not to choose a text that is too short. The shorter the text, the greater the danger of exploiting the text for our own ends. For example, it is problematic to take one of the beatitudes in isolation, Barth argued. One should not preach on "Blessed are the sorrowful, for they shall be comforted," already knowing in advance what this "sorrow" is and what such "comfort" might mean (KS4, P60).

What did Barth suggest with this reference? In the context of preaching in the Third Reich, one can easily imagine the sermon that set out from

---

85. The same German term, *"wählen,"* which Kirschbaum sometimes puts in quotes, can mean "choosing" or "voting." In contrast to Kirschbaum's account, the student notes omit this general discussion of *"wählen"* as a part of life, moving immediately to the specifics of "text choice."

Karl Barth's Predigtvorbereitung *in Context: Summer Semester 1933*

the "sorrow" of war, the "stab in the back," Versailles, and the "decay" attributed to Weimar, only to arrive triumphantly at the "comfort" of the national awakening.

Second, Barth continued, one should avoid certain passages, specifically, certain "much quoted, supposedly easy and universally understood" texts (KS4). To preach on such texts, Barth warned, is almost always a disaster. He proceeded to cite two examples: On Reformation Day "distorting" a text like Galatians 5:1 is perilous, as is "coercing" something like 1 John 3:16 on *Volkstrauertag*, or Memorial Day (KS4, P60)![86] These students had no doubt heard sermons citing these particular texts on the occasions Barth indicated, probably more than once. The illumination of the Word will be greater in the fullness of its context in the Scripture rather than in our speeches, Barth argued, which may be "beautiful and captivating" but which "rape" the Word (KS5, P60).

Third, one should not set out to find a text that will facilitate a particular allegorical scheme, to seek out a word in order that the preacher can imbue it with a more or less beautiful or witty meaning. Preaching ought not to serve our artistic aspirations (KS5, P60).

And finally, Barth told them, repeating the now familiar injunction, preachers should not choose a text that simply facilitates a kind of propaganda, that is, a speech designed to accomplish an independent and predetermined goal. Preaching on Psalm 96:1 to improve church singing is a mistake, for example. So is exploiting John 4 to "aggrandize" the *Erntedankfest* (harvest festival) (KS5, P61).

It is, Barth reminded them, a matter of obedience. As a preacher one is servant of the Scripture, not its lord. All of our own "powerful reaching into the Scripture is therefore forbidden" (KS5).

With these four safeguards in mind, Barth asked, how then is a preacher to go about making the decision regarding what text to choose week by week? There are three possibilities for a preacher who wants to avoid caprice, Barth advised.

The first is to seek the counsel of the church, namely, to preach from the lectionary. This is above all a wise choice for the novice preacher, to turn to the church, which Calvin called "the mother of believers," for guidance (KS5, P61). Of course the lectionary is a church custom, a human cus-

---

86. Galatians 5:1: "For freedom Christ has set you free. Stand firm, therefore, and do not submit again to the yoke of slavery" (NRSV); 1 John 3:16: "We know love by this, that he laid down his life for us — and we ought to lay down our lives for one another" (NRSV).

tom, Barth conceded, but a custom which is based on experience, and as such can be "calmly affirmed" (KS5).

A second possibility is one that is shaped by the form of the Scripture itself: series-preaching. With this option one commits to the movement of a biblical book, preaching continuously from text to text, week by week (KS5, P61).

And the final and "most lively" possibility is one that springs from the "living communication" of the preacher and the Holy Scripture. Preachers should not engage the Bible only for the purpose of preaching (P61). The pastor who practices thorough Bible study can then select a particular text not arbitrarily, but in the context of a close life-connection with the Bible. But this requires a long life with the text, Barth cautioned, and "in no case stands open to young theologians" (KS5).

In the ensuing discussion, one student's question was highlighted. It did indeed move the conversation onto "dangerous" ground. How is a preacher to behave, a student asked, when his church administration dictates a particular Sunday theme to him (KS5)?

In the context of the spring of 1933, this was not a hypothetical question but a feature of pastoral life. Preachers in the German Protestant church had long been given statements from their superiors to be read from the pulpit or "themes" to be expressed on a given Sunday.[87] In some cases these were fairly innocuous, but in the period following the *Machtergreifung*, many pastors were instructed by administrators or church boards as to the degree of enthusiasm and thanksgiving they ought to exhibit with regard to the "national awakening" in their proclamation and prayer, and it would only get worse.[88] At this time in particular, showing support for the regime in the pulpit could be justified on the basis of evangelistic or "missionary" concerns alone — after all, people were finally coming back to the Protestant church, and the church should express its gratitude to God for the "national renewal" all around them.

How did Barth respond to the student's question? Barth explained that one should by all means listen to what the administration had to say, and turn to the text to see whether such an emphasis was found there. But

---

87. In his text, Deggeller embarks on a discussion of the practice of having themes for Sunday, which "under all circumstances" should "sharply be opposed." Even the church year with its themes is "open to question" (D9).

88. The letter Dibelius sent out to his pastors is unusual for its reticence with regard to expressions of partisanship, but, as we have seen, still counsels that pastors offer thanks for the salvation of Germany in the national revolution.

we do not have the authority in the church, Barth argued, to talk about "Christian principles" or other themes, but only to listen to what a particular scriptural text has to say. "There is no way that leads past God's Word," Barth insisted (P61). Even if one "wants to win outsiders," even if the request in question concerns "evangelism or missionary activities," even then the church is not allowed to neglect "the service commanded of it" — that is, to listen for the Word (P61).

If a church authority prescribes some "special reference" for the day, the question of whether or not to include that suggestion in the sermon can be answered only "in the claim of the divine Word" (P61). Only what remains valid *after an engagement with the text* (in the rigorous sense in which Barth understood such engagement) can be said (KS5). The Scripture should "purge all of one's own opinions, wishes and thoughts," Barth insisted. We want to hear "what the Word says, not what the great public, the smaller *Gemeinde*, or one's own heart might like to hear" (P61).[89]

The final arbiter of what was preached in the spring of 1933, then, according to Barth, should not be the church administration, but a local preacher who listens deeply, with *respicere*, to the particularity of the witness of a biblical text in its context. This would become more and more critical in the months, even years, to come.

May 16 to 23, 1933

Contextual Developments

The awareness that the decisions now being made by Hitler's advisor for church affairs, Ludwig Müller, and the Committee of Three in Berlin would change the Protestant church forever sparked discussion, debate, excitement, and anxiety throughout the country in the spring of 1933. The *Deutsche Christen* continued to insist, loudly, that they, of all people,

---

89. That Deggeller heard an implicit critique of preaching during the Great War during this discussion is apparent from his account: "Especially in cases (suppositionally: the outbreak of war) the text must always be set above the theme of the mentioned days. . . . More than ever exactly in such situations [one] is to preserve obedience in relation to the text and to the Word of God. For the church can only then fulfill its actual task, if it is not moving toward the general [situation] with agitation, but seeks to become its lord, in that it announces something that stands above all human fuss. On the same basis are all manner of slogans (*Stichworten*) of so called casual talks (*Kasualreden*) strictly to be avoided" (D9).

should play a part in the negotiations now under way in Berlin. And many Protestants agreed with them. Since the party was founded in 1932, their numbers had increased exponentially. Like their NSDAP counterparts, they looked like the young, vigorous, passionate Germany that few in the church wanted to discourage in general, regardless of doubt in the details. Telegrams and letters began to arrive in Berlin, urging Müller and the Committee of Three to include *Deutsche Christen* representatives in the discussion.

But by this time the more radical wing of the *Deutsche Christen,* personified by Hossenfelder, had begun to be a problem for Ludwig Müller. In public statements Hossenfelder and his cohorts made it clear that they wanted nothing less than the *Gleichschaltung* of the Protestant church, and, confident the *Deutsche Christen* would triumph, demanded new elections in all the *Landeskirchen*.[90] But Müller's goal was to reach a compromise on a new constitution with the leaders of the *Landeskirchen,* hopefully a compromise that would include his, Müller's, appointment to the office of Reich Bishop.

But compromise with the old guard was not what Hossenfelder had in mind. When the Committee of Three relented and invited Hossenfelder and his colleagues to present their ideas in Berlin, the ten "points" they laid out there depicted a state-controlled, *völkisch* church — something absolutely unpalatable to the Committee of Three. From Müller's perspective, this sort of provocation by the *Deutsche Christen* had to stop. To get the compromise he desired, Müller needed to tame the radical wing of the *Deutsche Christen,* and he needed to come up with his own alternative to the revolutionary proposals of Hossenfelder. But Müller had to find a way to do this while retaining the basic vision of the *Deutsche Christen:* a Protestant church in harmony with the new state.

The person who came to Müller's rescue in the latter regard was a theologian, Professor Karl Fezer of Tübingen, the very Fezer whom Barth discussed in the winter semester of the *Predigtvorbereitung*.[91] It was Fezer

---

90. The leadership of the *Deutsche Christen* in Berlin made the following announcement on April 30: "The enemies of the Third Reich are hiding themselves behind the church . . . the church can receive true life only through the mass of Protestant church people who are still strangers to the official church. This mass, however, already stands behind our Faith Movement and demands more and more vigorously the co-ordination of state and church. . . . We therefore call for immediate new elections on the basis of an equal, secret and direct vote." Scholder, *Churches and the Third Reich*, vol. 1, p. 315.

91. Fezer's involvement in the matter originated with a meeting in Berlin between the

who, along with his own ad hoc advisory committee of theologians, produced a new and (relatively) moderate set of guidelines for the *Deutsche Christen* in the spring of 1933.[92]

The "Fezer Guidelines," as they were called, were undeniably based on the presuppositions of Political Theology, namely, that the German *Volk* must be understood as a direct creation of God, that the church was bound to the German *Volk* and must help it flourish, and that the will of God is not revealed only in Jesus Christ or the Bible, but also in the history of the *Volk*. The guidelines rejected any democratic form of governance in the church, embraced a vague "spiritual" version of the *Fuhrerprinzip*, and called for united *Landeskirchen*. In the spring of 1933, this was a vision the majority of Protestant leaders could support.[93] With some reluctance, the Berlin leadership of the *Deutsche Christen* agreed to the new guidelines on May 15 (at least temporarily), and the next day Müller showed them to Hitler for his seal of approval, which was given. A few days later Müller undertook concluding negotiations with the Committee of Three. Things seemed to be coming together. But at just about that time, the first organized opposition church party made its presence known.

The Young Reformation Movement was born early in May in reaction to the *Deutsche Christen* claim to leadership in the Protestant church.[94] Like the *Deutsche Christen*, the Young Reformers were convinced that the National Socialist revolution was a gift from God, they were enthusiastic supporters of the *Führer*, and they wanted comprehensive reform of the church. But in contrast to the *Deutsche Christen*, they did not

---

deans and assistant deans of all Protestant faculties of German universities in late April, to discuss the task of theology in the new situation. The conference was deeply divided between the minority who were disturbed by the injustice and loss of freedoms in the Third Reich and a majority, especially marked among the younger professors, who argued that the National Socialist state merited their "unconditional solidarity." Among the more prominent of these was Karl Fezer, who was sympathetic to the *Deutsche Christen*. The conference commissioned Fezer to serve as "liaison officer" to approach Müller's group in Berlin and presumably to influence the new constitution. Scholder, *Churches and the Third Reich*, vol. 1, p. 317.

92. Fezer's theological working group was comprised of Emanuel Hirsch, Friedrich Karl Schumann (Lutheran systematics professor, Halle), and Wilhelm Goeters (Reformed professor of church history, Bonn).

93. On the "Fezer guidelines," see Scholder, *Churches and the Third Reich*, vol. 1, pp. 318-19.

94. Among the flood of younger pastors who joined the movement in May was Barth's dialectical colleague Friedrich Gogarten and the dynamic nationalist Martin Niemoeller.

want a porous boundary between church and the National Socialist state, a position grounded in the Lutheran doctrine of the two kingdoms. The church must make decisions based on its nature as the church, without interference from the state or the National Socialist Party.[95]

In May of 1933, the Young Reformers wanted the Committee of Three to appoint a bishop immediately, to quash the increasingly strident *Deutsche Christen* and NSDAP grandstanding for the *Gleichschaltung* of the Protestant church. They even had a candidate for bishop in mind: the Director of the Bodelschwingh Institutes in Bethel — a Christian organization that provided aid to the poor and disabled — the fifty-six-year-old Friedrich von Bodelschwingh. Meanwhile reports came in from various quarters that the *Deutsche Christen* were demanding Müller himself for Reich Bishop. This news panicked the Young Reformers. They worked feverishly to get the attention of the powers that be, writing letters, releasing statements, and making contacts, with some success. By the time the Committee of Three, Müller, and Fezer's contingent met in Loccum on May 17, the Lutheran member of the Committee of Three (Marahrens) argued that they should not ignore the concerns of the Young Reformers, especially since Müller was an official representative of a church-political party (the *Deutsche Christen*) himself. Thus the negotiations continued, even as statements, counterstatements, theses, announcements, confessions, and other such efforts to stake a claim sprouted up everywhere, the fruit of the many gatherings, large and small, that Protestants of all sorts attended in those days.[96]

By the middle of May, Barth confessed that he was very worried about the "church question," and he described his involvement in the conflict, as he would for some weeks, as "primarily *behind* the scenes." "The chaos is outrageous," he wrote to his brother Peter on May 18.[97] The planned and impromptu late-night meetings in the Barth house contin-

---

95. For one example, the YRM rejected the application of the Aryan paragraph to the church, on the grounds that "the state is to judge, the church is to save." Scholder, *Churches and the Third Reich*, vol. 1, p. 321.

96. The most famous of the documents produced in these months include *"Aufruf an alle Lutheraner"* by General Superintendent Zoellner (April 13, 1933), *"Osnabrucker Bekenntnis"* (April 27, 1933), *"Aufruf der Jungreformatorischen Bewegung"* (May 9, 1933), *"Richtlinien der Glaubensbewegung Deutsche Christen"* by Joachim Hossenfelder, and the revised version, the *"Müllerish"* or *"Fezerish Richtlinien"* of the *Deutsche Christen* (May 16, 1933).

97. Karl Barth to Peter Barth, May 18, 1933, in *Briefe 1933*, p. 208.

ued without interruption. Earlier in the spring, Barth began meeting with a small group of Reformed theologians, pastors, and laypeople in Düsseldorf to discuss the theological issues involved in the question of church reform. On May 20 they met from three in the afternoon until ten in the evening, ultimately producing a document (largely written by Barth) known as the Düsseldorf Theses, which was then published in the Reformed *Tagesblättern* on May 22.[98]

In addition to the Düsseldorf project, Barth was also in close communication throughout this period with the Reformed representative on the Committee of Three, Hermann Albert Hesse of Elberfeld. It was and would remain a frustrating situation for Barth, for although Hesse regularly sought Barth's advice on the matters before the committee, often summoning him to Elberfeld to confer, he rarely took the advice in the pressure of the moment.[99] By this time Barth was aware of the basic content of the nationalist document about to be released by Müller and the Committee of Three, though the organizational implications were not yet visible.

Worries about the fate of friends and former students in the Third Reich continued as well. On May 20 Barth learned that his old friend from Switzerland Wilhelm Vischer (then lecturer in Old Testament at Bethel in Germany) had been dismissed for having "hidden 'Jewish-Bolshevist' propaganda" in his Old Testament lectures. If he tried to take the lectern again, Vischer was warned, he would be placed in *"Schutzhaft"* (protective custody).[100] In Bonn, Barth's students remained "loyal and well-behaved in their work," though there was reportedly the occasional "diatribe" from members of the *Deutsche Christen*.[101] A sense of the atmosphere in Bonn is captured by Charlotte von Kirschbaum in a letter to Barth's mother on May 21:

---

98. Barth said of the meeting: "The four non-theologians who signed it were not just there, by the way, as decoration, but they really honestly collaborated in the seven-hour meeting in which the thing came to be, especially the farmer named in the fourth place from Vörde who demonstrated an astonishing knowledge of the Bible and the catechism. The little conference already made quite an impression on me, in spite of all kinds of trouble which [came] after the fact." Karl Barth to Karl Gerhard Steck, May 28, 1933, in *Briefe 1933*, p. 227.

99. Though Hesse, as Reformed, rejected the idea of a bishop, for example, in a compromise with the Lutherans, he voted for it anyway in the course of the negotiations. *Briefe 1933*, p. 211, n. 4.

100. Charlotte von Kirschbaum to Anna Barth, May 21, 1933, in *Briefe 1933*, p. 212. *Schutzhaft* is the first entry in Victor Klemperer's notebook of Nazi terminology, which formed the basis for his *Lingua Tertii Imperii*. Evans, *Coming of the Third Reich*, p. 440.

101. Charlotte von Kirschbaum to Anna Barth, May 21, 1933, in *Briefe 1933*, p. 211.

we live in a mysterious time, externally identified by countless uniforms and countless *Heil* Hitler calls in the streets and in the hallways of the university. Karl keeps far away from the *"Feiern"* [celebrations] of this university. They begin or end with the Horst-Wessel song and are little triumphs of *Gleichschaltung*. In the faculty meetings he pleads for his standpoint in great things and in little things, and the present dean, Professor Pfennigsdorf, appears no match for the situation. Everything thus rolls along at an unprecedented tempo, each day the situation changes again, and no one knows, what will be tomorrow.[102]

Session 3: May 23, 1933

The third class meeting of the semester was dedicated to the next aspect of sermon preparation, something Barth called "the receptive task." It could also be called "passive" in contrast to "active" or "objective" in contrast to "subjective," Barth observed, though none of these terms can be used without caution. The receptive indicates a "simple but not unproblematic" activity: listening to the text (KS6, P62). This means *reading* the text, absorbing it word by word, attending to what is there. "What is there" will become the content of the sermon — which should be obvious, Barth noted, to anyone who has been paying attention (KS6, P62).

This close reading must begin with the original text, because any translation (even Luther's!) is already a commentary (KS6, P62). Therefore, Barth told the class, the whole enterprise presents us with the problem of *language*. On the one hand, we do not say that Hebrew and Greek as such are "the language of the Holy Spirit" by virtue of some special aptitude. But on the other hand, "revelation *happens* in these languages," and that must be acknowledged (KS6; P62).[103] If one does not begin with the original language, certain connections are lost, and, Barth told the students, one is able to observe this in the sermon (KS6, P62).

After reading the original text, one can then read the translations of others. Barth named Adolf Schlatter in this regard, "even if one does not follow him in everything," as well as Weissäcker and Stange, and then he turned to the translation of Luther. Luther's translation is the one known

---

102. *Briefe 1933*, p. 212.
103. Deggeller writes: "To the question of *why* this linguistic predestination one can only respond: it is just so" (D11).

in the *Gemeinde*, Barth explained — it had been read in the church for centuries. It is *their* text. Therefore this text warrants a particular hearing, and should be read from the pulpit, rather than a translation of one's own. When Luther has missed the nuance, Barth suggested, this provides an opportunity for discussion in the sermon (KS6-7).

After a careful reading of the text, then, one must ask about its content. Barth offered a number of questions: What is the context of this text?[104] What comes before and after it? What is the goal of this entire address? How do the proportions of the statements relate to each other? How are the ideas ordered? What is the *curve* of the text (KS7, P63)? Only after considering such questions should one turn to commentaries (P63).[105]

A commentary, Barth explained, is distinguished from a translation in that it examines the text in its constituent parts. There are two types of commentaries from which to choose. The modern ones from the eighteenth century to the present provide the necessary insights of historical-critical research. The older commentators also understood that the Bible has a "historical mortal form" and sought to understand the text in its "concrete *Sosein*" (in-the-time-being), but took the constraints that might come with such historically bound readings "less seriously" than modern interpreters (KS7, P63).

In our time, Barth commented, one often thinks the historical meaning of the text is *the* meaning of the text. Where that happens, Barth insisted, we stand before a dogma — an "extra-ecclesiastical, heathen dogma" — which sees all of this simply in terms of the aspect of the human being and the human world and the human activities called religion (KS7, P63).[106]

---

104. Deggeller adds: "For every text has its organic binding with the collective corpus of the Bible and has no distinct existence.... The *Woher* and *Wohin* of a text does not stand in the foreground in scientific exegesis, but it is also not to be overlooked with any homiletical work" (D11-12).

105. Deggeller notes that once the "line" of the text is found and established, then "we can go a step further and consult the commentaries for orientation, which are not only translations and content statements, but also have something to say about the *Sache*, above all to clarify the historical context" (D12).

106. Deggeller's notes describe the argument as follows: "The [historical-critical] quest is in itself so natural and warranted that it needs no mention. One must know in all times that the Bible is not fallen from heaven, but has its completely natural history of development, that, for example, Paul was a child of his time and thus only as such could speak and has spoken. The tragic development in biblical science thus does not lie in the fact that it has a historical research method, but in the overemphasis on its meaning, in the regrettable error, to have made the historical side of biblical research into the main issue" (D12-13).

But preaching cannot happen with the presupposition of such a dogma. If this dogma is true, then it makes no sense to grant the Bible any privileged place — there are other texts that might serve just as well. But the Holy Scripture involves the unique and exclusive revelation of God. This does not mean we do not learn from historical-critical research! Modernity attends to the human form of the Bible, and the preacher must "respect this situation and take it seriously" (KS8).[107] Barth named the handbook of Lietzmann, the *Göttingen Bibelwerk,* and the commentaries of Jülicher, Zahn, and Holtzmann as possible resources (KS8, P63).

If it is true with regard to revelation that the word becomes flesh, then "how could we have the Bible otherwise than in its human form?" This is a serious problem but also a "hopeful one": "To what extent is this entire concrete human word God's Word, a witness to God's Word? To what extent will this text also say something which points beyond humanity to God?" To what extent is "a movement carried out in which the writer looks beyond his deepest agitation and points to Immanuel" (KS8, P64)?

No amount of critical work can prevent us from seeing these problems. "The Word became *flesh* but the *Word* became flesh: that is the Christian dogma of the Bible" (KS8). Human speaking is subordinated by a truth which comes over them, a speaking from revelation about revelation. Precisely as a "mortal vessel" preachers must take the Bible seriously as "the vessel of *revelation*" (K8). With regards to the question of revelation, the "decisive question for exegesis," "the *old* exegetes have been more openminded than the moderns" (KS8).[108] What are some worthy commentaries from the older interpreters? Bengel's *Gnomon* [*Novi Testamenti*], Calvin, Luther, and also (with some caution) Augustine (KS8, P64).[109]

After reading the text, translations, and commentaries, one might also read sermons on the text, Barth suggested. But with modern ser-

---

107. From Deggeller: "We should read [commentaries] with all peace and without fear, to go to them without prejudice. We know it well: the biblical text is a document, but only *also* a document. This situation is to be taken very seriously" (D13-14).

108. Deggeller includes the comment: "But also the so-called positive exegetes of the last century are to a large extent like the liberals, even if they are different from them by some more anointing and a certain religious trimming" (D14).

109. Deggeller on Calvin: "Calvin had his eyes open, even for historical things, even if his attempts in this direction remain hidden in the beginning. Above all he preserved the concern of the church, in that he [preserved] the church dogma that only one thing needed to be said: Scripture concerns God." And on Augustine: "But with him a certain caution is yet required. For he was not only a theologian, but also a great philosopher and stood under the influence of the platonic world of ideas" (D14-15).

mons, Barth warned, "special caution is demanded," because they "almost all stand under the fatal sign of theme preaching" (P64).[110] Sermons that have "the clear character of Scripture interpretation" include Calvin, Hermann Friedrich Kohlbrügge, and Gottfried Menken, Barth advised the class (P63).

In the final discussion many questions were raised, including the issue of the "busyness" of the pastor, which Barth, as in the first semester, lamented, arguing that the preaching task should be at the center of pastoral work, and would certainly come at a price of other "valuable and important society-work." The pastor should begin the sermon by Wednesday at the very latest! And the absolute minimum preparation must include a basic study of the text, including the original text itself (KS9).

Barth's antidote to the superficial, utilitarian, "theme" approach of his contemporaries is the difficult, thoughtful work of exegesis. How odd this attention to the details of words, of dead languages, of dusty sermons must have seemed in the context of the "national awakening"!

May 23 to 30, 1933

Contextual Developments

The agreement reached by Müller and his collaborators in mid-May on the outline of the new constitution of the Protestant church — known as "the Loccum Manifesto" — called for one German Protestant church with a Lutheran Reich Bishop and a National Synod. It would be a federation, not of *Landeskirchen*, but of confessions, though "vigorous" *Landeskirchen* were to be preserved.[111] It was rather sketchy on the details. But

---

110. Deggeller adds: "For our modernity stands unfortunately under the fatal sign of theme preaching, and what this, its *Wesen* (essence), presents accordingly, is the distortion and vilification of the true mode of preaching, of which an important word is to be said later in a particular place. But there are really good contemporary sermons in print, which one could choose without qualms, to read them like one might read a commentary. It is still true: wrestling over an understanding of the Bible has always taken place in the study of the pastor. Why should we not go to their school and learn from them? Thus we will in conclusion make ourselves the rule, the old as well as the new exegesis to zoom in on, to keep them close to one another, to test everything and to keep hold of the good" (D15).

111. The language of "Reich church" was dropped in favor of "German Protestant church" on the grounds that the former excluded Germans outside the legal borders of the Reich. Scholder, *Churches and the Third Reich*, vol. 1, p. 319.

how was this vision to be implemented? Namely, how would they choose the bishop?

Ludwig Müller, not surprisingly, thought the *state* should be involved in this decision, but, at least on this, he was overruled. Instead, the Committee of Three sketched out their own plan, which Müller finally accepted: the Committee of Three would meet with the various church "parties" (mainly they thought of the *Deutsche Christen* and the Young Reformers), then they would secure agreements on the new constitution and on the nominee for bishop (confidentially) from official representatives of the *Landeskirchen*, and *then* they would tell Hitler. The plan called for celebrations all over Germany on the day the results were announced. *No* election, *no* state participation.[112]

The problem with the plan was that the *Deutsche Christen* were already proclaiming that Müller was to be bishop, and this claim was plastered all over the newspapers. Feeling themselves railroaded by the *Deutsche Christen* and having some sympathy for the impassioned arguments of the Young Reformers, the Committee of Three caused an uproar by announcing that their choice for bishop was . . . Bodelschwingh.

The headlines changed overnight. The fury from the *Deutsche Christen* was almost matched by the terror of the leaders of the various *Landeskirchen*, who were now all summoned to a meeting on May 26 for the purpose of voting to affirm the outline to the new constitution and the selection of the bishop. All eyes were upon them. While a group of Lutheran bishops pleaded Müller's case in the course of the May 26 deliberations (as did Müller himself), in the end Bodelschwingh prevailed.[113]

Why was this a momentous event in the context of the Third Reich? Because it marked perhaps the first time since the *Machtergreifung* that Hitler's will was thwarted. And this could not be.

The *Deutsche Christen* and Müller himself were up in arms. On the very night that Bodelschwingh was elected by the representatives of the *Landeskirchen* as their bishop, Müller went on the radio to make it clear that this was not over. He scolded the Protestant leaders who rejected him:

> You have not heard the voice of God which, through the movement in our *Volk*, calls us to daring action. . . . The Reich Bishop ought to be a

---

112. Scholder, *Churches and the Third Reich*, vol. 1, p. 324.

113. Though the first round of voting was quite close, by the final round Bodelschwingh won 91-8. Scholder, *Churches and the Third Reich*, vol. 1, p. 330.

man whose name arouses a response in our fighting groups, a man whose the whole awakening *Volk* looks on with trust with all its heart. He ought to be the church's leader for a new birth and a new energy.[114]

Müller ended his radio address with the surprisingly democratic demand that the bishop must be called by the *Volk*, not elected by men who were mere "advocates for the status quo."[115] A few days later Müller met with Hitler, who, temporarily abandoning his policy of non-engagement, promised to help him prevail. For the next four weeks, Müller would have all the resources of the National Socialist Party at his disposal. With that, the next massive propaganda campaign began.

For Barth, a Reformed theologian, the question about *who* would be bishop was simply the wrong question, and it was being asked for the wrong reasons in the spring of 1933. As he explains the Reformed position in a letter to his former pupil Karl Gerhard Steck:

> Our opposition against the "bishop" is . . . a theological one. We protest — and we will certainly protest irreconcilably — against the possibility that we, that any, who confess to "a church reformed by God's Word," should allow our dogmatics to be enriched by a *locus de Episcopo* (placing of a bishop) by reason of the present heresies and chaos. It concerns the condition that the bishop is endowed with spiritual authority, especially with the authority to proclaim doctrine or even simply to adjust [it]. It concerns the bishop as "spiritual *Führer*" above the individual *Gemeinden* and the ordinary *Ministerium Verbi*. The idea of *this* bishop arises in the momentary situation doubtless from the ideology of the insane and wicked sect of the so-called *deutschen Christen*. It is also as such, barely in disguise, identical with the currently rampant political *Führeridee*. This political *Führeridee* translated in theological terms results without fail in the specified bishop.[116]

---

114. Scholder, *Churches and the Third Reich*, vol. 1, p. 334.
115. Scholder, *Churches and the Third Reich*, vol. 1, p. 334.
116. Karl Barth to Karl Gerhard Steck, May 28, 1933, in *Briefe 1933*, p. 228. As he had written to Hans Asmussen a couple of days earlier: "For us Herr von Bodelschwingh, or whoever thus may be the chosen one, under no circumstances [could] be more than simply still 'president' and an outwardly decorative figure." Karl Barth to Hans Asnussen, May 26, 1933, in *Briefe 1933*, p. 219.

Regardless of the outcome of the question now gripping the Reich — "Müller or Bodelschwingh?" — already in May Barth felt he could only exist in opposition to the new and improved German Protestant church.[117]

Along with the institutional and legal pressure to conform to the Third Reich, there were also continuing incidents of more personal pressure to do so. Barth had known his Bonn colleague, Church History Professor Wilhelm Goeters, since 1923, and though they disagreed, they on occasion talked of politics. (Goeters had been member of the right-wing *Deutschnationalen Volkspartei* [DNVP] prior to the National Socialist Revolution.) But on May 25, Goeters wrote to Barth to tell him that the time had come for Barth to desist from expressing his political opinion. Barth should not openly discuss his "Swiss-democratic state ideology" and should withdraw from the SPD immediately. Barth, Goeters wrote, had done enough for his party, and now that it was "in liquidation" there was no reason to jeopardize his future. The hour had arrived when Barth needed to do something to demonstrate visibly that he was not using his civil service office "for political opposition goals."[118]

Barth responded that it would be impossible for him to abandon "his own political hypothesis" for the reasons Goeters indicated. "You could ask me now, first of all, whether I am so certain of the good thing which I call my 'political hypothesis,' that I do not treat it as *adiaphora* and thus, for example, 'for the sake of love' could now take up the *Hakenkreuz* in some form."[119] Of course, Barth continued, every political decision is a relative thing before God, and subject to error.

> I can, yes, be wrong. I can, yes, by thinking through or thinking after the facts still be taught other things.... But until then you would have to knock me in the head ... to dissuade me of the view, that the German *Volk* have not justly and not to its health thrown its arms around this current system.[120]

Finally Barth concluded:

---

117. See, for example, Karl Barth to Wilhelm Goeters, May 27, 1933: "But so much is already clear to me, that I thus could only live in this new church to be in opposition." *Briefe 1933*, p. 225.
118. *Briefe 1933*, p. 222.
119. *Briefe 1933*, p. 223.
120. *Briefe 1933*, p. 224.

You could ask me in the second place, whether I then could not and must perform the desired *"Gleichschaltung"* for example, for the sake of the church, that is, for the sake of my further work in the church — a fat burnt offering [cf. Amos 5:22]. I see well, how many now have intended to come to help the dear God in this way. But I beg your pardon: To me the train of thought that leads there is Jesuitical. The goal does not sanctify the means. In contrast I think that it applies even and precisely to the church as well — and perhaps still might come to good again, if now here and there one of its representatives in the profane region of political decisions, where it "only" can concern civil-courage, provides the *concrete* evidence that *Gleichschalterei* has its limits, as it is also possible of a heathen.[121]

The exhausting cycle of teaching, writing letters, following the various developments in church and politics, navigating the minefield of the University campus, and engaging in long hours of discussion continued.

Of his existence in Germany Barth wrote to a former student in Japan at the end of May:

> It is certainly a very amazing time, in which one must unavoidably spend many, many hours a day reading the newspaper and in conversations of all sorts. One must really each day exert oneself just to realize what has come over us here since 30 January. Again and again one is surprised by the trains of thought, which now may still perhaps be correct in themselves in the fascist-becoming-world, but practically have no more meaning [here]. *"Rechtstaat"* (rule of law), *"Menschenwürde"* (human dignity), *"Gedankenfreiheit"* (freedom of thought), "mail and telephone privacy," the possibility of an honest word from strangers — oh dear, where has everything gone?
>
> But thus one lives in opposition, [one] lives in the entirely pompous style of a state in which one party put the entire *Volk* in their pocket with marvelous technique; [one] lives in it, to be dispensed the wisdom and the good will of this party and respectively its *Führer* of mercy and unmercy; [one] lives in it, never to know what could still be possible in, for example, 14 days, on the whole and in detail. From the Jewish boycott to the giant fireworks display on 1 May, already a little of everything has become possible. It was, yes, not even very much dif-

---

121. *Briefe 1933*, p. 224.

ferent in Babylon or Rome or even in the absolutist state of the eighteenth century, and people still lived through [it]. The true miracles of a lack of character are very painful, which now in this transitional period are ongoing everywhere — really wherever you look. Thereby one learns to know his peers and will be poorer concerning a few illusions: it is entirely awesome, how promptly especially the theologians of the different schools have learned, to *'gleichschalten'* themselves . . . !"[122]

Session 4: May 30, 1933

Though there is no trace of this in the official or unofficial notes for this session, Barth began the session with "a long, very thoughtful and very commanding little speech" to the class, before he took up the subject of the day. The speech was about "the responsibilities of students of theology (among whom he thoroughly reckons himself!) in the summer of 1933."[123]

The talk was prompted on the one hand by the "now so obvious distraction" in the form of political and church developments, and on the other by a remark Georg Merz made in a letter to a student, suggesting that, in the present moment, theological work had little significance. Barth told the preaching students that "right now, only entirely serious theological work could be meaningful action and that their participation in the development of their *Volk* and their church could only go through there."[124]

How did the *Predigtvorbereitung* students respond? Kirschbaum wrote: "They have understood [it] well, and I have heard some thankful comments about this call. They could unify, yes, actually endure, these poor young people, who from all sides only get mottos and slogans and yet simply must do without any real guidance to a large extent."[125] After this "speech," Barth turned to the material for the day.

The previous session dealt with the "receptive" activity of considering "what is there" in a biblical text, its words, its structure, its biblical context.

---

122. *Briefe 1933*, pp. 224, 231-32. A student protocol of the speech is printed in Hinrich Stoevesandt's introduction to the new edition of *Theologische Existenz heute!* (1933) (Munich: Chr. Kaiser Verlag, 1984), pp. 10-11.

123. Charlotte von Kirschbaum to Eduard Thurneysen, June 2, 1933, in Karl Barth, *Gesamtausgabe*, ed. Hinrich Stoevesandt and Hans Anton Drewes (Zürich: Theologischer Verlag, 1971), V.34, pp. 420-21.

124. Barth, *Gesamtausgabe* V.34, p. 421.

125. Barth, *Gesamtausgabe* V.34, p. 421.

Karl Barth's Predigtvorbereitung in Context: Summer Semester 1933

In this class meeting Barth turned to what he called the "spontaneous" task of sermon preparation. What did he mean by this? The spontaneous or subjective task involves the exploration of two issues, Barth explained. One is the discernment of the "peculiar way of witness" of a text; the other is the "present situation" of this "peculiar way of witness." The former is the subject of this class session.

Barth began with the claim that the Bible is both a historical monument and a living document. As a monument it is "a piece of the history of human piety," as modern commentaries have "sharply and rightly" emphasized (P65). But for the preacher and the people, who exist in the "space" of the Christian church, the Bible as a monument, a remembrance of a past that once was, is not adequate. In the event "church" the Bible is a document, a charter, that still has validity, that places us before a decision in the present (P65). As this living document it is "the one unique and sufficient witness of God's revelation"; "we call it the Word of God" (KS9). When we read the Bible in the space "church" — as witness — then it is "impossible" to turn to the text asking: What is the "theme" or "*Skopus*"? The "theme" of the Holy Scripture can only be one: Jesus Christ himself (KS9). And Jesus Christ "himself speaks" (KS10).[126] What we can pass along on the basis of the text can only be the "witness" of this speaking of Jesus Christ. This witness is not some "theme" from the Holy Scripture, but rather is the human statement of the prophets and apostles, a human statement which did not arise from their "own inner necessity" but because "Yahweh was too strong for them"; it was "given under a burden that was laid on them," under "a Word that was spoken to them" (KS10). In relation to this burden, this Word, they responded in the presence of the people and "a piece of their human response lies before us in our text." The way which this text will go — not just then, but in the "repetition" (*Wiederholen*) of its way now — "is the content of preaching" (KS10, P66). To read the text in view of its "way of witness" is to read beyond "individual words" — it stands in a context! Barth then repeated his warning about preaching on texts that are too short, "because with them one more easily disregards the situation" (P66).

The sermon, then, does not primarily concern "familiar truths" such

---

126. Deggeller writes: "What would the mischief of theme-setting be other than an arrogant, but impotent attempt to lead to Jesus Christ by our thought, so to speak, by a plan? We guard ourselves, therefore, from hauling out a theme from some section of the Bible and speaking on that" (D16).

as "the glory of faith" or "the Christian and the *Vaterland*" or "any other familiar or relatively less familiar truths as its subject" (P66-67). The truth that concerns the preacher is not "familiar" at all but "absolutely unknown" and "hidden" — to theologians just as much as to laypeople (P67)! The preacher's task, Barth continued, is to point again and again to this "not only relatively but absolutely unknown truth in the hope and with the prayer" that Jesus Christ himself — through the service of this human pointing — will make this absolutely unknown truth (the *aletheia* of Jesus Christ) *known* to the people (KS10).[127] The church is called to this service of pointing, stepping "in the ranks of the prophets and apostles as their students, their hearers, as those who are altogether dependent on them" (KS10). It is a "simple and humble thing," to travel the way of witness taken by the text again with the *Gemeinde* (P67). What the prophets and apostles heard, we attempt to say-after (P67).

Barth then alerted the students to three "technical" issues that arise with the problematic of the "way of witness."

First, Barth returned to the question of the *other* identity of the Bible, to its witness as a monument of human piety in contrast to its witness as a document for the church. As in the previous week, Barth affirmed that consideration of the Bible as a historical text is necessary, for "we could not thus understand it as a document, if we did not also see it as a monument" (KS10). This monument is the *form* of the witness, and there will be times in a sermon that aspects of the text which belong to its historical relativity must play a certain role, Barth explained, though this cannot be elevated to an "independent meaning"[128] (KS11). After all, the purpose of preaching is not to explore ancient history, but to go the way of the text today, Barth remarked. Therefore there is a limit to too much emphasis on historical events. A preacher might ask: Does this history belong to the way of witness in the present (P67)?

Second, Barth warned the students against constructing all their sermons according to "one particular schema" (P68). The Bible is diverse, Barth asserted. Not every sermon should follow the pattern: "the human being is a sinner, but now Christ is there, now the human being should be

---

127. Deggeller adds: "Theologian and *Gemeinde* do not have it in their power to disclose this truth. It will happen entirely sovereignly and without our questionable interference. To that we have to humble ourselves and to concentrate on the only task: the interpretation of Scripture" (D17).

128. Deggeller: "the subject of the repetition is not the outer form of the witness, not the historical garment in which the witness is clothed" (D18).

better!" for example (P68). Guard against such "well-worn tracks," Barth advised the young preachers (P68). Every Sunday should be "a new thing" that points to the "one great new thing," to the "great new beginning that we can make with God, on the basis of his great new beginning with us" (P68). There is a "richness" to the Scripture in regard to the "possibilities of its ways of witness," Barth affirmed (KS11).[129]

Finally, Barth reminded them, every preacher belongs to a church with a certain confession, a certain dogma. Dogma can be compared to "buoys" which "point the ships in the sea in the right direction" (P68). Then Barth continued more pointedly: "Many bad things would not be said; much would be said better, if the preacher knew what is permitted to be said of Christ, of the Holy Spirit" (P68). But this does not mean one should literally quote dogma in the sermon! Dogma is a guidepost that can guard against presumption and caprice; it is like a "good pair of glasses, with whose help the preacher can look confidently and joyfully in the text" (P68). One is not to be a "savage" in exegesis, Barth admonishes, but attentive to the direction dogma can provide.[130] Therefore, continuous study of dogmatics is of "extraordinary importance" for preachers (KS11). This is a matter of "discipline," of "chastity," in the consciousness of a responsibility that is "firmly established on the basis of the church" (P68).

In a time when the value of such things as theology and dogmatics was openly questioned and "savagery" was all the rage, Barth continued to underline the message of his "speech" at the beginning of the session.

But what is it actually like to discern the way of witness of a text? To help the students discover that for themselves, Barth led them in a workshop of sorts on three biblical texts, in each case listening for its way of witness. There was time for only one of these examples in this session, Psalm 121, and the class traced its "way of witness" as the meeting ended.[131]

---

129. Deggeller continues: "It is comparable to an entire forest or an ocean, where each tree, each drop is something completely special" (D18).

130. Deggeller writes: "We are not permitted to be savages in the great wood of the Bible, who shoot wherever and whatever comes to mind, but we have to keep ourselves to completely particular rules of action" (D19).

131. Kirschbaum did not write anything down about this exercise, and the student protocol includes only a brief comment for each set of verses (P68). Both include much more detail with the remaining two examples the following week, so discussion of the psalm may simply have been cut short. Deggeller provides a fuller discussion of Psalm 121 in his manuscript, though it is impossible to know whether what he wrote is primarily Barth's commentary, a record of the overall discussion including student observations, or Deggeller's own reflections on the text (D20-21).

May 30 to June 13, 1933

Contextual Developments

On May 30 the NSDAP received its marching orders with regard to the controversy over the bishop in the Protestant church. They were to support the *Deutsche Christen* in their effort to seat Müller as Reich Bishop. As an official of the party put it: "the *Führer* wishes to drive reaction from its last bastion."[132] This meant a steady flow of telegrams, meetings, letter campaigns, mass demonstrations, petitions, flyers, and — since the press was now almost completely controlled by the government — constant and exclusively favorable press attention for the *Deutsche Christen* cause.

But the aggressive use of such means in the church sphere made even some *Deutsche Christen* uncomfortable. There were a number of supporters who questioned whether the instruments of political power belonged in this struggle. A few of those who complained about these tactics resigned from the *Deutsche Christen* in protest; others were expelled from the party.[133] At some universities, the *Deutsche Christen* staged large gatherings and attempted to persuade the student body to declare its support for Müller. This worked in Karl Fezer's home territory in Tübingen but did not run smoothly everywhere.[134]

Meanwhile, Bodelschwingh gathered some assistants around him and started work. He received an overwhelming number of letters and telegrams expressing support from all kinds of people during this period, but also there was quieter pressure from some quarters to spare the church from the spectacle now unfolding and resign. This pressure would only increase as the days and weeks went by. For Pentecost, Bodelschwingh sent out a greeting to be read from the pulpits of all the churches in the nation during Sunday worship. *Deutsche Christen* leader Hossenfelder immediately called for "spontaneous protest demonstrations during worship," though little came of it. More common was the decision of some Lutheran church administrators not to distribute the greeting to their pastors at all, on the grounds that the legality of Bodelschwingh's election had not been established.[135]

---

132. Scholder, *Churches and the Third Reich*, vol. 1, p. 336.

133. Scholder, *Churches and the Third Reich*, vol. 1, pp. 338-39.

134. In Berlin, for example, Bonhoeffer led most of the students out of the hall before the vote could be taken. Scholder, *Churches and the Third Reich*, vol. 1, p. 341.

135. Scholder, *Churches and the Third Reich*, vol. 1, pp. 343-44.

The decision of whether to support Bodelschwingh or Müller was a difficult one for many Protestant pastors. The newspaper headlines called those who accepted the decision of the *Landeskirchen* representatives, "The Bodelschwingh Front against Hitler," suggesting that to take this path was to oppose the *Führer* himself, the last thing most Protestants, including the Young Reformers, wanted.[136]

Barth watched these developments "with growing worry." Was this what the Protestant church would be like from now on, with decisions made behind closed doors and agitation to follow?[137] He continued to ask about the *theological* basis of the church "reformation" now under way, in constant conversation with others. Charlotte von Kirschbaum reported, for example, on June 11, that she, Barth, Hellmut Traub, and Helmut Gollwitzer worked all afternoon searching for the writings of Luther that endorsed the office of bishop and finding none — though conceding there was such a doctrine in Luthera*nism*. Then, she wrote, they debated "late into the night" about the relationship between the office of the preacher and that of a deacon and the exegetical basis of such distinctions, among other things. And, she told her friend, they will

> talk further this afternoon, and Gollwitzer will bring with [him] worked out theses about the bishop. . . . Thus you must just believe that here perhaps we do not see through this complete chaos. Only one thing is actually clear and unambiguous, that Karl tenaciously holds fast to a specifically *theological* orientation and all attempts to theologically justify a church-political step after the fact must be rejected, because to him this reversal of precedence is most deeply ominous.[138]

Around this time, Barth also started up an ongoing "working group" among the students to talk about the fourteen Düsseldorf Theses, in addition to his other responsibilities.

Barth's letters now as in previous weeks contain pleas for information. He wrote to trusted correspondents asking what was *really* going on, and for news of the latest defections, dismissals, and disciplinary actions.

---

136. Scholder, *Churches and the Third Reich*, vol. 1, p. 341.

137. "As first fruit and test of what we now have to expect in future even in the church field after the successful collapse of the democratic system into cabinet politics, I find in these procedures little convincing and promising, which thus may finally be its more illuminating meaning and harvest." Karl Barth to Wilhelm Niesel, June 1, 1933, in *Briefe 1933*, p. 240.

138. Charlotte von Kirschbaum to Erica Küppers, June 11, 1933, in *Briefe 1933*, p. 252.

The word came late in May that Professor Werner Richter (history of literature), who had appointed Barth to Göttingen and was later involved in the decision to bring him to Bonn, was dismissed from Berlin.

Two days before the next meeting of the *Predigtvorbereitung*, Ludwig Müller delivered his Pentecost sermon about the "boisterous Spirit" of the day, which then graced the front page of *Evangelium im Dritten Reich* the following morning. The sermon argued that the Spirit of Pentecost is

> the very Spirit which passes through our age as a gift of God — [it] again runs through the songs of the young awakened German fighters. That is what makes men of us, to pledge ourselves utterly.... To be triumphant bridges to the new era, ready to make the final sacrifice in victorious anticipation![139]

Session 5: June 13, 1933

The fifth meeting of the *Predigtvorbereitung* returned to the second and third of the three "test cases" Barth put to the students — an exercise in the "spontaneous" task of listening for the way of witness of a biblical text.[140] We will not recount the details here, but it is clear with each example that Barth drew their attention to the context of the text, to its movement, its reversals, its rhetorical features, and certainly to its theological nuances and implications.

In the discussion that developed after these examples, a question about the Old Testament, namely Psalm 121, was asked. Could the intercession at the end of Psalm 121 be understood on the basis of the intercession of Jesus Christ? Barth answered that in the Christian church we could not read the text without our "constant memory of our faith in Christ." We could say, in reference to the fact that in the text people are interceding for other people, that this happens because Jesus Christ has "advocated for them all beforehand before God." This is the truth that the psalm says to us (P71).

A second question was then asked about the parables of Jesus —

---

139. Quoted in Scholder, *Churches and the Third Reich*, vol. 1, p. 337.

140. The remaining examples are John 13:31-35 and Ephesians 2:1-10. Given that Psalm 121 was the first example, this meant Barth gave them an Old Testament text, a gospel text, and an epistle text.

don't they have an intentional *Skopus,* a theme, a plan?[141] In some places the way of witness is more direct than in others, Barth answered. But we want to say what is really there. As soon as the thought of a *Skopus* (or a theme) *determines* our preaching preparation, our attention is divided between the theme we have in mind and what the text actually says (P71). Barth acknowledged the arguments in favor of such practices (KS13). But even the most moderate sort of *Skopus* (such as Fezer's), Barth argued, breaks up the *action* of the text.

After this discussion, Barth turned to the second aspect of the "spontaneous" task of sermon preparation: understanding the peculiar present-day situation of the sermon. What is the way of witness of the text today for a particular *Gemeinde* "in the Germany of the year 1933"? Barth asked them (P71).

The witness of the Scripture is given to the church of the present, he told the class, to people who are called by God's Word and should be called anew, people who are baptized or should be baptized, people who know that Jesus Christ died and is raised for them and the people who do not know it. In this sense there is no separation between church and world: "the church is always also world and the world can be addressed as the becoming church" (KS13-14).[142] Note that the witness of Scripture is given to the *world,* to the baptized or those who ought to be baptized, *not* to the *Volk.*

Of course there is something that stands over the entire human situation, Barth explained, in all its conditions and relationships: the fact that we must die. But I must not only know these people in the solidarity of mortality, Barth told them. I must know them also in their "particular individuality," in their history, in their abilities, in their good or evil will — I must consider everything about them (P71). These people under this word should now hear what the apostles and prophets once said; the preacher should pass on the witness to them. This raises the whole problem of *Gemeindemässigkeit* again, Barth said, and the question about language.[143]

---

141. The term *Skopus* can indicate a particular two-part structure or plan for the sermon. First the theme is discussed; then the text is exegeted in relation to that theme.

142. Deggeller writes: "This being-addressed [by the Scripture] is not [just] valid for one particular chosen people — all people should be given the witness" (D25).

143. The student notes include in parentheses: "the basic question of whether a person can actually speak to another at all . . . cannot interrupt our presentation of this" (P72). This is a likely reference to Emil Brunner's argument that the human capacity for language is itself a "point of contact."

Thus explication must become application. What was heard must be said in relation to all the associations of ideas, feelings, attitudes, assumptions that hearers bring. "The preacher then is bound not only to the text," Barth insisted, "but also to the people" when the preacher "speaks after the text *today*" (KS14).[144] The preacher must not embark on a monologue that for all its beauty is not fitting for the *Gemeinde* (P72).[145] As the preacher writes the sermon he must think concretely of his hearers, and as he thinks through the way of witness of the text he will notice at once "very easily" that associations arise, what Barth called "contemporary material" (KS14).

This "contemporary material" can only be an "unsettled factor" in preaching preparation, but even so one is not to avoid it out of fear, Barth told the class.[146] Such material arises "as a predicate to the subject of the interpretation of the text" (KS14). It is the "invisible and flexible element" in the development of our Christian speech. Barth would return to this issue in the following session.

June 13 to 20, 1933

Contextual Developments

On June 12, an anxious Müller met with Hitler, telling his *Führer* that he should not approve the nominee for bishop unless the *Volk* were consulted. Müller left the meeting with the response for which he had hoped. Three days later Müller triumphantly released the following statement to the press:

> The Chancellor has expressed to me his extraordinary regret that the labors for the reconstruction of the German [Protestant] church have taken a difficult and thoroughly disagreeable turn. He has rejected my

---

144. The word Kirschbaum uses for "people" is *"Menschen,"* not *"Volk."* From Deggeller's notes: "With regard to the question of the how of proclamation, regard for the hearer and his particularity must appear large and important to us" (D25).

145. Deggeller: "Again and again we must remind ourselves that the sermon is never a monologue" (D25).

146. Deggeller continues: "We must without delay pull a warning signal. This contemporary material, that we in more or less rich fullness have perhaps accumulated, bears the features of a very unsure and changeable factor within preaching presentation" (D26).

Karl Barth's Predigtvorbereitung in Context: Summer Semester 1933

request to receive its authorized representatives. He also refuses to receive Pastor Dr. von Bodelschwingh.[147]

Everyone knew what this announcement meant: the Reich Government rejected what the Protestant church had done. Bodelschwingh and the Committee of Three who selected him were now completely cut off from the center of political power. Müller, with the *Führer's* ear, blocked them at every turn. With an air of concern, Müller urged the Committee of Three either to call for church elections in all the *Landeskirchen* to resolve the matter or "find another way out," that is, get rid of Bodelschwingh.[148] The *Deutsche Christen* onslaught would stop immediately if the bishop from Bethel dropped out, Müller assured them. And in the aftermath of Müller's press release, some of the leaders of the *Landeskirchen* — especially the Lutherans who were dragging their feet to begin with — started to defect from Bodelschwingh.

As in nearly all communities in that tumultuous summer of 1933, the Protestant citizens, pastors, professors, and students were consumed with the question regarding the bishop and bombarded with propaganda from all sides.

On June 14, the prominent Political Theologian Wilhelm Stapel, who also published the popular NSDP paper *Deutsches Volkstum*, spoke to a packed lecture hall at Bonn University — invited by the "coordinated" members of the Protestant faculty.

Stapel's speech of that summer, which he also delivered at the universities of Tübingen and Königsberg, contained his justification for the totalitarian state and his longstanding claim that it is the state, not the church, that decides moral or ethical questions. Every *Volk*, he argued, has its own unique "law" *(nomos)*, its sense of what is good. A state that is truly connected to the *Volk* is the absolute and unquestionable arbiter on all moral and ethical matters, not just for the nation, but for the church. The church, recognizing its limits, can only confirm the *Volksnomos* embodied by the state. In addition, while the church certainly has the right and responsibility to preach the gospel and administer the sacraments, *how* it is to do this is a matter for the *state* to decide. What order or method of proclamation is best for this *Volk*? The state determines the answer to this question.[149]

---

147. Scholder, *Churches and the Third Reich*, vol. 1, p. 346.
148. Scholder, *Churches and the Third Reich*, vol. 1, p. 346.
149. For a discussion of Stapel's views and his influence on Gogarten at this time, see Scholder, *Churches and the Third Reich*, vol. 1, pp. 420-24.

Barth did not attend Stapel's lecture, but he heard all about it nonetheless. Apparently Stapel was not as well received as some on the Protestant theological faculty had hoped. Charlotte von Kirschbaum gave the following account of the event:

> Yesterday evening Stapel from *Deutschen Volkstum* spoke here in the university. This occasion showed very clearly how little Karl's students — he himself obviously did not attend — are now disposed to abandon everything they have learned theologically, and a *Deutscher Christ* [German Christian] must have the experience of a speech [that] was repeatedly interrupted by resounding laughter in the lecture hall. How long this "disruption center" [*Störungszentrum*] is in fact allowed to continue, and how long Karl can still swim in this German soup as a still indigestible [but] at least easier to digest lump, that is the question. But we want to wait and see that in peace. Thus it is good how sober-mindedly and contemplatively he is now able to put his step and how amid all this agitation he really is the calming influence.[150]

A few days later another meeting occurred on the Bonn campus, this one apparently intended to be a rally in support of Müller, though the event was advertised as a purely informational gathering. When it became clear to the students in the hall that this was really a "confidence demonstration" for Müller, approximately one hundred and twenty of them left the room, "among them also countless Nazis and even a few uniformed SA people."[151] This group of Bonn students then organized themselves under the leadership of Gollwitzer and Traub and proceeded to fire off a telegram to the relevant *Staat* Mininster (Rust) to complain about the deceptive way the event was presented.

But for Barth, the formation of yet another action group within the church solely in reaction to the struggle over the bishop was only a political-tactical matter that did not address the root of the problem in the German Protestant church.[152] And over the course of these June days, Barth decided it was time for him to tackle that root, publicly. His decision to say something now was prompted by yet another late night conversation with suspended lecturer Wilhelm Vischer, Bonn Privatdozent Fritz Lieb,

---

150. Charlotte von Kirschbaum to Anna Barth, June 15, 1933, in *Briefe 1933*, pp. 257-58.
151. Charlotte von Kirschbaum to Heinz Otten, June 17, 1933, in *Briefe 1933*, p. 259.
152. Charlotte von Kirschbaum to Heinz Otten, June 17, 1933, in *Briefe 1933*, p. 259.

and former student (now a pastor) Hans Fischer, all of whom were urging Barth to join the fray and take up the cause of Bodelschwingh. But in the course of the conversation, Barth persuaded them that this narrow, circumstantial kind of protest did not dig deeply enough; it "drained" the "church" from "church politics."[153] At the urging of these friends, who said they and many others "longed for a word from Karl Barth in this general confusion and instability," Barth proposed to write "a word" on the situation. It was to be, as Kirschbaum explained, "an appeal to the theologians not to now abandon their *theological* existence amid contemporary things. Naturally [it] cannot be otherwise [than] that; at the same time, this appeal must mean a sharp boundary vis-à-vis all '*Gleichgeschalteten*,' and thus as well [cannot be otherwise] that he perhaps opens a very agitated debate."[154]

Barth's work on the "word" that would become *Theologische Existenz heute!* had to be squeezed into the brief "*Zwischenpausen*" now available to him — the leftover moments between his preparation for lectures and exercises, reading and writing letters, and the many conversations with the visitors who descended on the Barth house at all hours.[155]

Session 6: June 20, 1933

The sixth meeting of the exercises returned to the question of the hearer and the "contemporary material" of the sermon — again in the context of the spontaneous task of discerning the "way of witness" today. The student protocol used the term "application" to describe the matter at hand (P72).

The contemporary person who is addressed by the sermon is not a person "in an empty room," Barth reminded the class, but the person "in his joys and in his sorrows," who is baptized or should be baptized (KS14). The "application" of the witness of the text to the person of the present is directed neither to the preacher abstracted from the *Gemeinde*, nor to the *Gemeinde* abstracted from the preacher, but to the preacher *in* the *Gemeinde* or to the *Gemeinde in which the preacher stands* (KS14, P72). Bengel's famous dictum to preachers, "Apply yourself totally to the text; apply the text totally to yourself," does not tell the whole story, Barth ar-

---

153. Charlotte von Kirschbaum to Anna Barth, June 15, 1933, in *Briefe 1933*, p. 256.
154. Charlotte von Kirschbaum to Anna Barth, June 15, 1933, in *Briefe 1933*, pp. 256-57.
155. Charlotte von Kirschbaum to Heinz Otten, June 17, 1933, in *Briefe 1933*, p. 260.

gued. If it did, then preaching would just be a "self-conversing"; it would suggest "the abolishment of the church" (KS14-15).

But there is also the other danger, Barth continued, that the preacher addresses the *Gemeinde* as a separate entity, something he stands over against, rather than something to which he belongs (P72-73). Knowledge of the real situation of the preacher — that the preacher as office-bearer is the "last and simplest" member of the *Gemeinde* — is the basic prerequisite for proper application (KS15).[156] From this starting point — of preacher in *Gemeinde* — we now ask after the way of witness into the present, Barth told the students. In the positive sense, a sermon written with the criterion of *Gemeindemässigkeit* really engages the life of the church, and without such "congregation-temperedness" remains "stuck in explication." On the other hand, an orientation to *Gemeinde* and "contemporary material" can lead almost unawares to the theme sermon, Barth warned. How does one navigate this dilemma, the relationship of "closeness to life" and "closeness to the text" (P73)?

First it must be said: "woe to the preacher who is comfortable and contents himself with exegesis which does not become address," Barth preached. "Woe to the preacher who does not see how newsworthy *(aktuell)* a respective biblical word is for the people of today" (P73). "Woe to the preacher who has heard a word from the text that must be said now, today," but does *not* say it — not because the preacher didn't hear it, Barth explained, but "because he didn't have the courage to let the explication become application" (KS15).[157] Something might be said to us in the Bible that "affronts us," that "may shake us to the foundations of our existence," which sounds "behind the times" to us. The Bible is "an unsettling book," Barth declared.[158]

---

156. Deggeller writes that when the preacher includes himself in the *Gemeinde*, "then he speaks as one who has not already heard, but every moment listens again in the *Gemeinschaft* with those who are entrusted to him. . . . Thus one arrives at the clear knowledge concerning one's own littleness and smallness. The proper precondition for right application is only given from this radical humiliation" (D27).

157. Deggeller: "Woe to the pastor, who sees with seeing eyes and hears with hearing ears as well what must be said today in this entire concrete moment, but who then out of certain considerations does not want to arouse offense in the public or from entirely egotistical reasons has qualms about the security of his position and his office" (D28).

158. Deggeller writes: "For a conscientious responsible pastor there is actually no time and no situation where the text could not be threatening and full of danger. What the text has to say, that must be said unconditionally, and even if it may under the circumstances cost the preacher's neck. Thus openness to the text and then courage in its proclamation — that is stressed at this point with all insistence" (D28).

Karl Barth's Predigtvorbereitung *in Context: Summer Semester 1933*

A preacher who "fears for his position in the *Gemeinde* or the church" may be tempted to become "a coward in the pulpit," letting "the secret of God" be "covered up once again." This is to be a "deserter" in the pulpit (KS15, P17)! Application requires — among other things — "civil courage," Barth told the young German preachers at the beginning of the Third Reich (KS16, P73).[159] They are to bring the word of Scripture to expression in relation to "all outer life relationships under all circumstances," with a "civil courage" which "ventures to seize the concrete situation in obedience to the text" and in this obedience to the witness of the text they are thus "relieved of responsibility for all outcomes" of this venture. The word of Holy Scripture bears the responsibility (P73).

Then there is the other side of the problem, Barth transitioned. There is, yes, the danger of not being bold enough, of lacking the necessary courage, as was described, but there is also the danger of preaching that is dominated by the preacher's opinions and intentions, that is, "theme" preaching. As one intensively meditates on a text, thoughts and feelings arise, things that seem to have "a certain necessity," Barth explained, which can take over the sermon. In the memory of the *Gemeinde* these thoughts and opinions can remain "as the 'meaning' of the whole" (KS16). Yes, now the preacher has avoided the "mistake" of being "out of touch with life" (*Lebensfremden*), but now there is the "greater and more fatal mistake" of "blowing spiritual bubbles," the "rape of the text," of confusing the "beautiful thoughts of our self-serving 'I'" with the "less comfortable" and "less timely" thoughts of the text (P74).

In light of this possibility, the "contemporary material" that "thrust itself" upon the preacher during preparation must be "winnowed." It may be that the text finally and ultimately rules out particular material. The preacher's thoughts must "bend" to the text; the preacher's "convictions and opinions" must be "trained like a wild horse." It may be that "very dear, important things" must "remain behind, yes, that the 'main thought' of the sermon named in expectation at the beginning must be sacrificed" (KS16). A sermon that is thus "broken" by the text is "at the same time courageous and humble" (KS16).

But the tension between closeness to life and closeness to the text can

---

159. The English translation of this sentence in *Homiletics* (1991) renders the word "*Zivilmut*" as "ordinary courage," thus obscuring its public import. Karl Barth, *Homiletics*, trans. G. W. Bromiley and D. E. Daniels (Louisville: Westminster John Knox, 1991), p. 114. Barth used the same language in his letter to Wilhelm Goeters only days earlier. See Karl Barth to Wilhelm Goeters, May 27, 1933 in *Briefe 1933*, p. 224.

never be dissolved — it is only possible for the preacher to be "always on the way from courage to humility and vice versa"[160] (P75). In response to the question, "which is more important, modesty in relation to the text or courage in relation to the *Gemeinde* and its present wishes," one must slightly favor the first, Barth said: humility. Think of it in analogy to the command, "You should love God your Lord . . . and your neighbor as yourself" (KS16).

Barth concluded the class by highlighting three further considerations. First, Barth asked, what does it mean "to apply"? Sometimes application is reduced to the use of *Stichworten* (catchwords) in the sermon.[161] But it is a "superstition" to think that *Gemeindemässigkeit* must consist of such direct references. Sometimes a sermon whose "outer form" seems "very unpractical" turns out to be "the truly practical." A sermon will have "closeness to life" when a responsible and called preacher, whose heart "is full of the need of the present," interprets the text, Barth tells them (KS17, P75).[162] Second, "every preacher has his favorite areas and thoughts," Barth explained. To "apply" is not to let these favorites come to expression.[163] "They belong to the flesh," Barth warned, and we are not to bring them into the pulpit. There are "legitimate ways" such thoughts might be said, namely, "when the text pronounces these thoughts." But "the strictest discipline" is necessary in this regard. Barth told the class about his own sermons on socialism in Safenwil to illustrate the point (KS17).[164] The third

---

160. Deggeller adds: "A guarantee for success can naturally not be given" (D30).

161. What was indicated by the reference to *"Stichworten"* can be discerned from Deggeller: "In any case, one should not excavate the contents of newspapers with more or less relevant quotations, or even to allude to them with *Stichworten*. . . . The entirely practical *'landschaftlichen'* (scenic, beauty of nature) sermons or *'heimatlich'* (patriotic) sermons in many cases praised as especially effective can often be very unhealthy" (D30).

162. Deggeller continues that one should not assume that the *Gemeinde* is "so alien from the world" and so "far from life" that "they do not know the needs of the present." Rather, "they know life intimately and really do not need an orientation by the pastor" (D30-31).

163. Deggeller: "These favorite thoughts belong to the flesh and to the old, unbaptized humanity. There is as well here and there a situation where they could be pronounced, but the danger of misuse is tremendous. The fad for teetotalism, for example, or also with social, ethical, or other problems again and again seductively affect [us] each time to fire off in the sermon in these directions. Be warned of it" (D31).

164. Deggeller reports that Barth confessed the way "he often succumbed to this danger of a falsely understood *Gemeindemässigkeit* in Safenwil, citing his sermon on the sinking of the *Titanic* and his incessant preaching on the Great War, "until finally a woman came to him and begged him that he might once speak of 'something else other than this dreadful war.' She was right. The subordination to the text had been outrageously forgotten. It should

Karl Barth's Predigtvorbereitung *in Context: Summer Semester 1933*

and final issue Barth raised in this session is the demand that application must "always be entirely up-to-date/newsworthy" (KS17). If there is a fire in the *Gemeinde* it is not imperative that it appear in the Sunday sermon.[165] The sermon is to press the *Gemeinde* forward, not to repeat the everyday again on Sunday (KS17). These can simply be distractions (P75).

In this session, Barth navigated treacherous waters. On the one hand, for those who would put down their weapons, who would regard the witness of the text, who were willing to let themselves be questioned, he wanted to call them to courageous proclamation in a time when it would surely be required. But for those who were confident, those who already had an agenda in mind, those overflowing with the *Geist* of the revolution, Barth returned to the theme of humility.

---

not get to the point that a *Gemeinde* member must call the pastor to order and admonish the conscience. All honor to timeliness, but like the artillery, the pastor should, as a good shot, shoot over the hills of timeliness" (D32). Deggeller does not mention socialism.

165. Deggeller's notorious reference to the fire reads as follows: "The approach and the references are not always to be *a jour;* [one] need not always bring the very latest and most sensational things. Had a fire occurred in the *Gemeinde* the previous week, for example, the *Gemeinde* members still standing under the frightful effects, take care only suggestively to start up with this theme in the sermon." The English translation of *Homiletics* (1991) offers the more extreme: "For instance, if a fire broke out in the community last week, and church members are still suffering under its awful impact, we should be on guard against even hinting at this theme in the sermon." Barth, *Homiletics,* p. 118. Fortunately a way to adjudicate the competing renditions of Barth's comment here is provided by Barth himself in an address to students in Kaiserswerth on January 9, 1935. There we have (in Barth's own words) a similar reference: "The situation is only too well known and frequent, where the preacher is fraught with a certain event in the sermon, a certain train of thought, of which he believes the *Gemeinde* is also fraught. Perhaps just now a blaze raged through the village. Should he now give a sermon: Christ and the blaze? Naturally he must be busy with it, but should the blaze therefore be his ulterior speech or his open theme? Also on this day he must interpret the text to this *Gemeinde.* Just now the *Gemeinde* that takes [things] seriously desires to hear God's Word. And God's Word is then quite simply to be what is available to us in the Holy Scripture as today's text. It can certainly happen that reference is made to this event in the *Gemeinde,* but perhaps that is not absolutely necessary. Under all circumstances it must remain: even now God's Word is essential, exactly now. The more the people are filled by something or other, ever so more does the church owe to them the comfort and the help of the Word of God." Karl Barth, "Die Gemeindemässigkeit der Predigt," in *Aufgabe der Predigt,* ed. Gert Hummel (Darmstadt: Wissenschaftliche Buchgesellschaft, 1935), pp. 173-74.

June 20 to 27, 1933

Contextual Developments

All doubts about the "legality" of the election of Bodelschwingh as Reich Bishop were ostensibly to be settled at the joint meeting of the *Kirchenausschuss* and the *Kirchenbundesrat* of the German Protestant church on June 23-24 in Eisenach. Unlike the May 23 ad hoc meeting of representatives of the *Landeskirchen*, these were official governing bodies, which supposedly made their decisions unquestionably binding. Naturally this event was regarded with a mixture of anticipation and dread throughout the country. If German Christian agitation was intimidating now, some wondered, what would it be like if this vote, too, did not go to Müller?

The Lutheran delegates arrived early for a strategy session, as they had done before the May vote. Now, more than ever, they felt they must make the case for Müller to the *Kirchenausschuss* and the *Kirchenbundesrat*. In the course of the first day's tense deliberations, the Lutherans presented their argument. "The question is," urged the Bavarian bishop, "whether we are serving the NS movement as we should. Let us not be deceived about the power of this movement. Something has to be done to bring about calm in our communities."[166] But the Lutherans were still greatly outnumbered by the delegates who supported Bodelschwingh.

No doubt this majority would have at least enjoyed a temporary victory that June, had not the whole proceeding been disrupted by the frantic news now coming out of Prussia. To explain the nature of this news requires a bit of background.

On June 8, the ailing Hermann Kapler — President of the Prussian *Oberkirchenrat* and thus President of the *Kirchenausschuss*, the leading member of the Committee of Three, and Bodelschwingh's most reliable champion — retired. Normally the Prussian *Oberkirchenrat* would have simply followed established procedure and nominated a replacement for Kapler. But something — rightly, as it turned out — gave the Prussian church leaders pause in the summer of 1933. It was a tiny clause in a 1931 treaty between the Prussian Protestant church and the Prussian state government which suggested that the civil authorities in Prussia ought to be consulted before such a replacement was named. And this was something that the church administrators wanted to avoid at all costs under

---

166. Quoted in Scholder, *Churches and the Third Reich*, vol. 1, p. 352.

the circumstances. So, they decided to name a *provisional* administrator to the post, and they went out of their way to pick a nationalist (Ernst Stoltenhoff) as a precaution. After an assurance from an official in the state *Kultusministerium* that a provisional appointment was of no interest to the state, on June 21 the Prussian church senate gave Stoltenhoff its blessing.

But this was just the opening for which *Deutsche Christen* zealots in Prussia had been waiting. On June 23, the very day the Protestant *Kirchenausschuss* convened in Eisenach, the Prussian *Kultusminster*, Bernhard Rust, sent a letter to be printed in the morning papers, which not only suspended the hapless Prussian official who had not objected to the appointment of Stoltenhoff, but installed in his place the unscrupulous and power-hungry *Deutsche Christen* leader August Jäger, who would now take over the church department at the *Kultusministerium*.[167] Jäger's goal was nothing less than the "coordination" of the Prussian church.

At first it was not clear to the leaders of German Protestantism now gathered in Eisenach what Jäger's appointment meant. After the official meeting on June 23, the Committee of Three (with Friedrich Seetzen taking Kapler's place) talked late into the night with Professors Fezer and Schumann, who had come to Eisenach to plead for Müller. Again the argument was made that if the Protestant leaders would just acknowledge Bodelschwingh as a *provisional* candidate, then the NSDAP would withdraw from the conflict.[168]

But it was not until two o'clock the following afternoon that the really decisive thing happened. Word reached the assembly that the Prussian *Kultusminister* had announced that, in order to eliminate the "present confusion" in the church for the sake of "*Volk*, state, and church," August Jäger — in addition to his responsibilities at the *Kultusministerium* — was appointed as State Commissioner of all Protestant *Landeskirchen* in Prussia, "with authority to take any necessary steps."[169] Bodelschwingh, recog-

---

167. Scholder, *Churches and the Third Reich*, vol. 1, p. 350. August Jäger (1887-1949), lawyer, member of the NSDAP, *Deutsche Christen* leader, later an officer in Poland. Jäger was ultimately executed for war crimes and crimes against humanity on June 17, 1949.

168. Scholder, *Churches and the Third Reich*, vol. 1, p. 353. Meanwhile, at a secret meeting of their own, the Lutheran bishops decided to abandon the Protestant establishment. From then on they began quietly communicating to the powers that be of their willingness to represent the Protestant church in future negotiations, should the present Protestant leadership prove "incapacitated." Scholder, *Churches and the Third Reich*, vol. 1, p. 354.

169. Scholder, *Churches and the Third Reich*, vol. 1, p. 355.

nizing that such a "Commissioner" made his office obsolete (at least in Prussia), resigned that very evening.

The *Kirchenausschuss* ended in confusion, desperation, anger, and despair. It would never meet again.

Almost immediately Jäger started suspending church administrators in the Prussian *Landeskirchen* and replacing them with *Deutsche Christen*.

Barth was nearly finished with *Theologische Existenz heute!* when he heard of Jäger's appointment, and the news prompted him to revise the text to respond to the new development.[170] He completed the manuscript on June 25. The manifesto was addressed to preachers and theologians, and it spoke frankly about (among other things) the church's reform efforts, the bishop question, the *Deutsche Christen*, the Young Reformers, Political Theology, and the church in the totalitarian state, but at its heart it was a call for spiritual resistance. This resistance would not take up the weapons "of pollings and placards and protests, with mobilizations and 'fronts'" — it would not resist by trying to *protect* preaching but by *practicing* it.[171] Though the pamphlet did not criticize the NS regime *directly*, in the context of the church/state situation of June 25, 1933, it stood to reason that a critique of the *Deutsche Christen* could be considered an attack on the Reich government itself, and it is with this awareness that Barth sent it off. Of the document itself and the whole situation he wrote to Thurneysen:

> You must take account in Switzerland that I still could have said very much more, but partly had to "be silent," just to be able to say *that* at least. And even that can lead to my undoing since the situation created on Saturday, which quite simply means that the [*Deutsche Christen*] hold a kind of dictatorship in the church through the arm of the state. . . . Oeri was *very* right when he recently wrote: "The brown *death* goes through the German land"! That exactly expresses the mood in which we [have lived] for weeks and now thus even live in the church. Humanly speaking it is simply desperate. I read without interruption my history of theology and the gospel of John (glad, this time to have usable old notebooks for both — dear me, now when one should produce!) and the three seminars (of late yet a working group on the 14 theses of Düsseldorf . . .). The students are there in great

---

170. Karl Barth to Eduard Thurneysen, June 27, 1933, in *Briefe 1933*, p. 262.
171. Karl Barth, *Theological Existence Today! A Plea for Theological Freedom*, trans. R. Birch Hoyle (London: Hodder & Stoughton, 1933), p. 74.

hosts and very serious, but alas, the whole thing greatly reminds [me] however of the sinking of the *Titanic*, when the music also still played to the last: "nearer my God to thee . . ."[172]

Barth also followed the developments in Prussia closely, and just before the next meeting of the sermon exercises, he heard the news that Jäger had suspended General Superintendent Otto Dibelius. Barth commented:

> We have already experienced here unbelievable things for eight days in the perversion of justice with the propaganda of the *Deutsche Christen*, and one must be composed in many, many things. . . . Even the newspaper comes with the news that Hitler is an instrument of God, the church only exists through the nation and now even Dibelius is discharged. Who would have dreamed, that he, the preacher of Potsdam, my old enemy and now almost friend, must yet fly *before* me!! *Vanitas vanitatum* [Ecclesiastes 1:2], the ranks will yet come to me as well. But what should become of all those among my disciples and students who remain *firm*? They walk about here with unsettled faces and do not know what should be.[173]

Session 7: June 27, 1933

This session was devoted to the actual design of the sermon, how it should be "carried out" — but only in keeping with the scope of the course. These are exercises in sermon *preparation*, Barth reminded the students. The course would not consider the actual delivery of the sermon (P76).

Barth proceeded to set forth some general rules of art for these young preachers in the Third Reich. But he began with what he called "a prerequisite" to this aspect of preaching preparation, namely, that it is vital that they write their sermons down. "A sermon is a *speech*," Barth said, but is not the kind of speech in which one just assumes that "the Holy Spirit or perhaps even another spirit" will "supply" the words, regardless of whether one has arranged them or not (KS18, P76).[174] Rather, preaching is a speech

---

172. Karl Barth to Eduard Thurneysen, June 27, 1933, in *Briefe 1933*, pp. 263-64.
173. Karl Barth to Eduard Thurneysen, June 27, 1933, in *Briefe 1933*, pp. 264-65.
174. Cf. the opening sentence of Johann Lorenz von Mosheim's homiletic: "A sermon is a speech." See Johann Lorenz Mosheim, *Anweisung erbaulich zu predigen*, 2nd ed., ed. Christian Ernst von Windheim (Erlangen: Bey Wolfgang Walther, 1771), §I.

that should be prepared and recorded verbatim (KS18). "That should be held as an unconditional rule, also and even for the so-called 'gifted' orator!" Barth declared (KS18).[175]

To preach a sermon is to participate in an act of worship, the central act of worship in the Protestant worship service, which corresponds to the sacrifice in the Mass of the Catholic Church (P76). And whoever is to conduct this "sacramental act," Barth said, should not undertake it "indiscriminately" but "under exertion of the greatest labor" (KS18). It must be done with the "fullest consideration" according to the preacher's "best knowledge" and as the preacher's conscience permits (P76). Each word should be accounted for. This exertion is part of the "sanctification" of the pastor, and next to justification it should not be forgotten (P76). Such responsible preaching is also expressed by the practice of *writing the sermon down*. "Each sermon should be ready for press," Barth told the students, "that is, it could bear up under even the closest and most sustained test" (KS18). And this is not only important for young preachers, he insisted, something to be discarded once the preacher has experience. "Hundreds and thousands of pastors" have such experience, "but in spite of or just because of this their sermons are only religious speeches" (P76). It is not a matter of judging others, Barth told them, but we have to ask: What is proper for a person who is not a prophet, and who prepares his sermon with prayer and effort (P76)?

The preacher, then, writes down what he has heard — for himself and for his *Gemeinde*. But what form should this take? In what followed Barth did not prescribe any particular form, but cleared a space, offered boundaries, suggested limits.

First, one should not think of a sermon as something that consists of "parts" but as something that consists of "limbs." "The sermon is a body," Barth said, "a corpus which is formed by the unity of the text" (KS18). This unity "must be visible" in the sermon, in the "movement which the text itself designs, whose 'life' — for it is to be understood as a part of life — should be repeated in it" (KS18).[176] It is not a "sequence of parts" but "a saying-after the one thing" the text says, the Word of God in Jesus Christ (KS18). It is not really a matter of deciding what is to be said first, second,

---

175. Deggeller: "Even the gifted orator, for whom it is an effortless thing to give his thoughts perfect expression ex cathedra, should here contain himself and write out his sermon word for word" (D32).

176. Deggeller writes: "The text is rather a living piece of existence *(Dasein)*, and this life-being should be reproduced by us" (D33-34).

Karl Barth's Predigtvorbereitung in Context: Summer Semester 1933

and third, but to ask, how do I speak-after the one thing, the way of witness, I heard in the text (P76)?

Second, Barth argued, the sermon should really have no introduction.[177] Only one sort of introduction is conceivable for sermons, he said, and that is to have a sort of "pre-sermon" after the Scripture reading, a short analysis of what was read, that would then connect it to the sermon itself (KS19, P76).

But why would we not have a formal introduction? The length and intensity of the following discussion indicates the fact that Barth's instruction in this regard was a minority report. The practice of beginning sermons with elaborate introductions was widespread, and something these students not only heard regularly but were almost certainly instructed to do in their *Predigerseminars*. So why should they abandon this pattern?

There are several "practical" reasons, Barth said, or, if you want, call them "psychological."[178] First: Why do people come to church? To hear the Word of God that approaches us in the sermon, which as explication is always also at the same time application. The whole worship service already leads into the sermon! Any other "introduction" can only mean a "delay," a "setback of the decisive event of proclamation." It is "lost time" (P77).[179]

According to the student protocol, at this point there was a discussion about the length of the sermon in general, with some arguing that "brevity is the soul of wit" (P77). This may well be the case for speeches in general, Barth responded, but it cannot be applied to sermons. If a sermon is to "create space for the Word of God," it takes as long as it takes. It can certainly happen in a short time! But if this activity is the most vital part of our Sunday, Barth asked the students, why would we be particularly concerned about the time (P77)?

Barth returned to his second argument against the introductions of his day: they impede the necessary concentration on the text. They do not lead people into the Word of God but distract them when they are already

---

177. Deggeller: "One is wary of any introduction" (D34).

178. "Psychological" is a likely reference to the use of psychology in modern homiletical theories. It was invoked as a means to understand the mental state of the modern hearer. What was the mental state of hearers in Germany in the summer of 1933? One thing is certain: there were distractions, crises, and "fires" everywhere!

179. Deggeller adds: "Indeed in such introductions there is occasion of spirit and wit, but in all cases it is to be said that through these mental somersaults precious time is lost, when on average preaching is already in and for itself too brief. Twenty to twenty-five minutes are often dawdled away with such preliminaries, before one gets to the main matter" (D34).

distracted enough (P77)![180] Whether one wins the attention of the hearers (to the text) is decided in the first ten minutes — as a rule — and it is hard to recover when they are distracted from the text by introductory remarks (KS19). Listeners who were ready and eager to "hear a call" are now "disappointed" — why would we want to detain such serious listeners (P77)?

What kinds of "introductions" are to be rejected? Barth made it clear: First, a "popular beginning point is our time, to which the pastor expresses his positive or negative attitude"[181] (P77). These popular introductions "tend to consist of opinions or attempts by the preacher to interpret the events of the time, perhaps also with the quotations of the sayings of famous men" ("Goethe!" Kirschbaum wrote) (KS19).[182] After we have heard the text and prayed, Barth wondered, why would we steer listeners off in such a direction (P77-78)? Do we need to make the Bible "commendable" by suggesting that someone (German!) once said something similar? "That is unworthy of the matter," Barth insisted (P78).

Another possibility often heard is the negative introduction: one "indulges in the description of the sins and weaknesses of humanity" so the Word of God can "shine all the more brightly" against this background (KS19). One should not "besiege" a Christian or becoming-Christian *Gemeinde* with "such an outpouring of bitterness" (P78).[183] A student suggested that one might "aim at the old Adam in people" and then "oppose" to this old Adam the "great 'but!'" of God. But Barth argued that one should not see the hearer primarily "in his wrongness." This then becomes the "secret theme" of the sermon, regardless of the biblical text. Let the Word itself show the way, Barth suggested (P78).

---

180. From Deggeller: "To begin the sermon the hearers are still curious and attentive. But if one at first talks about something different, perhaps very interesting, then it can happen that some person or other positively winces when one finally gets to the main issue" (D34).

181. Deggeller writes: "A beloved beginning to such obscene sermon introductions is for example the phrase, 'our time.' ... Then there follows a detailed description of this 'our time.' Either the signs of the times are agreeable to the pastor, then the introduction is positive, or he rejects them, then it is negative" (D35).

182. Deggeller offers: "Or another, very beloved sermon beginning: 'the great statesman Bismarck ...' One should always be clear that already by the mere mention of such names carried in from outside almost automatically tends to set off the most incredible thought-associations with the hearer, and these thoughts then are an occasion to go wandering off" (D35).

183. Deggeller: "We are not permitted to greet the hearer with a cold shower. For then the great danger develops that we use the word of the Bible only as a club, which we swing with growing passion against these sinful people" (D35).

Karl Barth's Predigtvorbereitung *in Context: Summer Semester 1933*

Yet a final type of introduction gives a "situation report" about the text, in the name of being "biblical," Barth explained, or gives a lecture on theology or an "introduction" to the Old or New Testament. These things do not belong in the sermon, at least not as "distinct components" (P78).

The theological argument often given in favor of introductions, Barth observed, is the doctrine of the *Anknüpfungspunkt*, the belief that there is some analog to the Word of God in human beings, something in them by virtue of creation that corresponds to the event of revelation.[184] Adam in paradise. A *gratia praeveniens*. An *analogia entis* (P78). But, according to Reformation doctrine, Barth argued, the only *"Anknüpfung"* is the miracle of revelation alone, "the reality of God's action" (KS20). A human being is not "disposed" to hear the Word of God — "we are children of wrath by nature," Barth said (citing Ephesians 2:3). But the preacher addresses people *as those who are called through baptism in Christ*. Therefore we have no right to regard people with a negation, for "now John 3:16 is in force. We believe in the miracle of God, which occurs in our midst. That miracle is the *Anknüpfung*" (P79).[185]

Barth concludes with this: that a human being is allowed to speak about this is an "immense thing" and yet "it is only humble service." We have only to take up "the attitude of a messenger *(Boten)*, who has something to say."[186] We do not need to build a ramp — it will come down from above. Let the Bible speak from the beginning. "Then we have done what we could" (P79).

While Barth did speak to the theological arguments for and against the "introduction" at the end of the session, his designation of his arguments against introductions as "practical" indicates that *he was speaking to their present situation*, not offering a theological rationale for the banishment of introductions from sermons in every time and place.[187] It is clear that Barth had particular examples in mind, most prominently the sermon

---

184. Deggeller: "One believes that this little door to the inward parts of human beings must first be found and pushed open, before one can effectively bring the message" (D36).

185. "That applies also to the most corrupt people, even the criminal and the murderer. A pointer to this confidence, that on the basis of baptism a miracle happens to us, that is the best introduction to any sermon" (D37).

186. Deggeller writes: "We only have to take up the attitude of a messenger, who does not have to create a mood for the message. All that appears like a wild destruction of the little garden of our sermon, from which we thought to gather so many flowers" (D37).

187. Cf. how Barth talks about the "practical" decision of joining the SPD. It is a *practical* decision, a "political hypothesis," not an absolute, ideological, once-for-all decision.

that with its opening words situates the hearer in the great stream of German history, German culture, and, in the summer of 1933, the "national renewal." He spoke about the *Anknüpfungspunkt* because that was the theological argument that undergirded this local practice. It was not a time to explore all possible techniques, all possible introductions, all possible contexts — time was short. It was enough to challenge what the students had been taught about how to begin a sermon, and perhaps change the way they would listen next Sunday as well.

June 27 to July 11, 1933

Contextual Developments

By this time in the summer of 1933, Hitler had nearly achieved a one-party state. On July 1, agreement was reached on a final text for the Concordat between the Third Reich and the Roman Catholic Church, and it was signed a week later. By that time the Centre Party had dissolved itself. On July 6 Hitler gave a speech to a group of leading Nazis, declaring that the National Socialist revolution was successful, and now they must work to consolidate their power. This message and its implications were communicated to all levels of the Reich government over the next few weeks. In concrete terms it meant that the violence of the brownshirts, still a regular feature of German life, must come to an end. A clear demonstration of a stable and orderly Reich would encourage investors to entrust their money in the still struggling German economy.[188]

But in the massive territory of Prussia, the *Gleichschaltung* of the Protestant church continued at a revolutionary pace. From the time he took office, August Jäger fired off dismissals, appointments, decrees, and actions at every turn. In short order, all elected church bodies in Prussia had been disbanded.[189] Protestant church leaders were hustled out of their offices even as their newly appointed DC replacements were moving in. In addition, Jäger took over the two largest private Protestant institutions, the Press Association and the Inner Mission. Objections to this completely illegal takeover by the Director of the Press Association were met with the declaration that it was "a revolutionary act."[190]

---

188. Evans, *Third Reich in Power*, p. 21.
189. Scholder, *Churches and the Third Reich*, vol. 1, p. 358.
190. Scholder, *Churches and the Third Reich*, vol. 1, p. 21.

But the Prussian General Superintendents were not about to take this outrage quietly. Dibelius commissioned Martin Niemöller to write a statement of protest against the use of political power in the church and called for congregations and pastors to join them in holding services of repentance and prayer regarding the situation the following Sunday (July 2). "If God be for us, who can be against us?" the statement concluded, an ironic echo of Dibelius's Potsdam sermon. Though no newspaper would print the statement for fear of reprisal, it was swiftly mimeographed and distributed all over Prussia.

At the point when Jäger ousted Dibelius, the ever-aggressive Hossenfelder — now Clergy Vice President of the Old Prussion Union — issued his own message to be read in Prussian churches the following Sunday. Congregations were to place themselves enthusiastically at the disposal of "the great work of church reorganization" now underway "in praise, prayer, thanksgiving, and action." On a more ominous note, the new President of Old Prussia wrote to all pastors that any type of church political activity carried with it "the danger of prosecution because of the criticism of government measures which might be connected with it."[191] Later the new Prussian overlords would also demand that on Sunday, July 2, all churches were to be decorated with the black-white-red flag and the swastika flag. Thus every pastor was faced with a decision one way or the other.

Dibelius and the other deposed *Landeskirchen* administrators made two further moves in rapid succession. First, Dibelius wrote a letter to Jäger essentially refusing to give up his post — they could take away his administrative functions, Dibelius argued, but not his episcopal and priestly ones, which only the church could revoke.[192] This declaration was widely circulated. Second, the suspended council members of the Prussian *Oberkirchenrat* filed a lawsuit against the state of Prussia in civil court.

This unexpected move infuriated Jäger. He mobilized the full power of the state to defend his position and enforce his orders. The state "cannot tolerate any kind of resistance," he instructed state officials and chiefs of police. Any attempts at resistance should be considered "treason against the *Volk* and the state."[193]

On June 28, Ludwig Müller, emboldened by the situation in Prussia, declared a "state of emergency in Church and *Volk*" and announced that he

---

191. Scholder, *Churches and the Third Reich*, vol. 1, p. 359.
192. Scholder, *Churches and the Third Reich*, vol. 1, p. 360.
193. Scholder, *Churches and the Third Reich*, vol. 1, p. 361.

was taking over the presidency of the Protestant *Kirchenbundesamt* and control of all its subsidiary bodies. He revoked the authorization for the Committee of Three and would now replace them with a new committee that would continue the work on the new constitution of the German Protestant church.[194]

Most Protestants were stunned by these developments. Many were torn between their disapproval of what they considered unjustified state interference and their continuing enthusiasm for the new regime. Three main groups can be discerned in relation to this developing situation: first, there was the radical group that wanted full coordination of the Protestant church, a group that included Jäger, Hossenfelder, the Berlin Reich leadership, the radical wing of *Deutsche Christen*, Prussian *Kultusminster* Rust, and the NSDAP; second, there was the group in opposition to Jäger, which was comprised of the Prussian *Oberkirchenrat*, the Prussian General Superintendents, the Young Reformation Movement, and many pastors. And finally, there was the "compromise" group, namely, Müller, the Lutheran bishops, the Reich ministry of the Interior, and, significantly, Hitler.

By the end of June, these groups seemed locked in a power struggle with no resolution in sight. And by now reports about the disaster in the German Protestant church were regularly appearing in the foreign press. But this ecclesiastical knot was about to be loosened in a way no one had anticipated.

Of course, the unrest in the Protestant church was troubling to many people, but to the elderly Reich President Hindenburg — a Protestant himself — it was especially troubling that this spectacle was taking place on his watch. And he resolved to do something about it. On June 30, Hindenburg spoke to Hitler about the matter and secured Hitler's promise that he would take immediate steps to bring about reconciliation between the church parties. And to make sure Hitler kept his promises, Hindenburg did a surprising thing: he outlined his concerns about the Protestant church in an open letter to Hitler and had it printed on the front page of all the morning papers the following day. In it, Hindenburg expressed concern about the freedom of the church, rejected the interventions by the Prussian government, and declared his confidence that Hitler would keep his promise and restore peace in the church by facilitating ne-

---

194. This new constitutional committee was to consist of Müller himself, August Jäger, four Lutheran bishops, four *Deutsche Christen*, one Young Reformer, and one representative of the Old Prussian Church. Scholder, *Churches and the Third Reich*, vol. 1, p. 363.

gotiations with "both trends," so that work on the new constitution could continue.[195]

Even before Hindenburg's letter was made public, Hitler summoned the appropriate administrators (Frick, Rust, and Müller) and, after some heated debate, gave them their marching orders. Frick was to take charge of the negotiations overall, while Müller was instructed to get compromise agreements on the constitution from all parties as quickly as possible. As for the mayhem in Prussia, the newly minted *Deutsche Christen* administrators could stay where they were for the present, but as soon as there was agreement on the constitution, they were to be withdrawn. This sounded promising enough to the opposition in Prussia when the word got out, but it came with a caveat — Hitler's plan for the Protestant church called for new church elections in all *Landeskirchen* soon after the constitution was ratified. Hitler and his negotiators were confident that the *Deutsche Christen* would prevail in such a contest, especially since they would have the full support of the National Socialist Party in their respective election campaigns.[196]

Hindenburg's letter not only put pressure on Hitler to follow through on his promises, but it also put pressure on the church-political parties to cooperate in the ensuing negotiations. No one wanted to be seen as an obstacle to the President's obviously heartfelt desire for peace in the church, not to mention the *Führer*'s will.[197] Even Müller had to give up his ideal constitutional committee and accept the banished Committee of Three back into the negotiations; though in the end it was the opposition who would sacrifice the most in the name of peace and unity. On July 7, Müller convened this compromise committee to continue work on the constitution.

But in spite of this "progress" on the question of the Protestant church constitution, not much changed with regard to the general chaos and agitation on the ground, especially in Prussia. On July 2, Sunday services in Prussia reflected the church-political tensions, with reports of some churches following Jäger's instructions, others those of the opposition. In the days that followed, Jäger continued to "coordinate" at will, enforcing his orders with the state apparatus when needed. Thus the unrest continued.

195. Scholder, *Churches and the Third Reich*, vol. 1, p. 367.
196. Scholder, *Churches and the Third Reich*, vol. 1, p. 368.
197. Scholder, *Churches and the Third Reich*, vol. 1, p. 367.

What was Barth doing during these strange days? On July 1, Barth sent copies of *Theologische Existenz heute!* both to Prussian Kultusminster Rust and to Hitler himself. A few days later he would send a copy to the Prussian State Commissioner of the church of the Rheinland as well. The response to Barth's manifesto was so dramatic that a second edition was printed on July 8.[198]

As a result of the revived constitutional negotiations prompted by Hindenburg's intervention, Barth was again called to consult with the Reformed representative on the Committee of Three, the ever-ineffectual H. A. Hesse. This meant train rides back and forth to Berlin during the week of July 2 (there were no classes at Bonn that week) and an odd "on-call" existence in a local Berlin hotel, waiting to confer with Hesse between the official negotiations. While Hesse was in meetings, Barth had conversations with Young Reformers and other resisters, including Dietrich Bonhoeffer and Martin Niemöller.[199] But Barth was disappointed with the "compromise" proposal now moving quickly through the committee in Berlin, and lamented its embrace of the *Führerprinzip* in the form of a "Reichbishop." As he wrote to Hesse of this constitution-in-progress on July 9: "The moment will come once again when the church must carry the edifice arising here with united shame."[200]

Amid all the other challenges of the week, Barth was also scheduled to preach at the University worship service at the *Schloßkirche* back in Bonn on Sunday, July 9. His text was Luke 6:36-42, from the lectionary for the day.[201] In a letter to Charlotte von Kirschbaum from Berlin, Barth asked her if she would read through relevant sermons of Luther as well as Calvin's commentary on the text and see if there was anything he should look at when he got home.[202] He knew he would not have much time to prepare.

The sermon began with words from the text: "your Father is merciful!" Soon Barth was asking the congregation questions they could not fail to hear in relation to the church controversy: "What has brought us together here, gathered to serve God in the space of our Protestant church?

---

198. Eberhard Busch, *Karl Barth: His Life from Letters and Autobiographical Texts* (Philadelphia: Fortress, 1976), p. 227.
    199. Karl Barth to Charlotte von Kirschbaum, July 4, 1933, in *Briefe 1933*, p. 275.
    200. Karl Barth to Hermann Albert Hesse, July 9, 1933, in *Briefe 1933*, p. 289.
    201. The sermon may be found in Barth, *Gesamtausgabe* I.31, pp. 287-95.
    202. Karl Barth to Charlotte von Kirschbaum, July 4, 1933, in *Briefe 1933*, p. 277.

What is the sum of the confession of faith of this church? What may and should we know as Christians?"[203]

Barth answered: "Just these main and central words of our text: your Father is merciful!" The sermon unpacked those four words, beginning with the idea that Jesus Christ names God as our Father. Earthly fathers give us our parentage, our life, our way of life, Barth said, but Jesus Christ gives us a new Father, which means "an empty room, a new beginning." In relation to this new beginning the parentage, the life, the way of life we have "from our natural and spiritual fathers" "fades and is finally unimportant."[204] Those things are radically relativized. In case anyone might miss the implications of this, Barth continued:

> [Jesus Christ] gives us an entirely other Father, other than our natural and spiritual fathers, a Father from whom we have parentage, life, and manner neither in the *Gemeinschaft* of nature, of *Blutes*, of family, of *Volkes* and race, nor in the free *Gemeinschaft des Geistes,* but rather as we can have it now only from God, who created us, but now raised us from the dead by his Word and thus created us anew, an event which is unique in the entire natural and intellectual world.[205]

The sermon (like the text) turned from the question of God's mercy toward human beings to consider the way human beings are called to be merciful to one another. It explored the ways human beings seek to live by something other than mercy, setting ourselves up as *"Helden"* (heroes) or *"Kämpfer,"* (fighters), as "good people" who judge and condemn and punish "this person" or "that group."[206] We choose to make ourselves the representatives and champions of an unmerciful — and therefore imaginary — god. "But," Barth asked finally,

> Why should we not wipe our eyes now and say to ourselves that all this, this entire fall from mercy to un-mercy is only an evil ghost? Is it not so: We dream when we go on the way which begins here and stops there, where we encounter one another as punishing gods and must make life into hell. . . . But [it is] only a dream and not life.[207]

---

203. Barth, *Gesamtausgabe* I.31, p. 288.
204. Barth, *Gesamtausgabe* I.31, pp. 288-89.
205. Barth, *Gesamtausgabe* I.31, p. 289.
206. Barth, *Gesamtausgabe* I.31, pp. 290, 292.
207. Barth, *Gesamtausgabe* I.31, p. 295.

Real life is "the life in and with the Word: Your Father is merciful!" Why should we with our judgment, our "madness," our "evil dream" try to open up the hell "that Jesus Christ has closed once and for all"?[208] That is over.

The sermon concluded with words reminiscent of the end of *Theologische Existenz heute!*:

> Do we still dream, or are we already awake? God knows it of each one of us. But who among us here doesn't need to hear it again and again, that we need to wake up? See, it is itself the mercy of God, that he allows us time, more time, than we allow each other, time, in which we can hear it again and again: Your Father is merciful![209]

Hitler, the Third Reich, the *Deutsche Christen* — none of them were mentioned by name. But no one who heard this sermon in Bonn, Germany, on July 9, 1933, could miss the fact that this was a sermon of resistance. And it was resistance, not in spite of, but because of, its disciplined attention to the way of witness of the biblical text.

Session 8: July 11, 1933

The July 11 session was the last class meeting in which material was presented to the students, and it seems to have been a day designed to gather up any loose ends. Barth first offered an "addendum" to the discussion in the last session regarding the need to produce a written record of the sermon; namely, he wanted to return to the issue of *language*. We need culture in our lives, Barth said, and we need to cultivate our facility with language. There is a grinding away of language that occurs over time, he observed, a tendency to simply repeat certain set phrases. This "seduces" one into "missing" things; it means the death of words (KS20, P79). But the writing out of the sermon is a "practical" kind of "protection" against the "corrosion and ruin of language (as it especially happens through much sordid reading)." Kirschbaum wrote, "newspaper reading!" (K20). "Sordid reading and newspaper German are a danger," Barth said, "because they could lead to a poison of the language from outside, with their general ex-

---

208. Barth, *Gesamtausgabe* I.31, p. 295.
209. Barth, *Gesamtausgabe* I.31, p. 295.

pression and fashionable phrases, which often are entirely mindless" (P79). But there is "fitting antidote" to this "shipwreck" for preachers (KS79).[210] The discipline of producing a written record helps with the necessary constraint, Barth advised them. Readers were reminded that by this time, all newspapers, even church newspapers, were controlled by the Nazis.

Further, Barth continued, recall that the sermon is a body, which does not have parts but limbs. As such it stands closer to the structure of the homily in contrast to that of the theme sermon with its set principles of arrangement and division. These set divisions do not grow from the text! As examples of common templates Barth offered the following: "I. faith as theory; II. The praxis of life," or a division that severs the sermon into law and gospel, or to tear explication and application from each other in the manner of Schleiermacher. These patterns are indeed comfortable! Barth conceded (P80). Instead, Barth argued, "the body of a sermon must be composed in the repetition of the text's own rhythms and proportions," which unfold in the course of interpretation (KS20). This does not necessarily mean moving verse by verse, Barth told the class, but rather that "the movement peculiar to the text arises again"; the important things are accentuated, the less important subordinated (K20, P80). He took a biblical text, John 1:43-51, and demonstrated what he meant.

Then there is the question of a separate "conclusion" to the sermon, Barth said. But why would one need to embark on a summary there at the end? Hasn't everything already been said? Or maybe the sermon has just been exegesis, for example, and the preacher thinks he can turn it into application "by a closing attack on the hearer." But the sermon must be address from the beginning! Barth asserted (KS21). One should also not make a habit of invoking "a Hallelujah in the style of Romans 8 and such passages" at the end of every sermon (KS21, P81). As for the "important, comforting, and dangerous little word," *Amen*, Barth told the class, it "confesses before God" what one has said; it is "a comfort in the weakness of what has been said" (KS21). It also prompts the preacher to look ahead to the next sermon — it calls the preacher to get back to work. It is both comforting and unsettling — "this little word unfurls the entire doctrine of preaching" (KS21, P81).

Barth then offered the group five further rules of art for engaging

---

210. Deggeller writes: "In quick, shallow writing down we run the danger of basically bungling the language and letting general phrases degenerate to a downright sickness" (D38).

the biblical text. Many of them were already familiar, but clearly Barth wanted to stress them again. First, be careful that nothing "alien" is carried into the text, that the "thread of the text is not broken" (KS21, P81). Second, it is good to say no to the inclusion of any sentence that is solely explication or solely application. The sermon is not to report about the text but to say what is said there (P81)! This is difficult work, Barth acknowledged. Third, Barth repeated the claim: one should not try to be master of the text. To a true interpreter the Bible always becomes more mysterious, with "depths and secrets" before which theology resembles "playing in the tides of the sea with a teaspoon" (KS22). The interpreter stands vis-à-vis the Bible like a child, who wanders in awe through a "wonderful garden" and not like an advocate "who has seen all of God's files" (KS22, P81). Fourth, the pulpit is not the place to report about the meaning of specific words in the text. That is "necessary spadework" that "belongs in the preacher's study" (KS22, P81). It is the "fruit of in-depth and diligent work" that should be brought to the *Gemeinde* (KS22). Finally, Barth repeated, the sermon must not have the *intention* of discussing current events. It can have more to say about current events if it follows the way of witness in the text, even if it does not include concrete references to the latest headline.

The closing discussion returned to the problem of language. One often hears a sermon criticized because it is too "high," too "abstract," too "theological." When this kind of linguistic incomprehensibility occurs, Barth told the class, it is vanity and "mostly nothing other than a forbidden laziness" on the part of the preacher (KS22). But it is sometimes an unjust criticism, namely, when the *hearer* is lazy! The language of the sermon must correspond "to the seriousness of the subject matter *(Sache) and* the seriousness of life" (KS22).[211]

Barth ended the session with "a final warning." We have to speak as servants of the Word of God. Of course "our individuality codetermines the sermon." But we want our "curves" to be swept up in the "great curve" of the text — we don't want to speak independently (KS22, P82). Therefore, we should be cautious with images and making parallels to the text. These are good only when they are *disciplined* — "especially when refer-

---

211. Deggeller writes: "The problem of understandable language cannot be solved. In no case should one climb down in the language of the *Volk* and think to have found a solution with it. Really the question about a high and humble language should just be dropped. Preaching should be earnest. That is all" (D40).

ring to histories experienced by oneself" (KS22, P82).²¹² We also should be careful about trying to interfere or be invasive in the lives of our hearers. The silence that tends to arise in such situations is certainly a loaded silence (KS22, P82)!

In the final moments the students raised a number of questions. Can you end a sermon with an interrogative sentence? It depends on whether such a sentence is proclamation, Barth said (P82). How about "free prayer" after the sermon? Such prayer is often "idle chatter" that gives the impression that the pastor is not prepared, Barth suggested (P82). Should a sermon — a joyful message — be delivered with a manuscript? Is that in keeping with its character? There are different thoughts about that in different places, Barth explained. Whatever is done should be responsible — otherwise it depends on the individual (P82). What about a hymn stanza as the conclusion? This must be judged like the "Hallelujah." Is there a good reason to do this? Barth asked (P82). Then a student asked if one should give the hearers a question to take with them. It must be a serious question, Barth responded, and one that is "in the shadow of the answer" that the sermon already offered (P82). Finally someone argued that the practice of sermon divisions helps the hearer retain the sermon. Isn't that a rather "schoolmaster-ish" concern? Barth asked. The goal of preaching is not that people walk away with a couple of thoughts, but that they opened the Bible and followed the way of witness (P83).

July 11 to 18, 1933

Contextual Developments

By July 10, the committee gathered around Müller in Berlin concluded their negotiations on the new constitution. An eleventh-hour attempt by a minority to weaken the bishop's power and shape the new organization in a more collaborative direction was defeated. The document was then signed, with objections noted in the minutes.²¹³ The next day, commissioners from the various *Landeskirchen* descended on Berlin to ratify the

---

212. Deggeller comments with the more restrictive: "images and stories are to be used chastely, at best to be avoided. For the eagerness of the *Gemeinde* in the moment of the story cancels the receptivity for the actual word of the sermon" (D40).

213. Scholder, *Churches and the Third Reich*, vol. 1, pp. 376-77.

constitution. The large Prussian delegation specifically included both the dismissed commissioners and their DC replacements.[214] Müller addressed the gathering, urging the delegates in conspiratorial tones that they needed to act quickly before the Catholics (with *their* treaty) gained the upper hand.[215]

Only a few hours and a few minor corrections later, the constitution was passed without a single negative vote. Minister Frick assured the commissioners that he would immediately begin the process of reversing the actions taken by the Prussian state against the *Landeskirchen* within the week, and the delegates headed home to plan for the new church elections, scheduled for August 20. The constitution was then presented to Hitler at the cabinet meeting on July 14, where the Roman Catholic Concordat was ratified as well.

For this brief window of time, many Protestants felt relieved, even elated, about the way things had turned out. Even the Young Reformers expressed their "deep joy" that "the way has become free for the *Volkskirche* under the gospel."[216] But the *Landeskirchen* delegates had barely returned home from the vote on the constitution when telegrams arrived from the Reich Ministry of the Interior calling them back to Berlin. On July 14 they reassembled and were promptly presented with a new law, soon to pass the Reich cabinet, which included the provision that the church elections were now to be held on July 23 — a mere nine days later — on Hitler's orders.[217] Though this was a violation of the election rules of the *Landeskirchen* and a logistical disaster, the representatives did not have the will to put up much of a fight. That very day, Hitler authorized two sets of directives: the governments of all the *Länder* were to be instructed to make sure the church elections were carried out in an "impartial" manner, *and* the Reich propaganda office was to mobilize forces on every level "to secure a victory" for the *Deutsche Christen*.[218] And so another feverish election campaign began.

By the middle of July *Theologische Existenz heute!* was in its fourth

---

214. Reichminister of the Interior Frick included the new and the old Prussian church administrators as a precaution — to rule out possible legal objections in future. Scholder, *Churches and the Third Reich*, vol. 1, p. 377.

215. Scholder, *Churches and the Third Reich*, vol. 1, p. 377.

216. F. Söhlmann, *Junge Kirche 1*, 1933. Quoted in Scholder, *Churches and the Third Reich*, vol. 1, p. 380.

217. Scholder, *Churches and the Third Reich*, vol. 1, p. 441.

218. Scholder, *Churches and the Third Reich*, vol. 1, p. 442.

printing, and some 12,000 copies had been distributed. Barth received numerous letters from friends and strangers, clergy and students, thanking him for his words.

But the work also provoked criticism from the expected quarters. Emanuel Hirsch, Barth's former colleague at Göttingen, was so disturbed by the manifesto that he wrote his own in response to Barth's "attack."[219] In it Hirsch repeated his belief that Barth would understand the proper relationship between church and *Volk* if "he were German from top to toe, like us; if he had experienced as his own the fate of our *Volk* in war and defeat and self-alienation, and the National Socialist revolution in the way we did, with trembling and joy."[220]

But as for the Bonn students who crowded Barth's lecture hall, they greeted their professor on the day after *Theologische Existenz heute!* appeared with a *"Spektakel"* (loud stomping of the feet) — "as if I had my seventieth birthday," Barth reported.[221] He took comfort in such small hopeful moments in the unpredictable days before the church elections. Barth wrote to Emil Brunner the day before the next meeting of the sermon exercises:

> We live here in a curious, incessant dramatically moving world, in which each day, as it were, has its small or great sensation, which one must handle without being *able* to worry about the next [cf. Matthew 6:34]. Always with the possibility that yet one day some *entirely* unpleasant thing could also happen. In these months I have seen and heard much that until now I only read about.[222]

Session 9: July 18, 1933

This session, like much of the one that followed it, was a sort of practicum, where a student read out a sermon he composed, and then the sermon was discussed by the whole class. There is no information about how exactly

---

219. Emanuel Hirsch, "Zur Beurteilung des Angriffs von Karl Barth," in *Das kirchliche Wollen der Deutschen Christen* (Berlin-Steglitz: Evangelischer Pressverband für Deutschland, 1933), pp. 5-17.
220. Hirsch, "Zur Beurteilung des Angriffs von Karl Barth," p. 7. Quoted in Scholder, *Churches and the Third Reich*, vol. 1, p. 439.
221. Karl Barth to Emil Brunner, July 17, 1933, in *Briefe 1933*, p. 297.
222. Karl Barth to Emil Brunner, July 17, 1933, in *Briefe 1933*, pp. 295-96.

this last part of the course took place. The notes from Kirschbaum and the student protocol suggest that only a few representative students read sermons to the class for the purposes of the discussion, but it is certainly possible that each student wrote a sermon, even if it was not presented to the class. At any rate, the notes perhaps give a sense of Barth's reaction to the representative sermons, but we do not have the sermons themselves. For our present purposes, we will simply observe the following: the sermons were (not surprisingly) discussed in great detail in terms of their relationship to the dynamics of their respective biblical texts, but the critique was not limited to that. Barth praised the first sermon (by Herr Johannsen) for its "honest attempt to interpret the text" and for its "genuine religious earnestness," but criticized it because it lacked "closeness to life." "The explication does not become application," he observed, "no claim takes place," "the sermon is more like a lecture" (KS25, P83-84). The second sermon (by Adolf Horn) received Barth's approval with regard to its "succinct, pregnant language" and "good biblical insights," but he suggested that it was too short and seemed to concern "general biblical insights" rather than interpreting its particular text (KS25, P85).

July 18 to 25, 1933

Contextual Developments

Both the *Deutsche Christen* and the Young Reformers launched frantic campaigns in anticipation of the July 23 church elections. The Young Reformers initially called their "list" — meaning their slate of candidates — "*Evangeliche Kirche*," but Hossenfelder managed to procure an injunction against the use of the title on the grounds that the name "defamed" the *Deutsche Christen*.[223] The Young Reformers settled for "*Evangelium und Kirche*" instead, and threw themselves into the fight.

But they were swimming upstream from the start. Once the word from the Reich leadership that the NSDAP was to make every effort to help the *Deutsche Christen* to victory reached the local party officials, they immediately began canvassing the country, registering all Protestant party

---

223. Ostensibly because it implied that *Deutsche Christen* were then *not* the "*Evangelische Kirche*," though if one follows this line of reasoning the name "*Deutsche Christen*" would imply *its* opponents were neither German nor Christian. See Scholder, *Churches and the Third Reich*, vol. 1, p. 443.

Karl Barth's Predigtvorbereitung in Context: Summer Semester 1933

members, recruiting Nazis as *Deutsche Christen* candidates, and making it clear that a failure to vote in the church elections, or a failure to vote for the *Deutsche Christen*, would result in expulsion from the NSDAP. Naturally, party members were also forbidden to become a candidate for any election list other than the *Deutsche Christen*. At the same time, both the *Deutsche Christen* and the NSDAP made every effort to persuade (or intimidate) local church bodies to vote to utilize a long-standing provision in the election rules of the *Landeskirchen*, a provision that allowed for communities to agree ahead of time to have only one list, thus eliminating the need for an election at all. Most Protestants, still shaken after the events of the last few months, relieved that the constitutional question was now settled, and deeply loyal to the *Führer* and the President, just wanted peace. Thus in the majority of communities there was one list, that list was at least two-thirds *Deutsche Christen*, and there was no election on July 23.[224]

But this plan did not work everywhere. In Berlin, there were vigorous elections in over half the districts, and in Bonn, despite efforts to the contrary, the *Deutsche Christen* faced not just one but two oppositional parties.[225] The first was the Young Reformers (*"Evangelium und Kirche"*). The second was a list that came into being only three days before the election. It was called "For the Freedom of the Gospel." Its "list" included three professors, an attorney, and a woman. Its lead candidate was Karl Barth.

Why did Barth decide to run in the local church elections? For Barth and the other like-minded Protestants surrounding him, it was an obligation, a duty, a calling, to participate in the church election of July 1933. But what "list" could they support?

Naturally the *Deutsche Christen* was out of the question, but why not throw their lot in with the Young Reformers? At least they were also opposed to the *Deutsche Christen*!

To understand why that was impossible for Barth, and what that impossibility had to do with the very questions Barth raised with his students in the *Predigtvorbereitung,* one only need listen to the statements made by the Young Reformers in the Rheinland in the days leading up to the election. As Annette Hinz-Wessels has established, the group emphasized its

---

224. For a careful examination of Protestant attitudes in the church elections of July 23, 1933, see Shelley Baranowski, "The 1933 German Protestant Church Elections: *Machtpolitik* or Accommodation?" *Church History* 49, no. 3 (1980): 298-315.

225. This occurred in only one other community in the Rheinland: Remscheid. Annette Hinz-Wessels, *Die evangelische Kirchengemeinde Bonn in der Zeit des Nationalsozialismus (1933-1945)* (Cologne: Rheinland-Verlag, 1996), p. 141.

"unconditional loyalty" to the Third Reich and its *Führer*. Hinz-Wessels summarizes their election platform:

> As *German* Protestant Christians we want to establish that the church serves the German *Volk* in deepest solidarity, and to struggle for the inner renewal of the German *Volkes*. As German *Protestant* Christians we advocate for action with the power of the gospel by the grace of God in Jesus Christ alone.[226]

The primary difference between the Young Reformers and *Deutsche Christen* in the Rheinland was the insistence of the former that the church had a right to self-determination without state interference and, for some, a desire to preserve the presbyterial-synodial order.[227]

But in its basic stance, the leaders of the Young Reformers in Bonn affirmed the *Deutsche Christen* desire for "a sharper defense against all modern heresies, materialism, mammonism, Bolshevism and Christian pacifism" and clearly accepted the premises of Political Theology and its implications for the proclamation of the church. The lead candidate on the Bonn *"Evangelium und Kirche"* list, General Superintendent Klingemann, argued that Christian preaching must "assume the peculiarity of a *Volk* and it must be for the good of the *Volk*. Thus we have experienced it in the history of our *Volk*, and because our German Christian peculiarity will be best secured where the gospel is preached without abbreviation."[228]

The unconditional loyalty to Reich and *Führer*, the embrace of Political Theology, and the narrow view of the nature and purpose of Christian preaching were all, of course, unacceptable to Barth and the group around him. Sometime on Wednesday, July 19, Karl Ludwig Schmidt and Ernst Wolf persuaded Barth that they needed to mount their own list. Even if it was not successful, it would at least be, as Charlotte von Kirschbaum put it, "a demonstration — for general astonishment."[229] Immediately they set

---

226. Hinz-Wessels, *Die evangelische Kirchengemeinde Bonn*, p. 143.

227. This did not necessarily mean the abandonment of the *Führerprinzip*. According to one of the candidates on the list of the Young Reformers, this presbyterial-synodical order was "in no way democratic or parliamentary, but leadership growing out of faith and a working *Gemeinschaft* beneficial for the life of the *Gemeinde*." Quoted in Hinz-Wessels, *Die evangelische Kirchengemeinde Bonn*, p. 144.

228. Hinz-Wessels, *Die evangelische Kirchengemeinde Bonn*, p. 144.

229. Charlotte von Kirschbaum to Eduard Thurneysen, July 20, 1933, in Barth, *Gesamtausgabe* V.34, p. 473.

about all the necessary arrangements. Colleagues, students, and friends came to help. Flyers and posters were printed and distributed. Soon the Barth household was host to "a very strange society" of people working, planning, and debating.[230] The election was three days away.

On July 21, even as complaints about NSDAP interference in the church elections poured in to the office of the Reich Ministry of the Interior, Ludwig Müller decided to do one final thing to secure a *Deutsche Christen* victory and, he hoped, his own future as Reich Bishop. He pleaded with Hitler to personally intervene on behalf of the *Deutsche Christen*:

> The reactionaries in their final fury are using all — and I mean all — means, including the most vile slander, to deprive us of control of the new Reich Church. I urgently need your help, because otherwise the instrument of power we have forged will fall into the hands of the enemy. And it is essential to be clear that in the final analysis this so-called "church-struggle" is none other than a struggle against you and against National Socialism.[231]

The following evening, late on the eve of the election, Hitler made a well-publicized speech that was broadcast on every radio station in Germany. In it he explained that the church and the state were dependent on each other. The church needed the protection of the state, and in exchange for that protection it owed the state its support. The church could have its "inner freedom," but it should therefore play its part "in standing up for the freedom of the nation." In the Protestant church today, Hitler concluded, it was the *Deutsche Christen* who had "deliberately trodden the ground of the National Socialist state."[232]

The same night in Bonn, Barth spoke to a large crowd about the election. The subject: what does "the freedom of the gospel" *mean*?[233] Above all, Barth said, the gospel is something that is said *to* us; it is not something we can say to ourselves.

> No human being can discover that God is for us and with us in nature or in history or in the treasure of his life experience. But it is heard in

---

230. Barth, *Gesamtausgabe* V.34, p. 474.
231. Ludwig Müller, quoted in Scholder, *Churches and the Third Reich*, vol. 1, p. 445.
232. Scholder, *Churches and the Third Reich*, vol. 1, p. 446.
233. Barth's speech may be found in Karl Barth, "Für die Freiheit des Evangeliums," *Theologische Existenz heute!*, vol. 2 (Munich: Chr. Kaiser Verlag, 1934), pp. 3-16.

the freedom in which God himself has spoken his Word to human beings and will speak again. He has not spoken it always and everywhere but to a particular time and place: to the prophets of the Old and to the apostles of the New Testaments, which now on their part give us witness to his Word.[234]

Nelly Barth described the scene that night in a hurried note to a friend:

> Saturday evening — about 1000 people fill the great hall of the Bonn "Bürgerverein," *Deutsche Christen* and SA people are present. But my husband speaks undisturbed, strongly and with impact — freely, but prepared. It was really an hour of great import. It was now *possible* — that the gospel in its freedom and completely and entirely was shown in faith! It was possible, that the hearer ever and ever gave his consent and went along until the end. [How] gladly like-minded persons pressed each other's hand[s]! It was simply beautiful! That my husband was able to secure this peaceful maturity, that the truth was communicated by him before the public, and his young men who trust him listen respectfully before they now disband from each other and do not know which teacher in which university they will have later, was that not beautiful![235]

On July 23 the general elections for the German Protestant church were held. Overall, they were a resounding victory for the *Deutsche Christen*, in part because of the large numbers of NSDAP members who voted for the first time. In Bonn, the *Deutsche Christen* won the majority of seats in the Presbyterium, with thirty-five, the Young Reformers earned nineteen, and Barth's group, *"Für die Freiheit des Evangeliums,"* six.

And so the last week of classes began.

Session 10: July 25, 1933

There is little record of this, the final meeting of the sermon exercises. For whatever reason, Charlotte von Kirschbaum's notes and the student proto-

---

234. Barth, "Für die Freiheit des Evangeliums," p. 5.
235. Nelly Barth to D. Stoevesandt, July 23, 1933. Quoted in Barth, *Gesamtausgabe* V.34, p. 478, n. 2.

col are very brief and, for the first time, identical. One is clearly a direct copy of the other. As in the previous week, two students read their sermons, which were then discussed. Of the first sermon (by a Herr Röhrig) Barth noted among other things the "energetic pushing-forward exegesis" of the sermon and the way the preacher managed to concentrate on "the essential thing" without giving the impression that everything that could be said was said. The sermon should have avoided some of the repetitions, "a certain breadth," and "some scholasticism" (KS26, P87). The second and final sermon (by Herr Vogt) "drifted too far from the text" and "abandoned its basically joyful tone." Barth also expressed concern about its "too great pessimism with respect to the hearer" as well as "a certain unmercifulness" (KS26-27, P87).

The notes provide only a rather cryptic description of Barth's final words to the students on their last meeting. There was first "a vivid warning about theological onesidedness," then "a pure statement of the propositions of dialectical theology" — the Godness of God! — and finally "a call to an always *new* hearing of the Word of Scripture: the reconciliation happening in Jesus Christ" (KS27, P87).

With that, the sermon exercises were over.

Conclusion

Barth's classroom in the summer of 1933 was like the eye of the hurricane — a place of relative calm amid the roar and bluster of the Third Reich. But its calm was not indifference or "inner immigration" or acceptance in relation to the winds howling outside the doors. It was a place of resistance.

Barth's specific task for the semester was to offer practical guidance to those novice preachers, that is, a formal homiletic that corresponded to the principle and material work of the previous semester. But what sort of preaching would correspond to the affirmation of the Godness of God in the context of the Third Reich? What specific practices might serve to challenge and subvert the homiletic exaltation of *Volk, Blut,* and *Führer* all around them? What concrete strategies might help prepare these young people to preach under the wide horizon of God's way with and for all humanity in Jesus Christ in a totalitarian state and in a "coordinated" church?

In simplest terms:

Preach from the Bible, that is where God's witnesses speak. *Not anywhere else.*

Follow the lectionary, or preach through a book of the Bible. Don't preach on a text that's too short. Start with the original language — the details matter. Pay attention to the words, the context, the history behind the text. Read what others have to say about it. Trace its way of witness, its movement, its reversals, its curves, the one thing that is there. Follow that way of witness into the present. Be open. Be attentive. Be disturbed.

What does the text say to you and to these specific people who listen to you? Not to *Germans,* but to these people who belong to God, who are addressed by God, who are called by God. These people are baptized or should be baptized. Speak after the text to *them,* but speak after the *text,* not after your own vision, plan, opinion, theme, or scheme. To do the latter is to rape the text. You are a *servant* of the Word, not its *lord.*

A sermon is alive, so let it grow from the way of witness. Don't smother it with prefabricated structures. Follow the curves of the text in the *form* of the sermon too.

Do not *begin* the sermon in a way that denies the deepest identity of your hearers. Do not address them as *Volk,* or sinners, or even students, and do not begin with an introduction that confines the gospel to your ideological template. Speak to the *real* hearer, under the wide open heavens, right from the beginning.

Do not feel obliged to talk about every current event in the sermon. There are plenty of "fires" in Germany, every day, and plenty of people to talk about them, but who else will speak after the witness to God's Word? Our only comfort in life and in death?

When you are ready, write the sermon down. Every word. Watch its rhetoric. Guard against the language of death that greets us with every headline.

Be original. Be courageous. Be humble.

Barth's practical advice to his students in the summer of 1933 undermined just about everything they had learned from Professor Pfennigsdorf about how to prepare a sermon — a minority report in relation to the homiletical theory and practice on display all around them. As such, it was an emergency homiletic, a return to theological basics even with regard to practical questions, at a time when theological basics were in short supply.

But in the end, the *Predigtvorbereitung* was part of another kind of resistance as well. In contrast to the strident environment of marches, rallies, boycotts, and book burnings, in Barth's preaching classroom, substantive, thoughtful, critical theological conversation continued. Issues were discussed between those walls that prompted riots elsewhere. That Barth managed to facilitate such an atmosphere as a member of the Social Democratic Party in a room that included Nazis, *Stahlhelmer*, and *Deutschen Christen* surprised even him.

How did that experience change these young people, how did it form them, how did it prepare them for ministry in the disturbing months and years to come?

Though its legacy is difficult to trace in this regard, surely Charlotte von Kirschbaum was right when she said that the sermon exercises were a beautiful thing.[236]

---

236. Charlotte von Kirschbaum to Karl Barth, March 21, 1933, in Barth, *Gesamtausgabe* V.1, p. 270.

POSTSCRIPT

Rereading Karl Barth's "Homiletics"

The "trouble with Barth" has almost always been framed in binary terms. Critics charge that his theology exhibits an imbalance in the relation between "above" and "below," between heaven and earth, between the shadow of a very big God and the humanity eclipsed thereby. When Barth turns his attention to the task of preaching, it has been argued, he is particularly unhelpful. Barth is so focused on God's action that he ignores the human preacher, he is so fixated on the Bible that he disregards the situation of the hearer, he is so passionate about the Word that he has no concern for the words that make up sermons, and, worst of all, his theology leads to a pulpit that is "politely silent," even cowardly, with regard to public and political issues.[1]

A contextual reading of the artifacts of the *Übungen in der Predigtvorbereitung* paints a very different picture.

Barth, as we have seen, was himself influenced by the modern preaching movement that emerged in Germany around the turn of the century, and his earliest sermons show him to be a skilled practitioner of the genre. While he came to question many of the assumptions of the modern preaching movement, what he did not abandon was its attention to the hearer of the Word, even as he insisted that the hearer of Christian preaching was more than the sum of her demographic data — not reducible to gender, race, age, class, political affiliation, or "worldview."

But what Barth did object to, among other things, was the instru-

---

1. See for example David Buttrick, *A Captive Voice: The Liberation of Preaching* (Louisville: Westminster John Knox, 1994), p. 2.

mentalization of the sermon in the homiletic of his day. "Theme preaching" by the end of Weimar often functioned as a tool — or a weapon — that the preacher used to convince hearers that the Protestant church (and, indeed, the Protestant *God*) was fully behind the national awakening and that the church, as the dispenser of grace and the guardian of the *Volkseele*, had an indispensable part to play in the new order. The sermon, then, was unapologetically apologetic. As such, preaching — like everything else in the whirl of German political life — was often a matter of persuasion, or, to put it more cynically, propaganda.

It is certainly true that Barth rejected this approach to the matter. The *Predigtvorbereitung* artifacts demonstrate that Barth steadily, repeatedly, relentlessly worked to decenter these young preachers, urging them to lay down their weapons and their agendas, to listen with empty hands and open hearts for an unsettling Word from the Lord at the dawn of the Third Reich. They were not called to be Protestant propagandists, but servants of the Word, pointing as clearly as possible to something they neither possessed nor controlled. Almost from the beginning of the exercises Barth relentlessly deconstructed one sort of "preacher": the confident prophet with an unquestioned and unquestionable agenda, armed for battle — a pope, a visionary, an enthusiast, an idealist with "great thoughts," a little Luther, a tyrant.

But this deconstruction was not an end in itself. It cleared the field for another vision of the preacher, and yes, the *ēthos* of said preacher, to emerge. Anyone who reads through the *Predigtvorbereitung* artifacts cannot miss the catalogue of "virtues" — or, better, "charisms" — everywhere in evidence: preachers are called to humility, openness, regard *(respicere)* in relation to the Word of God, courage, diligence, prayerful expectancy, discipline, flexibility, love, and hope. The preacher is one who comes to the task of sermon preparation with open hands, willing to be called into question, willing to be pressed to the ground (K9, P12). Preaching in the space between incarnation and eschatology means that every "having" is a "full-fledged trembling not having," a wealth that is poverty (K22). This preacher "with all humility and seriousness" should engage in theological work, making every effort to "direct the Word rightly" (K33, P44). It is a "running ahead" in the command and blessing of the God who has promised to follow. In this sense the preacher is a "herald" who ventures out, who listens well, who tries to speak after what is heard as address to the people of the present (K36, P47).

But in the midst of this attentiveness, this *respicere*, this being "caught up" in that to which the Scripture points, Barth insisted that *the preacher as a person does not disappear.* The human being who is called to attempt this work must do so as a complex individual in a context with a history (K42, P53). This preacher must love the *Gemeinde,* be open to them, and share a life as one of them. To be a preacher is not to play a part or to imitate others but to be one's self. It is to interpret a biblical text "in free speech" to people today, "not at all mere recitation of the words of Scripture." Such preachers should be resistant to borrowed rhetoric, the poison of newspaper-speak, and prefabricated forms. They should employ "free speech." It is an emphasis with particular relevance at the dawn of a totalitarian regime.

After all, the purpose of preaching is not to explore ancient history, Barth told his students. It is to travel the way of witness of the text in the Germany of 1933, pointing where it points. This means explication must become application, Barth insisted. In fact, nothing in the sermon should be mere explanation of some "past-tense" event — it is address from the very beginning (K43, P53). This, he told the students, is a risk. For this "application" requires "civil courage." It has public import. Preachers are to witness to the way of witness of a biblical text in relation to "all outer life relationships under all circumstances" with the "civil courage" that "ventures to seize the concrete situation" in obedience to the way of witness of the Scripture (P73).

Such preachers can only go about their work with soberness, without pretension, and in constant prayer.

This, then, is the *habitus* Barth encouraged in his preaching students. Preachers are to wear these "graces" not in order to win a hearing, but because this is what it looks like to be claimed by the God who is God. It is a faithful and fitting response to the preacher's commission.

The Barth who led "exercises in sermon preparation" in the lecture hall at Bonn University in the tumult of 1932-33 bears little resemblance to the "neo-orthodox Barth" — the Barth oblivious to the human dimension of things. The flesh-and-blood Barth did not ignore the hearer of the Word, the person of the preacher, or the language of the sermon in his protest homiletic. His insistence on the Godness of God does not underwrite a politely apolitical pulpit.

The question for Barth was not whether or not preachers speak a word to "the situation," political or otherwise — one way or another all preachers do that.[2] The question for Barth was *how* the preacher does this.

---

2. Sometimes a "strange silence on public issues" is itself a form of resistance. In the

Postscript: Rereading Karl Barth's "Homiletics"

Faced with a hall full of young German Protestants in the early 1930s, at least some of whom were sympathetic to the *Geist* of national renewal and mesmerized by its *Führer*, it is hardly surprising that Barth stressed the need for humility, "chastity," open hands, again and again. But even then, the call for "civil courage" was there, and Barth continued to engage the question of the "how" of preaching and politics for the remainder of his time in Germany.

Read in their multilayered context, the *Predigtvorbereitung* artifacts tell a compelling story of emergency practical theology, one that is worth remembering. The notes that were left behind do not reveal some kind of timeless universal homiletical blueprint we might label "Barthian" and then discard. Instead, they offer a glimpse at a self-consciously contextual, dialectical, theological, and temporary homiletic forged in the midst of political and personal turmoil.

There are, of course, vast differences between the advanced democracies of the twenty-first century and the Germany of the early 1930s, but those charged with preaching the gospel today in many parts of the world know something of what a partisan and media-saturated environment is like. We know something of economic turmoil. We know something of the pathos that rails against enemies, foreign and domestic. We know something of a church that longs for full pews and public influence. Surely Karl Barth's efforts to teach young people to preach in a time of political, ecclesiastical, academic, rhetorical, and homiletical turmoil have continuing relevance for everyone who walks into a seminary classroom or steps into a pulpit today.

In 1946 Barth gave permission for his lectures on Protestant theology in the nineteenth century, which he delivered first in Münster and then again in Bonn, to be published. In his foreword, he explained his reasons for doing so:

> I have constantly had occasion to wish and suggest that the attitude and approach of the younger generations of Protestant theologians to the period of the Church that is just past might be rather different

---

course of the sermon exercises, Barth argued that it is not always necessary to name "the situation" explicitly. Especially in a media-saturated environment, where fanning the flames of outrage and playing to fears sells newspapers, preachers must not simply accept popular interpretations of what "situations" are most pressing. The refusal to make the Reichstag fire the centerpiece for a sermon on God's deliverance in the Germany of 1933 would be an example of "prophetic" silence on a "public" issue.

from that which they now often seem to regard, somewhat impetuously, as the norm — misunderstanding the guidance they have received from me. I would be very pleased if they were (to put it simply) to show a little more love towards those who have gone before us, despite the degree of alienation they feel from them.... We need openness towards and interest in particular figures with their individual characteristics, an understanding of the circumstances in which they worked, much patience and also much humour in the face of their obvious limitations and weaknesses, a little grace in expressing even the most profound criticism and finally, even in the worst cases, a certain tranquil delight that they were as they were.[3]

No doubt there will be just as much disagreement with the new interpretation of Barth's "Homiletics" as there was with the old. But perhaps we could go about rereading the sermon exercises the way Barth urged his students to read those who came before them. Perhaps we could reread Karl Barth with a richer understanding of the circumstances in which he worked, with much patience and much humor in the face of his limitations and weaknesses, a little grace in expressing even the most profound criticisms of his ideas, and even, when we are most unconvinced, a certain tranquil delight that he was the way that he was.

---

3. Karl Barth, *Protestant Theology in the Nineteenth Century: Its Background and History*, trans. Brian Cozens and John Bowden (Grand Rapids: Eerdmans, 2002), p. xii.

Appendix

Source Documents

The extant artifacts of the *Übungen in der Predigtvorbereitung*, conducted by Karl Barth at the University of Bonn in the winter semester 1932-33 and the summer semester of 1933, are as follows:

A. The handwritten protocols from the winter semester 1932-33 and the summer semester 1933, most sessions bearing the signature of the designated student recorder.
B. A typewritten copy of the student protocols (A) of the two semesters.[1] It is unclear when this typed text was produced and by whom, but it may have been the work of Charlotte von Kirschbaum.
C. A typewritten account of each of the two semesters, almost certainly the work of Charlotte von Kirschbaum, though no name appears on the documents.[2] Kirschbaum mentioned more than once that she was taking and preparing notes of the sessions to send to Eduard Thurneysen.[3]

---

1. The typewritten transcript of the student protocols is designated in this study as (P).

2. Because Kirschbaum's accounts of the two semesters are numbered separately, her notes of the winter semester are noted as (K), the summer semester as (KS).

3. See Charlotte von Kirschbaum to Eduard Thurneysen, November 25, 1932, in Karl Barth, *Gesamtausgabe*, ed. Hinrich Stoevesandt and Hans Anton Drewes (Zürich: Theologischer Verlag, 1971), V.34, p. 302; Charlotte von Kirschbaum to Eduard Thurneysen, December 7, 1932, in Barth, *Gesamtausgabe* V.34, p. 307; Charlotte von Kirschbaum to Eduard Thurneysen, January 3, 1933, in Barth, *Gesamtausgabe* V.34, p. 338; and Charlotte von Kirschbaum to Karl Barth, March 21, 1933, in Barth, *Gesamtausgabe* V.1, p. 270.

APPENDIX

Copies of these notebooks were found among Thurneysen's papers.[4]
D. A copy of the "free elaboration" of the sermon exercises by Werner Deggeller, a student who was present for the summer semester 1933 only. Deggeller describes his manuscript as "bound to the material" as far as content was concerned, but formulated "wholly independently."[5] Deggeller prepared and distributed his notes privately beginning in August 1933.

The interpretation of the *Predigtvorbereitung* lectures presented in this study is based on the student protocols and the notes attributed to Charlotte von Kirschbaum. Due to its character as an "elaboration," Werner Deggeller's account is cited in the footnotes when his interpretation expands on or departs from the other accounts, but is not included in the body of the text. The originals of each of these texts may be found at the Karl Barth-Archiv in Basel, Switzerland, and are used in this study with the gracious permission of the Karl Barth-Stiftung.

Initial Circulation

As early as 1934 there were requests by students to distribute notes of the sermon exercises. In April of 1934 Ulrich Bergfried, who had been a student in the Bonn sessions, wrote to Barth from the Netherlands, asking for his blessing to distribute copies of his (Bergfried's) notes from the sessions to the theology students there.

Barth's response to Bergfried did not survive, nor have any copies of Bergfried's notes surfaced. The following year, however, Charlotte von Kirschbaum wrote to Barth (who was away in Switzerland) concerning a request from some students to copy (and presumably distribute) notes from the sessions, and she reports that she gave the students permission to do so.[6] Whether the notes in question were copies of A, B, C, or even some other compilation of notes taken by individual students is not indicated. What is clear is that artifacts of the *Übungen in der Predigtvor-*

---

4. See Charlotte von Kirschbaum to Eduard Thurneysen, January 3, 1933, in Barth, *Gesamtausgabe* V.34, p. 338, n. 9.

5. Deggeller's text is indicated by (D) in the study. The quotations come from Deggeller's opening comments, which he gives under the heading "Zum Verständnis."

6. Charlotte von Kirschbaum to Karl Barth, January 14, 1935, in Barth, *Gesamtausgabe* V.1, p. 423.

bereitung were circulating informally among students in some form from that time forward.

Earliest Publication

Credit for first formal publication of an artifact of the *Predigtvorbereitung* appears to belong to Regin Prenter (1907-1990), a student at Bonn in the winter of 1933, who translated Werner Deggeller's notes into Danish and managed to have them published in Denmark in 1938.[7] But circulation was small, and it would be a very long time before the notes resurfaced in print again.

La proclamation de L'évangile (1961)

In 1961, nearly thirty years after the sermon exercises were held, a French translation of the student protocols (A/B) was published in Switzerland as *La proclamation de L'évangile* on the occasion of Karl Barth's seventy-fifth birthday. Barth appeared to have had minimal involvement in the endeavor and even wrote in the preface to the book that he did not remember when or where he delivered the material! He asked that practical theologians not judge the work too harshly and that readers remember that he was still relatively young when he gave the lectures — though he did not want to make any changes to the text.[8] Young theologians might find it interesting, Barth concluded, to compare some of his sermons with the principles developed in the notes "and see to what extent I have remained faithful to them."[9]

The text of *La proclamation de L'évangile* is based on the student protocols, portions of which were prepared for publication by a Swiss pastor, A. Roulin. As such, it is a sampling of the notes rather than a complete transcript. *La proclamation de L'évangile* does not include the historical survey at the beginning of the course, for example, and Roulin omits any contextual traces from his redaction, such as Barth's *zeitgemäß* reference at

---

7. Werner Deggeller, *Professor D. Karl Barths Øvelser over Praedikenens Forberedelse: En Homiletisk Øvelse Afholdt Ved Universitetet I Bonn Sommeren 1933*, trans. Regin Prenter (København: Theologisk Oratorium, 1938).

8. Karl Barth, *La proclamation de L'évangile: Texte Reconstitué par le Pasteur A. Roulin d'après des Notes d'étudiants* (Neuchâtel: Delachaux et Niestlé, 1961), p. 5.

9. Barth, *La proclamation de L'évangile*, p. 5.

one point to "the Germany of 1933" (P71). Roulin excises such references in an effort, one presumes, to give the text a more universal flavor.

A few months after these selected notes were published in French, Barth received a request that they be translated back into German and that the book then be published in Germany as well. But Barth was staunchly opposed to this idea. He did not want the text published at all, not even the original German notes, since "it has in it many crudities and blunders which might not make it totally impossible in the French sphere but which should not be allowed on the scene in today's German sphere."[10]

While at Barth's insistence it did not appear in Germany, in 1963 *La proclamation de L'évangile* was translated from French into English by B. E. Hooke and published in the United States as *The Preaching of the Gospel*. Naturally this English text shares in the limitations of its redacted source, now compounded by the fact that *The Preaching of the Gospel* is a translation of a translation, and thus even further removed from the *Predigtvorbereitung* artifacts themselves.

The Origin of *Homiletics* (1991)

The next major development with regard to the publication of the *Predigtvorbereitung* notes occurred a few years later in the summer of 1965 when Günther Seyfferth, then a theology student at the University of Bonn, discovered the file containing the notes of the sermon exercises. Seyfferth thought at first of distributing these notes informally; but soon, with the support of the Bonn *Dozenten* and Barth's consent, Seyfferth began preparing a manuscript for publication. The text he produced, *Homiletik: Wesen und Vorbereitung der Predigt* (1966), is based on three documents: the handwritten student protocols (A), the typewritten version of the student protocols (B), and Werner Deggeller's "free" interpretation of the second semester (D).

Seyfferth wrote in his afterword to the book that he compared the two versions of the protocols (A and B) and "when necessary smoothed out the style."[11] He also integrated Deggeller's text with his version of the

---

10. Karl Barth to Otto Weber, December 4, 1961, in Karl Barth, *Letters, 1961-1968*, ed. Jürgen Fangmeier, Hinrich Stoevesandt, and Geoffrey W. Bromiley, trans. Geoffrey W. Bromiley (Grand Rapids: Eerdmans, 1981), p. 24.

11. Günther Seyfferth, "Nachwort," in Karl Barth, *Homiletik: Wesen und Vorbereitung der Predigt* (Zürich: EVZ-Verlag, 1966), p. 114.

Appendix

protocols, rearranging material by subject when he felt it would simplify matters, and adding various titles and headings for the sake of clarity. As in the case of *La proclamation de L'évangile,* most contextual references are excised from Seyfferth's version of the notes.¹²

It was Seyfferth's redaction that was then translated by Geoffrey Bromiley and Donald E. Daniels and published in the United States in 1991 as Karl Barth's *Homiletics.*

The text published as *Homiletics* inherited all of the problems of the Seyfferth text and then added a number of translation issues. How does one translate terms such as *Offenbarungsmässigkeit* and *Gemeindemässigkeit,* so crucial to Barth's argument? Or words like *Wohin* and *Woher?* Or *Zivilmut?* Or the perilous *Vorläufigkeit,* which is misleadingly rendered in *Homiletics* as "heralding"? Bromiley himself observed that "the relatively unpolished original posed some problems in achieving the necessary balance between accuracy and readability."¹³

Ad Fontes!

The surest remedy to this state of affairs is a new, critical edition of the *Übungen in der Predigtvorbereitung* artifacts, one that begins again with the source documents, includes what is likely the most authoritative source, that of Charlotte von Kirschbaum (K, KS), retains the week-by-week structure of the original lectures, clarifies the nature of Deggeller's "free" contribution, features excursuses on key terms such as *Gemeindemässigkeit,* and places the whole work in its unique and ever-changing context.

A new hearing for Barth's emergency homiletic requires a new text, beginning again from the beginning.

---

12. Werner Deggeller's description of "the very beloved" kind of sermon introduction that celebrates Bismarck, for example, is not included in Seyfferth's redaction (D35).

13. Geoffrey W. Bromiley, "Preface," in Barth, *Homiletics,* pp. 14-15.

Glossary of Selected German Terms

Alltagsgeschichte: an approach to history that tries to balance analysis of the broad political and social factors with close research into the daily lives of "regular" people.
Anknüpfungspunkt: literally, point of contact. In the debate between Barth and Brunner, the term denotes the belief that, by virtue of creation, there is some analog to the Word of God inherent in human beings.
Auseinandersetzung: argument, debate.
Bekenntnis: confession.
Bonzen: a derogatory term for those with power or doing well financially, sometimes translated "fat cats" or "suits." In the Weimar years, it was often directed at prominent Social Democrats.
Boulevardzeitung: tabloid newspaper.
Bundesrat: the upper house of the German parliamentary body, comprised of representatives appointed by each state government.
Bürgerverein: civic organization.
Denkformen: patterns of thought.
Deutscher Evangelischer Kirchenbund: the German Evangelical (Protestant) Church Confederation, the formal federation of the *Landeskirchen* from 1922-1933.
Deutschnationale Volkspartei (DNVP): prior to the rise of the National Socialist Party, the DNVP was the largest nationalist/conservative political party in Weimar Germany.
Dozenten: unsalaried university lecturers.
Erbauung: edification, building up.
evangelisch: Protestant.

Glossary of Selected German Terms

Freiheit: freedom.

Führerprinzip: the "leadership principle" cherished in National Socialist ideology. It claims that certain individuals are naturally gifted to lead, an idea that resonated with the ethos of social Darwinism. Organizations and societies are to be governed by hierarchies of such individuals, who command absolute obedience from subordinates.

ganz andere: completely different, wholly other.

Gauleiter: the leader of a regional branch of the NSDAP.

Gemeinde: congregation, religious community.

Gemeindemässigkeit: in the context of the *Predigtvorbereitung* lectures, means that a sermon should be "measured" by the congregation, that is, "tempered" by it, or we might say, the sermon should be appropriate for it, though this loses the sense of congregational agency the term implies.

Glaubensbewegung Deutsche Christen: the "German Christians"; the pro-Nazi party within the Protestant church.

Gleichschaltung: "coordination"; nazification. The process through which the NSDAP systematically instituted a totalitarian state after the *Machtergreifung*.

Hakenkreuz: swastika.

Kampf: fight; struggle. The National Socialists used the language of *Kampf* with its social Darwinistic and racial connotations to highlight their gladiatorial disposition. *Kampf* was often code for spiritual and physical violence.

Kirchenwahlen: church elections.

Kriegspredigten: war sermons.

Kultus: worship; liturgy.

Kultusminister: minister for education.

Landeskirchen: regional churches.

Machtergreifung: seizure of power. A term used to describe Hitler's ascension to the position of chancellor and the eight-week process in which a dictatorship was established in Germany, culminating in the Enabling Act of March 23, 1933.

Nationalsozialistische Deutsche Arbeiterpartei (NSDAP or "Nazi" Party): National Socialist German Worker Party.

Oberkirchenrat: the highest administrative body of a *Landeskirche*.

Offenbarungsmässigkeit: in the context of the sermon exercises, the idea that revelation shapes or tempers the sermon.

Pfarrer: pastor.

Predigerseminar: the practical supplement to the theoretical instruction German theology students received at the University. Each *Landeskirche* had its own *Predigerseminar,* offering classes designed to help theology students make the transition to the parish.

Reichstag: the elected portion of the German parliamentary body.

Sache: subject matter, object.

Schlagwort: catchphrase; rallying cry.

Seelsorge: pastoral care; moral guidance. In the time of Weimar, *Völkseelsorge* meant providing moral guidance to the German people, combatting the immorality and materialism of modern society.

Sozialdemokratische Partei Deutschlands (SPD): Social Democratic Party of Germany.

Sozietät: discussion groups.

Stahlhelm: literally "steel helmet"; a paramilitary organization that formed after World War I and eventually affiliated with the right-wing *Deutschnationale Volkspartei.*

Stichworten: slogans.

Stoff: content; subject matter.

Vergangenheitsbewältigung: overcoming, or coming to terms with, the past.

Volk: in the context of Weimar, *Volk* was often a specific reference to the German people, a people constituted not on the basis of geographical proximity, citizenship, or constitutional loyalty, but by shared blood, history, culture, "spirit," and language.

volkfremd: alien to the German Volk, unGerman.

Volksgeist: the German way of thinking/feeling.

Volksgemeindschaft: the national community. It includes the idea that the community puts the common good before individual, party, or class interests, in contrast to the selfishness of Western and Marxist "materialists."

Volkskirche: in its most basic sense, the term indicates that one belongs to the church because one has been born into the *Volk.* The *Volkskirche* as an ideal often included the hope of a church where the laity participated in governance and/or the affirmation that the church played an indispensable role in German society as steward and custodian of public morality and culture.

Volkskirchenbund: the German *Volkskirche* Federation, formed in 1919. It was designed to unify Protestants, making them a cohesive political force in Weimar.

Volksseele: the distinct collective identity of a people; an ethnic soul.

Volkstum: German folklore, identity.
Vorläufigkeit: provisionality; tentativeness.
Wissenschaft: science.
zeitgemäß: timely; up to date.

Bibliography

Althaus, Paul. *Der Herr der Kirche*. Vol. 1. *Von der Kirche*. Gütersloh: C. Bertelsmann, 1934.

———. *Der Lebendige, Rostocker Predigten*. 2nd ed. Gütersloh: C. Bertelsmann, 1926.

Anderson, Clifford Blake. "The Crisis of Theological Science: A Contextual Study of the Development of Karl Barth's Concept of Theology as Science from 1901-1923." Ph.D. dissertation, Princeton Theological Seminary, 2005.

Aune, Michael B. "Discarding the Barthian Spectacles, Part 3: Rewriting the History of Protestant Theology in the 1920s." *Dialog* 45, no. 4 (2006): 389-405.

Bailey, Charles Edward. "Gott mit Uns: Germany's Protestant Theologians in the First World War." Ph.D. dissertation, University of Virginia, 1978.

Baranowski, Shelley. "The 1933 German Protestant Church Elections: *Machtpolitik* or Accommodation?" *Church History* 49, no. 3 (1980): 298-315.

———. *The Sanctity of Rural Life: Nobility, Protestantism, and Nazism in Weimar Prussia*. New York: Oxford University Press, 1995.

Barnett, Victoria. *For the Soul of the People: Protestant Protest Against Hitler*. New York: Oxford University Press, 1992.

Barth, Karl. *Against the Stream: Shorter Post-War Writings, 1946-52*. Translated by Ronald Gregor Smith. New York: Philosophical Library, 1954.

———. *Briefe Des Jahres 1933*. Edited by Eberhard Busch. Zürich: Theologischer Verlag, 2004.

———. "The Christian in Society." In *The Word of God and Theology*. Translated by Amy Marga. London, New York: T&T Clark International, 2011.

———. "Church and Culture (1926)." In *Theology and Church: Shorter Writings, 1920-1928*. Translated by Louise Pettibone Smith. Edited by T. F. Torrance. New York: Harper & Row, 1962.

———. *Church Dogmatics*, ed. Geoffrey W. Bromiley and T. F. Torrance. Edinburgh: T&T Clark, 1956-75.

———. "The Desirability and Possibility of a Universal Reformed Creed." In *Theology and Church: Shorter Writings, 1920-1928*. Translated by Louise Pettibone Smith. Edited by T. F. Torrance. New York: Harper & Row, 1962.

———. *The Epistle to the Romans*. 6th ed. Translated by Edwyn Clement Hoskyns. London: Oxford University Press, 1968.

———. "Für die Freiheit des Evangeliums." *Theologische Existenz heute!* 2 (1934): 3-16.

———. "Die Gemeindemässigkeit der Predigt." In *Ausgabe der Predigt*. Edited by Gert Hummel. Darmstadt: Wissenschaftliche Buchgesellschaft, 1935.

———. *Gesamtausgabe*. Edited by Hinrich Stoevesandt and Hans Anton Drewes. 46 vols. Zürich: Theologischer Verlag, 1971-.

———. *The Göttingen Dogmatics: Instruction in the Christian Religion*. Vol. 1. Edited by Hannelotte Reiffen. Translated by Geoffrey W. Bromiley. 1st English ed. Grand Rapids: Eerdmans, 1991.

———. *"Der Götze wackelt": Zeitkritische Aufsätze, Reden und Briefe von 1930 bis 1960*. Edited by Karl Kupisch. Berlin: Käthe Vogt, 1961.

———. *The Holy Spirit and the Christian Life: The Theological Basis of Ethics*. Translated by R. Birch Hoyle. Foreword by Robin W. Lovin. Louisville: Westminster/John Knox, 1993.

———. *Homiletics*. Translated by G. W. Bromiley and D. E. Daniels. Foreword by David G. Buttrick. Louisville: Westminster John Knox, 1991.

———. *Homiletik. Wesen und Vorbereitung der Predigt*. Zürich: EVZ-Verlag, 1966.

———. *Karl Barth Zum Kirchenkampf: Beteiligung, Mahnung, Zuspruch*. Theologische Existenz Heute (New Series). Edited by Ernst Wolf. Munich: Kaiser, 1956.

———. *Letters, 1961-1968*. Translated by Geoffrey W. Bromiley. Edited by Jürgen Fangmeier, Hinrich Stoevesandt, and Geoffrey W. Bromiley. Grand Rapids: Eerdmans, 1981.

———. "Die Not der evangelischen Kirche." In Karl Barth, *"Der Götze wackelt": Zeitkritische Aufsätze, Reden und Briefe von 1930 bis 1960*. Edited by Karl Kupisch. Berlin: Käthe Vogt, 1961.

———. *The Preaching of the Gospel*. Philadelphia: Westminster, 1963.

———. "The Principles of Dogmatics According to Wilhelm Herrmann." In *Theology and Church: Shorter Writings, 1920-1928*. Translated by Louise Pettibone Smith. Edited by T. F. Torrance. New York: Harper & Row, 1962.

———. *La proclamation de L'évangile: Texte Reconstitué par le Pasteur A. Roulin D'après des Notes D'étudiants*. Neuchâtel: Delachaux et Niestlé, 1961.

———. *Protestant Theology in the Nineteenth Century: Its Background and History*. Translated by Brian Cozens and John Bowden. Grand Rapids: Eerdmans, 2002.

———. "Quousque Tandem?" In *"Der Götze wackelt": Zeitkritische Aufsätze, Reden und Briefe von 1930 bis 1960*. Edited by Karl Kupisch. Berlin: Käthe Vogt, 1961.

———. "The Strange New World within the Bible." In *The Word of God and the Word of Man*. Translated by Douglas Horton. Boston: Pilgrim, 1928.

———. *Theological Existence Today! A Plea for Theological Freedom*. Translated by R. Birch Hoyle. London: Hodder & Stoughton, 1933.

———. *Theologische Existenz heute!* (1933). Edited by Hinrich Stoevesandt. Munich: Chr. Kaiser Verlag, 1984.

---. *Theologische Fragen und Antworten*. Zollikon: Evangelischer Verlag, 1957.
---. *Theology and Church: Shorter Writings, 1920-1928*. Translated by Louise Pettibone Smith. Edited by T. F. Torrance. New York: Harper & Row, 1962.
---. *The Way of Theology in Karl Barth: Essays and Comments*. Edited by Martin Rumscheidt. Allison Park: Pickwick Publications, 1986.
---. "The Word of God and the Task of the Ministry." In *The Word of God and the Word of Man*. Translated by Douglas Horton. Boston: Pilgrim, 1928.
---. *The Word of God and the Word of Man*. Translated by Douglas Horton. Boston: Pilgrim, 1928.
---. *The Word in This World: Two Sermons*. Translated by Christopher Asprey. Edited by Kurt I. Johanson. Introduction by William H. Willimon. Afterword by Clifford B. Anderson. Vancouver: Regent College, 2007.
---. *Das Wort Gottes und die Theologie*. Munich: Chr. Kaiser Verlag, 1925.
---. "Zwischenzeit." *Kirchenblatt für die reformierte Schweiz* 118 (1962): 38-39.
Barth, Karl, and Rudolf Bultmann. *Karl Barth–Rudolf Bultmann Letters, 1922-1966*. Edited by Geoffrey W. Bromiley and Bernd Jaspert. Translated by Geoffrey W. Bromiley. Grand Rapids: Eerdmans, 1981.
Barth, Karl, and William H. Willimon. *The Early Preaching of Karl Barth: Fourteen Sermons with Commentary by William H. Willimon*. Translated by John Elbert Wilson. Louisville: Westminster John Knox, 2009.
Barth, Marcus. "Current Discussions on the Political Character of Barth's Theology." In *Footnotes to a Theology: The Karl Barth Colloquium of 1972*. Edited by Martin Rumscheidt. Waterloo: Corporation for the Publication of Academic Studies in Religion in Canada, 1974.
Beintker, Michael. *Die Dialektik in der "Dialektischen Theologie" Karl Barths: Studien zur Entwicklung der barthschen Theologie und zur Vorgeschichte der "Kirchlichen Dogmatik."* Munich: Chr. Kaiser Verlag, 1987.
Bessel, Richard. "The Rise of the NSDAP and the Myth of Nazi Propaganda." *Wiener Library Bulletin* 33, no. 51 (1980): 20-29.
Bestian, Hans. "Redeübungen im Deutschunterricht." *Wirkendes Wort* 1, no. 3 (1950): 166-75.
Blackbourn, David. *Populists and Patricians: Essays in Modern German History*. London: Allen & Unwin, 1987.
Borg, Daniel R. *The Old Prussian Church and the Weimar Republic: A Study in Political Adjustment, 1917-1927*. Hanover: University Press of New England, 1984.
Brakelmann, Günther. *Protestantische Kriegstheologie im ersten Weltkrieg*. Bielefeld: Lutherverlag, 1974.
Brunner, Emil. "Die andere Aufgabe der Theologie." *Zwischen den Zeiten* 7 (1929): 255-76.
---. *The Mediator: A Study of the Central Doctrine of the Christian Faith*. Translated by Olive Wyon. Philadelphia: Westminster, 1947.
Burleigh, Michael. *The Third Reich: A New History*. Basingstoke: Macmillan, 2000.
Burnett, Richard E. *Karl Barth's Theological Exegesis: The Hermeneutical Principles of the Römerbrief Period*. Grand Rapids: Eerdmans, 2004.

Bibliography

Busch, Eberhard. *Karl Barth: His Life from Letters and Autobiographical Texts.* Translated by John Bowden. Philadelphia: Fortress, 1976.

———. *Karl Barth and the Pietists: The Young Karl Barth's Critique of Pietism and Its Response.* Translated by Daniel W. Bloesch. Downers Grove: InterVarsity, 2004.

Buttrick, David. *A Captive Voice: The Liberation of Preaching.* Louisville: Westminster John Knox, 1994.

Chapman, Mark. *Ernst Troeltsch and Liberal Theology: Religion and Cultural Synthesis in Wilhelmine Germany.* Oxford: Oxford University Press, 2001.

Childers, Thomas. *The Nazi Voter: The Social Foundations of Fascism in Germany, 1919-1933.* Chapel Hill: University of North Carolina Press, 1983.

———. "The Social Language of Politics in Germany: The Sociology of Political Discourse in the Weimar Republic." *American Historical Review* 95, no. 2 (1990): 331.

Classen, Christoph. "Thoughts on the Significance of Mass-Media Communications in the Third Reich and the GDR." *Totalitarian Movements & Political Religions* 8, no. 3/4 (2007): 547-62.

Cochrane, Arthur C. *The Church's Confession under Hitler.* Philadelphia: Westminster, 1962.

Conway, John S. "National Socialism and the Christian Churches during the Weimar Republic." In *The Nazi Machtergreifung.* Edited by Peter D. Stachura. London: Allen & Unwin, 1983.

———. *The Nazi Persecution of the Churches, 1933-45.* New York: Basic Books, 1968.

Cremer, Douglas J. "Protestant Theology in Early Weimar Germany: Barth, Tillich, and Bultmann." *Journal of the History of Ideas* 56 (1995): 289-307.

Crouter, Richard. "Shaping an Academic Discipline: The *Brief Outline on the Study of Theology*." In *The Cambridge Companion to Friedrich Schleiermacher.* Edited by Jacqueline Mariña. Cambridge: Cambridge University Press, 2005.

Crowner, David, and Gerald Christianson, eds. *The Spirituality of the German Awakening.* Classics of Western Spirituality. New York: Paulist, 2003.

Dahm, Karl Wilhelm. *Pfarrer und Politik: Soziale Position und politische Mentalität des deutschen evangelischen Pfarrerstandes zwischen 1918 und 1933.* Dortmunder Schriften zur Sozialforschung. Cologne: Westdeutscher Verlag, 1965.

Deggeller, Werner. *Professor D. Karl Barths Øvelser over Praedikenens Forberedelse: En Homiletisk Øvelse Afholdt Ved Universitetet I Bonn Sommeren 1933.* Translated by Regin Prenter. København: Theologisk Oratorium, 1938.

Diels, Rudolf. *Lucifer ante Portas: Zwischen Severing und Heydrich.* Zürich: Interverlag, 1949.

Dorrien, Gary J. *The Barthian Revolt in Modern Theology: Theology without Weapons.* Louisville: Westminster John Knox, 2000.

Dörries, Bernhard. *Die Welt Gottes: Ein neuer Jahrgang Predigten.* Göttingen, 1922.

Drews, Paul. *Die Predigt im 19. Jahrhundert: Kritische Bemerkungen und praktische Winke.* Vorträge der theologischen Konferenz zu Giessen. Giessen: J. Ricker, 1903.

Eberle, Joseph. *Grossmacht Presse, Enthüllungen für Zeitungsgläubige: Forderungen für Männer.* 3rd ed. Vienna: Verlagsanstalt Herold, 1920.

Edwards, Bela B., and Edward Amasa Park, eds. *Selections from German Literature.* Andover: Gould, Newman, and Saxton, 1839.
Ericksen, Robert P. *Theologians under Hitler: Gerhard Kittel, Paul Althaus, and Emanuel Hirsch.* New Haven: Yale University Press, 1985.
Evans, Richard J. *The Coming of the Third Reich.* New York: Penguin, 2004.
———. *In Hitler's Shadow: West German Historians and the Attempt to Escape from the Nazi Past.* London: I. B. Tauris, 1989.
———. *The Third Reich at War, 1939-1945.* New York: Allen Lane, 2008.
———. *The Third Reich in Power, 1933-1939.* New York: Penguin, 2005.
Faulenbach, Heiner, ed. *Das Album Professorum der evangelisch-theologischen Fakultät der rheinischen Friedrich-Wilhelms-Universität Bonn: 1818-1933*, Academica Bonnensia. Bonn: Bouvier, 1995.
Feige, Franz G. M. *The Varieties of Protestantism in Nazi Germany: Five Theopolitical Positions.* Toronto Studies in Theology. Lewiston: E. Mellen, 1990.
Fezer, Karl. *Der Herr und seine Gemeinde.* Stuttgart: Calwer, 1930.
———. *Das Wort Gottes und die Predigt: Eine Weiterführung der prinzipiellen Homiletik auf Grund der Ergebnisse der neuen religionspsychologischen und systematischen Forschung.* Stuttgart: Calwer, 1925.
Forstman, Jack. *Christian Faith in Dark Times: Theological Conflicts in the Shadow of Hitler.* 1st ed. Louisville: Westminster/John Knox, 1992.
Frankel, Richard Evan. *Bismarck's Shadow: The Cult of Leadership and the Transformation of the German Right, 1898-1945.* Oxford: Berg, 2005.
Fritzsche, Peter. *Rehearsals for Fascism: Populism and Political Mobilization in Weimar Germany.* New York: Oxford University Press, 1990.
Fulda, Bernhard. *Press and Politics in the Weimar Republic.* New York: Oxford University Press, 2009.
Fürst, Walther. *Predigt und Gebet: Theologische Beiträge.* Edited by Klaus-Peter Jörns. Göttingen: Vandenhoeck & Ruprecht, 1986.
Gallin, Alice. *Midwives to Nazism: University Professors in Weimar Germany, 1925-1933.* Macon: Mercer University Press, 1986.
Gassert, Philipp, and Alan E. Steinweis. *Coping with the Nazi Past: West German Debates on Nazism and Generational Conflict, 1955-1975.* New York: Berghahn Books, 2006.
Geck, Albrecht. *Kirchengeschichte im Religionsunterricht — Wie und Warum?* Göttingen: Vandenhoeck & Ruprecht, 2010.
Goeters, J. F. Gerhard. "Karl Barth in Bonn 1930-1935." *Evangelische Theologie* 47, no. 2 (1987): 137-50.
Gogarten, Friedrich. "Das Problem einer theologischen Anthropologie." *Zwischen den Zeiten* 7 (1929): 493-511.
———. "Staat und Kirche." *Zwischen den Zeiten* 10 (1932): 390-410.
Goldhagen, Daniel Jonah. *Hitler's Willing Executioners: Ordinary Germans and the Holocaust.* 1st ed. New York: Knopf, 1996.
Gordon, Frank J. "Liberal German Churchmen and the First World War." *German Studies Review* 41, no. 1 (1981): 39-62.

Bibliography

Gorringe, Timothy. *Karl Barth: Against Hegemony*. Oxford: Oxford University Press, 1999.
Gräb, Wilhelm. *Predigt als Mitteilung des Glaubens: Studien zu einer prinzipiellen Homiletik in praktischer Absicht*. Gütersloh: G. Mohn, 1988.
Haendler, Otto. *Die Predigt: Tiefenpsychologische Grundlagen und Grundfragen*. Berlin: A. Töpelmann, 1949.
Hammer, Karl. *Deutsche Kriegstheologie (1870-1918)*. Munich: Kösel-Verlag, 1971.
Hancock, Angela Dienhart. "Preaching 'As If Nothing Had Happened': Karl Barth's Emergency Homiletic, 1932-1933." Ph.D. dissertation, Princeton Theological Seminary, 2011.
Hart, John W. *Karl Barth vs. Emil Brunner: The Formation and Dissolution of a Theological Alliance, 1916-1936*. New York: Peter Lang, 2001.
Helmreich, Ernst Christian. *The German Churches under Hitler: Background, Struggle, and Epilogue*. Detroit: Wayne State University Press, 1979.
Herzog, Johann Jakob, Philip Schaff, Albert Hauck, Samuel Macauley Jackson, Charles Colebrook Sherman, and George William Gilmore. *The New Schaff-Herzog Encyclopedia of Religious Knowledge: Embracing Biblical, Historical, Doctrinal, and Practical Theology and Biblical, Theological, and Ecclesiastical Biography from the Earliest Times to the Present Day*. New York: Funk and Wagnalls, 1908.
Heyer, Helmut, and Karl Gutzmer. "Kultur in Bonn im Dritten Reich." In *Veröffentlichungen des Stadtarchivs Bonn*. Bonn: Stadtarchiv und Stadthistorische Bibliothek, 2002.
Hinz-Wessels, Annette. *Die evangelische Kirchengemeinde Bonn in der Zeit des Nationalsozialismus (1933-1945)*. Schriftenreihe des Vereins für rheinische Kirchengeschichte. Cologne: Rheinland-Verlag, 1996.
Hirsch, Emanuel. *Das Evangelium: Predigten*. Gütersloh: C. Bertelsmann, 1929.
———. "Zur Beurteilung des Angriffs von Karl Barth." In *Das kirchliche Wollen der Deutschen Christen*. Berlin-Steglitz: Evangelischer Pressverband für Deutschland, 1933.
"Historicism." In *Dictionary of the History of Ideas Online*. New York: Charles Scribner's Sons, 1974.
"Historicism." In *Routledge Encyclopedia of Philosophy Online*. London: Routledge, 1998-2011.
Hitler, Adolf. *Mein Kampf*. 13th ed. Translated by James Murphy. London: Hurst & Blackett, 1942.
Hoad, T. F., and Oxford University Press. *The Concise Oxford Dictionary of English Etymology*. Oxford: Oxford University Press, 1996.
Hoover, Arlie J. *The Gospel of Nationalism: German Patriotic Preaching from Napoleon to Versailles*. Stuttgart: F. Steiner Wiesbaden, 1986.
Höpfner, Hans-Paul. *Die Universität Bonn im Dritten Reich: Akademische Biographien unter nationalsozialistischer Herrschaft*. Academica Bonnensia. Bonn: Bouvier, 1999.
Horn, Curt, ed. *Grundfragen des evangelischen Kultus*. Neue Folge von "Kultus und Kunst." Berlin: Furche-Kunstverlag, 1927.

BIBLIOGRAPHY

Hornig, Ernst. *Die Bekennende Kirche in Schlesien 1933-1945: Geschichte und Dokumente*. Göttingen: Vandenhoeck & Ruprecht, 1977.

Hummel, Gert, ed. *Aufgabe der Predigt*. Darmstadt: Wissenschaftliche Buchgesellschaft, 1971.

Hunsinger, George. *Disruptive Grace: Studies in the Theology of Karl Barth*. Grand Rapids: Eerdmans, 2000.

———. *How to Read Karl Barth: The Shape of His Theology*. New York: Oxford University Press, 1991.

———. *Karl Barth and Radical Politics*. Philadelphia: Westminster, 1976.

Jehle, Frank. *Ever Against the Stream: The Politics of Karl Barth, 1906-1968*. Translated by Martha Burnett and Richard E. Burnett. Grand Rapids: Eerdmans, 2002.

Jowett, Garth, and Victoria O'Donnell. *Propaganda and Persuasion*. Thousand Oaks: Sage Publications, 1999.

Jüngel, Eberhard. *Barth-Studien*. Zürich: Benziger; Gütersloh: Mohn, 1982.

Kershaw, Ian. "Ideology, Propaganda, and the Rise of the Nazi Party." In *The Nazi Machtergreifung*. Edited by Peter D. Stachura. London: Allen & Unwin, 1983.

———. *The Nazi Dictatorship: Problems and Perspectives of Interpretation*. New York: Oxford University Press, 2000.

Klemperer, Victor. *The Language of the Third Reich: LTI, Lingua Tertii Imperii; A Philologist's Notebook*. Translated by Martin Brady. London: Athlone, 2000.

Kocka, Jürgen. "Asymmetrical Historical Comparison: The Case of the German Sonderweg." *History & Theory* 38, no. 1 (1999): 40.

Krause, Gerhard, Gerhard Müller, and Siegfried Schwertner, eds. *Theologische Realenzyklopädie*. 36 vols. Berlin: W. de Gruyter, 1977-.

Kretzenbacher, Heinz L. "Language Reveals All." *Monthly Review: An Independent Socialist Magazine* 55, no. 7 (2003): 47-51.

Krumwiede, Hans-Walter. *Evangelische Kirche und Theologie in der Weimarer Republik*. Grundtexte zur Kirchen- und Theologiegeschichte. Neukirchen-Vluyn: Neukirchener Verlag, 1990.

Künneth, Walter. *Der grosse Abfall, eine geschichtstheologische Untersuchung der Begegnung zwischen Nationalsozialismus und Christentum*. Hamburg: F. Wittig, 1947.

Lehmann, Hartmut, and Manfred Gailus. *Nationalprotestantische Mentalitäten: Konturen, Entwicklungslinien und Umbrüche eines Weltbildes*. Göttingen: Vandenhoeck & Ruprecht, 2005.

Lindsay, Mark R. *Covenanted Solidarity: The Theological Basis of Karl Barth's Opposition to Nazi Antisemitism and the Holocaust*. Issues in Systematic Theology. New York: Peter Lang, 2001.

Lischer, Richard. "Preparation for Preaching: A German Model." *Homiletic* 9, no. 1 (1984): 1-4.

Lohmann, Johann Friedrich. *Karl Barth und der Neukantianismus: Die Rezeption des Neukantianismus im "Römerbrief" und ihre Bedeutung für die weitere Ausarbeitung der Theologie Karl Barths*. Theologische Bibliothek Töpelmann. Berlin: W. de Gruyter, 1995.

Bibliography

Loofs, Friedrich. *Akademische Predigten. Die Predigt der Kirche: Prediger der Gegenwart.* Dresden: Verlag von C. Ludwig Ungelenk, 1908.

Marquardt, Friedrich-Wilhelm. *Theologie und Sozialismus: Das Beispiel Karl Barths.* 3rd ed. Munich: Kaiser, 1985.

Matheson, Peter. *The Third Reich and the Christian Churches.* Edinburgh: T&T Clark, 1981.

McCormack, Bruce L. *Karl Barth's Critically Realistic Dialectical Theology: Its Genesis and Development, 1909-1936.* Oxford: Clarendon, 1997.

McDowell, John. "Timothy Gorringe's Contextualised Barth: An Article-Review." *Evangelical Quarterly* 74, no. 4 (2002): 333-50.

McKelway, Alexander Jeffrey. "Magister Dialecticae Optimarium Partium: Recollections of Karl Barth as Teacher." *Union Seminary Quarterly Review* 28, no. 1 (1972): 93-97.

Meier, Kurt. *Der Evangelische Kirchenkampf.* 3 vols. Göttingen: Vandenhoeck & Ruprecht, 1976.

Michael, Robert, and Karin Doerr. *Nazi-Deutsch/Nazi-German: An English Lexicon of the Language of the Third Reich.* London: Greenwood, 2002.

Migliore, Daniel. "Karl Barth's First Lectures in Dogmatics: Instruction in the Christian Religion." In Karl Barth, *The Göttingen Dogmatics: Instruction in the Christian Religion,* vol. 1. Edited by Hannelotte Reiffen and translated by Geoffrey W. Bromiley. Grand Rapids: Eerdmans, 1991.

Militärgeschichtliches Forschungsamt, ed. *Germany and the Second World War.* Oxford: Oxford University Press, 1990.

Moose, George L. "Bookburning and the Betrayal of German Intellectuals." *New German Critique* 31 (1984): 143.

Morgan, D. Densil. *Barth Reception in Britain.* London: T&T Clark, 2010.

Mosheim, Johann Lorenz. *Anweisung erbaulich zu predigen.* 2nd ed. Edited by Christian Ernst von Windheim. Erlangen: Bey Wolfgang Walther, 1771.

Müller, Hans Martin. *Homiletik: Eine evangelische Predigtlehre.* Berlin: W. de Gruyter, 1996.

Niebergall, Friedrich. *Die moderne Predigt: Kulturgeschichtliche und theologische Grundlage; Geschichte und Ertrag.* Tübingen: J. C. B. Mohr, 1929.

———. *Wie predigen wir dem modernen Menschen?* Tübingen: J. C. B. Mohr, 1909.

Nitzsch, Carl Immanuel. *Praktische Theologie.* 2 vols. Bonn: Adolph Marcus, 1847.

Norden, Günther van. *Der deutsche Protestantismus im Jahr der nationalsozialistischen Machtergreifung.* Gütersloh: Mohn, 1979.

Nowak, Kurt. *Evangelische Kirche und Weimarer Republik: Zum politischen Weg des deutschen Protestantismus zwischen 1918 und 1932.* Göttingen: Vandenhoeck & Ruprecht, 1981.

Palmer, Christian. *Evangelische Homiletik.* 6th ed. Stuttgart: Steinkopf, 1887.

Paul, Gerhard. *Aufstand der Bilder: Die NS-Propaganda vor 1933.* Bonn: J. H. W. Dietz, 1990.

Peukert, Detlev, Jürgen Reulecke, and Adelheid Castell Rüdenhausen. *Die Reihen fast geschlossen: Beiträge zur Geschichte des Alltags unterm Nationalsozialismus.* Wuppertal: Hammer, 1981.

Pfennigsdorf, Emil. "Gottes Botschaft zum nationalen Aufbruch unseres Volkes." *Der Geisteskampf der Gegenwart: Monatschrift für christlische Bildung und Weltanschauung* 6 (1933): 201-6.

———. *Praktische Theologie: Ein Handbuch für die Gegenwart.* 2 vols. Gütersloh: C. Bertelsmann, 1929.

———. *Wie lehren wir Evangelium? Ein Methodenbuch auf psychologischer Grundlage für die Praxis des Religionsunterrichts in Schule und Kirche.* 2nd ed. Leipzig: A. Deichertsche Verlagsbuchhandlung, 1925.

Pressel, Wilhelm. *Die Kriegspredigt 1914-1918 in der evangelischen Kirche Deutschlands.* Arbeiten zur Pastoraltheologie. Göttingen: Vandenhoeck & Ruprecht, 1967.

Rasmusson, Arne. "'Deprive Them of Their Pathos': Karl Barth and the Nazi Revolution Revisited." *Modern Theology* 23, no. 3 (2007): 369-91.

Ricœur, Paul. *Freud and Philosophy: An Essay on Interpretation.* New Haven: Yale University Press, 1970.

Ritchie, J. M. "The Nazi Book-Burning." *Modern Language Review* 83, no. 3 (1988): 627-43.

Ritschl, Otto. "Vierundzwanzigsten Brief." *Die Christliche Welt* 41 (1927): 844.

Ritter, Karl Bernhard. *Von dem der da kommt.* Schwerin: Fredrich Bahn, 1925.

Robinson, James McConkey, ed. *The Beginnings of Dialectic Theology.* Richmond: John Knox, 1968.

Ross, Corey. "Mass Politics and the Techniques of Leadership: The Promise and Perils of Propaganda in Weimar Germany." *German History* 24, no. 2 (2006): 184-211.

Rumscheidt, Martin. *Revelation and Theology: An Analysis of the Barth-Harnack Correspondence of 1923.* Cambridge: Cambridge University Press, 1972.

Safranski, Rüdiger. *Martin Heidegger: Between Good and Evil.* Cambridge: Harvard University Press, 1998.

Sasse, Hermann. *Kirchliche Zeitlage.* Gutersloh: C. Bertelsmann, 1932.

Schian, Martin. *Wider die Perikopen.* Leipzig: J. C. B. Mohr, 1897.

Scholder, Klaus. *The Churches and the Third Reich.* Philadelphia: Fortress, 1988.

Schott, Heinrich August. *Die Theorie der Beredsamkeit mit besonderer Anwendung auf die geistliche Beredsamkeit in ihrem ganzen Umfange dargestellt.* 2nd ed. Leipzig: Johann Ambrosius Barth, 1828.

Schütz, Werner. *Geschichte der christlichen Predigt.* Berlin: De Gruyter, 1972.

Smith, B. Wesley Warren. "Pastoral Care to the Soul of the Nation: Ludwig Ihmels and Germany's Domestic Crises, 1902-1933." Ph.D. dissertation, Princeton Theological Seminary, 1998.

Sneeringer, Julia. *Winning Women's Votes: Propaganda and Politics in Weimar Germany.* Chapel Hill: University of North Carolina Press, 2002.

Spieckermann, Ingrid. *Gotteserkenntnis: Ein Beitrag zur Grundfrage der neuen Theologie Karl Barths.* Munich: C. Kaiser Verlag, 1985.

Stachura, Peter D., ed. *The Nazi Machtergreifung.* London: Allen & Unwin, 1983.

Stange, Carl D. *Unser Glaube: Predigten.* Gütersloh: C. Bertelsmann, 1926.

Bibliography

Steigmann-Gall, Richard. *The Holy Reich: Nazi Conceptions of Christianity, 1919-1945*. Cambridge: Cambridge University Press, 2003.
Stengel, Friedemann. "Wer vertrieb Günther Dehn (1882-1970) aus Halle?" *Zeitschrift für Kirchengeschichte* 114, no. 3 (2003): 384-403.
Stephan, Horst, and Martin Schmidt. *Geschichte der evangelischen Theologie in Deutschland seit dem Idealismus*. 3rd ed. New York: de Gruyter, 1973.
Strauss, David Friedrich. *Der alte und der neue Glaube: Ein Bekenntniss*. Leipzig: S. Hirzel, 1872.
Sutherland, Arthur Marvin. "Christology and Discipleship in the Sermons of Karl Barth, 1913-1916." Ph.D. dissertation, Princeton Theological Seminary, 2000.
"Theologians: Barth in Retirement." *Time Magazine*, May 31, 1963.
Theremin, Franz. *Eloquence a Virtue; or, Outlines of a Systematic Rhetoric*. Translated by William Greenough Thayer Shedd. Andover: W. F. Draper, 1860.
Tholuck, August. *Gespräche über die vornehmsten Glaubensfragen der Zeit: Zunächst für nachdenkende Laien, welche Verständigung suchen*. 2nd ed. Gotha: Friedrich Andreas Perthes, 1867.
Thurneysen, Eduard. "Die Aufgabe der Predigt (1921)." In *Aufgabe der Predigt*. Edited by Gert Hummel. Darmstadt: Wissenschaftliche Buchgesellschaft, 1971.
———. "Das Wort Gottes und die Predigt: Im Anschluß an Karl Fezers gleichnamiges Buch." *Theologische Blätter* 5 (1926): 197-203.
Trillhaas, Wolfgang. "Die wirkliche Predigt." In *Wahrheit und Glaube: Festschrift für Emanuel Hirsch zu seinem 75. Geburtstag*. Edited by Hayo Gerdes. Itsehoe: Verlag Die Spur, 1963.
Troeltsch, Ernst. *The Absoluteness of Christianity and the History of Religions*. Translated by David Reed. Richmond: John Knox, 1971.
Vahanian, Gabriel. "Karl Barth as Theologian of Culture." *Union Seminary Quarterly Review* 28, no. 1 (1972): 37-49.
Verhey, Jeffrey Todd. "The 'Spirit of 1914': The Myth of Enthusiasm and the Rhetoric of Unity in World War I Germany." Ph.D. dissertation, University of California Berkeley, 1992.
Vinet, Alexandre Rodolphe. *Homiletics; or, the Theory of Preaching*. Translated by Thomas Harvey Skinner. New York: Ivison & Phinney, 1854.
———. *Pastoral Theology; or, the Theory of the Evangelical Ministry*. Translated by Thomas Harvey Skinner. New York: Ivison & Phinney, 1856.
Watson, Francis. "The Bible." In *The Cambridge Companion to Karl Barth*. Edited by J. B. Webster. New York: Cambridge University Press, 2000.
Watt, Roderick H. "Landserprache, Heeressprache, Nazisprache? Victor Klemperer and Werner Krauss on the Linguistic Legacy of the Third Reich." *Modern Language Review* 95, no. 2 (2000): 424-37.
Webb, Stephen H. *Re-Figuring Theology: The Rhetoric of Karl Barth*. Albany: State University of New York Press, 1991.
Webster, J. B. *Barth's Moral Theology: Human Action in Barth's Thought*. Edinburgh: T&T Clark, 1998.
Welch, David. *The Third Reich: Politics and Propaganda*. New York: Routledge, 1993.

Wiggermann, Karl-Friedrich. "Leonhard Fendt als Lehrer der praktischen Theologie in Berlin." In *Zwischen Volk und Bekenntnis*. Leipzig: Evangelische Verlagsanstalt, 2000.

Winter, Friederich Julius, ed. *Apologetische Predigten*. Die Predigt der Kirche: Prediger der Gegenwart. Dresden: C. L. Ungelenk, 1905.

Winter, Friederich Julius, ed. *Arbeiterpredigten*. Die evangelische Predigt an der Schwelle des 20. Jahrhunderts. Dresden: Fr. Richters Verlag, 1904.

Wintzer, Friedrich. *Die Homiletik seit Schleiermacher bis in die Anfänge der dialektischen Theologie*. Göttingen: Habilitationsschrift, 1969.

Wright, Jonathan Richard Cassé. *"Above Parties": The Political Attitudes of the German Protestant Church Leadership, 1918-1933*. Oxford Historical Monographs. New York: Oxford University Press, 1974.

Young, John Wesley. "From LTI to LQI: Victor Klemperer on Totalitarian Language." *German Studies Review* 28, no. 1 (2005): 45-64.

Index

Aeschbacher, Robert, 176
Althaus, Paul, 69-70, 73, 81, 158-59, 167-69, 171, 207
analogia entis, 29, 186, 303
analogia fidei, 2, 29-30
Aryan paragraph, 170, 258, 270n.95

Barth, Fritz, 176
Barth, Karl: on anti-intellectualism, 86, 124, 280, 283, 322; on anti-Semitism, 70, 132, 252, 279; attention to hearer (of preaching), 182-84, 287-88, 291-92, 321-22, 324, 326; as "biblicist," 13n.24; and Brunner, 186-87, 207, 212; as candidate in church elections, 317, 319; and the Committee of Three *(Dreimännerkollegium)*, 271, 308; on contemporary context (and preaching), 26, 231, 281, 287-88, 291-95, 312-13, 316, 322, 326; as contextual theologian, 2, 30, 37, 39, 61-62, 76, 127-29, 190-91, 322, 327; critiques of, xiv, 13, 16n.33, 23-25, 30-31, 324, 326; on culture, 18, 28, 31-33, 57, 182, 186, 187n.147, 218-19, 310; definition of preaching, 211; and dogmatics, 18, 21-26, 198, 283; ecclesiology, 33; and ethics, 34-36; and ethos of preacher, 205-6, 221, 225, 228-29, 231-33, 235, 259, 283, 293-95, 300, 311, 322, 325-26; and existentialism, 128, 212, 215, 232; formation as preacher, 176-79; on the *Führerprinzip*, 308; on the German Christians, 271, 290, 298-99, 320; and Hitler, 299, 308; on humility, 22-23, 67, 74, 124n.108, 190, 199-200, 202-4, 206, 212-15, 223, 227-28, 232-36, 259-60, 264-65, 267, 294-95, 303, 312, 322, 325; influence of Herrmann, 6-7; on interpretation, 24-26, 128n.123, 226-27, 229, 231, 272-74, 281-83, 286-87, 293, 312, 327-28; on language of preaching, 21-22, 188, 231, 272, 294, 310-12, 316, 322, 326; and the modern preaching movement, 178-84, 187, 205, 212, 324; on nationalism, 55n.37, 59-60, 62, 69, 73, 123-24, 186-87, 249-53; on natural theology, 124, 184n.138, 186, 249; and the NSDAP, 60-62, 196, 251, 253, 255, 272, 290, 298; and "parables of the kingdom," 12, 32-33; on pathos, 57, 120-24, 128, 129, 134, 136, 191, 249, 250; on Political Theology, 128, 264; and politics, 55-

61, 121, 124-25, 126n.112, 134, 179, 195-96, 208, 236, 250, 253-55, 263, 272, 278-79, 290-91, 327; as preacher, 177-79, 187, 208, 294, 308-10; on propaganda, 120, 131, 188, 208, 298, 325; and the Protestant church in Germany, 68n.81, 73, 76, 123, 129-32, 136, 180, 210-11, 249, 252, 270-71, 278-79, 285, 290-91, 298-99, 325; *Quousque Tandem*, 67-68, 109n.59, 115n.81, 130, 184; on the Reich bishop, 246, 277, 285, 308; on "religion," 8, 31, 121-22; and religious socialism, 52-53, 55, 123, 252; on revolution, 55, 57, 120, 122-23; and rhetoric, 57, 119-31, 133-34, 136, 201; *Romans* I, 8, 55, 58, 125, 180; *Romans* II, 20, 28, 29, 31, 57-58, 120, 123, 125, 127; in Safenwil, 7-8, 52, 177-78, 294; on Scripture, 127, 179, 187-88, 217, 316, 320; and the Social Democratic Party, 56, 60, 123, 125, 126n.112, 132, 134, 253-54, 278; and socialism, 52-55, 57, 178-79; and the task of theology, 18, 20-23; as teacher, xiii, 38-39, 57-59, 61, 81-82, 86, 88-90, 120, 133-34, 136, 190-91, 197-99, 206, 209-10, 235-36, 256, 262, 271, 280, 283, 285-86, 298-99, 313, 315-16, 320-21, 323, 327; and "theme" preaching, 187-89, 208, 264-67, 275, 281-82, 287, 292-93, 311; *Theologische Existenz heute!*, 133-34, 291, 298, 308, 314-15; theology of proclamation, 17-18, 182, 188, 192, 209, 211; on the Third Reich, 279-80, 321; at the University of Bonn, 23, 32, 34, 38, 61, 81-82, 89-90, 133, 136, 175, 197, 254, 271-72, 320; at the University of Marburg, 3-7; war preaching, critique of, 121, 167; war theology, critique of, 7-8, 18, 31-32, 34, 54; and Weimar democracy, 56, 58, 60, 119n.93, 121n.95; on the Young Reformation Movement, 285, 298, 308, 317

Bauer, Johannes, 154, 166n.88, 204-5, 210

Baumgarten, Otto, 66, 70n.90, 87n.160, 154, 166n.88

Bible: canon of, 228; and historical-critical method, 14, 16, 227, 273; interpretation of, 13-17, 226-29; Luther's translation of, 272-73; Old Testament, 68, 229n.54, 260, 271, 286; and preaching, 179, 188n.148, 213, 225-26, 231, 235, 272-74, 281-83, 286-87, 293, 310, 312; secularity of, 11, 16; as witness, 217; as Word of God, 11-16, 188n.148, 204, 281, 295n.165, 320

Bismarck, Otto von, 40-41, 47, 107n.52, 125n.109, 161, 171, 245, 251; in the *Übungen in der Predigtvorbereitung*, 302n.182, 333n.12

Blumhardt, Christoph, 18-21, 179

Blumhardt, Johann, 18-21, 179

Bodelschwingh, Friedrich von, 270, 276-78, 284-85, 289, 291, 296-97

Bonhoeffer, Dietrich, 89, 284n.134, 308

Bonn, University of, 38, 81-82, 171, 315; and book burning, 261-62; faculty, 89-90, 171; and German Christians, 90; and *Gleichschaltung*, 254, 262, 271-72; and NSDAP, 88, 256, 289-90; and student body, 82, 88n.161, 133, 271; in Third Reich, 262

Bonn church election results, 320

Book burning, 260-63, 322

Brüning, Heinrich, 194

Brunner, Emil, 24, 129n.124, 167, 197, 207-8, 232n.59, 287n.143, 315; and eristics, 184-87, 207, 212n.34, 214; and natural theology, 185-86; and point of contact (*Anknüpfungspunkt*), 184, 186, 208

Index

Bultmann, Rudolf, 24, 82n.138, 84n.149

Calvin, John, 23, 35, 197, 234, 256, 265, 274-75, 308
Catholic Church in Germany, 41, 44, 245-46; and Centre Party, 41, 45, 109-10, 238, 304; and Concordat, 246, 304, 314; and NSDAP, 72n.97, 246
Committee of Three *(Dreimännerkollegium)*, 248, 267-71, 275-76, 289, 297, 306-8, 313
Communism, 42-44, 47; and the Russian revolution, 42-43, 45, 51, 55
Communist Party in Germany, 48-51, 109-10, 196, 221, 230, 238-40, 243; and propaganda 109; and violence, 195

Deggeller, Werner, 193n.1, 237, 330
Dehn, Günther, 61, 82-88, 124, 132, 250
Deutsche Christen. *See* German Christians
Dialectic, 8-9, 27-30, 32, 37, 56, 89n.166, 211, 215, 327
Dialectical theology, 24, 58, 61, 83, 86, 129, 207, 321; and German homiletics, 164n.83, 166-67; and the NSDAP, 75-76; and the Protestant church in Germany, 70-71, 75, 116-17
Dibelius, Otto, 67-68, 73-74, 115n.81, 168, 243, 245n.24, 250-52, 266n.88, 299, 305; preaching of, 251-52
Dörries, Hermann, 85-86
Düsseldorf Theses, 271, 285

Ebert, Friedrich, 45-46
Ecclesiology, 33, 215-16, 218, 222, 225
Enabling Act, 220n.43, 239, 242, 244
Ethics, 34-36

Fendt, Leonhard, 209-11

Fezer, Karl, 165-66, 204-6, 208-11, 268-70, 284, 287, 297
Frick, Wilhelm, 248n.33, 307, 314
Führerprinzip, 246n.28, 248, 254n.54, 269, 277, 308, 318n.227

Gemeindemässigkeit, 154, 233, 258-59, 287, 292, 294-95, 333
German Christians *(Deutsche Christen)*, 129n.124, 185n.140, 200, 247-48, 252n.46, 254, 267-71, 276, 284, 289, 297-98, 307, 314, 316, 318-20; and anti-Marxism, 75, 131; and anti-Semitism, 75; and church elections, 314, 317; guidelines of, 75, 196; and propaganda, 314; and the Protestant church in Germany, 249
German populace: and boycott of Jewish businesses, 241-42; and fear of revolution, 49, 51, 104, 112, 230, 239, 243n.18; and international press, 241; militarism of, 44; nationalism of, 41-42; and the NSDAP, 47-49, 94, 110-12; and political engagement, 41, 78, 95-97, 101n.26; and "the power of the press," 102-3; and propaganda, 111, 241-43; and *Vergangenheitsbewältigung*, 93-94, 164; as "victims" of Hitler, 95, 96n.10; and Weimar Republic, 46; and World War I, 42-45
German Protestant Church. *See* Protestant church in Germany
German universities. *See* Universities, German
Gleichschaltung, 137, 242-43, 254-55, 304
God: Godness of, 8, 30, 123, 134, 181, 213, 215, 235-36, 326; Holy Spirit, 10, 17-18, 128n.122, 209, 223-34, 299; Jesus Christ, 10-12, 27, 214-15, 222, 249, 259, 281-82, 300, 309, 310, 321; knowledge of, 8-11, 22, 28, 29, 32;

351

Triunity of, 9-10, 36; Word of, 11-12, 17-18, 36, 202-4, 228, 235, 303
Goebbels, Joseph, 105-6, 246n.25
Goeters, Wilhelm, 269n.92, 293n.159
Gogarten, Friedrich, 24, 84n.149, 129n.124, 167, 185-86, 207, 232, 250n.38, 269n.94
Gollwitzer, Helmut, 53n.30, 285, 290
Göring, Hermann, 220, 248n.33

Harnack, Adolf von, 7, 25, 31-33, 35
Harnack, Theodosius, 146-47
Heidegger, Martin, 128n.119, 254
Herrmann, Wilhelm, 3, 6-8, 22-24
Hesse, Hermann, 248n.31, 272, 308
Hindenburg, Paul von, 42, 44-46, 50-51, 108n.55, 171, 194-95, 197, 200, 207, 219, 230, 242n.14, 245, 306-8
Hirsch, Emanuel, 58n.47, 69, 73, 81-82, 85-87, 124, 167-71, 250n.38, 269n.92, 315
Historicism, 4-7
Historiography, 40, 94
Hitler, Adolf, 48-49, 51, 71, 105-6, 110, 134, 137-38, 186, 194-95, 207, 219-20, 229-30, 239-42, 249, 276-77, 288-89, 304, 306-8; anti-intellectualism, 86; anti-Semitism of, 47, 111, 240n.8, 241-42; and Catholic church, 244-46; and German Christians, 319; as "magical," 95; *Mein Kampf*, 47, 221; and "positive Christianity," 136n.141, 244; and propaganda, 100, 105-6, 243; and the Protestant church in Germany, 136n.141, 243-48, 269, 276, 284, 314, 319; use of religious rhetoric, 244; violence, 49n.20, 238-40
Hollaz, David, 198-201, 203
Homiletics, German, 138; and anti-Semitism, 170; apologetic/missionary preaching, 143, 155-56, 165, 169, 201; and Barth, 180; and the Bible, 142, 151, 155, 157-59, 169; and Dialectical Theology, 164, 167; and edification as goal of preaching, 202, 204, 219; and Enlightenment Rationalism, 141-42, 144; and the *Gemeinde* (congregation), 154; and homiletics as "applied" theology, 141; and *Kultpredigt*, 146; and lectionary preaching, 142, 155, 158; and Lutheran Orthodoxy, 141-42, 144, 146-47; and "mediating" homiletics, 144-51; modern preaching movement, 152-57, 161, 164-66, 172, 180, 182-83, 187, 191, 212, 232, 234, 265, 324; and nationalism, 160, 165, 168, 170, 172-75, 257; and need for reform, 153; and philosophy, 154; and pietism, 141-42, 144, 148; and Political Theology, 167-70; and politics, 170; principle, material, and formal homiletics, 145, 189, 198, 236, 259; and the Protestant church in Germany, 152; and psychology, 146, 149, 153-54, 156, 166, 171, 183; and rhetoric, 141-42, 144-51, 155, 183n.133, 201; and sermon form, 141-43, 145; and sermon introductions, 169n.95; and "theme" preaching, 142, 150-51, 155-56, 158-59, 163, 172, 188, 264-65, 311, 325; and war sermons, 157-61, 163, 165, 169, 234, 265
Hossenfelder, Joachim, 248-49, 268, 284, 305-6, 316

Jäger, August, 297-99, 304-7

Kapler, Hermann, 248, 296
Kirschbaum, Charlotte von, 133n.133, 207, 255, 263, 285, 290-91, 308, 316-18, 320, 323, 329-30
Klemperer, Victor, 92-93, 96
Kube, Wilhelm, 75, 248n.33, 252n.46
Kutter, Herrmann, 53-55, 166n.88, 178

Lamparter, Eduard, 70n.90, 132n.132

Index

Ludendorff, Erich, 42-44, 59n.49
Luther, Martin, 23, 25, 34, 40, 81, 139, 146-47, 161, 171, 197, 251, 256, 285, 308; in the *Übungen in der Predigtvorbereitung*, 228-29, 231, 272-74
Lutheranism: law and gospel, 34-46, 139, 147; two kingdoms, 34, 56, 60, 62, 270

Machtergreifung, 220-21, 224-25
Marahrens, August, 248n.31, 270
McConnachie, John, 189-91, 210
McCormack, Bruce, 2, 28-29, 54-55, 61
Mediating Theology, 144-45
Merz, Georg, 24n.53, 126n.113, 252, 280
Müller, Ludwig, 247-48, 267-71, 275-78, 284-86, 288-90, 296-97, 305-7, 313-14, 319

Nationalism, 41-42, 58-59, 62
National Socialist German Workers' Party. *See* NSDAP
Natural Theology, 118, 124, 185, 249
Nazi Party. *See* NSDAP
Neo-Kantianism, 4-5, 15, 35
Niebergall, Friedrich, 142, 154-55, 166
Niemöller, Martin, 269n.94, 305, 308
Nitzsch, C. I., 145-46, 201-6, 232
November criminals, 44, 106, 109
NSDAP (National Socialist German Workers' Party or "Nazi" Party), 46-47, 50-52, 137, 189, 248, 297, 307; and anti-Semitism, 109, 111, 240-42; and boycott of Jewish businesses, 241-42; and the Catholic Church in Germany, 72n.97, 244-45; and the civil service, 242, 253; and the Communist Party, 48-49, 240; concentration camps, 240; electoral decline, 197, 238-39; electoral success, 110; film, use of, 107n.53; and the Protestant church elections, 284, 316-17, 319; and the Protestant church in Germany, 74, 116n.84, 196, 230, 231, 244-45, 270, 284; and the press, 105-6, 108; propaganda of, 48-49, 92, 95n.7, 105-7, 110, 238, 240, 243, 261, 316-17, 319; and public events, 243, 245; public image of, 48-49, 105-7; reasons for electoral successes, 47-49, 51, 74, 112; rhetoric of, 47-49, 93, 105; and Social Darwinism, 48, 246n.28; and the Social Democratic Party, 240; "socialism" of, 48; and universities, 78n.122, 81, 86, 88, 254, 263, 268n.91; violence of, 48-50, 105, 195, 221, 230, 238-42, 263, 304; and Weimar government, 194; and women, 105

Orders of creation, 124, 128, 185-86, 191, 249
Overbeck, Franz, 8, 18-21, 126n.111

Palmer, Christian, 148-49, 201-2
Papen, Franz von, 194-97, 200, 207
Pathos, 122-24, 129, 134, 249-50
Pfennigsdorf, Emil, 38, 75, 90, 188-89, 191, 209, 234, 254, 260n.73, 272, 322; preaching of, 171-75
Point of contact *(Anknüpfungspunkt)*, 124, 184n.138, 186, 208, 215, 287n.143, 303
Political Theology, 69, 81, 116, 118, 129n.125, 185, 191, 216, 248, 252, 264, 269, 289, 298, 315, 318; anti-Semitism of, 70, 168-69; and ecumenism, 73; and the *Führerprinzip*, 70; and Hitler, 87; nationalism of, 85, 87; and preaching, 70, 167-70; and revelation, 69; and Volk, 69-70, 87
Politics, as "game," 33, 122-23
"Positive" Christianity, 68, 74, 75; and Hitler, 136n.141, 244
Predigerseminare, xiii, 188, 189n.150, 198n.17, 301

INDEX

Predigtvorbereitung. See *Übungen in der Predigtvorbereitung*

Press: in Germany, 101-5, 240, 245; international, 241-42, 306; perception of, 102-3; and politics, 101-2, 105-6, 108, 135; and the Protestant church, 65n.73, 276

Pressel, Wilhelm, 157-60, 163-64

Propaganda, 98-100, 135; in German press, 101-4; Hitler's philosophy of, 100; of right-wing parties, 108-9

Protestant church in Germany: as "above parties," 113-14, 116-17, 135, 250; and anti-Marxism, 65, 69, 73, 17; and anti-Semitism, 68-69, 258; and anxiety about influence, 63, 65, 71-72, 113, 117, 152, 170, 183, 187; and Catholicism, 71n.94, 246, 314; and church elections, 74-75, 196-97, 200, 234, 268, 284, 289, 307, 314, 316-20; and church press, 65n.73, 72, 114, 276, 285, 305; and church tax, 63, 113n.72, 152; confessional composition, 62, 65, 246; and *Deutscher Evangelischer Kirchenbund*, 65, 72, 114n.79, 246n.27, 248-49, 296, 306; and dialectical theology, 71, 167; and fear of revolution, 117, 135, 191; and the German Christians, 196-97, 249, 267-69, 284, 296-98, 306, 314; and Hitler, 244-48, 276-77, 288-89, 306, 318-19; *Kirchenausschuss*, 65, 246n.27, 248, 296-98; and labor movement, 117, 152, 184; *Landeskirchen*, 64-66; and membership decline, 63, 152; and nationalism, 62, 65, 69, 113-14, 117, 157, 160-64, 168, 183, 191, 236, 247, 252, 266, 305; and NSDAP, 71-73, 115-17, 191, 230-31, 244-46, 250, 252, 296-97, 306, 317; Old Prussian *Landeskirche*, 64n.68, 65, 196-97, 200, 296-98, 304-7, 314; and pacifism, 69; and Political Theology, 71, 116, 118, 167-68, 170; and politics, 65-66, 112-18, 170, 188, 191, 305; and post-war theology, 162; and preaching, 17-18, 72, 116, 137-38, 141-42, 152-53, 164-65, 183, 188, 191, 266; and the press, 305-7; and propaganda, 112, 114-15, 117-18, 131-32, 135, 138, 168, 183, 191, 197, 245, 277, 284, 289, 316-17; and the Reich bishop, 246n.28, 270, 275-77, 284-85, 288-89, 296-98, 313, 319; and the Reich Church, 64, 246-48; and rhetoric, 91, 118, 132, 183, 188; and *"seelsorgerlich,"* the church's task as, 66-67, 113, 115, 117, 161-62, 165, 168-69, 172, 183, 187, 217-18, 236; and the "Spirit of 1914," 63, 157, 165, 188n.148; and the state, 62-64; in the Third Reich, 247; and the *völkisch* movement, 71-72, 170; and war sermons, 63, 157-64; and the Weimar Republic, 63-64, 66, 68n.81, 112-13, 115

Rade, Martin, 8, 58, 64n.71, 66, 70n.90, 75, 85, 160n.73

Ragaz, Leonard, 53-55, 166n.88, 178

Reconciliation, 10, 35; in the *Übungen in der Predigtvorbereitung*, 216, 221, 321

Reich church, 244, 247-48, 275

Reichstag. See Weimar government: Reichstag

Reichstag fire, 230-31, 239, 243

Religious socialism, 7, 52, 55, 66, 74-75, 116-17, 178, 191

Revelation, 9-12, 16-17, 28-29, 36-37, 126n.112, 186, 188n.148, 249-50; actualism of, 10, 16, 18, 35, 228; in the *Übungen in der Predigtvorbereitung*, 212-15, 217, 218, 225, 228, 235, 257, 274, 303

Rhetoric: discipline of in homiletics, 150; as instrumental, 183; as pathos, 57, 120-24, 128, 129, 134, 136, 249,

327; 121; of political campaigns, 108-12
Rust, Bernhard, 253, 290, 297, 306-8

Sacraments, 11n.20, 17n.35, 202, 216-17, 246, 257, 289, 300, 303
Schleicher, Kurt von, 207, 219
Schleiermacher, F. D. E., 4, 14-15, 23, 89, 177; and German homiletics, 139-41, 143-52, 160n.74; in the *Übungen in der Predigtvorbereitung*, 199-200, 201, 203, 311
Schmidt, Karl Ludwig, 84, 254, 256, 318
Schweitzer, Alexander, 144-45, 147, 198n.17
Scripture. See Bible
Sermon Exercises. See *Übungen in der Predigtvorbereitung*
Social Democratic Party (SPD), 41, 43, 45-46, 48-49, 54, 60, 109-10, 135n.139, 163, 196, 221, 230, 238, 240, 253, 263; critique of Protestant church, 163; and propaganda, 110, 135n.139
Socialism, 41, 44, 53
"Spirit of 1914." See World War I: "Spirit of 1914"
Stapel, Wilhelm, 289-90

Theology: and church, 20-21; of "crisis," 37; as science, 3-4, 6, 18, 20-22; "without weapons," 22, 37
Third Reich, 107n.52, 239, 243, 247; book burning, 260-63, 322; and civil service, 242-43, 253; in international press, 241-42; propaganda of, 261; rhetoric of, 92, 95n.7; and universities, 254; use of violence, 238-41, 263
Tholuck, Friedrich August, 144n.10, 148
Thurneysen, Eduard, 24n.53, 60, 166-67, 178, 189, 196, 298, 329-30

Tillich, Paul, 24, 70n.90, 253n.49
Troeltsch, Ernst, 5-7

Übungen in der Predigtvorbereitung: analogia entis, 303; Bible, 202, 204, 208, 213, 217, 225-27, 229, 235, 257-58, 260, 264-67, 272-74, 281-83, 286-87, 292, 300-301, 303, 311-13, 321-22, 325; Bismarck, 302n.182, 333n.12; Brunner, 212n.34, 214, 232n.59, 287n.143; contemporary context and preaching, 231, 281, 287-88, 291-95, 312-13, 322, 326; courage, 231, 292, 322, 326; creeds and confessions, 218-19, 257; culture, 218; definition of preaching, 211-12; on dogmatics, 283; ecclesiology, 215-16, 218, 221-22, 225, 235, 259; on "edification" as goal of preaching, 202, 204, 219; eschatology *(woher)*, 205, 214, 216, 235, 325; ethics, 224-25; ethos of preacher, 205-6, 221, 225, 228-29, 231-33, 235, 259, 283, 293-95, 300, 311, 322, 325-26; existentialism, 212, 215, 232; formation of preachers, 198; the *Gemeinde* (congregation), 199, 201, 206, 223, 232-33, 258-59, 282, 287, 291-92; the hearer, 287-88, 291-92, 321-22, 326; historical-critical method, 227, 273-74; Holy Spirit, 206, 233-34, 299; humility, 199-200, 202-4, 206, 212-15, 223, 227-28, 232-36, 259-60, 264-65, 267, 294-95, 303, 312, 322, 325; incarnation *(wohin)*, 214, 235, 325; indirect communication, 294; interpretation, 226-27, 229, 231, 272-74, 281-83, 286-87, 293, 312; and justification, 224-25, 228, 300; language of preaching, 231, 272, 294, 310-12, 322, 326; lectionary, use of, 265-66; modern preaching movement, 265, 274-75, 301; on nationalism, 235, 257-58, 263, 266; office of preacher, 221-23, 258; Old

355

Testament, 210, 229, 256, 260; originality of preacher, 229, 231-32, 258; origins of, xiii, 38-39, 90-91, 191-92, 198; "point of contact," 215, 287n.143, 303-4; and politics, 256-57, 259-60, 263-64, 266, 293-94, 304; prayer, 234, 236, 266, 282, 300, 313, 325, 326; on propaganda, 310-11, 325; and the Protestant church in Germany, 257-58, 266-67, 325; publication of, xiv, 331-33; reconciliation, 216, 221, 321; revelation, 212-15, 217, 218, 225, 235, 257, 274, 303; sacraments, 216-17, 257, 303; sermon conclusions, 311, 313; sermon form, 282-83, 299-300, 311, 322; sermon introductions, 301-4, 322; sermon manuscript, 300, 311, 313, 322; source documents of, 193n.1, 237, 329-30; text selection, 263-64, 266, 322; "theme" preaching, 208, 264-67, 275, 281-82, 287, 292-93, 311; *völkisch* ideology, critique of, 215-16, 235; war preaching, 263, 265, 267n.89; Word of God, 202-4, 228, 235; worship, 300-301

Universities, German, 76-81; as "above parties," 79; and academic freedom, 76; and anti-Marxism, 77; and anti-Semitism, 77, 80; book-burning, 260-63, faculty attitudes toward democracy, 77-78, 80, 254; and the German Christians, 284; and nationalism, 26, 77, 80, 83-88; and the NSDAP, 78n.122, 81, 86, 88, 263, 268n.91; organizational structure, 78n.121, 79n.124; overcrowding, 80; and student activism, 80, 83-84, 87, 133n.133, 322; and student attitudes, 79, 132; theological faculties, 81; in the Third Reich, 242, 254

Vergangenheitsbewältigung, 93-95, 164
Versailles, Treaty of, 43-44, 46, 47, 79
Vinet, Alexandre, 148, 150-51, 201
Volk, concept of, 69n.84, 70, 108, 160, 168, 173, 174, 215-17, 226, 231, 257, 309; in Political Theology, 69
völkisch movement, 26, 68-69, 70, 71, 72, 75, 83, 90, 106, 111, 136n.141, 138, 170, 216
Volksgemeinschaft, 69, 107-10, 112, 118, 137, 160, 168, 262, 318n.227; and preaching, 216, 218, 309

Wandervogel movement, 79, 97
Weimar Republic: Article 48, 45-46, 50, 230; attitudes toward, 66n.76, 78; coalition government, 45; culture, 46; economic instability of, 46, 50-51, 134; and NSDAP, 195; office of Chancellor, 45; and propaganda, 98, 108-10, 135; *Reichstag*, 41, 194-95, 197; *Reichstag* elections, 47, 51, 194-95, 197, 238-40; and violence, 44, 195; Weimar Constitution, 45
World War I, 7-8, 42; the "Spirit of 1914," 42, 47, 63, 79, 97, 109, 157, 160, 165, 220, 224; "stab in the back" myth, 43-44, 79, 99, 162n.79; war sermons, 157-61, 163, 165, 169, 234, 265; war theology, 32, 34, 162-63

Young Plan, 47, 106n.50, 115
Young Reformation Movement, 269-70, 276, 306, 308, 314, 316; and preaching, 318

Zwischen den Zeiten, 24n.53, 67, 207, 221, 249, 255